Ronald M. Green

DARTMOUTH COLLEGE

THE

ETHICAL MANAGER

A NEW METHOD FOR BUSINESS ETHICS

Macmillan College Publishing Company
New York

Maxwell Macmillan Canada
Toronto

Maxwell Macmillan International
New York Oxford Singapore Sydney

Editor: Nina McGuffin
Production Supervisor: Ron Harris
Production Manager: Aliza Greenblatt
Text Designer: Hothouse Designs
Cover Designer: Robert Vega
Cover Art: © 1993 ARS, New York/ADAGP, Paris/SCALA/Art Resource, Wassily
Kandinsky, "Quadro con punte" ("Painting with Points"), 1919, St. Petersburg Hermitage

This book was set in Palatino by Compset, Inc. and was printed and bound by R. R.
Donnelley & Sons. The cover was printed by New England Book Components.

Macmillan College Publishing Company
866 Third Avenue, New York, New York 10022

Macmillan College Publishing Company is part
of the Maxwell Communication Group of Companies.

Maxwell Macmillan Canada, Inc.
1200 Eglinton Avenue East
Suite 200
Don Mills, Ontario M3C 3N1

Library of Congress Cataloging in Publication Data
   Green, Ronald Michael.
      The ethical manager : a new method for business ethics / Ronald M.
   Green.
      p.   cm.
      Includes index.
      ISBN 0-02-346431-3
      1. Business ethics.   2. Executives—Professional ethics.
   I. Title.
   HF5387.G72 1994   93-19865'
   174' .4—dc20   CIP

Printing: 1   2   3   4   5   6   7   8   Year: 4   5   6   7   8   9   0   1

For my son Matthew

PREFACE

✦ THIS IS A DIFFERENT KIND OF BUSINESS ETHICS TEXTBOOK. IF YOU ARE A MAN-
ager or aspiring manager, its aim is to teach you how to think through
difficult ethical decisions encountered in organizational life. For this purpose, it introduces a new method of moral reasoning, and it seeks to
develop skills in applying this method by taking you, the reader, the reader,
through a series of real-life cases drawn from many areas of business
experience.

Over the past two decades, as the field of business ethics achieved a
recognized place in business education, the number of textbooks published in the field grew accordingly. Many of these texts provide useful
factual introductions to topics that managers are likely to encounter in
the course of their work: drug testing, employee rights, whistle blowing,
or the ethics of advertising. But all these texts have been behind the times
with regard to current moral theory. Commonly, in their theoretical
introductions to ethics, these texts offer some combination of moral theo-

ries based on rights and rules, on the one hand, and consequentialist (utilitarian) theories, on the other. But despite occasional overlaps in their recommendations for concrete cases, these two approaches are fundamentally opposed. Small wonder that readers trying to apply both these theoretical approaches to tough decisions have been confused when the theories seem to produce divergent results. "Is it rights and rules that tell us whether something is ethical," they have asked, "or is it the beneficial consequences we produce by our choices and actions?"

This textbook aims at overcoming this core problem by introducing a new method—**NORM** or *Neutral, Omnipartial Rule Making.* **NORM** draws on the best current moral theory to overcome this theoretical impasse. By providing a unified and coherent approach to moral decisions, **NORM** helps us go beyond "gut feelings" to a reasoned account of our moral views. It also provides a framework for moral discussion, whether in the classroom or in organizational contexts, that facilitates reasoned moral debate.

Chapter 1, "Is Business Ethics an Oxymoron?" raises a vital preliminary question: Do managers have ethical responsibilities beyond those of maximizing bottom line profit? Using such influential thinkers as Albert Carr and Milton Friedman as opponents, I debate this question and argue that "business ethics," far from being a contradiction in terms, is currently one of the most important areas of managerial competence and responsibility.

Chapters 2 and 3 are the theoretical core of this book. Chapter 2 provides an overview of the main questions of ethics and brings the reader up to speed on some of the theoretical controversies that have long divided ethicists and philosophers. Chapter 3 goes beyond these historical debates to outline and explain the **NORM** method. Case illustrations and concise procedural advice help the reader to apply this method to difficult instances of organizational choice.

The chapters that follow apply the **NORM** method to the concerns of some of the major "stakeholder" groups facing managers today. Among these stakeholders are employees, customers, clients, competitors, and suppliers. Cutting across these groups are issues that crop up in a variety of business situations. These include conflict of interest, whistle blowing, employees' privacy rights, ethics and competition, product safety, ethics in advertising, overseas bribery, and sex discrimination.

Despite this coverage, not every current issue or area in business ethics is addressed. The primary aim is to offer a *means* of approaching issues, a *way of thinking*, that will serve no matter how complex the question or how novel the challenges it poses. Each day's news presents new quandaries in business or organizational life. No text can purport to provide current information on every issue in this fast-changing environment. Students of business ethics—whether undergraduates, MBAs, or those who are already managers of organizations—need to learn *how* to think ethically about novel and challenging issues. **NORM** seeks to provide a method for doing this.

The other distinguishing feature of this approach is the focus on cases. Virtually every chapter begins with a case, and these form the subject of most of the discussions. Almost every chapter also ends with one or more cases allowing the reader to test out her or his own skills of moral reasoning. These cases involve real problems. They represent reports by front-line managers who have chosen to share their experiences—and their dilemmas—with teachers, friends, or colleagues. While reading these cases, the reader should try to apply different theoretical options to resolving them. Take the "Questions to Consider" as a guide, and think through your answers before proceeding. If it helps, jot down your analysis of the case before reading the subsequent discussion of it. In this way, you can strengthen and test your grasp of the book's approach. In discussions that follow, what the **NORM** method brings to each case becomes evident. Throughout the text, theoretical observations of basic value are signaled by the use of italic type. These observations develop some aspect or application of the **NORM** method. In this way, chapter by chapter, case by case, a body of expertise in moral reasoning is built up, one that can be carried on to new cases and new dilemmas.

A final section of this book turns from the question of managers' responsibilities *in* organizations to their responsibilities *for* organizations. There the ways that organizational policies and structures can be molded to enhance ethical performance and to reduce the pressures for misconduct are explored. There is also a view of how an ethical "culture" can contribute to organizational excellence, even in terms of basic financial performance. The argument draws partly on recent studies of organizational success, but also refers back to insights produced by **NORM**. Understanding what moral reasoning requires helps all of us better see the ethical pitfalls and opportunities in corporate life. It can help design organizations that bring out the best—both ethically and professionally—in the people that make them up.

ACKNOWLEDGMENTS

This book owes enormously to the collaboration and creativity of Robbin Derry. She participated in the book's genesis and conception, edited drafts of the early chapters of the manuscript, and contributed to the development of key concepts in the book. For all of this, I offer my heart-felt thanks.

I also owe a special debt to my colleague John W. Hennessey, Jr. As the reader can see, many cases in this book were developed by Professor Hennessey during his years of teaching courses on organizational behavior and organizational dilemmas at Dartmouth's Amos Tuck School. John's invitation to me to co-teach a course on business ethics with him at Tuck was the stimulus for my own work in this field. I regard the several years that John and I worked together before he retired from Tuck as my "second Ph.D."—an intensive period of training in case method teaching at the feet of one of its acknowledged masters.

R. M. G.

BRIEF CONTENTS

CONTENTS

PART ONE

BASIC ISSUES

◆

CAN WE SPEAK OF "BUSINESS ETHICS"?

✦

✦ THE BHOPAL DISASTER, WHICH IS BRIEFLY RECOUNTED IN CASE 1.1 ON PAGE 4, is a sobering reminder of how much harm can result from a series of poorly made business decisions. Whether Union Carbide was primarily responsible for the tragedy or not, its U.S. and Indian managers contributed to a series of decisions that culminated in the events of that terrible December night. Although not all management decisions have this kind of potential for harm, the growing size, complexity, and interdependency of economic and industrial activity are hallmarks of modern society. In the wake of the Three Mile Island reactor emergency, Johns-Manville's handling of asbestos, A. H. Robins's marketing of the Dalkon Shield, and Dow Corning's experience with silicone breast implants, we are more aware than ever that poor decision making by managers threatens us all.

Text continues on page 5

Case 1.1

◆ THE BHOPAL TRAGEDY[1] ◆

Late in the evening of December 2, 1984, a cloud of deadly white gas descended on the shantytown homes of thousands of poor people living on the outskirts of Union Carbide's pesticide plant in the central Indian city of Bhopal. Within hours at least two thousand people were dead, thousands more lay gasping for breath with seared lungs and burned eyes, and many others faced the prospect of long-term impairment and disease.

The Bhopal disaster had begun innocently enough fifteen years earlier, when Union Carbide India Ltd. (UCIL), the majority-owned subsidiary of the American-based Union Carbide Corporation, had established a packaging facility for the pesticide Sevin in Bhopal. The Indian government favored this step as part of its drive to alleviate the country's chronic food shortages, while Union Carbide looked forward to securing a foothold in a potentially vast market. In 1978, under an agreement with the government that required it to share technology with its subsidiary, Carbide opened a $25 million Sevin production plant in Bhopal. Modeled on Carbide's U.S. facilities, the plant was designed to produce up to 5,000 tons of Sevin per year, using volatile methyl isocyanate (MIC) as a basic ingredient.

Events in the early 1980s frustrated Carbide's profit expectations. Economic recession led Indian farmers to seek cheaper alternatives to Sevin, and small-scale producers began to undersell Carbide's product. As early as 1981, the Bhopal plant was losing money; by 1984, management expected a $4 million annual loss. In response, Carbide and UCIL adopted extensive cost-cutting measures. Management cut staff at the MIC facility from twelve to six operators per shift and reduced the number of maintenance workers. Faulty safety devices went unrepaired for weeks at a time. A refrigeration unit designed for emergency cooling of the three large MIC storage tanks was shut down.

Union Carbide officials were aware of these growing safety and maintenance problems. A 1982 report by a group of Carbide's U.S. engineers itemized the problems, but the parent corporation made little effort to spur the Indian executives responsible for the day-to-day operation of the plant to correct them. The stage was set for disaster.

On December 2, 1984, a large quantity of water was somehow introduced into one of the MIC tanks. Carbide later claimed that this was a deliberate act of sabotage by a disgruntled worker, whereas others testified that it was an accident made possible by faulty equipment. Whatever the case, when the water combined with the MIC and contaminants in the tank, a powerful chemical reaction resulted, generating large amounts of heat and pressure. This led to massive, uncontrolled venting of MIC and other poisonous reaction products into the air. As staff and managers fled in panic, the next act began in what was to become the world's worst industrial accident.

THE MYTH OF AMORAL BUSINESS
✦

Against this background, how are we to understand why many people find it hard to take seriously the concept of business ethics? Often, when someone introduces the term *business ethics* in conversation, smiles come to people's faces and a knowing member of the group is likely to quip, "'Business ethics'? Isn't that an oxymoron, like 'jumbo shrimp' or 'military intelligence'?" In part, of course, this attitude derives from the hallowed American tradition of bashing business, government, and other large institutions. More fundamentally, it reflects a view that denies a role for ethical considerations in managers' daily decision making. Richard DeGeorge terms this view "the myth of amoral business."[2] Since our discussions in the chapters ahead presume that ethical judgment is a vital component of professional management, I want to begin by looking critically at this myth and its assumptions.

The "myth of amoral business" is partly a descriptive observation of business reality. From the overseas bribery practices exposed during the Lockheed and other scandals in the 1970s, to the insider trading investigations of the 1980s, to the more recent discoveries of fraud and deception in the savings and loan industry, business misconduct has fostered the view that businessmen and businesswomen are unconcerned with ethics and are even prepared to break the law if they can get away with it. Like many stereotypes, this one greatly exaggerates reality. Although some businessmen and businesswomen cut ethical corners, many more act with integrity and view their professional activity as fully consonant with their personal ethical values. Similarly, although some business organizations have seriously violated ethical and legal standards, the vast majority conduct their affairs responsibly. Indeed, it is precisely because of the uncounted daily instances of fair dealing, honesty, and trustworthiness on the part of businessmen and businesswomen that occasional episodes of unethical business practices draw our attention and capture headlines.

Even a moment's reflection suggests that moral integrity not only is but *must be* the norm for business conduct. Imagine a world in which businessmen and businesswomen commonly lie, cheat, and treat others without respect. Business as we know it would soon grind to a halt. In such a world, I would hesitate to give my credit card to a merchant, and I would insist on payment in advance before undertaking any task for an employer. Employers, in turn, would not trust their employees with valuable resources or information. Because this is not the way most of us conduct business, we can see the importance of the unnoticed expectation of moral behavior in daily business practice.

THE AUTONOMY OF BUSINESS

✦

The myth of amoral business is more than just stereotype and exaggeration. Like other myths, it draws its force not from a view of how the world *is* but of how it *ought to* be. If we want to understand why the myth of amoral business persists, we must look beyond the actual practices of businesspeople to the basic theories and self-understanding that characterize modern commercial activity. It is in these that we find the view that business and ethics are separable, that owners and managers conduct business best when they put moral concerns aside and single-mindedly attend to the pursuit of profit.

Historically, we can trace this view to Adam Smith's *The Wealth of Nations*. In his struggle to identify the laws inherent in economic behavior and to free commerce from the oppressive hand of the state, Smith stressed the positive role that individual initiative and the desire for profit play in economic progress. He was also confident that, in an economically free and competitive society, one person's excessive self-interest would be checked by the self-interest of others. In a frequently quoted remark, he urged his readers to replace their ethical distrust of self-interest with an appreciation of its positive role in economic life:

> It is not from the benevolence of the butcher, the brewer, or the baker that we expect our dinner, but from their regard to their own interest. We address ourselves not to their humanity but to their self-love, and never talk to them of our own necessities but of their advantages.[3]

Smith's position established what might be called the autonomy of business from ethics. According to this view, commerce is an independent sector of human activity governed by its own rules and standards. Left to themselves and allowed to operate freely, businessmen and businesswomen will produce maximum benefit for society. Efforts to impose external norms of conduct, especially ethical norms more appropriate to interpersonal relations, are doomed to failure and will only impede economic creativity and progress.

Adam Smith understood that there must be limits to business autonomy. He was aware that strict self-interest might lead those in business to conspire to reduce competition and he recognized that the "invisible hand" that otherwise checks destructive egoism in commercial affairs sometimes needs an assist from law or ethical teaching. Occurrences over the two centuries since Smith wrote have amply driven this lesson home. Most free-market societies have been forced to develop legal structures to control inherent instabilities caused by excessive greed in the drive for profit. Nevertheless, although most capitalist theorists would concede that there is a need for some legal supervision of markets and commerce, they also believe that an economic system works best when managers and owners are allowed maximal autonomy to pursue profit-maximization and are not saddled with ethical concerns inappropriate to commercial life.

In modern discussions of business ethics, two writers have powerfully expressed this view: Albert Z. Carr and Milton Friedman. Carr's position is set forth in a provocative article that appeared in 1968 in the *Harvard Business Review* under the title "Is Business Bluffing Ethical?" Friedman summarized his view, developed in his book *Capitalism and Freedom,* in the brief article reprinted here entitled "The Social Responsibility of Business Is to Increase Its Profits." Because Carr and Friedman emphasize slightly different facets of the argument for business autonomy, those seeking to defend the importance of ethics in the conduct of management today must come to terms with each thinker's views.

CARR'S GAME ANALOGY
✦

At the center of Carr's view is the claim that business has an ethic of its own, different from the one that governs our ordinary personal relationships and is taught to us at home or in church. For the sake of profits and economic success, this ethic permits conscious misstatements, concealment of pertinent facts, and exaggeration—what Carr calls "bluffing." Business ethics, Carr maintains, is a "game ethics" whose closest analogy is to poker:

> No one expects poker to be played on the ethical principles preached in churches. In poker it is right and proper to bluff a friend out of the rewards of being dealt a good hand. A player feels no more than a slight twinge of sympathy, if that, when—with nothing better than a single ace in his hand—he strips a heavy loser who holds a pair, of the rest of his chips. It was up to the other fellow to protect himself.... Poker's own brand of ethics is different from the ethical ideals of civilized human relationships.... No one thinks any worse of poker on that account. And no one should think any the worse of the game of business because its standards of right and wrong differ from the prevailing traditions of morality in our society.[4]

Carr does not believe this analogy means that in business "anything goes." Just as poker has its formal rules and informal standards of behavior, business conduct is constrained by legal regulations and some informal standards of fair play among competitors. He also points out that, as a simple matter of strategy, not ethics, "a wise businessman will not seek advantage to the point where he generates dangerous hostility among employees, competitors, customers, government, or the public at large." But, according to Carr, where neither law nor strategy counsel otherwise, business managers would be foolish not to engage in deceptive advertising or the marketing of harmful products if by doing so they could increase their profits.

What can we say about this view? First, perhaps, that it contains a grain of truth. Many businessmen and businesswomen undeniably view themselves as "game players" and derive some of their keenest satisfactions from playing the game well. Often, they are right to do so because business dealings *sometimes* approximate the conditions found in a game of poker, where mature players confront one another in a context where everyone knows and freely accepts the rules of the game. Labor negotiations offer a good example. It is common for each side to misrepresent its resources or its "minimum" bargaining position as part of a negotiating strategy. The same is true of many other kinds of "deal making" between relatively equal and informed participants.

Seeing where Carr's analogy applies also tells us where it doesn't. This is most clearly true when business decisions inflict serious harm on third parties who are not aware that they are involved in another's business game. It is also true when the "game" involves people who cannot be expected to understand its rules or who, for various reasons, are unable to play on an equal footing with others. Many consumers who rely on the truth of advertising claims regarding the value and safety of products aren't "game players" in Carr's sense. Neither are many managers, employees, and ordinary citizens caught up in the turmoil and dislocation of the giant takeover battles of the past decade. Nor, for that matter, were the thousands of sea otters, salmon, and wildfowl destroyed when oil from the Exxon Valdez spilled into Alaska's Prince William Sound. To the extent that situations of this sort comprise a major part of business activity today, therefore, Carr's argument, despite its grain of truth, ends by seriously distorting the reality of managerial ethical responsibility. Managers are sometimes validly thought of as game players. But game ethics must be replaced by more familiar moral standards when managers' actions seriously impact on persons not playing the business game.

Milton Friedman

The Social Responsibility of Business Is to Increase Its Profits*

When I hear businessmen speak eloquently about the "social responsibilities of business in a free-enterprise system," I am reminded of the wonderful line about the Frenchman who discovered at the age of 70 that he had been speaking prose all his life. The businessmen

* © 1970 by The New York Times Company. Reprinted by permission.

believe that they are defending free enterprise when they declaim that business is not concerned "merely" with profit but also with promoting desirable "social" ends; that business has a "social conscience" and takes seriously its responsibilities for providing employment, eliminating discrimination, avoiding pollution and whatever else may be the catchwords of the contemporary crop of reformers. In fact they are—or would be if they or anyone else took them seriously—preaching pure and unadulterated socialism. Businessmen who talk this way are unwitting puppets of the intellectual forces that have been undermining the basis of a free society these past decades.

The discussions of the "social responsibilities of business" are notable for their analytical looseness and lack of rigor. What does it mean to say that "business" has responsibilities? Only people can have responsibilities. A corporation is an artificial person and in this sense may have artificial responsibilities, but "business" as a whole cannot be said to have responsibilities even in this vague sense. The first step toward clarity in examining the doctrine of the social responsibility of business is to ask precisely what it implies for whom.

Presumably, the individuals who are to be responsible are businessmen, which means individual proprietors or corporate executives. Most of the discussion of social responsibility is directed at corporations, so in what follows I shall mostly neglect the individual proprietor and speak of corporate executives.

In a free-enterprise, private-property system a corporate executive is an employee of the owners of the business. He has direct responsibility to his employers. That responsibility is to conduct the business in accordance with their desires, which generally will be to make as much money as possible while conforming to the basic rules of the society, both those embodied in law and those embodied in ethical custom. Of course, in some cases his employers may have a different objective. A group of persons might establish a corporation for an eleemosynary purpose—for example, a hospital or a school. The manager of such a corporation will not have money profit as his objective but the rendering of certain services.

In either case, the key point is that, in his capacity as a corporate executive, the manager is the agent of the individuals who own the

corporation or establish the eleemosynary institution, and his primary responsibility is to them.

Needless to say, this does not mean that it is easy to judge how
well he is performing his task. But at least the criterion of performance is straightforward, and the persons among whom a voluntary
contractual arrangement exists are clearly defined.

Of course, the corporate executive is also a person in his own right.
As a person, he may have many other responsibilities that he recognizes or assumes voluntarily—to his family, his conscience, his feelings of charity, his church, his clubs, his city, his country. He may feel
impelled by these responsibilities to devote part of his income to causes he regards as worthy, to refuse to work for particular corporations,
and even to leave his job, for example, to join his country's armed
forces. If we wish, we may refer to some of these responsibilities as
"social responsibilities." But in these respects he is acting as a principal, not an agent; he is spending his own money or time or energy,
not the money of his employers or the time or energy he has contract-
ed to devote to their purposes. If these are "social responsibilities,"
they are the social responsibilities of individuals, not of business.

What does it mean to say that the corporate executive has a
"social responsibility" in his capacity as businessman? If this statement is not pure rhetoric, it must mean that he is to act in some way
that is not in the interest of his employers. For example, that he is to
refrain from increasing the price of the product in order to contribute
to the social objective of preventing inflation, even though a price
increase would be in the best interests of the corporation. Or that he is
to make expenditures on reducing pollution beyond the amount that
is in the best interests of the corporation or that is required by law in
order to contribute to the social objective of improving the environment. Or that, at the expense of corporate profits, he is to hire "hard-
core" unemployed instead of better-qualified available workmen to
contribute to the social objective of reducing poverty.

In each of these cases, the corporate executive would be spending
someone else's money for a general social interest. Insofar as his
actions in accord with his "social responsibility" reduce returns to
stockholders, he is spending their money. Insofar as his actions raise

the price to customers, he is spending the customers' money. Insofar as his actions lower the wages of some employees, he is spending their money.

The stockholders or the customers or the employees could separately spend their own money on the particular action if they wished to do so. The executive is exercising a distinct "social responsibility," rather than serving as an agent of the stockholders or the customers or the employees, only if he spends the money in a different way than they would have spent it.

But if he does this, he is in effect imposing taxes, on the one hand, and deciding how the tax proceeds shall be spent, on the other.

This process raises political questions on two levels: principle and consequences. On the level of political principle, the imposition of taxes and the expenditure of tax proceeds are governmental functions. We have established elaborate constitutional, parliamentary and judicial provisions to control these functions, to assure that taxes are imposed so far as possible in accordance with the preferences and desires of the public—after all "taxation without representation" was one of the battle cries of the American Revolution. We have a system of checks and balances to separate the legislative function of imposing taxes and enacting expenditures from the executive function of collecting taxes and administering expenditure programs and from the judicial function of mediating disputes and interpreting the law.

Here the businessman—self-selected or appointed directly or indirectly by stockholders—is to be simultaneously legislator, executive and jurist. He is to decide whom to tax by how much and for what purpose, and he is to spend the proceeds—all this guided only by general exhortations from on high to restrain inflation, improve the environment, fight poverty and so on and on.

The whole justification for permitting the corporate executive to be selected by the stockholders is that the executive is an agent serving the interests of his principal. This justification disappears when the corporate executive imposes taxes and spends the proceeds for "social" purposes. He becomes in effect a public employee, a civil servant, even though he remains in name an employee of a private enterprise. On grounds of political principle, it is intolerable that such civil servants—insofar as their actions in the name of social responsibility are real and not just window-dressing—should be selected as they are now. If they are to be civil servants, then they must be selected through a political process. If they are to impose taxes and make expenditures to foster "social" objectives, then political machinery must be set up to guide the assessment of taxes and to determine through a political process the objectives to be served.

This is the basic reason why the doctrine of "social responsibility" involves the acceptance of the socialist view that political mechanisms, not market mechanisms, are the appropriate way to determine the allocation of scarce resources to alternative uses.

On the grounds of consequences, can the corporate executive in fact discharge his alleged "social responsibilities"? On the one hand, suppose he could get away with spending the stockholders' or customers' or employees' money. How is he to know how to spend it? He is told that he must contribute to fighting inflation. How is he to know what action of his will contribute to that end? He is presumably an expert in running his company in producing a product or selling it or financing it. But nothing about his selection makes him an expert on inflation. Will his holding down the price of his product reduce inflationary pressure? Or, by leaving more spending power in the hands of his customers, simply divert it elsewhere? Or, by forcing him to produce less because of the lower price, will it simply contribute to shortages? Even if he could answer these questions, how much cost is he justified in imposing on his stockholders, customers and employees for this social purpose? What is his appropriate share and the share of others?

And, whether he wants to or not, can he get away with spending his stockholders', customers' or employees' money? Will not the stockholders fire him? (Either the present ones or those who take over when his actions in the name of social responsibility have reduced the corporation's profits and the price of its stock.) His customers and his employees can desert him for other producers and employers less scrupulous in exercising their social responsibilities.

This facet of "social responsibility" doctrine is brought into sharp relief when the doctrine is used to justify wage restraint by trade unions. The conflict of interest is naked and clear when union officials are asked to subordinate the interests of their members to some more general social purpose. If the union officials try to enforce wage restraint, the consequence is likely to be wildcat strikes, rank-and-file revolts and the emergence of strong competitors for their jobs. We thus have the ironic phenomenon that union leaders—at least in the U.S.—have objected to Government interference with the market far more consistently and courageously than have business leaders.

The difficulty of exercising "social responsibility" illustrates, of course, the great virtue of private competitive enterprise—it forces people to be responsible for their own actions and makes it difficult for them to "exploit" other people for either selfish or unselfish purposes. They can do good—but only at their own expense.

Many a reader who has followed the argument this far may be tempted to remonstrate that it is all well and good to speak of government's having the responsibility to impose taxes and determine expenditures for such "social" purposes as controlling pollution or training the hardcore unemployed, but that the problems are too urgent to wait on the slow course of political processes, that the exercise of social responsibility by businessmen is a quicker and surer way to solve pressing current problems.

Aside from the question of fact—I share Adam Smith's skepticism about the benefits that can be expected from "those who affected to trade for the public good"—this argument must be rejected on grounds of principle. What it amounts to is an assertion that those who favor the taxes and expenditures in question have failed to persuade a majority of their fellow citizens to be of like mind and that they are seeking to attain by undemocratic procedures what they cannot attain by democratic procedures. In a free society it is hard for "good" people to do "good," but that is a small price to pay for making it hard for "evil" people to do "evil," especially since one man's good is another's evil.

I have, for simplicity, concentrated on the special case of the corporate executive, except only for the brief digression on trade unions. But precisely the same argument applies to the newer phenomenon of calling upon stockholders to require corporations to exercise social responsibility (the recent G.M. crusade, for example). In most of these cases, what is in effect involved is some stockholders trying to get other stockholders (or customers or employees) to contribute against their will to "social" causes favored by the activists. Insofar as they succeed, they are again imposing taxes and spending the proceeds.

The situation of the individual proprietor is somewhat different. If he acts to reduce the returns of his enterprise in order to exercise his "social responsibility," he is spending his own money, not someone else's. If he wishes to spend his money on such purposes, that is his right, and I cannot see that there is any objection to his doing so. In the process, he, too, may impose costs on employees and customers. However, because he is far less likely than a large corporation or union to have monopolistic power, any such side effects will tend to be minor.

Of course, in practice the doctrine of social responsibility is frequently a cloak for actions that are justified on other grounds rather than a reason for those actions.

To illustrate, it may well be in the long-run interest of a corporation that is a major employer in a small community to devote resources to providing amenities to that community or to improving its government. That may make it easier to attract desirable employees, it may reduce the wage bill or lessen losses from pilferage and sabotage or have other worthwhile effects. Or it may be that, given the laws about the deductibility of corporate charitable contributions, the stockholders can contribute more to charities they favor by having the corporation make the gift than by doing it themselves, since they can in that way contribute an amount that would otherwise have been paid as corporate taxes.

In each of these—and many similar—cases, there is a strong temptation to rationalize these actions as an exercise of "social responsibility." In the present climate of opinion, with its widespread aversion to "capitalism," "profits," the "soulless corporation" and so on, this is one way for a corporation to generate goodwill as a byproduct of expenditures that are entirely justified in its own self-interest.

It would be inconsistent of me to call on corporate executives to refrain from this hypocritical window-dressing because it harms the foundations of a free society. That would be to call on them to exercise a "social responsibility"! If our institutions and the attitudes of the public make it in their self-interest to cloak their actions in this way, I cannot summon much indignation to denounce them. At the same time, I can express admiration for those individual proprietors or owners of closely held corporations who disdain such tactics as approaching fraud.

Whether blameworthy or not, the use of the cloak of social responsibility, and the nonsense spoken in its name by influential and prestigious businessmen, does clearly harm the foundations of a free society. I have been impressed time and again by the schizophrenic character of many businessmen. They are capable of being extremely far-sighted and clear-headed in matters that are internal to their businesses. They are incredibly short-sighted and muddle-headed in matters that are outside their businesses but affect the possible survival of business in general. This short-sightedness is strikingly exemplified in the calls from many businessmen for wage and price guidelines or controls or income policies. There is nothing that could do more in a brief period to destroy a market system and replace it by a centrally controlled system than effective governmental control of prices and wages.

The short-sightedness is also exemplified in speeches by businessmen on social responsibility. This may gain them kudos in the short run. But it helps to strengthen the already too prevalent view that the pursuit of profits is wicked and immoral and must be curbed and controlled by external forces. Once this view is adopted, the external forces that curb the market will not be the social consciences, however highly developed, of the pontificating executives; it will be the iron fist of Government bureaucrats. Here, as with price and wage controls, businessmen seem to me to reveal a suicidal impulse.

The political principle that underlies the market mechanism is unanimity. In an ideal free market resting on private property, no individual can coerce any other, all cooperation is voluntary, all parties to such cooperation benefit or they need not participate. There are no "social" values, no "social" responsibilities in any sense other than the shared values and responsibilities of individuals. Society is a collection of individuals and of the various groups they voluntarily form.

The political principle that underlies the political mechanism is conformity. The individual must serve a more general social interest—whether that be determined by a church or a dictator or a majority. The individual may have a vote and a say in what is to be done, but if he is overruled, he must conform. It is appropriate for some to require others to contribute to a general social purpose whether they wish to or not.

Unfortunately, unanimity is not always feasible. There are some respects in which conformity appears unavoidable, so I do not see how one can avoid the use of the political mechanism altogether.

But the doctrine of "social responsibility" taken seriously would extend the scope of the political mechanism to every human activity. It does not differ in philosophy from the most explicitly collectivist doctrine. It differs only by professing to believe that collectivist ends can be attained without collectivist means. That is why, in my book *Capitalism and Freedom,* I have called it a "fundamentally subversive doctrine" in a free society, and have said that in such a society, "there is one and only one social responsibility of business—to use its resources and engage in activities designed to increase its profits so long as it stays within the rules of the game, which is to say, engages in open and free competition without deception or fraud."

✦   ✦   ✦

ASSESSING FRIEDMAN'S ETHIC OF SHAREHOLDER WEALTH

✦

On the surface at least, Friedman's views are similar to Carr's. Like Carr, Friedman believes that managers' foremost objective should be "to make as much money as possible" for the owners of the firm. Like Carr, Friedman maintains that this responsibility is constrained only by the need to obey the law, to respect a minimal set of ethical values (what he calls "ethical custom"), principally the avoidance of fraud and force, and to keep in mind the firm's longer-term, strategic interests. Apart from this, managers shouldn't worry about exercising "social responsibility" to promote social benefit or to prevent social harms. But whereas Carr's basic aim is to ease managers' moral qualms, Friedman's view rests on a complex and strongly held ethical position.

♦ THE AGENCY ARGUMENT ♦

Friedman's argument has two main thrusts. One focuses on a manager's moral obligations to his or her firm's owners or shareholders. The second stresses the manager's relative incompetence to make moral decisions about the use of the firm's resources. The first argument draws its force from the view, rooted in business law, that a corporate executive or manager is an "agent" of the firm's owners. Having freely entered into an employment contract with them, the manager is obligated to serve their lawful interests, which generally will be the maximization of profits. Although a manager may use his or her personal time or money to pursue other goals, including moral objectives like reducing poverty, cleaning up the environment, or educating the inner-city poor, he or she may not divert corporate resources for this purpose unless doing so somehow clearly contributes to long-term profitability. Friedman describes the manager who misuses corporate resources as wrongly assuming the role of an elected political official and imposing taxes on the firm's owners without their consent. But his argument is really far more pointed. Ordinarily, we call a person who appropriates others' goods without their permission a "thief." This, in effect, is what Friedman would call a manager who uses corporate resources (including managerial time and effort) for any purpose other than profit maximization.

THE SHAREHOLDER–MANAGER CONTRACT

Although this is a powerful argument, it draws on a series of questionable assumptions. For example, how accurate is Friedman's reading of the implicit "contract" he believes to exist between a firm's owners and its managers? Looked at closely, Friedman's conception of this contract is more appropriate to a small, private business firm than a large public corporation. Imagine someone setting up a company, gathering capital, and hiring a manager for a designated purpose (such as maximizing profit). If the manager then violates the terms of this contract and puts the firm's capital to personal use, the owner will feel deceived and robbed. But the shareholder in a large corporation is in a very different situation. He or she typically buys into an *ongoing* organization whose objectives, values, and priorities are well known and have been shaped by board members, the CEO, and senior executives long before the prospective shareholder entered the scene. Although a small owner may rightfully be indignant if a manager employs resources for purposes outside the framework of their mutual agreement, does a shareholder who freely and knowingly buys into a firm committed to certain objectives, including adherence to ethical standards apart from considerations of profit, have any contractual grounds to object if the firm continues on the course it previously pursued?[5]

Nor for that matter are the shareholders of a modern public corporation as vulnerable to managerial abuse as is the owner of a small, private firm. Whereas the smaller owner is hostage to the manager's use of the firm's capital, today's shareholders (many of whom are large institutional investors) usually operate in a well-established stock market. Shareholders who disagree with the way a firm is managed can join with others to persuade the board and management to change their conduct, a potentially significant course of action where powerful institutional shareholders are involved. Or they can promptly sell their shares and invest in a corporation with a more congenial management style. This does not mean that shareholders in public corporations have no right to rely on reasonable norms of managerial conduct, including the expectation that business decisions will ordinarily be made with satisfactory shareholder return in mind. This expectation is built into existing capital markets and practices. A firm that persistently neglected shareholder return would violate legitimate shareholder wishes and would ultimately fail to secure the capital it needs through public offerings of its stock. But it is one thing to say that managers must give satisfactory shareholder return an important place in their thinking and another to say they may never put ethical considerations before profit. To the extent that corporations are ongoing entities that develop their values over time and make these values known to prospective shareholders, nothing in Friedman's contractual argument rules out considerable room for managerial initiative in establishing a firm's ethical objectives and priorities.

MANAGERIAL CONDUCT AND LIMITED LIABILITY

If Friedman's contractualist approach does not rule out corporate managers' bringing ethical considerations to bear on their decision making, a more complete understanding of the contractual obligations in this area may *require* managers to maintain independent moral oversight of their business dealings and occasionally to subordinate profit to ethics. Another way of putting this is to say that although Friedman is right to stress the importance of managers' contractual obligations, he construes these obligations too narrowly and misses the larger framework in which they stand.

The basic idea is that the corporation and its managers have an implicit contractual relationship to society that follows from the grant of limited liability corporations enjoy.[6] Over the years, society has bestowed on corporations a significant set of powers and protections, one of the most important of which is the provision in business law limiting shareholders' financial liability to the extent of their equity in the firm. At first sight, this may not appear to be much of a benefit. Which of us, after all, wants to see the value of stock we own wiped out if the company does poorly or goes bankrupt? As bad as this may be, how much worse is it to be held personally responsible for every financial obligation of the firm, including damages for which it is liable? In a world where investors run the risk of seeing everything they own—their savings accounts, homes, and pensions—go down with the financial shipwreck of a large corporation in which they hold a few shares, no one would be willing to invest in stock.

To prevent this from happening, society evolved the idea of the limited liability corporation. In doing so, it provided a benefit to corporations and shareholders by protecting the noninvolved assets of individual investors from whatever legal and financial liabilities the firm incurs. Although shareholders can lose their total stock investment in a company, thanks to limited liability they cannot be forced to "ante up" out of their own resources for costs or penalties that exceed the company's net capitalization. Limited liability can thus be likened to a subsidy in the form of an unpaid insurance policy protecting investors' other assets and minimizing, as well, the liability of corporate managers for their organization's failures.[7]

What responsibilities do the corporation and its managers incur in accepting this benefit? Until recently this question may not have been too pressing. Business failures have usually harmed only investors or creditors knowingly involved with the firm. But, more and more, we see business decisions inflicting massive harms on parties often not directly involved in a company's dealings. The financial costs of these harms sometimes exceed the resources of the firm and sometimes the harms continue for generations after the firm has ceased to exist.

The Bhopal case provides a vivid illustration of this problem. Following the disaster, a complex series of legal questions faced U.S. and Indian courts. Was the U.S. parent corporation responsible for compensating the victims, or should UCIL—the Indian subsidiary—bear these costs? Whereas the former had net assets of $10 billion, UCIL's estimated worth was only $250 million. Another question concerned the appropriate level of damages. Should awards be pegged at the level paid to victims and survivors of similar disasters in India during this period, or should Carbide be responsible for damages at the level of recent U.S. awards? If the primary purpose of payment is to compensate survivors or the injured victims for economic losses they suffered, the first approach makes sense. On this reckoning, Carbide's maximum liability might be $500 million, not much more than the company's insurance. One also could argue for a U.S. level of payment on the grounds that an Indian life is no less valuable than an American one and that a lesser payment might encourage multinational corporations like Carbide to "export" hazardous activities to poor third-world nations. If this reasoning prevails, Carbide might be liable for anywhere from $15 billion to $35 billion in damages.[8]

The final resolution of these questions is still uncertain. In 1989, Carbide and the Indian government reached an out-of-court settlement of $470 million, but the government has since come under pressure to rescind what many victims believe is an unfair agreement. Whichever way matters finally go, the Bhopal incident graphically illustrates how important the social subsidy represented by limited liability can be. If Carbide is able to confine responsibility for the disaster to its Indian subsidiary, UCIL's assets of $250 million would be well below the sum needed to meet the victims' most urgent needs, and both Carbide's and UCIL's investors will have been spared a large part of this expense. Should Carbide lose on all its major contentions, and courts hold the parent corporation liable up to the sum of $15 billion, limited liability will still have prevented the victims from obtaining billions of dollars in damages legally due them. Sheltered behind limited liability, Carbide's owners and managers could inflict great suffering on many people and themselves remain protected from the consequences of their decision making. As Christopher Stone has observed, thanks to limited liability, "We have arranged things so that the people who call the shots do not have to bear the full responsibility."[9]

The lesson of the Bhopal case also applies today to many other companies in the chemical, transportation, mineral extraction, energy, pharmaceutical, and financial services industries. Repeatedly, the size, complexity, and scope of corporate decision making threaten harms to society that exceed the financial resources of single firms, causing victims to go unaided or forcing society to step in as a protector of last resort. Sometimes, in addition to the general immunity afforded by limited liability, society fashions additional "safety nets" protective of corporate investors or managers. The U.S. federal deposit insurance program is an example. Acting within the security of its provisions, managers of U.S. savings and loan corporations mishandled assets totaling hundreds of billions of dollars, eventually forcing the federal government to step in to protect depositors and the U.S. banking system as a whole. The Bedlington Federal Savings case, presented at the end of this chapter, illustrates some of these dynamics. As you read this case, try to evaluate how well Bedlington's managers upheld their part of the explicit and implicit "contract" between their firm and society.

Even in industries where there is no explicit insurance program of this sort, limited liability exists as a sign of society's commitment to protect and promote corporate enterprise. In the normal course of things, the enhanced productivity made possible by corporations probably compensates us all for the costs involved in limited liability. But clearly there are limits to what corporations may do. A social commitment to protect the corporation would cease to make sense if corporate owners or managers willfully abused their responsibilities. The implicit social contract behind the existence of the modern corporation, in other words, assumes that corporate owners and managers will exercise substantial responsibility for the conduct of their firm's business. Friedman is right to stress the moral and legal duties managers owe a firm's shareholders. But because his discussion tends to dwell on the simple model of a small firm with its owners and managers instead of the modern limited liability corporation with unprecedented capacity to produce social harms, Friedman ignores or dismisses the larger context of social expectations within which both owners and managers of today's large corporations operate.

✦ THE COMPETENCE ARGUMENT ✦

Friedman's second major argument against the concept of business ethics is that managers are not competent to exercise moral oversight of their business. Because managers are not trained to make socially responsible decisions and companies do not hire them for this purpose, these decisions are better made by public officials accountable to those who elect them. Friedman assumes that a strict division of labor best serves society's needs, with managers singlemindedly pursuing profit within the limits of the law while governments impose constraints on this pursuit by forbidding certain forms of conduct or by levying taxes to fund public goods.

MANAGERIAL ROLE CONFLICT

This view has considerable support in the experience of managers, who often find it compelling to understand themselves as professionals performing a highly specialized function. This is particularly true whenever managers experience a sharp conflict of roles. Sometimes, for instance, they find themselves in painful situations where their responsibility to an organization on whose survival and success many people depend runs directly counter to other roles they play as friends, advisors, or ordinary members of the community. A tempting way of resolving role conflicts of this sort is to put personal values aside, give priority to one's organizational role, and justify doing so by appealing to one's professional identity. A manager might argue, for example, that just as lawyers must place their clients' interests above their own personal judgments of right and wrong, managers must place profit above all personal considerations. Hasn't our society learned that justice is best served by an adversarial legal system, where defense attorneys and prosecutors each singlemindedly perform their specialized function and forget about larger ethical questions? Why, then, is society's best interest not served if managers give priority to their organizational role, place profit first, and leave ethical matters entirely to legislators or government regulators?

   This emphasis on managers' performance of a specialized role and Friedman's related view that managers should leave ethical questions to elected officials both proceed from the assumption that managers are not competent to exercise broad moral judgment about their functions and that government officials or legislators can better identify and address the moral problems created by business. Is this true? Let us consider the case of Bhopal. A striking feature of this incident is that government intervention did not work and may even have contributed to the disaster. This was partly because Carbide's management, like that of many

multinational firms, faced a variety of conflicting legal and political jurisdictions, ranging from the U.S. government to national and local governments in India. Caught within this web of law, regulations, and political
pressures, Carbide's management repeatedly had to make decisions.
Should the company yield to the Indian government's pressure to share
complex technology, or should the parent company and UCIL resist this
pressure in the name of public safety? Should Carbide seek a larger
American presence in its Bhopal facility, or would this send an unfortunate message to its Indian managers? Although there are no simple
answers to these or the many other questions Carbide faced, the
unavoidable need for managerial decision making here contradicts the
simple division of labor that Friedman proposes or the view of managerial role specialization he upholds.

TECHNICAL COMPLEXITY AND MANAGERIAL RESPONSIBILITY

The Bhopal incident illustrates another key feature of modern economic
activity that runs counter to the idea of role specialization and calls on
managers to develop a substantial degree of moral initiative: the increasing technical complexity of business life. In a host of industries, managers are often far better equipped to understand and control the consequences of their activities than are nonspecialists or government officials.
Often—and the Bhopal case, again, is only a striking example—if managers do not attend to the harms created by their choices, no one will. It
is ironic that Friedman, who usually maintains that government officials
ought to refrain from meddling in business matters they do not understand, should advocate total reliance on government and law for the ethical direction of business conduct. Friedman's competence argument
thus works against him. Although managers may not generally be the
best agents of social reform, they are frequently the people most knowledgeable about the specific harms and benefits created by their industry
or firm.

Comparison with other specialized roles bears this out. It is true that
society usually permits lawyers to ignore larger social and moral questions as they defend their clients' interests. This makes sense because in
law a clear adversarial system exists to root out the facts and establish
justice. Nothing like this exists in business, and we have seen that the
increasing complexity of managerial decision making suggests that a
purely adversarial system is not likely to be very effective. Furthermore,
even in law (as in medicine and accounting), professional autonomy is

being increasingly challenged and constrained as pressing new social needs emerge. For example, the lawyers' code of ethics requires attorneys to breach confidentiality whenever illegal behavior by a client threatens the physical safety of other persons.[10] Recently, there have also been proposals to extend this requirement to specific instances of fraudulent behavior in the securities markets.[11] In the field of medicine, courts have limited psychiatrists' duty of confidentiality to patients when serious injury to others might result,[12] and there is a growing tendency to hold accountants legally and financially responsible for violations of law they encounter in the course of performing their professional duties.[13] This suggests that even in the most highly specialized roles, society is asking professionals to assume a measure of independent moral oversight. If so, why should business managers, who potentially affect many people by their decisions, have less responsibility?

THE STAKEHOLDER ALTERNATIVE
✦

Taken together, these considerations suggest that Friedman is wrong to believe that managers' ethical responsibility can be limited to profit maximization. Both in terms of contractual obligations and the needs of society, managers cannot avoid paying attention to the ethical implications of their decisions. This is particularly true whenever managers' decisions or corporate activities risk imposing serious harms on persons. One way of confirming this is to look back on the Bhopal case from the perspective of Friedman's analysis. Applied to this case, Friedman's approach seems to support the policy of cost reduction at Bhopal that led to the disaster. Even if a proponent of Friedman's view tried to argue against this policy on the grounds that the increased risk of an accident threatened long-term liability costs, the relatively low economic value of "Indian lives" might have made these economies seem good business sense. Friedman's approach also seems to support efforts by Carbide in the aftermath of the disaster to deny any responsibility for the accident and to distance itself from its Indian subsidiary as a way of reducing financial liability. If we regard shareholder wealth as a manager's number one priority, this strategy makes good sense. But if this approach strikes us as inhuman and morally wrong because it deprives the accident's victims and their survivors of vital assistance, then we need an alternative model for thinking about managerial ethical responsibility.

✦ DEFINING STAKEHOLDERS ✦

This alternative is often called the *stakeholder* model. Stakeholders are those individuals or groups whose welfare may be seriously affected by a corporation's activities and thus have a "stake" (or claim) in managers' decision making. Stakeholders include the corporation's financiers (shareholders, bondholders, and other creditors or investors), its employees (executives and hourly workers, both active and retired), customers or clients, suppliers, competitors, governmental bodies, and the various communities, from the local to the national and international, in which it operates.[14] Whereas Friedman's shareholder view concentrates on only one line of moral responsibility—that of the manager to the Board and, through the Board, to shareholders—the stakeholder approach sees corporate management as involved in a network of relationships and lines of mutual moral responsibility. Figures 1.1 and 1.2 suggest the contrasts between these views. What is noteworthy is the *variety* of responsibilities the stakeholder model thrusts on managers and, as the two-way arrows in this model indicate, the relative *mutuality* of responsibilities between different constituencies in the corporation. Although it wouldn't be quite correct to say that in the older shareholder model (Figure 1.1) responsibilities were unidirectional, certainly the emphasis was on managers' responsibilities to the Board and, through them, to stockholders. The rights of managers, employees, and other elements of the corporate community were not emphasized. In the stakeholder model, in contrast, emphasis is on the mutual moral responsibilities that connect managers and the Board, managers and other employees, managers and suppliers, and so on.

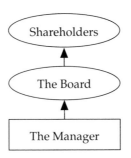

FIGURE 1.1
Friedman's Shareholder Model

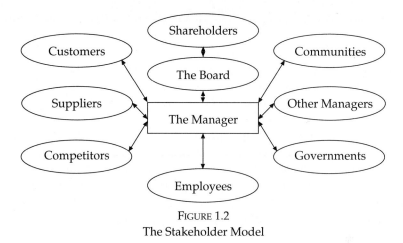

FIGURE 1.2
The Stakeholder Model

Sketching things this way raises several questions. Granted that managers have responsibilities to their organization's stakeholders or constituencies, what are these responsibilities and how do they relate to one another? It seems clear, for example, that managers do not have the same kind or the same degree of responsibility to their firm's competitors as they do to shareholders or employees. Whereas we normally think that the top managers of a firm must disclose financial information or policy decisions to the board of directors as representatives of the shareholders, no one would contend that competitors are entitled to such information. How do we establish the meaning of these different obligations or decide how extensive they are?

✦ CONFLICTS AMONG STAKEHOLDERS ✦

Another important question is what happens when responsibilities to stakeholders conflict. These conflicts are commonplace in daily managerial decision making. Senior managers, seeking to protect their firm against a hostile takeover, for example, may feel compelled to take on additional debt to repurchase stock, but this may injure bondholders by lowering the value of their securities. A decision to recall a harmful product may protect consumers, but only at significant cost to shareholders or employees. An aggressive commitment to affirmative action in hiring may greatly benefit members of a community where a plant is located, but may slow the advancement of some employees previously hired by the firm.

One way of approaching these questions is to itemize in advance the specific obligations owed by managers to each constituency and then rank them in order of importance. For example, one might say that customers have a right to safe products, employees deserve full and frank disclosure of information affecting their safety, compensation, and job security, and shareholders are entitled to a reasonable return on their investment. One might then suggest rough priorities among these obligations or stakeholder rights—for example, by arguing that employees' right to a safe working environment normally takes precedence over shareholder return, and so on.

This is an appealing way of approaching managerial decision making and one that has an established place in the literature of business ethics. In the next chapter, we will see that ethical theorists have formalized a related approach to moral decision in terms of what are sometimes called *deontological* and *rights-based* theories of ethics. But, despite its prevalence and its appeal, this approach has some serious drawbacks. Can we really specify in advance of decisions the meaning of obligations owed to various persons or corporate stakeholders? It may be true that customers have a right to safe products, for example, but what does this mean in view of the different categories of things that corporations produce and consumers purchase? Safety in a motorcycle is not the same thing as safety in a child's toy, nor is the meaning of safety for an experimental drug the same as that for an over-the-counter medication. How, then, do we provide a definition of safety in all the contexts where it may be relevant?

Nor is it clear that we can always rank obligations in advance. Although employees may generally have a right to information that bears on their job security, will this be true in cases where providing such information threatens the firm's survival—and employees' own job security? Ordinarily, shareholders' right to a reasonable return on their investment when profits permit will take very high priority in managers' decisions. This is so because shareholders' willingness to maintain their investment is a condition of the firm's survival and continuing activities. But it is not hard to imagine extreme situations where dissolution or sale of the firm might be the only way of compensating customers or communities for harms done. The experiences of A. H. Robins and Johns-Manville provide examples from recent history. Robins lost its financial independence as a result of the financial costs of settling lawsuits caused by its defective Dalkon Shield intrauterine contraceptive device, and

Manville has been compelled to devote a major portion of its ongoing profits to a trust fund that compensates individuals injured by exposure to asbestos.[15]

✦ BALANCING STAKEHOLDER CLAIMS ✦

The stakeholder view, then, represents only the beginning of our thinking about managerial ethics. It provides a solid alternative to the views of those who deny the existence of managerial ethical responsibility or who, like Friedman, would reduce that responsibility to one stakeholder group alone. In Chapter 10 I argue that a stakeholder perspective is not just a constraint on managerial decision making. Providing value to stakeholders is essential to long-term business success and profitability. But for the stakeholder view to become applicable, it must be supplemented by a more complete account of how we define and establish the moral obligations owed to various constituencies and how we resolve the conflicts between these obligations when they crop up. Traditionally, this task of defining and ranking ethical obligations has been the focus of ethical theory. In the next chapter, we turn to some leading ethical theories that have been developed to guide our thinking about moral conflicts. We do so with this question in mind: If managers and firms are responsible to the various stakeholders they affect, how do we sort out and balance the claims of stakeholders in the real world of managerial decision making?

Case 1.2

✦ BEDLINGTON FEDERAL SAVINGS[16] ✦

In April 1989, William (Bill) Cole, president of Bedlington Federal Savings (BedFed), spoke about the challenges his bank was facing in the short term:

> We're in a bit of a bind right now. There's no question but that we're going to have to recognize some major losses on some loans that have gone bad. We've also got to deal with this accounting rule change [FAS No. 91] that requires us to defer our loan origination fee income. That's

going to cost us several million dollars in income this year alone, and the change comes at a time when we are least able to make up for the income loss. Adding urgency to the problem, there are signs that a corporate raider has targeted us for a takeover. To protect the independence of the entity, we've got to find ways to increase our stock price quickly.

Unfortunately, what we will have to do to get out of this bind will not be particularly pleasant. We can implement some takeover defenses, but they are not totally effective. Our best protection is to get our earnings up. To do so, we may have to make some deep expense cuts, trim our reserves, sell some of our good loans, and, ironically, make some more high-yielding loans which have caused part of our problem. In taking these steps, we will probably be sacrificing some longer-term performance. We believe, however, that our shareholders and employees will be better served if BedFed remains independent.

Bill called for an April 24 meeting of the BedFed Management Committee (comprised of the bank's senior managers). The purpose of the meeting was to discuss ways of signaling the corporation's full value to the stock market.

COMPANY BACKGROUND

Bedlington Federal Savings was a federally chartered savings and loan company headquartered in Bedlington, Florida, a suburb of Orlando. It operated twelve branches in central and northern Florida. At the end of 1988, total assets were $1.4 billion.

Until 1984, BedFed had followed a traditional savings and loan strategy. Deposits came primarily from small savers. Assets were mostly long-term fixed-rate single-family residential mortgage loans made to customers in the greater Orlando area. BedFed's managers prided themselves on knowing their customers well and on providing them with both access to financing and good service.

BedFed's organization structure had always been primarily functional (see Figure A). The branch network generated the bank's deposits and loans. Centralized staff groups provided financial, marketing, and administrative support to the branches. Corporate

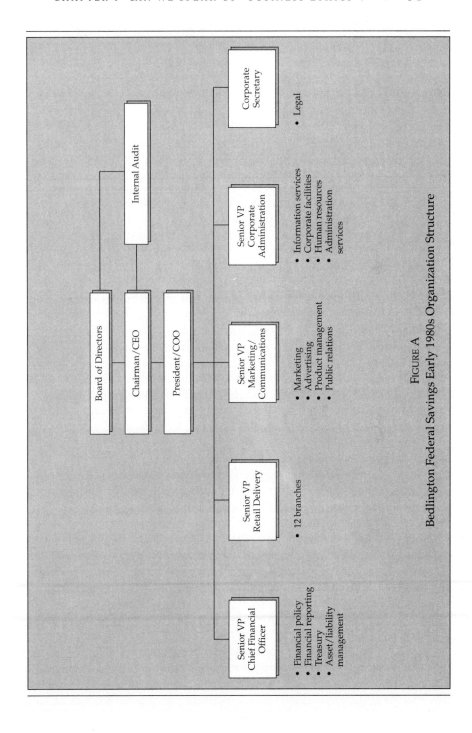

FIGURE A

Bedlington Federal Savings Early 1980s Organization Structure

committees comprised of many of the top-level bank managers made or approved many of the bank's most important decisions, including choices of marketing strategies and decisions to make specific loans.

BedFed suffered major financial problems in the early 1980s. Depositors slowly began moving their money out of passbook accounts, which paid 5.25 percent interest, into certificates of deposit (CDs) that paid market rates of interest. This movement accelerated when interest rates soared to 16 percent (and even higher). BedFed's interest costs rose sharply. The bank's average cost of funds rose from approximately 7 percent in 1978 to more than 11 percent by the end of 1981 with almost no corresponding increase in revenues due to the preponderance of fixed rate mortgages in the bank's asset portfolio.

The higher interest costs and reduced loan demand caused earnings to drop sharply. Even though the cost of funds exceeded the return on mortgages by approximately 1.5 percent, BedFed managers continued to make loans to qualified customers because of a sense of obligation. Then, as interest rates rose and the economy moved into recession, the percentage of BedFed's loans going bad increased. In 1978, the bank's "scheduled items," loans with delinquent interest payments, were only .15 percent of assets. This rose to one percent of assets by 1982. BedFed reported significant losses in 1981 and 1982 because these borrowers defaulted. Earnings began to turn around in 1983 when interest rates began to decline.

In September 1983, BedFed converted from a mutual association to a publicly held stock corporation. Management believed the corporate form of organization would enable BedFed to obtain additional capital from external sources, and would provide the additional funding necessary to participate fully in the rapid growth taking place in the Orlando area. The initial public offering of stock was at $7.50 per share, but the price fell to $6.50 by the end of the fiscal year (March 1984).

In late 1983, BedFed's long-time president retired because of bad health. The Board of Directors hired a new president, William W. "Bill" Cole. Bill, then thirty-four years old, had been a top performer in the mergers and acquisitions department of a New York investment bank. Bill accepted the job, even at a considerable loss in expected compensation, partly because he was attracted by the possibility of returning to live in his native Florida. But, more importantly, he wanted a career change. He said he wanted to work in and build an organization rather than just "do deals" for the rest of his life. He saw a real opportunity at BedFed. At the time he made the career change, Bill told his friends:

> Over the years, BedFed muddled along, as did most savings and loans, in a highly regulated environment. Now the environment has changed. The regulations have been relaxed, and I see the possibility of doing some exciting things.

BILL COLE'S PLANS FOR THE FUTURE

Most people who had worked with Bill Cole characterized him as a born leader. Bill had been successful in every venture in which he had become involved. He served as officer in the Marine Corps during the Vietnam war and was awarded several combat medals. In New York, he had been on the investment banking firm's "fast track." Bill worked hard and played hard. For example, even while working seventy-hour weeks, Bill found time to race his ocean speedboat competitively.

Consistent with his personality, Bill Cole brought aggressive ideas to BedFed. He felt that most savings and loans, including BedFed, had limited their growth potential because they had chosen to generate deposits and loans through their branch organization in their limited geographical areas.

Bill had two primary goals for BedFed: (1) to protect the bank as much as possible from the risks and earnings swings caused by vagaries of interest rate changes; and (2) to make BedFed the largest savings and loan in Florida by the end of the century. His five-year financial goals were annual increases of 20 percent in revenues and 25 percent in profits. At the time he announced these goals to the bank's employees, Bill also remarked:

> I'm aware that BedFed's primary mission, like that of most S&Ls, has been to give people in its geographical area a place to borrow mortgage money. We're not changing that. We're still trying to help people get into a home. But this is now a stock company, so we have another

important mission—to make profits for our shareholders. I don't see any major conflicts in these goals. The better we are at generating profits, the more money we will be able to make available to the community.

THE "REACH FOR THE TOP" PROGRAM

Soon after his arrival, Bill decided to challenge BedFed's employees with a new strategic program. He called it "Reach for the Top." His program consisted of four main parts: First, an emphasis was placed on adjustable-rate mortgages, which the Federal Home Loan Bank Board (FHLBB) had allowed savings and loans to offer only since April 1981. This was intended to shield BedFed somewhat from interest-rate risk. BedFed would still offer fixed-rate mortgages to customers who insisted on them, but loan prices would be set to emphasize adjustable rates. Bill explained this part of the program:

> I'm not terribly concerned about the overall risk. Our capital is above the minimum set by the FHLBB, and I'm confident we will improve over our current position. I am concerned, however, about the high earnings volatility caused by interest rate swings. Those swings are not so costly to a mutual association, but they are unacceptable for a publicly held corporation. They make it look like we can't manage our business. We can't control interest rates, but we can take steps to reduce the effects rate changes have on us.

The second part of the Reach for the Top program was to extend the bank's range of lending to increase the average yield on the bank's loan portfolio. Bill hired Mike Toohey, an old college friend, who had been working as a lending officer in a Philadelphia commercial bank, to start a new investment-lending department. The department was to make loans for the acquisition, development, and construction of real estate ventures. Many apartment and condominium projects were being developed in Florida, and Bill wanted BedFed to become a major player in lending to this market. As compared to single-family residential mortgages, these so-called ADC loans (for *a*cquisition, *d*evelopment, and *c*onstruction) were larger (in the range of $1–10 million, as compared to an average mortgage of $80 thousand), more profitable (fees plus spread over average cost of money of 4 to 10 percent, and sometimes even higher, as opposed to a total of 3 percent for mortgages), and more risky.

Third, the Reach for the Top program involved aggressive marketing. Bill Cole planned to throw a series of gala parties for large current and prospective customers and to sponsor local sporting events to keep BedFed's name in front of the public.

Fourth, Bill implemented a new incentive plan for personnel who could measurably affect BedFed's success. Included in the plan were senior managers, branch managers, and those personnel in the organization directly responsible for generating deposits and loans. About this plan, Bill Cole said, "We want to reward the people who are making us money. It's as simple as that." BedFed had previously provided no incentive compensation for these people.

The new plan provided incentives based on the achievement of management-by-objectives targets tailored to each individual's responsibilities. For a branch manager, for example, the bonus potential was 25 percent of salary, and the targets were for deposit growth, asset growth, and expense control. For the senior vice-president, retail delivery, the bonus potential was 40 percent of salary, and targets were set for lending margin, market share, expense control, net income growth, and personnel development. The specific targets to be achieved were negotiated as part of BedFed's annual planning process.

THE PERIOD 1985–1987

The subsequent three years (1985–1987) were good ones for BedFed (see financial summaries in Tables 1 and 2). The bank's capital/asset ratio (the FHLBB's principal measure of capital adequacy) improved from a dangerous 3 percent in 1983 to over 4 percent by the end of 1987. The increased marketing expenditures generated revenue growth, and earnings were helped by a sustained period of declining interest rates. BedFed's cost of funds declined from 11 percent in 1982 to below 8 percent in 1987.

Table 1

BEDLINGTON FEDERAL SAVINGS INCOME AND EXPENSE SUMMARY FOR YEARS ENDED MARCH 31 (DOLLARS IN MILLIONS)

	1980	1981	1982	1983	1984	1985	1986	1987	1988
Revenues									
Interest income	$56	$59	$60	$65	$77	$ 94	$114	$137	$164
Fees and charges	4	1	2	4	5	6	7	7	9
Investment income	3	2	2	4	4	5	6	6	8
Other income	2	2	3	4	5	6	7	7	7
Total revenues	$65	$64	$67	$77	$91	$111	$134	$157	$188
Expenses									
Interest expense	$49	$59	$70	$69	$72	$86	$94	$116	$141
Other expense	6	7	7	8	9	11	13	18	19
Total expenses	$55	$66	$77	$77	$81	$97	$107	$134	$160
Income before income taxes	$10	$(2)	$(10)	$ 0	$10	$ 14	$ 17	$ 23	$ 28
Income tax expense	4	(1)	(4)	0	4	5	6	9	11
Net income	$6	$(1)	$ (6)	$ 0	$6	$ 9	$ 11	$ 14	$ 17

Table 2

BEDLINGTON FEDERAL SAVINGS SUMMARY STATEMENTS OF FINANCIAL CONDITION AT MARCH 31 (DOLLARS IN MILLIONS)

	1980	1981	1982	1983	1984	1985	1986	1987	1988
Assets									
Cash and securities	$ 43	$ 46	$ 47	$ 48	$ 52	$ 51	$ 57	$ 55	$ 57
Loans receivable	399	420	426	462	548	777	922	1,101	1,302
Other assets	35	37	37	38	44	53	58	66	74

	1980	1981	1982	1983	1984	1985	1986	1987	1988
Total assets	$477	$503	$510	$548	$644	$881	$1,037	$1,222	$1,433
Liabilities and stockholders' equity									
Deposits	$304	$320	$323	$348	$386	$429	$ 473	$ 527	$ 595
Borrowings	151	162	172	185	237	422	524	643	771
Other Liabilities	—	—	—	—	—	1	1	1	1
Surplus/Stock- holders' Equity	22	21	15	15	21	29	39	51	66
Total Liabilities and Surplus/Stockholders' Equity	$477	$503	$510	$548	$644	$881	$1,037	$1,222	$1,433

The growth in loans and deposits generated through the branch organization, even with the opening of some new branches, was limited during this period to about 10 to 15 percent per year. The remainder of BedFed's asset growth during this period was provided through the investment lending organization and financed primarily by institutional sources, including deposits from pension funds, governments, corporations, and high-net-worth individuals. Although the cost of these funds was higher than on branch deposits, there was still a positive spread between these deposits and most loans.

Bank noninterest expenses rose as a percentage of revenues during this period. Corporate marketing expenses rose sharply, as the increased promotions became more expensive. In addition, BedFed purchased two corporate airplanes to allow executives and officers in the investment lending department to visit remote sites and return in the same day. On the other hand, branch administrative expenses declined as Bill Cole pushed the branch managers to cut fat from their organizations.

BedFed's managers took advantage of the sustained period of profit growth to increase its reserves for potential losses on the more lucrative but riskier investment loans. At the end of 1987, Harvey Wooten, BedFed's chief financial officer (CFO), commented:

Over the last few years, we bumped up our reserves quite significantly. Our loan portfolio is certainly more risky than it used to be, but we more than reflected that risk in our reserves. We wanted our judgments to be quite conservative, as long as we could afford the earnings hit. Just recently we did an internal study showing areas where we thought we were over and under reserved. Our auditors did a study and drew the same conclusion. They told us they were pleased with our position.

BedFed's management decided not to take one potential income-reducing action during this period. In 1985, regulations were changed to allow savings and loans to offer money market accounts paying market rates. These rates, usually in excess of 7 percent, were considerably higher than the 5.5 percent rates offered on passbook accounts, yet the money market accounts offered no loss in liquidity and little increase in risk. BedFed's managers considered either eliminating the passbook accounts that they now considered obsolete or implementing an aggressive informational campaign to convince their customers of the superiority of the money market accounts. They rejected both ideas, however, because they feared the increased interest expense would adversely affect the bank's ability to compete. At this time, one of the bank's long-time employees remarked:

> I think the old BedFed would have tried to convince its customers to move their money. In those days we were more interested in providing good service for our customers and less interested in profits.

Over the 1984–87 period, it was clear that Bill Cole had changed BedFed's organizational culture significantly. Many of the long-term employees had left the bank. They were replaced with younger, better educated, more aggressive employees. Total compensation had increased for most management personnel. With incentives, even some of the top investment lending and institutional sales personnel were earning over $100,000 per year.

THE SITUATION IN 1988

In 1988, BedFed's managers became concerned about a flattening of the earnings trend. Interest rates had stopped declining, so the bank was no longer enjoying the boost to their lending spread caused by longer-term lending than borrowing.

To attempt to maintain the bank's recent earnings growth trend, Bill Cole took several actions, proven to be successful, that he felt would complement the Reach for the Top program. At midyear, he instituted a 6-percent across-the-board cut in branch general and administrative expenses. The branch managers complained that this was not a wise decision. They pointed out that revenues had increased sharply over the last four years, yet the branches were operating with fewer employees than in 1984. The result was that customer service was declining even while most employees were working longer hours. The workload had increased to the point where some long-time employees quit. The bank replaced them with new, inexperienced employees whose lack of skills caused further customer-service problems.

Bill also called for a series of meetings in the last half of the year to discuss other actions that might be taken. Following are the major ideas that were implemented:

1. Steps were to be taken to reduce the bank's year- and quarter-end deposits to save Federal Savings and Loan Insurance Corporation (FSLIC) fees. FSLIC fees were charged at the rate of one twelfth of one percent of savings capital at the end of the year and one thirty-second of one percent each quarter. BedFed managers reduced the fees the banks had to pay by setting abnormally low period-end deposit rates to discourage savings. The savings funds were replaced by borrowing short-term money, such as pension funds, from institutions.

2. When bank profits were below plan, lending officers boosted the loans made at the end of the accounting quarter or year. The boost was implemented by promising "teaser" rates on loans that were 100 basis points (and sometimes even more) below the rates paid for deposits. Even though these loans did not generate a positive interest rate spread for at least three years, they allowed the bank to recognize the loan origination fees (typically 2 to 4 percent of the loan principal) immediately as accounting profits.

3. Assets were sold to generate additional profits as necessary. Many loans were recorded on the books at less than market value, so accounting gains could be recognized when these

loans were sold. The only constraint the bank faced was that investment analysts routinely looked at loan sales volumes. If the sales volume was abnormally high, the analysts knew the reported profits were not all recurring.

4. Bank reserves, particularly for expected loan losses, were reduced by nearly one third just before year end, thereby increasing after-tax net income by nearly $1 million. BedFed's auditors questioned the decrease, but management explained to them that they had updated their loan-by-loan review and concluded that prior estimates had been too conservative. Harvey Wooten, BedFed's CFO, provided this rationalization for this action: "It's a little bit manipulative, sure. But I don't lose any sleep over it because our reserves are still in that broad range that must be considered acceptable. My feeling is that if I am aware of an action that helps the company and that is not a clear violation of law or a specific accounting rule, then it is my obligation to take that action."

Table 3

BEDLINGTON FEDERAL SAVINGS
STOCK PRICE HISTORY

	1983	*1984*	*1985*	*1986*	*1987*	*1988*
Low	6⅜	6⅜	7	8	5½	5⅝
High	7⅝	7¾	8½	10¼	11⅞	8½
Year-end	6½	6⅜	7¾	9½	5⅜	7⅝

THE SITUATION IN 1989

For several reasons, profit pressure became even greater in fiscal year 1989. First, BedFed's stock price, which had fallen at the time of the 1987 crash, remained low. This was partially due to the perception of a broad-based crisis in the savings and loan industry. Bank managers worried that the price, which was trading near $7.00 early in the year, would fall even further if earnings dipped. The low market price was especially worrisome because a corporate takeover specialist was rumored to have been acquiring BedFed shares. Concern was high because trading volume had

risen sharply, and because managers feared that the takeover specialist might be interested in using the bank's federally insured
deposits to fund his own development projects. As a partial
response, BedFed's Board of Directors implemented some anti-
takeover defenses, including a poison pill[17] and a plan to repurchase shares that, they explained, "appeared to be undervalued in
the market."

Second, BedFed was engaged with other banks in a deposit-rate
war. Such wars occur whenever there is a general expectation of
increasing interest rates because bank managers want to secure
increased deposits before rates peak.

Third, the Financial Accounting Standards Board (FASB) passed
a new rule (FAS No. 91) that prohibited the recognition of loan
origination and commitment fees, typically 2 to 4 percent of the
loan principal, at the inception of a loan. Instead, such fees were
required to be recognized as income over the term of the loan, as an
adjustment of yield.

Fourth, interest payments on two large ADC loans were not
current. It was likely that loan-loss reserves would have to be
increased sharply to cover these highly visible problems.

In response to these pressures, the Management Committee
agreed to continue the earnings management actions they had
begun during the last year. They also agreed to take some new
actions. To evade the FAS No. 91 ruling, they decided to sell virtually all the bank's loans shortly after they were made in order to
capture the loan origination fee income immediately in accounting
income.

The Committee also decided to tighten the bank's mortgage
lending requirements. This action was taken to free up funds that
could be used to make more higher-yielding ADC loans that would
yield more fee income and higher interest-rate spreads. Bill Cole
provided one lead. He stated that several of his investment-bank-
ing friends were now involved in real estate development. He felt
they might be willing to agree to loans with high early fees and at
high interest rates in exchange for a reliable source of capital for
their ventures.

In a meeting on April 27, 1989, after a lengthy discussion,
BedFed's Board of Directors concurred with the new planned
actions. During the meeting, when Bill Cole was asked if the
actions were excessively short-term oriented, he replied:

We must concentrate on the short term; we have no choice. We can't tell analysts we are suffering short-term interest rate pressures. That's not a good story. We're competing for funds with businesses who do not face such pressures. We've got to manage our business in a way that makes it look attractive to investors.

QUESTIONS TO CONSIDER

1. In your view, were any of the actions undertaken by BedFed's managers or Board of Directors unethical?

2. How do you think Albert Carr would view the conduct of BedFed's managers and Board? Among other things, how would he assess the Management Board's decision to evade the FAS No. 91 ruling?

3. How would Milton Friedman evaluate these actions? For example, what would he say about the decision to tighten the bank's mortgage lending requirements and the decision to concentrate on the short term?

4. What considerations might a stakeholder view present in this case? How would it assess the decisions regarding the FAS ruling and mortgage standards? How might it regard Bill Cole's history of leadership of the bank?

5. What does this case say to you about the ethical responsibilities of business managers?

$\mathcal{N}$OTES

1. This case is based on treatments by Arthur Sharplin, "Union Carbide of India, Ltd.: The Bhopal Tragedy," *Case Research Journal* 1985, pp. 229–48; and Thomas N. Gladwin, "A Case Study of the Bhopal Tragedy," chap. 10 in *Multinational Corporations, Environment and the Third World*, Charles Peason, ed. (Durham, N.C.: Duke University Press, 1986).
2. *Business Ethics*, 3rd ed. (New York: Macmillan, 1990), p. 3.
3. *The Wealth of Nations*, I.ii.2.
4. *Harvard Business Review*, 46, no. 1 (Jan.–Feb. 1968): 145.

5. For a discussion of the weaknesses in Friedman's contractual argument, see Richard Nunan, "The Libertarian Conception of Corporate Property: A Critique of Milton Friedman's Views on the Social Responsibility of Business," *Journal of Business Ethics* 7, no. 12 (December 1988): 891–906.
6. The concept of an implied social contract between the corporation and society is developed by Thomas Donaldson in his *Corporations and Morality* (Englewood Cliffs, N.J.: Prentice-Hall, 1982), chap. 3. The economic and public policy implications of limited liability for multinational corporations have been developed by K. John, L. W. Senbet, and A. Sundaram in their article "Cross-Border Liability of Multinational Enterprises, Border Taxes, and Capital Structure," *Financial Management* 20, no. 4 (Winter 1991): 54–67.
7. Christopher D. Stone views the legal doctrine of limited liability as partly representing a compromise in the struggle between managers and shareholders to pass accountability for financial liability off to one another. See his *Where the Law Ends* (New York: Harper & Row, 1973), pp. 16, 23.
8. The higher estimate is offered by R. Claton Trotter, Susan G. Day, and Amy E. Love in their article, "Bhopal, India, and Union Carbide: The Second Tragedy," *Journal of Business Ethics* 8 (1989): 439–54.
9. *Where the Law Ends*, p. 46. Contrast this argument with Michael Jensen's claim that stockholders should have total control of the corporation because they are the bearers of all its residual risk ("Takeovers: Folklore and Science," *Harvard Business Review* [November–December 1984]: 111). Stone's point, and mine, is that limited liability effectively transfers some of this risk to society as a whole.
10. American Bar Association, *Model Rules of Professional Conduct* (Chicago: American Bar Association, 1984).
11. The American Law Institute has suggested a rule in its "Restatement on the Law of the Law Governing Lawyers" requiring lawyers to break confidence when a client places fraudulent information in a stock prospectus if the fraud is likely to result in a "substantial financial loss" (*New York Times*, 14 May 1990: D2).
12. *Tarasoff* v. *Regents of the University of California*, 529 Fd. 2d 553.
13. Ahmed Riahi-Belkaoui, *Morality in Accounting* (Westport, Conn.: Quorum Books, 1992), chaps. 3 and 4.
14. For a comprehensive discussion of stakeholder theory, see R. Edward Freeman and Daniel R. Gilbert, Jr., *Corporate Strategy and the Search for Ethics* (Englewood Cliffs, N.J.: Prentice Hall, 1988).
15. Discussions of these episodes include Nicole Grant, *The Selling of Contraception: The Dalkon Shield Case, Sexuality, and Women's Autonomy* (Columbus: Ohio State University Press, 1992); and Paul Brodeur, *Outrageous Conduct: The Asbestos Industry on Trial* (New York: Pantheon Books, 1985). Manville's difficulties continue. See "Manville Payout Plan Back to Square One," *Business Insurance*, December 14, 1992, p. 2.
16. This case is based on Kenneth A. Merchant, "Instructional Case: Bedlington Federal Savings," *Issues in Accounting Education* 4, no. 2 (Fall 1989): 359–74. Reprinted by permission.

17. "Poison pill" is a name given to a protective strategy against "hostile" (or unwelcome) corporate takeovers. Poison pills work by saddling anyone who contemplates a hostile takeover with the prospect of burdensome new financial obligations. One type of poison pill, for example, requires the new owners of a firm to pay a substantial premium to existing shareholders once the takeover is accomplished.

ETHICAL THEORIES AND MORAL CHOICE

✦

✦In Case 2.1 Phil Cortez faces a moral problem. The conduct and demands of his boss run counter to Phil's sense of right and wrong. Phil also stands at the beginning of a series of decisions with consequences for his life and career. Should he cooperate with these organizational demands or should he resist them? If noncooperation is appropriate, what form should it take? Although this process of decision making is a complex one, shaped by many personal considerations, it begins with a single basic question: "Is what I'm being asked to do morally right or wrong?" Before he chooses a course of action, Phil must be reasonably sure he understands the moral issues in the situation he faces. Ethical theory exists to help with this basic question. Over the centuries, philosophers and theologians have sought to develop theories providing insight into the process of moral decision and guidance through it. In this chapter we look at some of the leading theories of ethics and see what bearing they might have on situations facing managers like Phil Cortez.

Text continues on page 47.

Case 2.1

✦ "THE COSTS OF KEEPING A SECRET"[1] ✦

Phillip Cortez reread the engineering director's memo with considerable anxiety. It read: "Call me at your earliest convenience about design specs for new radial."

"New radial"—that could mean only one thing: that his employer, National Rubber and Tire, wanted to beat its biggest competitor, Lifeworth, in getting an 80,000-mile, puncture-proof tire on the market.

Ordinarily such a memo would signal a challenge for an employee as conscientious and industrious as Phil Cortez. But until six months ago Cortez had been employed by Lifeworth. While there, he had been instrumental in drawing up designs for a similar tire that Lifeworth was not only interested in producing but was also counting on to revitalize its sagging profit posture. In fact, so important did Lifeworth consider Cortez's work that, when he had announced his departure, Lifeworth's president reminded him of an agreement which Cortez had entered into when undertaking his work with Lifeworth. He had promised to refrain from disclosing any classified information directly or indirectly to competitors for a period of two years after his termination with Lifeworth. In no uncertain terms the president indicated that he considered Cortez's work on the new radial highly classified. Cortez had assured the president that he anticipated no conflict of interests since National had given him every reason to believe that it wanted him in primarily a managerial capacity.

And now, the memo was staring him in the face. Cortez responded to it that very afternoon and had his worst fears realized. As he'd suspected, the engineering director solicited Cortez's input on the matter of a new radial.

Cortez unhesitatingly explained his dilemma. While sympathetic to Cortez's predicament, the director broadly hinted that refusal to provide constructive input would not only result in a substantial disservice to National but was bound to affect Cortez's standing with the firm. "After all," the director said, "it's very difficult to justify paying a man a handsome salary and expediting his movement up the organizational ladder when his allegiances obviously lie elsewhere."

The conversation ended icily with the director's advising Cortez to "think about it."

QUESTIONS TO CONSIDER

1. What do you believe to be Phil Cortez's moral obligations in this situation? Why does he have these obligations?
2. What would you recommend that Phil do?

"ETHICS" AND "MORALITY"

✦

Until this point I have used the terms "ethics" and "morality" interchangeably to designate the judgments we make about right and wrong behavior. This use of terms is historically warranted. "Ethics" is derived from the Greek word *ethos,* meaning the character or custom of a people. The Latin word *mos,* from which our term "morality" derives, also refers to the customs or regular practices of a social group. Hence, both these terms have to do with the expected practices of a community and, by extension, its individual members. They describe what a society believes to be right or wrong.

Some philosophers have tried to make a distinction between the terms "morality" and "ethics." The former, they maintain, should be used to describe the actual values, conduct, and norms of a community, whereas the latter should be reserved for the systematic study of these values. Ethics, on this understanding, is the "science" of morality. Nevertheless, we can see that in their etymologies and daily employment these terms are used interchangeably, and we will do so as well. In the discussions that follow I speak of "moral" or "ethical" judgments or of "immoral" or "unethical" conduct; whichever term is used, we will be dealing with the norms people use to evaluate one another's social conduct.

✦ THE SPHERE OF ETHICS ✦

Ethical or moral judgments are essentially normative: they tell us what people *should do* in specific circumstances and they lay down prescribed courses of conduct. In the words of one philosopher, ethics involves the "ought thought."[2] When we conclude that some form of conduct is unethical or immoral, we express our belief that people "ought not" act in that way. Ethical judgments are not the only "ought thoughts" we possess. By surveying the different types of normative judgments that bear on our lives and by seeing how ethical "oughts" are distinctive, we can arrive at a better understanding of the specific kinds of judgments ethics involves.

PRUDENCE

The most common kinds of normative judgment have to do with our own welfare or happiness. Frequently, friends, loved ones, or colleagues tell us that we "ought to" do something if we wish to secure some benefit for ourselves or that we "ought not to do" something else if we wish to avoid harm. For example, an acquaintance may tell us that we should lock our car securely in her neighborhood if we want to avoid theft. A tennis instructor may tell us that we are not holding the racket "the right way" or that our method of serving is "wrong."

These statements involve judgments of prudence because they seek to promote our personal happiness (or avoid our unhappiness). In each instance, those who counsel us suppose we have some goal connected to our well-being—the protection of our property, success at tennis—and their advice or counsel aims at that goal. Although the various words used in prudential statements have a moral ring to them, the "shoulds," "oughts," "rights," or "wrongs" of prudence may have nothing at all to do with ethics or morality in any larger sense and may even be used to convey crassly immoral advice. For example, it makes perfect sense for a drug dealer to counsel a younger protégé on the "rights" and "wrongs" of the street trade.

In contrast to the "ought" of prudence, the "ought" of morality has a social reference. Whereas prudence concerns our individual interest, morality concerns other persons' or society's welfare generally. When I act morally, I take others' interests into account. Advice is "moral" if it arises from a concern with the way our behavior affects other people. Of course, judgments of prudence and judgments of morality can overlap. A close friend may counsel us to treat others fairly in part because he fears the consequences of their anger for us. His ethical advice has a prudential component. Or, we might counsel someone to look after herself not only because we are concerned about her welfare, but because we value the contribution she can make to society. This interweaving of ethical and prudential concerns is common in business ethics because managers are most comfortable with personal ethical commitments that also serve a firm's business objectives. As we seek to understand moral judgments, it is important to keep these two kinds of "ought" separate in our minds, since they can sometimes lead in different directions. When we give or receive advice or make normative judgments, therefore, it is always important to know whether the "ought" involved is one of prudence or morality.

ETIQUETTE

A second type of "ought" also has a social reference: the norms governing manners, courtesy, and social propriety. For example, when we are planning to visit friends for a weekend, we may be reminded that it is "appropriate" to bring a house gift; and when we are planning to attend a wedding, we may learn that it would be "wrong" to toast the new couple before the best man does so. In matters of dress for business or social settings, prescriptive judgments like these abound. Judgments of etiquette have considerable force in our lives, and these are not unrelated to other types of prescriptive norms. Breaches of etiquette can be imprudent and, when they cause injury to others or frustrate important expectations, may also have a moral dimension.

But the "ought" of etiquette remains distinct from the "ought" of morality because it involves lesser stakes for human welfare. Although we may rebuke someone who acts impolitely or violates a matter of social propriety, we usually reserve our most serious judgments for immoral conduct. And, when the norms of etiquette conflict with those of morality, usually there is little question that moral conduct, because of its far greater impact on human welfare, takes priority. We see a moving illustration of this in the film *Out of Africa*, when the leading female character, played by Meryl Streep, interrupts a colonial governor's garden party to beg protection for a small native village threatened by development. Although the heroine's disruptive behavior scandalizes the English matrons looking on, we deeply sympathize with her, recognizing that moral concerns take precedence over matters of etiquette or decorum.

LAW

So far, we have identified ethics as the sphere of "oughts" dealing with matters of substantial social concern—significant goods and evils for members of society generally. There remains one final normative area and another kind of "ought" fitting this description that must be distinguished from ethics proper. This is the sphere of law.

It is very common to say that ethics and law are entirely separate. This view underlies the phrase "You can't legislate morality." But even a moment's reflection suggests that this separation is misleading. Most persons, for example, regard the willful taking of an innocent human life as morally wrong. Most also would regard sexual violence or the breaking of serious commitments to be immoral. Yet all civilized societies prohibit these forms of conduct through laws dealing with murder, rape, or the sanctity of contracts. We do, then, sometimes legislate morality, and we believe that certain moral rules deserve legal expression.

When people say "You can't legislate morality" they do not mean that *some* moral requirements cannot be enacted into law. Instead, they mean that we cannot enact into law *all* the requirements or ideals of our moral codes. There is a sphere of morality that is much wider than law. Figure 2.1 depicts these relations.

This figure lets us see that law is largely a subdomain of ethics and morality. It comprises those specific moral norms to which society attaches its most severe sanctions and penalties, including fines or jail terms. Thus, although we generally regard the keeping of promises as a

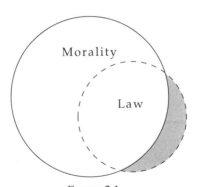

FIGURE 2.1
Law as a Subset of Morality

moral obligation, the law does not uphold all promises, but only those made in specific and designated ways—and these we call contracts. Similarly, although it is usually morally wrong to injure other persons, the law prohibits only the most serious forms of harm, attaching civil or criminal penalties to them.

One reason society legislates morality, attaching penalties to some forms of immoral behavior but not to others, has to do with the serious-ness of the issues involved. Law usually involves only the most impor-tant elements of a society's moral code. There are other reasons why we also sometimes abstain from legislating morality. Some prohibitions, no matter how important, are unenforceable. This explains why all but the most solemn promises made between lovers are not legally upheld. Certain aspects of morality are too much in dispute to warrant legal enactment. The United States' experience with Prohibition illustrates both this problem and the problem of enforcement. When people say "You can't legislate morality," therefore, they usually mean that a certain form of conduct should not be legally prohibited because it does not involve evils serious enough to warrant legal prohibition or because a ban on it is either too controversial or too difficult to enforce.

If Figure 2.1 accurately depicts our thinking about law and morality, it also suggests other important features of these two areas of normative judgment. For example, although law is largely a subset of morality, there may be legal enactments (the shaded area in the figure) that go beyond morality or defy moral expectations. Immoral laws fit here. History offers many examples of such laws. In the United States, the Southern "Jim Crow" segregation laws that prevailed until the 1960s were of this kind. Such legislation is usually notorious and widely con-demned, suggesting that this sector should not, ideally, be very large.

The broken line between the spheres of morality and law suggests that this boundary line is rarely definite and fixed. It is a permeable fron-tier, with matters in the sphere of morality sometimes moving into the sphere of law (or, less frequently, matters that were once legally enforced ceasing to be so). This can take place through any of the processes by which law is established: statutory enactment, administrative regulation, judicial reinterpretation of customary (or common) law, or constitutional reinterpretation or revision. Driving such changes are a community's developing moral perceptions, as when, in the light of experience, we reconsider a matter formerly believed not serious enough to justify legal attention and make it subject to legal penalties. This can sometimes happen even after the fact. A jury in a civil lawsuit, for example, may rule that a form of injury not previously prohibited by society should now be more strenuously discouraged, and it may do this by inflicting severe penalties on the perceived wrongdoer who acted under the assumption that his or her conduct was legal. The substantial damages now being awarded by some juries to women who contend that their health was damaged by silicone breast implants is one illustration of this dynamic.[3]

The relationship between law and morality and the permeability of the boundary between them is something of great importance to managers. There is a recurrent tendency in business organizations to limit one's normative thinking to the "hard" sphere of law and to believe that ethical questions can be delegated to the office of corporate counsel. We saw this brought out in the views of Carr and Friedman. This way of looking at things is understandable, since legal norms, because they are often recorded in public documents, usually seem clearer than those of ethics and have serious penalties attached to them. Nevertheless, Figure 2.1 shows us that there is no such thing as a fixed sphere of law separate from ethics. Law comprises the crystallized and enforced judgments of a community's evolving moral sensibility. As such, law is always changing and always shaped by moral perceptions. A manager who neglects ethics and tries to steer a course by the norms of law alone is likely to violate not only a community's moral sensibilities, but the law itself as it changes to reflect them. A capacity to make sound moral judgments, therefore, is as important to good management as is attention to legal norms.

The situation in which Phil Cortez finds himself illustrates these considerations. It would be tempting for Phil to try to assess his predicament solely in terms of the legal consequences of his choice. He might ask, for example, whether he would be likely to face civil penalties for violating the oral contract into which he entered with his former employer and he might try to let the answer to this question decide his course of action. But this approach has two serious drawbacks. First, in terms of law, Phil cannot avoid coming to terms with the moral issues raised by the misuse of proprietary information. Although American courts have often been reluctant to deprive persons of their ability to earn a living and have frequently sided with employees in cases like this,[4] the law in this area is not static. Phil may find to his dismay that the ethical issues in this case prove disturbing enough to alter the previous pattern of court rulings. Second, and more important, even if Phil could escape legal punishment for his conduct, there remains the serious moral question of whether it is right for him to break his word in this way. Unless Phil comes to terms with the ethical side of this issue he may emerge from this situation legally unscathed but ethically compromised in his own and others' eyes.

By a process of narrowing, therefore, we have arrived at a rough but useful understanding of the "ought" sphere unique to ethics. We can think of it as comprising *those normative judgments about social conduct involving significant matters of good and evil for members of society but not necessarily enforced or upheld by legal penalties.* Ethical judgments of this sort are logically separable from judgments concerning prudence, etiquette, and law. Of course, in reality, these areas of judgment are rarely separate, and managers must often make decisions that simultaneously involve matters of prudence, propriety, ethics, and law. But it is useful to maintain the distinction between these spheres in our thinking since, as we have begun to see, the considerations that shape judgment in each sphere may be very different and may even conflict.

THREE QUESTIONS OF ETHICS
✦

Just as it is important to distinguish ethics from other normative areas, so is it helpful to understand precisely what kind of ethical question is at stake in a particular instance of moral decision. Over the centuries, philosophers have identified at least three different questions bearing on moral conduct. A complete approach to ethics requires us to answer all three questions, although, as we will see, they may not be equally pressing when it comes to making ethical decisions in a managerial context.

✦ THE QUESTION OF "VALUE" ✦

When we think in a very basic way about right or wrong behavior in society, it is natural to ask which values or goods we want to promote through our moral norms. Do we cherish competitive achievement and human fitness to survive? If so, it seems that norms rewarding boldness and daring are appropriate. Do we value each person's unique personality and individual aspirations for happiness? If so, norms for a more nurturing and less competitive society might be a better choice.

Reasoning this way centuries ago, the great philosophers of Greece believed that a definition of ethics must begin by first identifying the basic values at which we aim and by specifying what they called "the good life." Only after this had been done, thinkers like Plato and Aristotle believed, could specific norms for human social conduct be defined. In their writings, these philosophers discussed a host of values, ranging from sensual pleasure and artistic enjoyment to the display of self-restraint and courage. Unfortunately, many of these discussions ended in stalemate, with competing visions of the good life set forth but with no single vision prevailing.

These problems in the Greek approach to ethics led some later philosophers to conclude that the Greeks had misconceived the essential task of ethics, focusing on the wrong question by emphasizing values at the beginning of their inquiry. There is no real agreement about what the "good things" in life are. Some of us are hedonists who cherish physical or sensual pleasures and have little interest in "loftier" pursuits. Others pursue intellectual enjoyments or forms of physical or mental self-discipline. But these discrepancies do not ordinarily prevent agreement on some basic norms of moral conduct. Just as a civilized society can establish legal norms without a clear consensus on the good or bad life, so can ethics identify certain basic ethical or unethical ways of acting regardless of people's personal visions of happiness. For the later philosophers, the question of "the good" or "the good life" is important, and each of us must confront it as we decide how to live our lives. But it is not the primary or central question of ethics.

◆ THE QUESTION OF VIRTUE OR MORAL CHARACTER ◆

When the focus of inquiry turns from different visions of the good life to basic ways of conducting oneself it becomes natural to ask what makes a person morally good or bad. This is the question of "moral character" or "virtue." A long tradition in ethics (and one that has recently reemerged with new vigor[5]) considers this the most important question of ethical theory. Those who hold this view observe that we not only distinguish between a particular act a person performs and the intentions or more basic motives that underlie it, but we tend to think that such intentions and motives are the most important factors in our moral assessment of that person's conduct. For example, I may try to help a friend by lending her money but, unexpectedly, she may use the funds in ways that harm her. Although my act proves harmful, my intentions and underlying motives were good, and, overall, we would not judge my conduct to be wrong.

Persons' intentions and motives enter into our judgments about their moral character. In the eyes of those who focus on the question of character, our judgments about a person's intentions and motives are more important than any we make about specific actions, since a person of good character will usually try to do the right thing, whereas someone whose character is vicious may sometimes do the right thing, but more often will not. For those who reason this way, this question of character—what it is that makes someone a morally good or bad person—is thus the central and foremost one with which ethics must deal.

This question of personal moral worth or character is undoubtedly an important, perhaps even the most important, part of moral theory. In managerial contexts, ethical decisions frequently require us to make careful judgments of character. No manager can be everywhere or make all decisions for a large firm. Hence, the major moral responsibility of ethical managers is to choose subordinates whose moral integrity can be relied on. Frequently, as well, complex moral decisions turn less on the specific rights and wrongs of the case, which are often hard to determine or assess, than on an evaluation of the moral character of various advisors or parties to the dispute. Sound judgments of character, therefore, are essential to ethical management.

✦ THE CENTRAL QUESTION: RIGHT CONDUCT ✦

Nevertheless, for all their practical importance, judgments about moral worth are probably not the first question of ethics. This is because we ultimately judge a person's character by the deeds one intends to perform. A good person, we normally think, is one who wants to and habitually tries to do what is right. Although we recognize that no one will always do the right thing (and hence are prepared to distinguish the person from the deed), we expect that a striving in this direction is the measure of moral character. If this is true, judgments about specific actions or forms of conduct logically precede judgments about personal moral worth: we must know what is the right thing to do before we can assess whether a person's intentions, motives, or character are morally praise-worthy.

LEADING THEORIES OF ETHICS
◆

This third question of ethics is the most pressing one we face and is also the focus of some leading theories of ethics. These theories aim to help us decide when an act is right or wrong. Typically, the philosophers who build them begin with a basic understanding of why we have and need morality. From this, they develop a method of moral reasoning meant to guide our thinking in difficult instances. Very often this method of reasoning also produces a moral principle or set of principles that we are called on to apply when choosing between courses of action.

It is important to recognize that these theories are not meant to replace our day-to-day, intuitive moral judgments. The best theories usually begin with the clearest of our commonsense moral beliefs and seek to analyze and extend their underlying logic to help us with new or perplexing situations of moral choice. A theory that defies moral common sense by suggesting that it is morally right to injure innocent persons gratuitously or to lightly break solemn promises would probably be regarded as an inadequate account of our basic moral thinking. Like any theoretical enterprise, a good moral theory tries to remain true to the data of our experience, correcting them only when there is a compelling reason to think that they are in error. A good theory also must provide a coherent account of our basic moral thinking, must help us explain and justify our moral views to others, and must yield conclusions in new areas that strike us as morally reasonable and consistent with our deepest moral beliefs.

◆ FOUR LESS-THAN-ADEQUATE VIEWS ◆

We will begin by looking at four basic theories of right conduct that have always enjoyed great popularity but which, on closer inspection, fail to meet the minimum criteria of an adequate theoretical position. We will see that each of these views—ethical egoism, ethical relativism, an ethics based solely on religious teachings, and the position that right or wrong is simply a function of each person's conscience—responds to important aspects of our moral thinking. But, as a complete theory of right conduct or a unique guide to moral decision, each is seriously deficient.

ETHICAL EGOISM

Ethical egoism is the view that holds that *an act is right when it best promotes the individual's long-term self-interest.* Proponents of ethical egoism maintain that, when trying to decide whether a course of conduct is right or wrong, each of us must look only to our own long-run advantage. If an action promotes our long-term well-being, it is morally the right thing to do. If not, it is morally wrong.

It is important to recognize that ethical egoists generally emphasize that it is one's *long-term* self-interest that must be taken into account in making moral decisions. Ethical egoism, its defenders argue, does not mean that each of us should "eat, drink, and be merry." Genuine egoists will usually be sober and responsible citizens because they must take into account the extended consequences of their actions. Egoists will also avoid intemperance or injuring others because they fear the various harms they may suffer as their reckless or antisocial behavior rebounds on them.

But what if the egoist can ignore such harms? What if I value short-term gain more than long-term harm or if I can injure others without jeopardizing my own long-term well-being? What if I am so powerful that I can evade the retaliation of others? In such cases, it seems, ethical egoism not only counsels me to pursue an aggressive course, but declares this the "right" thing to do. Although ethical egoists believe such situations are rare, they concede that even in such circumstances egoists must do what best promotes their self-interest.

A moment ago I said that a theory of ethics that markedly defies our moral common sense is probably unacceptable. We can see that ethical egoism is such a theory. By reducing moral judgments to matters of prudence, it makes social conduct depend on each person's particular wishes and desires and opens the way to a society riddled with conflict. It also leads to the odd conclusion that if two persons wish to pursue courses of conduct leading them into bitter conflict with one another, each may be morally right, since this view defines "right" only in terms of what each individual believes will best promote his or her long-term interests. Thus, according to the egoist account of right conduct, we may conclude that both the murderer and the murderer's resisting victim are morally right: the murderer because he believes this act of aggression will further his long-term interests, and the victim because he refuses to relinquish his life.

In view of these obvious absurdities, why would anyone seriously want to defend ethical egoism as a theory? There are at least several reasons why egoism has sometimes seemed a plausible guide to conduct. For one thing, it is an attractive philosophy whenever moral norms become too demanding or stray too far from the reality of what people can accomplish. Defenders of egoism are frequently reacting against some overly idealistic view of ethics, which, in their view, most people either ignore or reject. The defenders of egoism seek to encourage moral conduct, not by proposing even more stringent norms, but by appealing to people's *enlightened* self-interest as a way of encouraging sobriety and restraint. They maintain that if everyone acted like intelligent egoists, factoring into their reasoning the long-term consequences of their deeds and their unavoidable need to secure others' cooperation, the resulting social behavior would be far more harmonious than egoism's critics contend.

Some have defended ethical egoism because they are drawn to a position known as *psychological egoism*. This view holds that human beings are basically selfish and cannot do anything other than pursue self-interest. Psychological egoism, a theory of human motivation, is distinguishable from ethical egoism, a theory of what makes something right or wrong. One can be an ethical egoist and believe that selfish behavior is morally right without also holding that people can only act selfishly. Nevertheless, if psychological egoism is a correct account of human motivation, it seems to rule out any moral theory other than ethical egoism, since it makes no sense to ask people to act in ways beyond their power.

As an account of human motivation, psychological egoism is initially attractive. After all, we witness many instances of self-serving behavior around us in society. But it is also true that human beings sometimes act in generous or altruistic ways—even undergoing great sacrifice on others' behalf. Many who act this way maintain that they wish to help others. Doesn't this undermine the validity of psychological egoism as an all-encompassing account of human motivation? Defenders of psychological egoism typically respond by saying that, despite appearances, people are really motivated by self-interest in these instances of seeming generosity or altruism. They may be seeking public approval. Or, if they believe they are moved by concern for others, their deepest incentives may be unconscious desires, rooted in the wish for approval or in fears carried over from childhood. Claims of this sort convert psychological egoism from an empirical theory of human motivation into an assumption about human motivation that can be neither proved nor disproved. This weakens the case for both psychological and ethical egoism, as does the indisputable fact that, whatever their reasons, people often do act on others' behalf. Such instances of altruistic behavior open the way to the possible validity of other, nonegoistic, guides to conduct or theories of ethics.

Finally, we should note that ethical egoism holds a special attractiveness for people in business contexts. Because the pursuit of self-interest is such an important and legitimate part of economic behavior, it is natural to believe that the right thing to do in *all* moral choices is that which maximizes the satisfaction of one's self-interest. Nevertheless, it is important to note that the classical economists who defended the role of self-interest in economic affairs did not usually argue for the appropriateness of such behavior in all human relationships. Because they believed that economic laws work to constrain and channel self-interest in ways that lead to social welfare generally, the real objective of their economic counsel was maximum well-being for society as a whole. Their view of what makes something right, therefore, was much closer to the position known as utilitarianism, which I discuss below.

Egoism is also attractive to people in business contexts because of the related view that business firms may do whatever is needed to promote their interests. This form of group egoism is a powerful shaper of attitudes in the business and organizational worlds, where managers often feel compelled to give their primary loyalty to the needs of the organization they serve. In subsequent chapters, we look more closely at the psychological and organizational imperatives that make this view so prevalent and attractive. For now, I can say that collective egoism is no better as an ethical view than individual egoism. The consequence of this view is a world riddled with conflict and without any moral or principled way of bringing selfish behavior under review.

In sum, ethical egoism is an attractive position and one that has an element of truth in its vindication of the legitimacy of acting on self-interest in some circumstances. But as a complete account of what makes actions right or wrong and as a guide to conduct, it is not an ethical theory to be taken seriously.

ETHICAL RELATIVISM

Like ethical egoism, ethical relativism is a theory that has had defenders for as long as people have thought systematically about ethics. Ethical relativism is the view that right and wrong are a function of the moral teachings of each particular society. It holds that *an act is right when it is approved by the social group to which one belongs and wrong when it is not.* Ethical relativists usually begin with a position (sometimes termed *cultural relativism*) involving the descriptive observation that societies seem to differ fundamentally in their moral teachings and moral rules. One society, for example, permits polygamy, whereas another is strictly monogamous. One praises entrepreneurial behavior, another regards it as criminal. One is pacifistic and abhors violence, another esteems military prowess. Societies with such differing moral values also frequently believe that only their values are correct: that their moral norms are absolutely right whereas all other moral views are evil or wrong. These cross-cultural observations lead ethical relativists to conclude that there really is no single "right" moral viewpoint, that ethics is a function of group teachings, and that the very terms "right" and "wrong" are nothing more than reports of what one's society happens to value.

Because the reality of moral diversity is indisputable, many persons have come to regard ethical relativism as a compelling position. In addition, people sometimes defend ethical relativism because they fear the kind of intolerance and cultural imperialism that goes with nonrelativist views. Relativism, they argue, is a reminder that our own moral values may not be absolutely correct or accepted by other societies, and it warns against efforts to impose our views on others. Ironically, those who defend relativism this way usually possess at least one objective and universal moral value: tolerance. They believe that, except perhaps for the most urgent reasons, people should not be forced to act in ways that violate their own cultural norms.

This essentially moral argument for ethical relativism points up a basic incongruity in this view. If ethical relativism is correct, moral right or wrong depend ultimately on the teachings of each society. What, then, can the defender of relativism say about the teachings of a society that militantly opposes tolerance and that, if given the opportunity, would impose its beliefs and values on others? If "right" is a function of what each society teaches, then the ethical relativist must conclude that this society is morally right in rejecting relativism and forcing its views on others!

Of course, the ethical relativist may contend that her own society believes that intolerance of this sort is wrong. She is therefore right to criticize it and right actively to oppose it. But this illustrates the serious conceptual and moral difficulties to which ethical relativism leads. The relativist must also concede that, whatever her own moral beliefs, the members of the opposing, intolerant society are also right in holding their views and in forcibly imposing their claims. In a world of ethical relativists, therefore, moral judgment and discourse as we know it vanishes. Moral discussion becomes nothing more than an occasion for each community or subcommunity to trumpet its values, and there can be no appeal to objective values or norms that will adjudicate the dispute or bring a group's conduct under review. It follows that, if ethical relativism is correct, we lose the capability of judging that any particular forms of behavior—for example, genocide undertaken by one group against another, or forms of torture or abuse—are morally "wrong" in any objective sense of this word.

Ethical relativism thus pays a very high price, in conceptual and moral confusion, for whatever valid insights it contains. But this is not a price that has to be paid. We can retain the legitimate insights of relativism without accepting the conclusion that right and wrong are simply a function of an individual group's values. For example, it is possible to recognize the value of tolerance, and the need to respect the many differing norms of other social groups, without agreeing that all matters of right and wrong are defined by group values alone.

It is also possible to accept the fact of moral diversity without relinquishing the claim that there are some moral values that transcend cultures. We just saw that ethical relativists sometimes support their views by referring to the fact of cultural relativism: the seemingly wide diversity of moral values found from culture to culture. But disagreement over specific and concrete norms does not mean that societies necessarily disagree in their *fundamental* values or most basic moral teachings. All societies, for example, share the goal of ensuring the care and protection of children. In some circumstances these goals are achieved by norms requiring monogamy and restricting extramarital sex. In other societies—for example, those experiencing an imbalance between marriageable men and women—very different marital practices such as polygamy or polyandry may develop as a humane way of regulating sexual conduct and family life. Before we conclude that human social groups differ fundamentally in their moral teachings we should try to understand the basic norms involved in these cases and whether they really differ. Often they do not. It is possible, therefore, to recognize and respect the diversity of apparent moral teachings across cultures while rejecting ethical relativism and holding to the belief that there are some universal and objective moral values.

Although ethical relativism may be an incoherent and self-contradictory moral theory, it is often attractive in organizational or business contexts. Managers of global enterprises frequently encounter widely different moral practices in the countries in which they do business. Even within individual societies, organizations sometimes have internal "cultures" so different as to lend credence to the belief that right and wrong depend entirely on one's cultural group. For example, Phil Cortez might be led to abandon the previous commitment he has made in the belief that he must now adopt a new employer's culture and values. I have suggested that this would be a misleading conclusion. The difficult task for managers working in diverse cultural environments is to identify those moral norms or ways of thinking that transcend cultural boundaries. Without compromising these norms, they must then undertake the equally difficult task of trying to recognize and respect diversity where it is morally appropriate to do so. In Chapter 8 we look at some ways this challenge presents itself to managers working in a global context.

RIGHT IS WHAT MY RELIGIOUS TRADITION TEACHES

Many persons find the teachings of a particular religious tradition to be a major source of ethical guidance and instruction. Some even define right and wrong conduct in terms of these religious teachings. Many Jews and Christians, for example, maintain that right and wrong are determined by the teachings of the Bible. Muslims similarly look to the Qur'an, and Hindus and Buddhists to the sacred texts of their traditions.

One leading religious approach defines right as what "God wills or reveals as His will." This approach reflects the veneration religious believers have for sacred moral teachings and for the supremacy of these teachings as expressions of God's will. Since the days of Plato and Socrates, however, philosophers have asked whether right and wrong can be defined exclusively in religious terms. Critics of the view that right may be defined as "what God wills or reveals" point, for example, to the diversity of religious beliefs both within a tradition and among different traditions, and they ask how any one religious view can justify itself in the face of so many competing understandings of religious truth. Some critics point out that no tradition of revealed teaching is self-explanatory. Every sacred scripture or teaching needs interpretation, and when this is so there must be some independent rational basis for judgment. Finally, some critics maintain that the definition of morality in terms of what God wills undermines the moral praise and worship religious believers ordinarily bestow on God. When devout believers say that God acts righteously, these critics point out, they usually have in mind an independent and commonsense standard of morality. They believe that God is just and loving in the ordinary human meanings of these terms. But if we *define* right as "what God wills," then to say that God acts righteously is merely to say that God does whatever God wills to do.

We do not have to settle all these questions to see that a view defining right in purely religious terms is inadequate for managerial ethical decision making. In making such decisions, managers must be able to communicate and justify their views to others in their organization, but the diverse religious backgrounds of people in most large enterprises today rule out appeal to any single standard of religious teaching. Managerial decision making thus requires resort to a reasoned and secular standard of judgment.

Fortunately, this should not disturb managers who base their personal sense of right and wrong on a religious foundation. As Figure 2.2 suggests, the major ethical teachings of most religious traditions are largely compatible with various secular or rational ethical views. Religious traditions typically prohibit forms of conduct that secular culture also views as morally wrong. Almost all religious codes condemn violence against innocent persons, theft, and dishonesty. One need not resort to a sectarian perspective, therefore, to justify positions one takes in a managerial context. Reasons for conduct can and must be given that make sense to people regardless of their specific religious views.

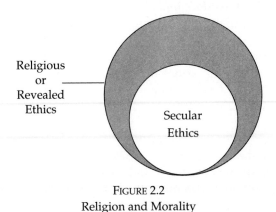

FIGURE 2.2
Religion and Morality

As the shaded zone in this figure suggests, religious teachings can sometimes go beyond the boundary of secular ethics. Usually this will not pose a problem for managers who base their ethics on religion. Many teachings in this shaded zone involve what is called "supererogatory" behavior, forms of conduct that are beyond the call of duty but not necessarily opposed to required secular standards. Jews, Christians, and Muslims, for example, often feel called to a higher standard of charity or justice than secular ethics seems to require. These higher standards do not have to create serious conflict for managers, who can usually separate the sphere of their organizational responsibilities from a private life governed by the higher personal ideals. For example, nothing prevents a religiously committed manager from supplementing her daily work with off-hours assistance to the homeless.

The only portion of this shaded area that can cause serious conflict for the religious manager involves those religious teachings that *violate* norms accepted in a secular and nonreligious context. For example, how is the Orthodox Jewish or Muslim rental manager of apartment buildings to respond to secular legislation that prohibits discrimination against gay persons? Does complying with this legislation amount to condoning a form of conduct condemned by the manager's religion? Can the Catholic researcher employed by a large drug company ethically cooperate in the development of a new abortion drug? These and other cases admit to no easy solutions. Religious and secular morality can sometimes diverge and even conflict. When this occurs, a manager will have to choose between the two, and may even choose to resign his or her position rather than violate a personal moral standard. Despite these complexities, we can see that ethical views that define right conduct *only* in terms of a particular religious teaching are not an adequate basis for managerial ethics. Although managers are fully entitled to hold religious views—to the extent that they must explain and justify specific moral decisions to others in their organization and society—they cannot rely on these alone but must develop and employ a reasoned, widely acceptable means of making and justifying moral decisions.

RIGHT AS CONSCIENCE ALONE

A final less-than-adequate view to consider is one that defines right or wrong in terms of the dictates of individual conscience—with nothing more said. The problem with this view is not its insistence that each of us must respect our conscience in the sense of those deep moral convictions within us that lead us to believe that some action is right or wrong. Moral theorists have long insisted that each of us must form our own moral judgments and not merely follow the opinions of others or unthinkingly obey some external authority. But they have also insisted that personal moral judgment is a reflective and reasoned act through which we actively try to understand and decide whether a course of action is right or wrong. Those who define right or wrong in terms of the dictates of conscience alone, but provide no counsel about how our conscience is to be informed or which principles or norms should guide it, do not really offer a theory of ethics. In this view, "conscience" remains an impenetrable black box that anyone can use to justify conduct of any sort.

If we define right action simply as *what my conscience tells me* and say nothing more about what constitutes a valid exercise of conscience, then any behavior in response to inner urgings or compulsions (whatever their source) becomes morally right by definition. We cannot really criticize the fanatic who commits a grave wrong while appealing to his "conscience," since he can always say "my conscience told me to do it." As was true concerning egoism and relativism, matters of moral discourse and judgment become utterly subjective and we lose the ability to bring our own or others' moral judgments under review. In contrast to this, the proper exercise of conscience involves a willingness to explain and justify our moral judgments, and this implies the need for a moral theory. The problem with the view we are examining here is that it is not really a moral theory; if it purports to be, it is a deficient account of the *reasons* why something is a matter of conscience in the first place.

✦ CONSEQUENTIALISM VERSUS
NONCONSEQUENTIALISM ✦

This brief excursion through less-than-adequate views suggests the criteria for an adequate ethical theory. Because a moral theory aims at helping us make moral decisions, it must provide clear guidance through the choices we face. It must be capable of resolving moral conflicts or disputes in a reasoned and principled way, and it must offer reasons for acting that are understandable to other persons and potentially acceptable to them. Although none of the views we just looked at meets these criteria, two major theories of ethics do. In one form or another, each of these views has long been regarded as providing the best insight into what makes conduct right or wrong.

NONCONSEQUENTIALIST (OR DEONTOLOGICAL) THEORIES

Very often, when we witness behavior that offends us morally it involves conduct we tend to think of as wrong because it violates some basic and important moral rule. We may be upset, for example, because an official acts "unfairly" or a salesperson "cheats" a customer. When thinking or speaking this way we usually have in the back of our mind some rules of behavior that we regard as defining moral conduct, rules whose violation we normally consider immoral. We also often think that these should be obeyed even when the immediate consequences of doing so are not always beneficial. This is because these rules seem to have an intrinsic weight or validity that we must respect regardless of consequences.

Moral philosophers have refined this way of thinking into a comprehensive approach to ethics known as *nonconsequentialism*. This view begins by identifying general types of behavior or rules of conduct as intrinsically right or wrong and then defines right action in a specific situation *as what best conforms to this set of moral rules*. Because of the importance this approach gives to this listing of moral rules or duties, it is sometimes called *deontology* (from the Greek *deon*, "duty").

Deontology or nonconsequentialism is really a family of ethical theories rather than a single ethical view. Deontological positions vary in terms of the specific set of moral norms or rules they espouse. Some are religious, beginning with a set of rules derived from sacred revelation and subsequently handed down or interpreted by a religious authority. The Ten Commandments are a good example, as are the Sermon on the Mount, and the many specific moral rules expounded by other religious traditions.

Other deontological views are secular and make no appeal to religious revelation or to beliefs depending on religious teachings. In his book *Morality*, the philosopher Bernard Gert provides a list of ten moral rules that he believes express our considered judgments about the basic norms governing the moral life. These rules are listed in Box 2.1. Gert himself is not a deontologist in the sense we are discussing, because he possesses a still more basic theory of how we derive these norms. But many secular deontologists subscribe to a list of rules like these. A secu-

---

Box 2.1

GERT'S TEN MORAL RULES[6]

1. Don't kill.
2. Don't cause pain.
3. Don't disable.
4. Don't deprive of freedom.
5. Don't deprive of pleasure.
6. Don't deceive.
7. Keep your promise.
8. Don't cheat.
9. Obey the law.
10. Do your duty.

---

lar deontologist, therefore, is one who assesses conduct by asking whether it conforms to a list of rules of this sort. In general, *an action is right if it respects these rules and wrong if it violates them.*

As we look at this set of rules, a problem appears. It is frequently impossible to act without violating one or another of these rules. For example, let us suppose that I am the supervisor in a firm and that one of my employees has proven so negligent in his work that I must dismiss him. I know this person is emotionally sensitive and that a full account of why he is being dismissed will cause him to become seriously depressed. I am tempted to lie about my reasons, perhaps by telling him that the firm has decided to reduce its work force. Morally speaking, can I lie to a subordinate in this way? Gert's list of moral rules tells us that it is wrong to deceive, but it also tells us that we should not cause pain, and I break this rule if I remain truthful.

Such conflict between moral rules divides deontologists into two camps. On one side are *absolutist* deontologists, who believe the moral rules, appropriately understood, are absolute and must always be respected. On the other side are the *prima facie* deontologists, who believe that each moral rule has intrinsic validity and exerts a force on our judgment. But when rules conflict, one can be outweighed by another that exerts greater moral force.

Absolutists do not deny that conflicts may *seem* to arise. But they regard these conflicts as only apparent, not fundamental. They insist that conflicts disappear when we recognize either that there are strict (and absolute) priorities between the moral rules or that the rules have specific meanings that limit their scope. For example, an absolutist deontologist might argue here that the rule against lying is more stringent than the rule against causing pain. No matter what good I might do by telling a lie, therefore, I should not do it. Alternatively, an absolutist deontologist might argue that the rule against causing pain has a more precise specification or meaning. It should read "Do not cause pain to those who have not incurred it by their own carelessness or neglect." As such, this rule does not extend to employees who have been negligent. Reasoning this way, some Christian thinkers who espouse a religious deontological absolutism and believe that killing is *always* morally wrong have sometimes justified capital punishment. They have done so by arguing that the rule "Do not kill" should properly be understood to read "Do not kill innocent persons."

Prima facie deontologists take a different tack.[7] They believe that each moral rule has intrinsic weight and exerts a particular moral force, but that when the force of another rule outweighs this, it may be overridden. Many prima facie deontologists would argue, for example, that it can be right to lie to another person when there are compelling reasons to do so. Thus, acting under the rule "Do not cause pain," we might choose to deceive this employee if we believe the truth might lead him into depression. But the force of a prima facie moral rule remains so great that these deontologists probably would not counsel lying for lesser reasons. The fact that we can make the employee somewhat happier by telling a lie, for example, would not count as a valid reason for breaking this rule.

Despite their important disagreements, there are many cases in which absolutist and prima facie deontologists will agree. Considering Phil Cortez's dilemma, outlined at the beginning of this chapter, both types of deontologists probably would conclude that Phil is morally obligated to keep his word to his former employer and to refuse to participate in National's radial tire project. For the absolutist deontologist, this is because the rule of keeping one's promise is unbreakable and because the competing and stringent rule, Phil's obligation as an employee to "do his duty," should not be construed to include complicity in illegal or immoral conduct. A prima facie deontologist might not take this definitional route. Phil has some moral obligation to follow his new employer's orders, this deontologist might concede, but this obligation does not outweigh the solemn promise he made to the previous employer.

Although deontological views often take form around a series of moral rules or duties that individuals must respect, deontologists also can base their judgments on an intrinsic set of "moral rights" they believe people possess. For the most part, moral rights are correlative to our duties to obey specific moral rules. This means that for each specific moral rule there is a corresponding entitlement on someone's part or "claim" to the behavior the rule imposes. If Gert is correct that there is a moral rule prohibiting the killing of other persons, this takes the form in a rights-oriented deontology of a corresponding "right to life." The rule against depriving others of their freedom becomes the "right to liberty," and so on. Like rule-oriented views, rights-based views can be religious or secular, absolutist or prima facie. Perhaps because of the example set by the Bill of Rights, American ethicists frequently approach moral issues by considering the competing rights involved.

Box 2.2 presents a listing of some basic human rights that many persons have found compelling. It distinguishes between *negative* rights, so

---

Box 2.2

SOME BASIC HUMAN RIGHTS

Negative Rights

- Life
- Physical security
- Personal liberty
- Free speech and conscience
- Privacy
- Due process
- Property
- Informed consent
- Participation in one's social groups

Positive Rights

- Food
- Shelter
- Employment
- Education
- Health care
- Legal counsel
- A safe environment

---

called because they usually impose nothing more than restraints on people's conduct vis-à-vis other persons, and *positive* rights, the fulfillment of which requires active efforts by individuals or governments. Thus, we can usually respect others' right to privacy by refraining from intruding in their personal affairs or by not disclosing confidential information about them. Satisfying someone's right to employment or education, however, may require individuals, firms, or governments to develop costly social programs. Of course, this distinction is not absolute, since protecting some negative rights, such as the provision of physical security or due process, may require substantial and active governmental efforts.[8]

Whether rule-based or rights-based, deontological views are attractive because they often correspond to our moral common sense. Many of us, for example, believe that lying, stealing, and cheating are intrinsically wrong, and although we are uncertain whether these rules are absolute or not, we characteristically feel a "tug" in our consciences when we break them. We also tend to believe that persons have certain rights, and we find ourselves criticizing immoral conduct as a violation of rights held by some person or group.

In approaching moral decisions, an understanding and identification of the relevant rules and rights can be helpful. Phil Cortez, for example, might organize his approach to his dilemma by looking at Box 2.1 or 2.2. He might ask himself whether National's conduct forces him to break Gert's seventh rule requiring the keeping of promises or whether he will be violating Lifeworth's right to privacy or property where confidential research information is involved. He also might ask what the rule "Do your duty" means in this context and whether his own right to employment should be factored into his decision. This kind of deontological assessment is a useful way to begin any process of moral reasoning.

PROBLEMS WITH DEONTOLOGICAL THEORIES

Despite its initial usefulness as a guide to thinking, deontology in all its forms has several serious problems. These have led many philosophers to criticize its adequacy as an approach to moral decision. One problem concerns the derivation of the specific rules or rights found on deontological lists. Where do these come from and how do we know that any specific rule or right should be there? The problem is most acute where religious deontologies are concerned, particularly where current sexual/moral rules are involved—witness the conflict between liberal and conservative Christians, for example, over such matters as the rules prohibiting contraception, abortion, or homosexuality. But the same problem can arise whenever the validity of any particular moral rule or right is questioned. Some of the hottest arguments in American society, for example, revolve around the question of whether there is a "positive" right to health care if this right involves massive governmental expenditures for its implementation. Deontological theories typically begin and end with a specification of the relevant moral rules or rights, but they usually do not explain why these exist or how they can be further justified. As a result, deontologists often disagree about whether a particular rule or right is important or whether it deserves a place on our moral lists. In the face of this kind of moral disagreement, deontologists sometimes insist that the rules or rights are "self-evident." Although this may be true, it stops reasoned discourse about right and wrong.

An even more serious problem occurs when moral rules or rights appear to conflict. Here deontologists usually offer little help. An appeal may be made to certain moral absolutes or various priorities and definitions may be voiced, but, either way, nothing within the deontological viewpoints explains why these specific views and rankings are correct. If pressed, deontologists may, again, insist that their priorities or definitions are "self-evident," but since people tend to disagree about the particular ranking of rules in cases of conflict, this appeal to self-evidence usually only aggravates a moral dispute.

The opposition between negative and positive rights in Box 2.2 illustrates this problem. Proponents of free-enterprise capitalism, on the one hand, and defenders of forms of socialism or social democracy, on the other, tend to disagree vehemently about the relative priority to be given to the negative versus the positive rights on this list. Free-market theorists usually regard the high rates of taxation needed to fund social programs as unjust or confiscatory and as violations of the right to property, whereas socialists see basic programs of social justice as necessary to serve the basic and "inalienable" rights of each citizen. These disputes go on within U.S. society and across national borders with little prospect of agreement.

This problem of conflict between rules and rights becomes especially severe in managerial contexts whenever cases are unusually difficult or complex. In the area of employee rights, for example, it has become common today to maintain that workers have a basic right to privacy that extends even to the workplace and to their individual work stations, files, and private conversations. Some managers argue, however, that an employee who commits theft or is suspected of doing so loses this right.

In such cases a different right, the employer's right to property, takes precedence. Reasoning this way, some employers have chosen to eavesdrop on employees' telephone conversations to learn whether they are misusing phone services for private purposes. Is this ethical? Many believe it is, that it is not morally wrong for firms to engage in surveillance of this sort, but others are not sure. Note that both sides to this argument agree on the basic list of rights, but strongly disagree on the relative weights these competing rights possess. One difficulty with the deontological approach is that it usually is unable to clarify or resolve disputes of this sort. Because of this, deontological discussions of ethical issues frequently end with sharp and seemingly irresolvable conflicts between persons who hold different rankings of the rules and rights.

CONSEQUENTIALIST (OR TELEOLOGICAL) THEORIES

The problems with the nonconsequentialist (deontological) view have called forth a competing *consequentialist* approach to ethics that measures acts, not in terms of their conformity to some "intrinsically right" set of moral rules, but solely in terms of their observable consequences for human beings. This approach is also known as *teleology* (from the Greek *telos*, "goal") because of the way it measures acts by their end product or effects. Teleology is an approach to ethics that declares an act to be right *if it produces a greater sum of desired value in the world than its alternatives.*

As with deontology, there are many specific forms of teleology. All share an emphasis on measuring an act in terms of its consequences for the production of some specific good or value. An aesthetic teleology, for example, might emphasize the value of works of art or other objects of beauty and might measure individual acts or policies by how much beauty they produce. A *hedonistic* teleology (from the Greek word for pleasure) measures acts in terms of the amount of pleasure they produce for persons, and so on. All teleologies agree, however, not to list moral rules or rights among the values we must produce, because this would render this position identical with deontology. Instead, they emphasize some morally neutral but widely shared value as the *goal* or *object* at which teleology aims.

Despite the diversity of teleological views, only one has commanded wide attention and loyalty: the position known as utilitarianism. Developed over the past two centuries by such philosophers as Jeremy Bentham (1748–1832) and John Stuart Mill (1806–1873), utilitarianism is a form of teleology whose central value is human happiness, understood in terms of the satisfaction of the various desires that we each have as human beings. As the most famous formulation puts it, an action is right for utilitarianism *if that action produces the greatest amount of happiness for the greatest number of persons.*

Behind this well-known utilitarian norm lies a comprehensive theory of morality. Utilitarians begin with the uncontroversial view that all persons seek their own happiness (which includes, perhaps, the happiness of others for whom they care), and tend to define happiness as that state of life in which our most important desires are satisfied. They observe, however, that right conduct cannot be what makes one or several of us happy, as egoism contends. Ideally, the right act must make *everybody* happy. But since this is impossible in any real social situation, where objectives often conflict, utilitarians conclude that the right act is one that makes as many people as possible happy. This leads naturally to the utilitarian "greatest happiness" principle.

It is important to recognize that although utilitarians seek to provide a basic understanding of the logic of the moral life, they have no wish to defy moral common sense. Utilitarians support the ordinary moral rules identified by deontologists and believe that, in most circumstances, one will not go wrong by using these rules as guides to conduct. Indeed, they believe that the basic utilitarian "greatest happiness" principle leads to these rules and explains the force they have in our consciences. It is wrong to lie, cheat, or break serious promises, utilitarians maintain, because human experience has repeatedly shown that such behavior usually produces serious harm. Thus, if I am tempted to tell a "benevolent" lie to an employee to spare his feelings, it is probably best that I not do so. The employee may well learn of my deception and be doubly injured; other employees also may learn what I have done and mistrust my future utterances.

Despite this bid to deontology and moral common sense, utilitarians believe that for several reasons their theory of ethics is a significant advance over these other views. First, utilitarians feel that their "greatest happiness" principle provides the rational basis for any specific rules deserving our attention. Utilitarians believe we can eliminate from deontological lists any rules whose consequences are bad. Thus, in the debates over certain religious deontological rules, especially those governing controversial areas of sexual conduct, utilitarians believe their approach simplifies rational discourse and decision. For example, if we wonder whether it is morally right or wrong to prohibit birth control, we do not have to engage in endless arguments over the validity or meaning of some sacred teaching, but merely ask which course of action is *now* likely to have the most beneficial consequences for human beings.

Similarly, utilitarians believe their method gives reason a place in the recurrent task of weighing and balancing conflicting moral rules. As mentioned above, this problem is the Achilles' heel of deontology. When moral rules conflict, deontologists have no clear way of settling disputes, which can go on interminably. But within a utilitarian framework, such conflicts, in the strictest sense, cannot occur. This is because *utilitarianism contains not a plurality of basic rules, like deontology, but a single high-order rule that decides all choices.* Thus, when any two specific moral rules conflict, utilitarians tell us that we must not fixate on the rules but ask which course of action is likely to produce the most happiness for the most persons. In the case of the negligent or incompetent employee, for example, we do not have to engage in the highly intuitive task of weighing the moral value of a rule of truth-telling against a rule of non-injury. We need only ask how we are most likely to maximize human happiness.

Utilitarians admit that reasoning about matters like this will often be difficult. Frequently we cannot identify all the consequences of our actions, and it is also very hard to assess how much good and evil we inflict on different persons. Utilitarianism compounds this difficulty by requiring us to be even-handed and impartial, or "omnipartial," in such assessments (the aim of morality, after all, is not just my happiness but *everyone's* happiness). This means that we must try to put ourselves in the shoes of all the persons affected by our deeds, both now and in the foreseeable future. We also must try to measure our choice in terms of its impact on everyone's conception of happiness and not our own. Anything else would amount to the imposition of our views on others and reduce happiness overall. Finally, whenever possible, we also must seek an accurate factual understanding of the issues and interests involved. This may require us to do research or conduct experiments to determine which course really maximizes human well-being. Box 2.3 offers a succinct statement of the utilitarian approach to decision making.

Utilitarians concede that all this is difficult. Nevertheless, although they acknowledge the difficulties of putting their norm into effect, they emphasize that these difficulties are practical rather than conceptual or moral. They stress that even the practical problems can often be overcome. By forcing us to pay attention to the empirical question of what makes people happier, something that can presumably be measured by tests or polls, their method avoids the need to make inscrutable judgments about the relative weights of competing moral rules. It is no small wonder that defenders of utilitarianism have regarded it as a great advance over other, less "rational" theories of ethics.

Box 2.3

THE UTILITARIAN METHOD
OF REASONING[9]

1. Accurately state the action to be evaluated.
2. Identify all those who are directly and indirectly affected by it.
3. Specify all the pertinent good and bad consequences of the action for all those directly affected—as far into the future as appears appropriate—and imaginatively consider various possible outcomes and the likelihood of their occurrence.
4. Weigh the total good results (the degree of happiness produced) against the total bad results, considering such matters as the quantity and duration of the harms and benefits involved.
5. Carry out a similar analysis, if necessary, for those indirectly affected, and for society as a whole.
6. Sum up all the good and bad consequences. If the action produces more good than bad, the action is morally right; if it produces more bad than good, it is morally wrong.
7. Consider, imaginatively, whether there are various alternatives other than simply performing or not performing the action and carry out a similar analysis for each of the other alternate actions.
8. Compare the results of the various actions. The action that produces the *most good* (or the least bad, if none produces more good than bad) among those available is the morally proper thing to do.

DIFFICULTIES WITH UTILITARIANISM

Utilitarianism does have problems. Critics have maintained that, in practice, it often leads to strange conclusions that seriously defy our moral common sense. They argue that this tendency to produce counterintuitive moral results means that utilitarianism is somehow a flawed theory and an inadequate account of the basic logic of our moral reasoning process.

Critics of utilitarianism point to two problems. The first has to do with the distribution of goods or evils in society. Critics observe that utilitarianism's counsel to produce the most happiness for the most persons leaves undetermined whether it is the widespread distribution of happiness or the intensity of happiness that counts. Because of this, a strict utilitarian reading will consider a society with a handful of billionaires living alongside thousands of persons in poverty to be morally equivalent to a society with a more equal distribution of wealth. More serious, the critics contend, is the problem associated with the distribution of evils. In principle, nothing prevents a utilitarian society from seriously mistreating a small number of persons, say a racial or religious minority or economic class, if this is the best way of increasing the well-being of many other members of society. If the sum total of happiness produced by this abuse outweighs the suffering of the minority (and this is true whenever the number benefitted grows large enough to outweigh the more intense suffering of the few), utilitarianism must declare this to be morally right. But this conclusion, say the critics, defies our common-sense moral belief that people have basic rights that cannot be taken away and that people should not be treated unjustly merely for others' gain. Utilitarian reasoning, they conclude, seems to provide moral support for the worst abuses of the totalitarian regimes of our time. If utilitarianism is right, the leaders of at least some of the political regimes of our century who slaughtered millions in order to build a utopian future for their societies may not have been vicious despots but moral heroes.

As we might expect, utilitarians have ways of replying to these criticisms. They argue, for example, that great economic inequities will not ordinarily maximize human happiness because, beyond some level of material comfort, each unit of income produces less real satisfaction (this is sometimes called the "principle of diminishing marginal utility"). Because of this, a society is best advised to distribute excess resources among those who have less, an approach leading to a more equalized division of wealth. The problem with this argument is that it is not clear that the principle of diminishing marginal utility is valid in all economic circumstances. Utilitarians also reject the claim that their principle would justify the abuse and mistreatment of minorities. Even if it were true that this conduct could enhance the well-being of many—and utilitarians point out that economic and social flourishing are not likely to occur in an atmosphere of victimization—the fear and terror inspired in all members of society by this violent exercise of power would provide a reason against it. If members of society were aware of the conduct of their leaders, utilitarians maintain, everyone's well-being would be seriously reduced, making this policy inadvisable on utilitarian grounds.

However valid this last argument may be, it points to the second major criticism of utilitarianism: that it permits morally repugnant behavior whenever public knowledge of this behavior is unlikely to occur or whenever such knowledge can be suppressed by policies of concealment or deception. In some instances, critics say, utilitarianism may even *require* concealment or deception, with the curious result that we morally improve vicious conduct by keeping it hidden! For example, in the cases just discussed, utilitarianism's critics agree that the generalized anxiety minority persecution produces is a powerful argument against it. But utilitarians do not have to conclude that it is therefore wrong to victimize minorities. Instead, they can counsel a despot to carry out these practices in secret in order to spare the majority knowledge of them.[10] This may prove impossible to do but, at least in principle, utilitarianism supports advice of this sort. Because of this, critics see something wrong in the whole utilitarian way of thinking. Do we really believe, they ask, that concealed terrorism is better than no terrorism at all? If we do not, something is wrong with utilitarianism's approach to ethical questions.

We can see this problem more clearly by focusing on a purely hypothetical case offered by the critics of utilitarianism. Case 2.2, "The Desert-Island Promise," is designed to eliminate public knowledge of a deed as a factor in its assessment.

In the eyes of its critics this case helps expose a basic flaw in utilitarianism's whole line of reasoning. According to the critics, the pilot here acts in a consummately utilitarian way. He is concerned, above all, with promoting the greatest happiness in each of his choices and deeds. Thus, he naturally assents to the passenger's dying request, since refusing to do so will make the passenger less happy. But because he does not intend to keep his word, he must make it *seem* as though he intends to do so. This leads him into deception and studied insincerity. On returning to civilization he continues this utilitarian line of reasoning. His only concern is how he can maximize human happiness. It is not clear on utilitarian grounds whether he should seek out a good cause—the local charity—or whether it is permissible to further his own well-being and buy a car. But one thing is certain: the pilot owes nothing to the deceased passenger or his orchids. They are out of his moral picture, the promise no longer has any binding effect (because respecting it will not contribute to anyone's happiness), and he acts as a good utilitarian in tossing the flowers on the trash heap.

Utilitarianism's critics point out that the pilot's conduct here runs directly counter to many of our everyday moral convictions. Not only does the pilot treat the passenger's wishes with disrespect, but he deceit-

Case 2.2

◆ THE DESERT-ISLAND PROMISE ◆

A charter pilot and his elderly passenger are flying across a distant tropical sea when the plane's engine malfunctions and it crashes in the water near a desert island. Managing to make it ashore, the pilot and his passenger are stranded for weeks.

During their stay, the passenger reveals to the pilot that as a hobby back home, he cultivates orchids in his backyard. The plants, which he admits are not rare or otherwise valuable, may survive a few more months on their own but will eventually need care.

Several weeks go by. The passenger falls ill and is near death. He tells the pilot that he is extremely worried about who will take care of his orchids in the future if he dies. He also reveals to the pilot that buried in a secret location in his backyard is a sack of coins worth several thousand dollars.

"If I die and you survive," he asks the pilot, "will you make me a solemn promise? Please, locate the money and use it to endow perpetual care for my orchids. It is deeply, deeply important to me that these flowers not perish."

Looking into the pained eyes of the passenger, the pilot solemnly agrees.

With a look of relief and gratitude on his face, the passenger dies.

The pilot remains on the island for several more weeks and is eventually rescued. Returning to civilization, he visits the orchid grower's home and locates the buried money. Debating in his mind whether he should donate the sum to a local charity or merely use it to buy himself a new car, he leaves the backyard—but not before ripping up the orchids and throwing them on the compost heap.

QUESTIONS TO CONSIDER

1. How would a utilitarian evaluate the pilot's conduct?
2. What does this evaluation tell you about utilitarianism?

fully makes and then breaks a solemn promise. Critics also argue that there seems to be no way for utilitarians to avoid the conclusion that the pilot has acted correctly. If they try to argue, for example, that the pilot's conscience will bother him after he breaks the promise, the critics point out that this assumes the pilot has a deontological conscience (one that regards promise-breaking and lying as intrinsically wrong). But as a good utilitarian, he always wishes to maximize human happiness, and his conscience should tell him he has done just that. Utilitarians also may try to argue that if others learn of what the pilot has done, human happiness may be diminished because from now on serious promises will be viewed as less secure. Members of society will know that in similar future circumstances on desert islands, no promises they elicit will be taken seriously, and this loss of a potentially useful social practice must be factored into the utilitarian equation. But the critics point out that this case is designed to exclude the factor of public knowledge since no one knows—or is even likely to know—what the pilot has done.

Utilitarians, finally, may object that this case is so abstract and so hypothetical that it provides no real test of a theory. We are inevitably connected to society, they insist, and we must always take public knowledge of our conduct into account in assessing its consequences. Yet this objection misses the point that the public impact of conduct is only a *contingent* feature of a utilitarian analysis of moral choice. It does not *necessarily* enter into utilitarian reasoning, whose only strict requirement is a consideration of what maximizes happiness. Furthermore, the small weight this case gives to the public impact of conduct is not a trivial feature of our moral experience, because there are many real-life cases of moral choice where, whether by accident or design, others may be unaware of one's deeds.

Take, for example, the choices facing Phil Cortez. He finds himself in a situation where the immediate balance of good and evil created by his choice is not clear or may even support complicity with his firm's immoral practices. If Phil were to break his promise to his former employer, Lifeworth, his new firm, National Rubber and Tire, would more quickly produce the radial tire. On a utilitarian calculus, Lifeworth would lose the benefit from its expenditures on research but National's gain might balance this out. Consumers would benefit by the prompt introduction of a safer tire and by the existence of two competing manufacturers, and Phil, of course, could keep his job with its handsome rewards.

In this case, utilitarians may concede that it is not the immediate calculus of benefits or gains that counsels against complicity with betrayal or deceit. Rather, what makes this behavior wrong are the longer-term consequences should the conduct become publicly known.[11] If Phil breaks his promise to Lifeworth, all firms that invest heavily in proprietary research will now feel threatened. They may cut back on research or resort to extraordinary security procedures to prevent employees from ever again having access to the kind of information Phil acquired. In either case, new projects will be handicapped or eliminated and net social well-being will decline. Utilitarians argue that these longer-term negative (or "indirect") consequences of such practices as promise-breaking and deception are what make them so clearly unwise and immoral.

The problem with this whole line of reasoning, of course, is that it hinges on people's learning of Phil's conduct, but none of this need occur if Phil and his firm actively strive to prevent it from happening. As a good utilitarian, Phil can agree to betray Lifeworth's secrets so long as he and National succeed in making it appear that he has not done so. For example, Phil can deceptively inform his previous employer that he refused to violate his agreement and then, covertly, give all sorts of aid to National's project. (To strengthen this ruse, he might even agree to "quit" his job under protest while secretly continuing as a paid consultant to National!)

This can occur, deontological critics of utilitarianism argue, because this position does not respect the moral rules. As moral persons, we tend to believe that lying, promise-breaking, and injustice are intrinsically wrong and remain so even if we can sometimes increase net happiness by ignoring them. Because utilitarianism loses sight of this and reduces all moral conduct to a question of maximizing the sum of human well-being, it is a poor guide to choice. Critics conclude that utilitarianism may seem to have many advantages over the older deontological view, but these advantages lead us into moral error and render the whole theory questionable.

Over the past few decades, some utilitarian defenders have taken these criticisms to heart and tried to modify their views. The result is a position known as *rule utilitarianism*. Rule utilitarians believe that the earlier form of utilitarianism, which they term *act utilitarianism*, made a mistake by applying the greatest happiness principle to individual moral actions when this standard should be applied only to the basic moral rules governing a society. These basic rules, they maintain, are measured in terms of whether they contribute to the goal of human happiness, but once we establish a rule, it should be respected regardless of its consequences in a specific case. For example, we should ask whether truth telling is generally advantageous, and, if it is, we should thereafter consistently strive to tell the truth. Rule utilitarianism is the position that defines a right action *as one that conforms to a basic rule whose existence produces the greatest amount of happiness for the greatest number of persons.*

Rule utilitarians offer a series of reasons for their emphasis on basic moral rules. Sometimes they reiterate beliefs they share with act utilitarians: human beings are fallible, we often err in our judgment of specific cases, and social welfare is probably best enhanced by following rules that have generations of human experience behind them. To this they add the argument that we need rules to secure and tie down human expectations. In a world where all people are free to act in ways they believe will maximize happiness, no one's conduct can be relied on. In an act utilitarian world, if I elicit a promise from another person, I have no guarantee that this promise will be kept, and, although this may maximize happiness in a particular situation, it introduces a major source of anxiety and uncertainty into social affairs. Rule utilitarians conclude that if I really wish to promote the greatest amount of happiness, I must regard rules as having intrinsic worth and insist that they be respected regardless of their consequences in specific circumstances. At the core of their reasoning, rule utilitarians remain utilitarians. They believe it is our highest duty to maximize the sum of human happiness, but they also believe that this basic concern leads us to insist on firm respect for many general moral rules.

Are they right? Will this reasoning support promise-keeping and truth-telling in situations where we ordinarily feel this is required of us? Critics argue persuasively that it will not. Why, they ask, if I am a rule utilitarian, whose highest duty is to maximize human happiness, should I respect a moral rule in a situation where breaking it will have no real impact on others' expectations? If our desert-island pilot were a rule utilitarian he might well believe that keeping death-bed promises is a generally useful social rule and better than its alternate of breaking them. He also may feel that a world without respect for these promises would be poorer, and he may mentally resolve to do anything that increases respect for such promises. But why should he now keep the promise, when *nothing* he does has any discernible impact on others' expectations and when he can increase the sum of human happiness by breaking the rule? If he is truly a utilitarian, shouldn't he now depart from his previous resolve and act to increase the sum of human happiness by using the funds made available to him for a genuinely useful social purpose?[12]

Some rule utilitarians reply to this objection by saying that, despite these considerations, it is simply right that we obey the rules. This is because the ultimate moral goal is not to maximize human happiness but to obey generally useful moral rules. This kind of rule utilitarianism is no longer a strictly utilitarian position. With its insistence on respect for rules, regardless of the impact of doing so on human welfare, it approximates a deontological position. To the extent that utilitarianism remains true to its origins and emphasizes the maximization of happiness as the ultimate goal of our moral conduct, therefore, it has no place for a view that stresses obeying the rules when doing so no longer contributes to human well-being.

To sum up, utilitarianism in all its forms seems to lead to conclusions that defy moral common sense. Earlier I said that although a moral theory does not have to uphold or support all our day-to-day moral beliefs, it cannot markedly and repeatedly violate these and still purport to be an adequate account of our moral reasoning process. But utilitarianism violates moral common sense, especially our belief that it is intrinsically wrong to do certain kinds of things, and it does this often enough in matters great and small to cause us to question its worth as a theory.

Utilitarianism's shortcomings seem to force us back to the deontological or nonconsequentialist view as the only viable theoretical option, since here, at least, we find support for some of our deepest moral convictions. Among these are the belief that even in circumstances where others will not learn of our conduct, we must do our best to keep promises (including promises made to absent or deceased persons), our belief that we must strive to tell the truth, and that we must treat people justly and fairly—even when it may not be generally "beneficial" to do so. Unfortunately, as compelling as these convictions are, they thrust us back onto the confused terrain of deontology with its endless disputes. Our review of these two leading theoretical options, therefore, seems to end in a muddle, with no clear theory emerging to guide our reasoning through complex moral decisions.

Faced with this kind of theoretical impasse, some scholars of applied ethics have argued that we should try to take the best from each of these two competing theories. We can use utilitarianism *most* of the time to decide which rules are most beneficial and which course to follow when rules conflict. But when utilitarianism violates our deepest moral convictions, we should temper it by appealing to deontological principles such as justice, fairness, honesty, and fidelity. For example, we should usually try to maximize happiness, unless doing so seriously infringes on people's rights or leads us into flagrant dishonesty.

The problem with this way of thinking, of course, is that it does not help us decide when one approach or the other should reign. How severe must a violation of rights be for me to regard it as morally unacceptable? How flagrant must dishonesty be before I judge it to be wrong? When utilitarianism begins to offend our moral sensibilities, we must decide what will finally govern our thinking—respect for rules or the maximization of happiness. This "mix and match" approach to ethics provides no real guidance and only postpones the moment when we must choose on what basis we will make our moral choices.[13]

At this point it is easy to despair about the usefulness of moral theory in helping us resolve difficult ethical questions. Although moral theorists have made great progress in clarifying the underlying presuppositions of our moral thinking, the net result of all this theorizing has been to sharpen a basic question: Does our moral thinking rest on certain indispensable moral requirements such as fidelity, honesty, fairness, and justice; or may these requirements be set aside when they interfere with the well-being of identifiable people?

Most existing discussions and texts in business ethics and other fields of applied ethics leave this basic question unanswered. For example, it is common in business and medical ethics texts to signal this theoretical difficulty but then to move on to the discussion of cases in the hopes that familiarity with real life decision making will somehow allow one to make up one's mind between competing deontological and utilitarian approaches.[14] But if ethicists themselves cannot resolve this dispute, how can students or practitioners do so when they face difficult theoretical options and the complexity of actual decisions? Cases may highlight the conflict between an approach based on rules and one based on consequences, but they cannot eliminate it. Nor is it true, as some writers of applied ethics texts maintain, that *in practice* deontological and utilitarian approaches will usually provide the same advice. As we will see in subsequent chapters, in many cases two individuals, one acting on utilitarian premises and the other maintaining basic moral rules or rights as a priority, will come to diametrically opposed moral conclusions.

Fortunately, despair is not our only option. In Chapter 3, I examine a third approach to moral reasoning that seeks to resolve the conflict between deontology and utilitarianism. I call this approach *Neutral, Omnipartial Rule-Making* (**NORM**). Although it embodies elements of consequential and rule-oriented reasoning, **NORM** is not just a combination of deontology and utilitarianism. Instead, it rests on an understanding of the nature and purpose of morality that is truer to our basic processes of moral reasoning than the one provided by either deontological or utilitarian accounts. In Chapter 3 we see that **NORM** helps us understand the appeal and the limits of these two theories, offering in their place a unified theoretical approach that can help us steer our way through tough cases of moral decision.

$\mathcal{S}$UMMARY

- *Ethics* and *morality* are terms we use to identify the norms governing human conduct in society that have a significant impact on human welfare. Ethics is like *law,* but society upholds legal norms by imposing severe penalties when they are violated, whereas it does not always do this where morality is concerned.

- Ethical theories typically address questions of value, right conduct, and personal moral character (what is sometimes called the question of "virtue"). The question of right conduct takes precedence in our thinking because the answer to it shapes our answers to the questions of value and moral character.

- *Ethical egoism, ethical relativism,* the view that *right is what my religion teaches me,* and the position that defines right conduct simply in terms of the *dictates of conscience* are attractive because they contain important elements of moral truth. But none of these positions by itself qualifies as a complete or acceptable theory of right conduct.

- Deontology defines an action as right if it respects the moral rules and wrong if it violates them. There are different kinds of deontology. Deontology reflects important features of our moral common sense, but it usually breaks down as a guide to conflict when lists of rules differ or when rules conflict.

- Teleology sees right conduct as what produces most of certain types of basic values in the world. The best known form of teleology is utilitarianism. It defines an action as right if it produces the greatest amount of happiness for the greatest number of persons.

- Because of its clear decision rule, utilitarianism is very useful in resolving conflicts about moral questions. But in cases where it is possible to conceal an individual's conduct, utilitarianism often produces moral conclusions that defy common sense and violate people's deeply held moral beliefs.

• This review of theories suggests that business ethics (and other fields of applied ethics such as medical or legal ethics) is in a quandary. Although progress has been achieved in clarifying the leading theoretical options, ethical decision seems caught between two irreconcilable and opposing approaches to moral decision.

𝒩otes

1. Adapted from Vincent Barry, *Moral Issues in Business* (Belmont, Cal.: Wadsworth, 1979). Reprinted by permission.
2. Kenneth Goodpaster, Public Lecture, Dartmouth Institute, August 11, 1987.
3. "Breast Implant Maker Hit with $27 Million Jury Award," *Business Insurance,* January 4, 1993, p. 2.
4. Kevin McManus, "Who Owns Your Brains?" *Forbes,* 131 June 1983: 168–79.
5. Recent proponents of "virtue ethics" include Alisdair MacIntyre in his *After Virtue* (Notre Dame, Ind.: University of Notre Dame Press, 1981) and his *Whose Justice? Which Rationality?* (Notre Dame, Ind.: University of Notre Dame Press, 1988); also Stanley Hauerwas *Character and the Christian Life* (San Antonio: Trinity University Press, 1975, 1985) and *Vision and Virtue* (Notre Dame, Ind.: University of Notre Dame Press, 1981).
6. Bernard Gert, *Morality* (New York: Oxford University Press, 1988), p. 157.
7. Classic statements of the prima facie deontological position are found in the writings of Sir W. David Ross, especially *The Right and the Good* (Oxford: Clarendon, 1939) and *Foundations of Ethics* (Oxford: Clarendon, 1939).
8. For a discussion of this matter, see Henry Shue, *Basic Rights* (Princeton: Princeton University Press, 1980), chap. 2.
9. This outline is adapted from Richard DeGeorge's *Business Ethics,* 3rd ed. (New York: Macmillan, 1986), pp. 57–58.
10. Bernard Williams and J. C. C. Smart, *Utilitarianism for and Against* (Oxford: Clarendon, 1973), pp. 123–26.
11. DeGeorge argues this way in *Business Ethics,* p. 294.
12. In *Forms and Limits of Utilitarianism* (Oxford: Clarendon, 1965), chaps. 3 and 4, David Lyons argues that, because they permit general rules involving beneficial exceptions for cases like this, the various forms of rule utilitarianism in practice are "extensionally equivalent" to act utilitarianism.
13. For a critique of these positions see Robbin Derry and Ronald Green, "Method in Business Ethics: A Critical Assessment," *Journal of Business Ethics* 8 (1989): 129–41.
14. Ibid.

NEUTRAL, OMNIPARTIAL
RULE-MAKING

✦

✦IN CHAPTER 2 WE EXAMINED TWO LEADING THEORIES OF NORMATIVE ethics and looked closely at their strengths and weaknesses. In this chapter, I explore a third theoretical approach to moral choice, an approach I call *Neutral, Omnipartial Rule-Making* (**NORM**). This approach aims at drawing the best from deontological and utilitarian theories. Like utilitarianism, **NORM** tries to develop the underlying logic of our moral reasoning process in terms of a basic principle or procedure for choice and then tries to carry this forward into new and difficult areas of moral decision. Like deontology, it tries to produce results more congruent with our moral common sense than does utilitarianism. But although this third approach seeks to capture the advantages of the two previous theories, it does not just combine them. It is a distinct method with its own clear guide to conduct.

NORM has deep roots in the philosophical tradition. It is very strongly suggested in the ethical writings of Immanuel Kant (1724–1804).

Kant's famous guide for ethics, the Categorical Imperative, is often interpreted as a deontological principle (primarily because it prohibits making happiness the primary objective of moral choice), but it also can be interpreted as an important early statement of a **NORM**-type approach.[1] More recently, this approach has been developed in the work of philosopher John Rawls and several other moral theorists.[2]

At the heart of this view is the idea that moral reasoning is meant to be a source we can appeal to when our interests conflict. Morality thus involves general and publicly known social judgments about which kinds of conduct we can tolerate in our midst and which we cannot. To say that an action is morally right, according to this approach, involves the judgment that it is a kind of conduct members of society would be prepared to accept in their midst. To declare it wrong is to say that it is a form of conduct society would not tolerate.

According to this view, the requirement that conduct must be publicly known and acceptable to all persons in society is the most basic consideration in the moral reasoning process—more basic, for example, than whether or not conduct promotes happiness. It may be that everyone would ordinarily accept promoting happiness as a valid social goal (although it is not clear that they would always do so). But even if this were true, promoting happiness is not what makes an action right—it is the fact that this is a publicly acknowledged form of conduct everyone would accept.

Another way of looking at this is to see that it conceives moral reasoning as a kind of legislative process that results in abiding rules of conduct or "moral laws" for society. This legislative process need not actually take place—it primarily transpires in our minds as a way of testing people's conduct. Nor are the resulting moral laws or rules always enforced by criminal or civil penalties (this is the chief difference between morality and law). Nevertheless, these moral "laws" or moral "rules" express serious and considered judgments about the kinds of conduct we believe society is willing to permit. To judge that something is "right," therefore, is to regard it as a type of conduct that all members of society would freely vote into existence—or at least would not prohibit. Conversely, to judge something as "wrong" is to say that it could not be thought of as becoming a publicly acknowledged and approved social practice. It could not move from "moral bill" to "moral law." These ideas allow us to offer a preliminary formulation of this moral view. **NORM** defines an action as right if *it might reasonably be thought of as being accepted by all members of society as a moral rule, that is, as* *an abiding form of conduct known by everyone and open to everyone in similar circumstances.*

As stated, this formulation raises at least two important questions. The first is whether this approach does not amount to a form of relativism, since it seems to make right or wrong depend on social approval. If it is a form of relativism, doesn't it then incur all the drawbacks of relativism examined in Chapter 2? For example, if we define right as what members of a society can accept, how can we morally criticize a society that, as a whole, abuses its minorities or aggresses against other groups?

The answer to these questions lies in the basic idea behind this view: morality aims at the fair and principled settlement of disputes. Because of this objective, we must think of moral principles as being approved by *everyone* in society. Acceptable moral rules are not the result of majority will but of a *free* consensus of all the people who live under them. This excludes the possibility of the victimization of subgroups within a community. According to **NORM**, members of these subgroups are always enfranchised "moral legislators" able to vote against conduct that harms them. For the same reason, moral rules potentially have no territorial boundaries. Because the purpose of morality is to resolve conflict between persons by providing a reasoned and public method of appeal, all parties to a dispute must be thought of as having a say in formulating and accepting the resulting moral rules that govern everyone's conduct. This means that morality is ideally universal in scope, embracing all possible parties to conflicts and empowering them as moral rule-makers. Far from legitimizing the imposition of one group's values on another's, **NORM** requires the free consent of *all* parties affected by a form of conduct.

The second major question has to do with its requirement of *everyone's* free consent to principles. How, some might ask, can we realistically expect all persons freely to agree to anything? People have different values and different beliefs, and they stand in such different positions of power that almost no form of conduct meets everyone's approval. Nor, as the sad history of our century reveals, is any particular act—no matter how wicked—universally condemned. Is it ever possible, then, to reach a free consensus on social conduct?

As we consider this objection, it helps to know that **NORM** does not require an actual vote by real persons. It is above all a conceptual test we apply to assess conduct or policies. Conceptually, however, we have a procedure for adjudicating conflict between opposing viewpoints and for arriving at a single conclusion even when confronted by competing claims. This is the procedure of impartiality. It requires us to take the position of each party to a dispute seriously, but not to identify with it uniquely, and then to do the same for all other positions in the controversy. After evaluating all positions, we are better able to arrive at a decision that is objective and fair to each party. In fact, "impartiality" is not the best word for this intellectual activity. Like its companion word "disinterestedness," it suggests a stance of coolness or detachment. "Omnipartiality" is a better word, as it suggests full, empathetic identification with the beliefs, feelings, and interests of each person our decisions affect. At the same time, omnipartiality requires a stance of neutrality before competing claims. Parents exercise omnipartiality whenever they must decide between the competing claims and needs of their children. It is this approach of engaged, involved neutrality and evenhandedness that the **NORM** method requires.

In the judicial system we have an actual social procedure based on this idea. Courts of law are a rational method societies have developed for settling complex social disputes. Although guided by preexisting codes, judges frequently "make law" by their rulings. In deliberating, however, a judge is not supposed to represent a single party in a dispute. Instead, a judge must consider the interests and claims of *all* parties. Judges must weigh and assess these different viewpoints as fairly, neutrally, and "omnipartially" as they can and render a fair and objective decision (we ask a biased judge to step down from a case). This process of neutral omnipartial assessment and balancing is aptly symbolized by the statue enshrined in virtually every American courthouse: blinded justice holding her scales. It is a sign of how effective neutral omnipartiality can be that judges or arbitrators often reach fair decisions in cases where the actual parties to the dispute are hopelessly deadlocked.

The agreement on rules that this third approach to ethics involves, therefore, should not be thought of as agreement by all the actual parties to a controversy, but as agreement by an omnipartial person called in to settle the dispute. We can think of this "judge" as putting herself or himself into the shoes of each contending party, omnipartially weighing and assessing each person's claims and interests, and then rendering a decision about whose interests shall be respected and whose shall not. The result is identification of a rule governing conduct in this case and in *all* similar future cases.

Sometimes it is possible to arrive at moral decisions through a real process of omnipartial reasoning involving many persons. This occurs when we are able to have full public discussion of a moral issue, when people can be reasonably omnipartial, or when they are roughly equal in authority and a consensus emerges. But most of the time we make moral judgments on our own and, when we do, we undertake this entire process in our minds. Each of us then becomes a judge weighing the claims of various parties to the dispute. We strive to examine each perspective as omnipartially as we can, putting ourselves in the shoes of each person, and we try to arrive at a resolution that is fair to everyone (although it may not be one that satisfies everyone's interests). When we are reasonably convinced that other omnipartial judges would agree with our thinking, the result is a ruling on the conduct at issue—a "moral rule" or a valid "moral exception"—and we then are able to say that we know what the "right thing" to do is in the case. Of course, no one is entirely omnipartial or infallible. We cannot know for sure what completely knowledgeable and truly omnipartial persons would decide in all cases. We reason morally, therefore, not when we are absolutely certain about our conclusions but when we have reasonable and well-founded confidence that our judgment is informed and omnipartial.

Against this background we can now consider a more complete statement of the test of conduct embodied by this third theory of ethics. **NORM** defines an action as right if *each person might reasonably think of that action as being accepted by anyone who looked at the matter in an informed and omnipartial way as a moral rule, that is, as an abiding form of conduct known by everyone and open to everyone in similar circumstances.*

NORM has some important features in common with utilitarianism. Like utilitarianism, it proceeds logically from a basic conception of morality (in this case not utilitarianism's view that morality aims to maximize happiness, but the view that morality is fundamentally meant to provide a public standard of acceptable conduct). Like utilitarianism, it takes the consequences of actions into account (since we can assume that omnipartial "judges" are concerned about the impact conduct has on people's lives). And, like utilitarianism, it has a single decision rule for moral choice. Whereas utilitarianism requires us to produce the "greatest happiness for the greatest number," **NORM** tells us that our conduct must be capable of becoming an omnipartially acceptable public rule. Which of these similar but contrasting approaches is better?

Earlier I said that the test of a moral theory is how well it helps us think about difficult moral choices. We also saw that utilitarianism produces its most troubling results in cases where no one is likely to learn of our deeds or when it is possible to conceal or cover up what we have done. How does *Neutral, Omnipartial Rule-Making* work in cases like this?

To answer this question, let us return briefly to a case we met in the previous chapter: our purely hypothetical case of "The Desert-Island Promise" (Case 2.2).

The key actor in this case is the pilot, who must decide how he will respond to the dying passenger's request. We saw that if he reasons as a utilitarian whose single goal is to maximize happiness, the pilot probably must deceptively make the promise and then break it. But **NORM** imposes an entirely different requirement on the pilot. It asks him to decide whether what he plans to do might *reasonably be thought of as being accepted by anyone who looked at the matter in an informed and omnipartial way as a moral rule, that is, as an abiding form of conduct known by everyone and open to everyone in similar circumstances.*

Can the lying and promise-breaking shown in this case be an acceptable moral rule? To answer this, the pilot might first state precisely just what the rule implicit in his conduct is. It seems to be something like the following:

✦

Proposed Moral Rule: Someone facing the choice of making a promise to a dying person may deceptively make the promise and then break it whenever he or she thinks more good can be done.

✦

According to **NORM**, in evaluating this rule, the pilot must omnipartially weigh whatever interests he identifies, strive to be neutral, and seek to arrive at a fair conclusion.

Clearly, there are good reasons for not accepting this proposed rule. Although it somewhat benefits people who think others' deathbed promises are foolish, it seriously harms anyone trying to have a dying promise taken seriously. Reasoning omnipartially, I must try to put myself in the shoes of people like this. I may someday want to elicit a solemn promise from another person, perhaps even from someone who does not understand or appreciate the reasons I want the promise made. If I accept this conduct as a valid moral rule for society, it becomes senseless for me to count on promises made in such circumstances. This proposed rule takes decision making out of my hands and renders my interests hostage to another person's calculations of net benefit. It even invites other persons to deceive me about their intentions! If I reject this rule, however, if I prohibit deception and generally hold people responsible for keeping such promises, I do little harm. No one is forced to make and keep a deathbed promise. People remain free to reject such requests, although they must be honest in doing so. They also remain free to try to persuade dying people not to make what they regard as foolish requests. Thinking omnipartially about these matters, and taking all interests into account, therefore, it makes sense to prohibit behavior like the pilot's in this case.

We can see that, in this case at least, **NORM** supports our common-sense intuition that it is ordinarily wrong to lie or to break solemn promises. This is so because, unlike utilitarianism, this approach builds the requirement that our conduct be publicly acceptable into our most basic way of thinking about moral choice. Utilitarianism also considers the public impact of our conduct—but only when this impact is actually likely to occur. In contrast, **NORM** sees moral choice as inherently public. Whether or not others happen to learn of what we have done, to say that something is "right" is the same as saying that others would accept it as a public rule for everyone in similar circumstances. This means that in the case of the "Desert-Island Promise" there is no opportunity for the pilot to conceal his conduct. To the very extent that he makes a moral judgment, *in his mind* he necessarily reasons omnipartially and turns to all other members of society (including, in a sense, the deceased orchid grower) for their approval.

If we move from a purely hypothetical case to the real choices facing a manager like Phil Cortez, whom we met at the beginning of the previous chapter (Case 2.1), we can see that **NORM** also provides useful insight into his decision. Facing the question of whether to break his promise to Lifeworth, for example, Phil must first formulate the moral rule implicit in his choice. This rule might read:

✦

Proposed Moral Rule: An employee who has promised not to reveal proprietary information and who has been given access to it may break this promise whenever a more lucrative offer comes along or whenever he is threatened with firing by a new employer for not doing so.

✦

Phil must then ask whether he would omnipartially accept this rule if he were to put himself in the shoes of all relevant parties: his previous employer and present employer, other employees, and members of society generally.

Returning to our earlier discussion, it is not hard to identify the good reasons for *not* accepting this proposed rule. In a society governed by it, employers would be far less able to trust employees, research and development would suffer or be replaced by industrial espionage, and a bidding war would ensue for employees' loyalties. Although Phil might find some support for this rule if he looked at it narrowly from his perspective or that of his new employer, there are overwhelming interests on the other side that oppose it. Ironically, in a society where this proposed rule governed everyone's behavior, the very information that Phil's new firm seeks would probably no longer be available, since companies would either halt research or would take costly steps to prevent employees from having access to its results. Reasoning in this way, Phil must conclude that what he proposes to do cannot become a publicly known and accepted moral rule and, hence, that he cannot morally break his promise.

We can see, then, that *Neutral, Omnipartial Rule-Making* helps us think about difficult and real choices of this sort. It also helps explain the force of many of the deontological rules we ordinarily respect by identifying our deep interest as members of society in the preservation of the *general* forms of behavior or standards of conduct that shape our expectations and affect us all. If we feel it is usually right to tell the truth, keep promises, and treat persons justly even when we can sometimes increase net happiness by not doing so, this is because these practices benefit us all, because they form part of the public expectations on which we build our conduct, and because any departure from them must be considered as being approved by all of us. **NORM** thus takes the mystery out of the intrinsic validity of these deontological rules and explains why deontology has been an attractive moral viewpoint.

But **NORM** takes us beyond deontology and provides us with a way of reasoning when the rules conflict. To see why this is so, we should recognize that **NORM** does not always require us to uphold the standard moral rules. In each instance of choice what is important is not whether a specific rule is upheld or violated, but whether our actions *might reasonably be thought of as being accepted by anyone who looked at the matter in an informed and omnipartial way as an abiding form of conduct known by everyone and open to everyone in similar circumstances.* Sometimes this reasoning can lead us to make exceptions to a moral rule or to restate the rule in more specific ways. For example, imagine the case of the "Desert-Island Promise" with a small change. The pilot has agreed to keep his promise and honestly intends to do so. He returns to civilization and finds the money, but, just as he is about to establish care for the orchids, he learns to his distress that they harbor a parasite that seriously threatens human health. Is it ethically justifiable for the pilot to destroy the plants? The pilot now sees himself as caught between the possibility of breaking his promise or violating the moral rule against harming others. What should he do—and why?

A prima facie deontologist might handle a case like this by arguing that the rule against injuring others takes priority over the rule against keeping a promise of this sort. An absolutist deontologist might argue that we may never break our promises, but that the "promises" must implicitly be understood as not requiring us to keep them when human life is in peril. These familiar arguments characteristically contain no further reasons for their claims and they strongly reflect their defenders' own interpretations of the issues, which other deontologists might—and often do—dispute. In contrast, if the pilot were to legislate omnipartially from the vantage point of all persons affected, it hardly seems likely that he could support a moral rule requiring him strictly to keep his promise in a case like this. Consider this in terms of the following moral rule:

✦

Proposed Moral Rule: Someone who has made a promise to a dying person to care for his cherished flowers may not break that promise, even if it later turns out that the flowers are a source of deadly contagion.

✦

For society to accept a moral rule like this would put everyone's life in peril. Oddly enough, even those with the greatest stake in this rule's being upheld, potential cultivators of orchids or those wishing someday to elicit deathbed promises, would find their lives and projects constantly threatened by a rigid moral rule of this sort. Reasoning omnipartially, we would not want to live in a world where this rule prevailed. This amounts to the conclusion that whenever matters are this grave we can break a deathbed promise of this sort. In place of the proposed moral rule above, therefore, we can imagine omnipartial persons accepting the following rule as an implicitly understood exception to the rule of promise-keeping:

✦

Proposed Moral Exception to the Rule of Keeping Deathbed Promises: Someone who has made a promise to a dying person to care for some cherished possession (such as flowers) may break that promise if keeping it is seriously likely to harm other persons' lives or health.

✦

Can we all live with the knowledge that this rule/exception is in place? I think so. Although this means we cannot have absolute certainty that deathbed promises made to us will always be kept, this exception represents a reasonable balance among our various interests as individuals likely to be affected by cases of this sort.

We can apply similar reasoning to the case of Phil Cortez. We saw that Phil is ordinarily bound to uphold the promise to his previous employer. Would this be true if the year were 1939 and Phil was a refugee to the United States whose previous employer was a German manufacturer of vital aircraft components? Would Phil be morally required not to disclose any proprietary information in his possession, even if this information would help the democracies ward off defeat? To argue that Phil is morally obligated to keep his promise in such circumstances is to conclude that members of society would accept something like the following rule:

✦

Proposed Moral Rule: An employee who has promised his firm not to reveal proprietary information may not break this promise even when the firm has been taken over and put into the service of an aggressive tyranny.

✦

It is not hard to see the problems with this rule. Meant to support the integrity of commitments and productive research, it contributes to the victory of a despotism whose aim is the destruction of integrity everywhere. We can see why rational, omnipartial persons might exempt Phil from having to keep his promise and why they would make a special exception to employee promise-keeping in cases like this.

NORM, then, offers a method for reasoning through difficult cases of moral choice. Like the deontological view, it provides grounds for ordinarily respecting the commonsense moral rules. But it also makes reasoned judgment possible when the rules conflict. It can do so because, like utilitarianism, it is based not on a plurality of different rules but on a single basic rule or decisional procedure that we apply contextually in new circumstances. It differs from utilitarianism, however, in that it can arrive at conclusions more congruent with our moral common sense, because its basic rule or procedure—the requirement of omnipartial acceptability as a publicly acknowledged moral rule or moral exception—is more solidly founded on what we mean by and how we think about morality.

We can now outline a method of moral decision making based on a moral theory that avoids the worst problems of its predecessors. Box 3.1 summarizes this method. This outline deliberately builds on and corrects the utilitarian mode of reasoning presented in Box 2.3. It is meant as a guide to reasoning and a framework for discussion in difficult cases, including many of those examined in the chapters ahead. But even the best of moral theories will not mechanically produce "correct" results. Applying any general guide to reasoning requires judgment and an ability to identify relevant concerns. This is particularly true of an approach like this one, which entails a series of judgments in order to arrive at each decision. Against the framework of this list, let us look more closely at some features of this approach that deserve special attention.

Step 1 is a crucial aspect of this decision process. It requires us to identify and formulate the general moral rule (or exception) implicit in our choice or conduct. Each time we act, we form a model of behavior that, however specific, should be morally available to anyone else in the same kind of situation. The danger here is that I may state this rule so specifically that I unfairly represent what I am doing or so generally that I confuse it with different forms of behavior.

Proper names, for example, obviously have no place in the statement of a general rule since what is morally permissible for me is also appropriate for all other similarly situated persons. It would be foolish to

Box 3.1

NEUTRAL, OMNIPARTIAL RULE-MAKING (NORM)

1. Accurately state the conduct to be evaluated as a moral rule (a form of conduct open to all persons in similar circumstances).
2. Identify all those who are directly and immediately affected by acting on this rule in this instance.
3. Reason omnipartially:
   a. Put yourself into the shoes of each of these persons.
   b. *Using as your guide their interests and all the facts you can obtain*, determine how each person would be benefitted or harmed by this conduct both now and in the foreseeable future.
4. Identify all those who would be affected, directly or indirectly, if this moral rule prevailed in society.
5. Reason omnipartially about this rule:
   a. Put yourself into the position of each person affected by this rule.
   b. *Using as your guide their interests and all the facts you can obtain*, determine how each person would be benefitted or harmed by this moral rule both now and in the foreseeable future.
6. Weigh *both* the immediate effects of this conduct *and* its impact as a moral rule, taking into consideration such matters as the quantity, duration, and likelihood of the harms and benefits involved.
7. Reasoning omnipartially, representing any and all the persons possibly affected, ask yourself whether on balance you would be prepared to see this moral rule come into being. If you would not, you should regard this conduct as *morally wrong.* If you would, you may regard this conduct as *morally right.*
8. If you have judged this conduct wrong but there are still good reasons for wanting to permit it, consider imaginatively whether there are various alternatives to simply performing or not performing the action, and carry out a similar analysis for each alternative.

formulate a rule like "I, John Q. Smith, may lie to customers" and believe that because I am the only John Q. Smith this rule will have limited negative impact. This rule really empowers anyone in my situation to lie, and it must be assessed accordingly. We can say the same of the many other specific and morally irrelevant features that cases often present. Generally, the only relevant features of a case are those having a recognizable impact on human welfare. Thus, it may be relevant for a rule to include the fact that a person is acting as the head of an organization when this responsibility shapes the impact of his or her conduct on others and when it would have a similar effect for anyone else acting on this rule.

A proposed moral rule also can be stated too generally. Take, for example, the hypothetical case discussed above, that of breaking a promise to a former employer in time of war. It would badly misrepresent what is proposed here if one were simply to render a moral exception permitting disregard for employment agreements "in urgent circumstances." The circumstances already stated are quite specific and, as such, are relevant to our evaluation of the conduct. In permitting promise-breaking in this case, we surely do not mean to authorize disregard for promises in other, very different cases. Confusion about this can lead us wrongly to prohibit an otherwise permissible practice. Worse, in other circumstances it can lead us into immoral conduct. A common moral mistake is the taking of a rule appropriate to one very specific context and using it in other contexts where its relevant features no longer apply. Thus, it would be an error to take a conclusion indicated for wartime circumstances and use it to justify breaking employment promises when dealing with commercial competition. We should always be on the lookout for mistakes of this sort in our thinking.

Steps 2 and 4, the identification *all* the people affected by our conduct, are crucial elements of sound moral reasoning. When the need for decision bears down urgently upon us, it is easy to become "morally myopic": to focus narrowly on parties near to us but to miss entirely those at the periphery of our vision. The discussions and cases in the chapters that follow offer many examples of how easy it is to overlook actors in a moral drama. To avoid moral myopia in these and in real-life decisions, it helps to begin thinking about a choice by writing down all the persons our decision will affect—or, in the case of a business decision, all the "stakeholders" involved. Especially important, because they are so easily neglected, are persons not directly involved in our decision but affected by the moral rule it yields. For example, if I choose to break my word to an employer, I not only affect the people I am currently dealing with, but I also establish a rule for similar cases. Step 4 tells us to consider the impact of such a rule on the owners, managers, and employees of companies, as well as everyone in society, should this practice be accepted in the business community.

Steps 3 and 5 involve the exercise of omnipartiality, one of the most difficult and demanding aspects of the moral reasoning process. It is important to note once more that omnipartiality does not mean detachment. This is why "omnipartiality" is a better word than "impartiality." Omnipartiality requires us to empathize imaginatively with each person we affect, to strive to assume her or his interests and beliefs, and to measure our proposed conduct in terms of its impact on ourselves were we in this person's position. Omnipartiality does not rule out intense involvement with each party's interest, but only a *unique* attachment to any one interest (including one's own) that prevents a person from similarly appreciating all the other positions involved. This explains use of the paired terms *neutral* and *omnipartial* in the description of this method.

None of us, of course, can ever be fully omnipartial. As human beings we interpret others' experience through the lenses of our own perceptions and needs. But it would be false to say that we cannot approximate omnipartiality and even falser to say that we do not expect this of one another when making moral judgments. We have seen that omnipartiality is the premise of every judicial proceeding. The court system protects omnipartiality by excluding judges or jurors with any direct involvement in a case. Unfortunately, in daily life when we reason morally we are often interested parties to the issue we must evaluate. Nevertheless, we do possess the ability to discern biased reasoning and to identify personal factors that distort judgment, and these are what omnipartiality asks us to avoid. We also can take steps to enhance our appreciation of others' perspectives. Education—including exposure to art, literature, and the different viewpoints and perspectives of other persons—aims at broadening our appreciation of areas of human experience other than our own and at increasing our capacity for imaginative understanding of others' needs and claims.

As we reason omnipartially in connection with steps 3 and 5, it is also important to note that we weigh people's *interests*, not their *moral views*, on the issue before us. For example, in trying to determine whether employees should be permitted to smoke on the job, we do not omnipartially evaluate different people's assessments of whether employees have a right to smoke in the workplace, or whether they believe that it is morally right or wrong to forbid them from doing so. Instead, we assess our own *interests* in each relevant standpoint, those aspects of the conduct at issue that affect our basic welfare. As possible smokers, we ask whether we will be harmed or burdened by being forbidden to light up on the job, and we balance this against the interests we might have as nonsmoking colleagues in remaining free from annoyance or injury caused by secondhand smoke or the interests we might have as shareholders in reducing the costs associated with fire or employee health insurance. If we do not factor in competing moral views at this point in reasoning, it is precisely because our aim is to *arrive* at a moral viewpoint. We can think of moral views as *conclusions* of complex reasoning processes based on an omnipartial assessment of interests. Because **NORM**'s aim is to bring this process to light, it goes directly to the interests that form the basis of competing views, seeking to identify a sustainable moral conclusion out of these interests.

Finally, steps 3 and 5 remind us that we should keep in mind that an empathetic appreciation of others' interests does not mean that we can ignore the facts of a case. Moral reasoning aims at rules of conduct protective of all our interests. This means that we must accurately understand the real consequences of what we propose to do. Empathetic omnipartiality may require us to tolerate people's unfounded beliefs or prejudices to the extent that these shape their interests. For example, I may regard another person's religious views as quaint and outdated, but because people do not ordinarily like their important beliefs brought under criticism, omnipartiality requires me to respect these beliefs and practices. But when beliefs or prejudices demonstrably cause harm to others, they must yield to views based on facts. Thus, I am not morally required to tolerate racist comments. I may be called on to speak out against them and actively to oppose racist behavior. In the chapters that follow, we will see that many moral disputes are really disputes about facts. Although moral reasoning alone cannot resolve these controversies—which usually require appeal to expert opinion or research—it does stress the importance of objectivity and the need to resort to evidence whenever relevant facts are in dispute.

Steps 6 and 7 initially seem forbidding. Can we really weigh and balance a variety of competing interests and come up with a coherent conclusion? In fact, we do this all the time. While making prudential judgments, we often weigh and balance different kinds of satisfactions against one another to arrive at practical conclusions. For example, when I decide to pass up a movie on the night before a crucial examination, I make the judgment that the satisfactions I associate with passing the test outweigh the enjoyment of an evening's entertainment. Sometimes, as in this instance, decision is helped by the fact that my competing goals are not simply opposed but embrace one another or share some common values by which they can be compared. For example, I may choose to study in the knowledge that access to a successful career promises greater opportunity for leisure in the future. Similar processes of reasoning enter into the making of moral decisions under conditions of omnipartiality. Omnipartial persons view it as permissible to break a desert-island promise in order to ward off a threat to human life, for example, both because life has a high value and because it is essential to our ability to elicit promises in the first place.

Such careful reasoning can help us approach the point where we believe that anyone who has looked at the matter omnipartially will agree with our assessment and balancing of the issues. When this is so, we can have confidence in the validity of our moral judgment and are better able to defend a course of action as right or wrong. Sometimes, however, other persons may disagree with us or maintain that they see the issues differently. Disputes of this sort can often be resolved by further discussion. Talking over our differences, we may find that one person has missed a relevant feature of the case or is employing erroneous information. Where the facts are in dispute, we can seek additional evidence for the various claims. Frequently, this process will lead to clarity and agreement on the rights and wrongs of the issue.

Sometimes, however, it will not. Occasionally, the utmost exercise of omnipartiality leaves us pulled by competing claims and interests and unsure, both as individuals and members of society, about the course to prescribe. This is an unavoidable consequence of human diversity and human limitations—of the fact that we cannot know everything with certainty and do not always see things the same way as another person. But this outcome does not mean that the moral reasoning process, as far as it goes, is not very useful. For one thing, omnipartial reasoning can significantly reduce the number of occasions where this kind of indecision occurs. Although it does not altogether eliminate the gray region of the moral life, omnipartial moral reasoning narrows it and helps us expand the region of moral "blacks" and "whites." For another, it is instructive to identify instances when moral issues are genuinely uncertain. If, when exercising our skills as omnipartial moral "legislators" or "judges" we arrive at the conclusion that no single course of action seems clearly right or wrong, this should be taken as a counsel of humility. It warns us that reasonable people can disagree at this point and tells us to be tolerant of competing views. This does not mean that we must always withhold judgment on the case. Circumstances sometimes deny us this luxury. For example, an organization often must have a policy on a disputed matter and not having one can itself be a policy. At times like this, various fair "political" procedures may help shape decisions. For example, we can decide to vote or select a qualified leader to choose for us. The value of having a grasp of the moral reasoning process is that it helps us see when these other modes of decision are permissible and appropriate. As we saw earlier in connection with relativism, moral wisdom involves knowing when decisions that shape our conduct should be left to the groups to which we belong—and when they should not be.

Sometimes we conclude that an action is morally wrong. Step 8 tells us that this is not necessarily the end of the matter. There may be morally acceptable alternatives open to us, and we can frequently identify these by reviewing the considerations that led to our initial moral conclusion. For example, Phil Cortez might respond to the Engineering Director's request by stressing to him (or, more likely to those above him who are responsible for National's performance) that Phil's value to the firm partly depends on his ability to respect agreements. A deeper understanding of the moral issues points the way toward a morally better course of conduct. Alternatively, Phil might consider leaving National and returning to his previous employer. Although this may close what had seemed a promising career opportunity, it could spare Phil unemployment and protect his moral integrity. An interesting question, which might be considered in terms of the **NORM** method of reasoning, is whether Lifeworth would then have a moral obligation to take Phil back.

APPLYING **NORM**

♦

The kind of problem that faced Omicron's managers in Case 3.1 is common in high-tech industries, where complex products are often developed under tight deadlines and in the shadow of competitors. Although Omicron makes office machines, similar marketing practices occur in the software industry, where competitive pressures lead firms to market or ship programs that are defective or incomplete. Omicron's experience gives us a chance to test the main normative approaches to business ethics we have discussed and particularly to exercise our skills in applying the **NORM** method.

Case 3.1

✦ SELLING LEMONS[3] ✦

The following letter was written by Sally J. Kasnik to a former business school classmate with whom she had taken a second year elective course on business ethics.

86 Milburn Avenue
Austin, Texas 68108
April 4, 1993

Dear Ken,

I want you to know I'm really enjoying my job. You may remember what mixed feelings I had about this offer during recruiting two years ago, but I don't regret a thing. Austin's a better place to live than I could have imagined. My boss and division are wonderful, and I love every day at work.

Omicron is a great company. The best. Of course that doesn't mean there aren't problems. Let me tell you about an experience I've had as Sales Manager for Texas. It's one that made me think about our ethics course.

Our newest copier model, the M-3100, seemed like a fine product when it was launched last year. Its characteristics fitted the needs of small businesses at a price we all thought was competitive. By September, we knew we had a winner. All areas exceeded sales quotas, and we had lots of new customers, plus dozens of happy old clients who bought the M-3100.

Then it happened. Overnight we realized we had a "lemon." Maintenance costs were off the chart. The machine had to be repaired about every ten hours of use, which is totally unacceptable. Customers began to complain nation-wide. The engineering division did a complete survey and concluded that the best option was to cancel the M-3100 and go back to the drawing board. Top management of the office machine division had a problem. There were thousands of M-3100's in warehouses in every region in the country. The company had at least $15,000,000 tied up in that inventory.

The decision came down: "Sell out the M-3100's. Use all the sales processes (deals, incentives, etc.) necessary to empty the warehouses of the machine by June 1, 1993." We sales managers were instructed to take sales representatives into our confidence, tell them everything, but make clear what had to be done. Further, we were given an attractive new pricing model. The lower price was justified by the new projection of profits on future maintenance revenue.

We planned an aggressive state-wide advertising campaign in Texas. We didn't tell our ad agency what we were really doing. It was not something they would have wanted to know. Some things are better left unsaid. Of course, we didn't explain what we were doing to newspapers or the broadcast media either. At times I wish headquarters hadn't told me what the truth was, or that I hadn't told the sales force. It was something that had to be done. Even with the high future maintenance costs (about which we said nothing), customers got a bargain at the lower prices. By the way, the M-3100's are selling like Cabbage Patch dolls. We can easily empty the warehouses by June.

So that's my report from the "real world." No complaints, really. I'm very happy in my job and dreaming about my next promotion.

Best wishes,
Sally

QUESTIONS TO CONSIDER

1. What do you think of the way Omicron handled sales of its defective copier?
2. How would a deontologist evaluate the decisions of Omicron's management? What would a utilitarian say about these decisions?
3. What light does **NORM** shed on the company's conduct?

How would a deontologist respond to this case? Although this depends, in part, on the particular rules a deontologist favors, we can limit our thinking for the moment to someone using Bernard Gert's list of ten moral rules (Box 2.1). At first sight, the matter seems clear: since defective M-3100's are being marketed as problem-free machines, Omicron's conduct seems to violate Gert's sixth moral rule prohibiting deception. Sally Kasnik may feel this way herself. She wrote this letter because of her sense that something about this episode was "out of character" for a company as good as Omicron. But when we try to understand exactly what is wrong here, things become less clear. There is no evidence, for example, that Omicron's management has actually lied to anyone about the condition of the machines. Instead, what they did is *fail to disclose* facts that some consumers might regard as important. Is this unethical? Are we morally required not only to avoid lying, as Gert requires, but also to disclose information actively to others? Surely not every failure to disclose relevant information in business or personal matters is morally objectionable. Do I act wrongly if I fail to tell someone interested in buying my house that I desperately need to sell it and will accept a much lower price than I have asked? Do I wrong them if I fail to mention every flaw and needed repair I know of? The point is that failures to disclose and active lying are not always the same, and our views on which requirement is applicable to a sales situation differ widely. Some people believe that a standard of caveat emptor, "buyer beware," is the right one for most sales relationships; others advocate a commitment to full and fair disclosure of anything that might affect a customer's interests. Before assessing Omicron's conduct, we have to decide which point of view is applicable here. This case shows that within a deontological framework even the *meaning* of moral rules is often unclear. Unfortunately, the deontological approach provides little help in interpreting and applying its own standards.

Deontology has the further problem of *weighing* conflicting standards. If we believe that Omicron's managers have some obligation to share product information with prospective customers, how are they to balance this against their other obligations? For example, Gert's tenth moral rule requires managers to "do their duty." If Omicron is a public company, managers have a duty to increase shareholder wealth. Does fulfilling this duty allow them to withhold important sales information from customers? It is not hard to imagine the heated debate this question might precipitate among Omicron's various stakeholders. This points up a persistent problem with deontology: even when the rules are clear, different weightings of the rules or priorities among them hamper moral discussion and make it hard to see how disputes can be settled.

Utilitarianism holds out the promise of greater moral clarity. Because utilitarianism has only one high-order moral principle, the requirement that in each choice we seek to maximize happiness, it spares us deontology's conflict of principles. For dedicated utilitarian managers at Omicron, one question is to the fore: Will their decision produce the greatest amount of happiness for the greatest number of people? By this calculation, much can be said for the way Omicron's top people handled this problem. By clearing their inventory, they increased shareholder wealth and prevented layoffs of Omicron personnel. These stakeholders are happier as a result. Many buyers of the M-3100 have benefitted from a lower sales price (even with the additional cost of service contracts factored in). Offsetting this, of course, is the annoyance and inconvenience caused to some buyers who thought they were getting a reliable machine but were repeatedly forced to cope with breakdowns and repairs. Although we probably would have to know more about how many buyers fit into these categories and the net impact of their positive and negative experiences, within a utilitarian framework Omicron's conduct at least seems defensible.

Of course, utilitarians also insist that we consider the larger, indirect consequences of our behavior. Particularly relevant here are the impact on consumer confidence *if Omicron's conduct becomes widely known*. Then, not only Omicron's customers but consumers everywhere will have reason to question the reliability of high-tech products. They may develop sales resistance to other new products in ways that harm the economy as a whole and reduce everyone's well-being. We find some evidence for these kinds of reactions in the software industry, where a history of bug-filled programs and the marketing of "vaporware" (incomplete or nonexistent programs) have given the whole industry a bad reputation and made consumers wary of new product claims. If Omicron's conduct is exposed, these larger negative consequences for many stakeholders tip the balance against this type of marketing practice.

Of course, the key word here is "if." Only *if* the public becomes aware of Omicron's conduct will all these adverse effects occur. In contrast, *if* the company is successful in keeping customers, advertisers, and others in the dark there will be no general impact of its handling of this product. Some may argue that Omicron will find it difficult to keep a lid on this episode. Too many people are already involved, and disgruntled buyers are likely to express their views to one another or to the media. But these outcomes are contingent. They may or may not occur. If Omicron's leadership can "manage" the public's access to the facts, they might avoid these worst-case scenarios. For utilitarians, such information management is one available moral strategy open to Omicron. In other words, although utilitarianism presents a warning to those who act in ways that might undermine public confidence, it does not necessarily prohibit such conduct. Since what matters is not whether we are honest or dishonest, just or unjust, but what degree of happiness or harm is *actually produced by our choices,* utilitarianism may even encourage efforts to conceal conduct whose only bad consequences occur when it is publicly exposed. From a strictly theoretical standpoint, therefore, in this case utilitarianism is neutral between Omicron's not taking the risk of exposure and taking the risk but making strenuous attempts to reduce it by concealment or the skilled use of public relations. Again we see that utilitarianism permits us to make questionable behavior "better" by covering it up.

How does **NORM** apply in this case? Box 3.1 tells us that our first step is to mentally identify the moral rule implicit in the conduct of Omicron's top management. This step is crucial. It is very easy to misstate this rule in ways that obscure the essential moral issues. Consider, for example, the following as an interpretation of Omicron's conduct:

✦

First Proposed Moral Rule: To avoid layoffs and financial reverses, a company's managers may market products such as defective office copiers as long as they believe they have adequately compensated buyers for additional repair costs by means of a lower price.

✦

Although it contains some features of Omicron's decision that would be important to omnipartial persons (the fact that a failure to act will be costly for the company; that the product is one whose defects are not life-threatening; that the price is lower), this rule does not entirely describe the kind of conduct Omicron engaged in. It leaves out other features of interest to stakeholders (especially the details of Omicron's marketing program). In justifying their conduct, Omicron's managers may have thought of their decision in this imprecise way, but if so they were mistaken. The following is a better candidate for the rule implicit in their conduct:

✦

Second Proposed Moral Rule: To avoid layoffs and financial reverses, a company's managers may market products such as defective office copiers *without informing customers of the nature and extent of the defects involved* as long as they believe they have adequately compensated buyers for additional repair costs by means of a lower price.

✦

NORM tells us that, to the extent that Omicron's behavior is morally justifiable, we must reasonably believe that this rule would be accepted by all those affected by it, at least to the extent that they examine the choice omnipartially. How well does this rule fare under this test? How would someone who could be any and all of these affected persons be likely to vote?

In answering these questions, our analysis in some ways parallels that of utilitarianism. For example, in terms of the interests of Omicron's managers, employees, and shareholders, as well as of those customers benefitted by the lower price, the conduct allowed by this rule seems acceptable. Against this, we must expect that customers subjected to unanticipated breakdowns whose inconvenience is not offset by the lower product cost will have reason to vote against anything authorizing this sort of conduct. Reasoning omnipartially in the position of any and all of these stakeholders, up to this point we find ourselves undecided and pulled in conflicting directions.

NORM takes us beyond the immediate stakeholders benefitted or harmed by this conduct, however, and requires us to look at *all* persons affected by the rule we act on. It asks us to regard conduct as a type of behavior open to anyone in similar circumstances and publicly known to us all. The test of Omicron's conduct, then, comes down to this: If I could be any and all of the persons it affects, would I want to live in a world governed by this rule?

Viewed this way, Omicron's mode of acting poses serious problems. First, it exposes each of us to such conduct in all cases where a company finds it attractive not to disclose defects in technically complex office products such as copiers. Because there are many such products prone to frequent breakdown whose defects cause inconvenience and annoyance, this rule creates a world of constant surprises, where products we count on to do a job fail to perform. Second, this rule places decisions regarding the trade-off between inconvenience and price entirely in the hands of the company. In a world governed by this rule, I may buy a copier (or typewriter or computer), and later find through experience that the "down-time" involved in using the machine far outweighs the slight reduction in the price of the machine. Had I known more about the product's defects, I may well have chosen to buy a costlier unit. But this rule has deprived me of the ability to make that choice.

It is not hard to see that the rule implicit in Omicron's conduct has many unwelcome implications for many people far beyond the boundaries of Omicron's sales network. Reasoning impartially, we would find it very hard to authorize this kind of behavior. Interestingly, many of Omicron's managers, shareholders, and employees can also be expected to dislike this rule since they are potentially harmed every time they purchase a complex machine for the company's use. In the conduct of its business, this rule exposes Omicron to defects in products purchased from its own suppliers.

None of the harms we have identified here depend on the public *actually* learning of Omicron's handling of the M-3100 problem. Reasoning in terms of **NORM**, Omicron's managers are not asked to assess the likelihood that their conduct will be exposed and the harm that will result if it is. This is the way utilitarianism proceeds. Instead, they are asked to imagine a world in which their conduct is a public moral rule, known by everyone and open to everyone. Whether such a world ever actually comes into being is beside the point. Paradoxically, Omicron's managers may be entirely successful in covering up their behavior, but from the point of view of **NORM** it would still be wrong unless they could reasonably think of it as being an acceptable public form of conduct. This emphasis on the consequences of our conduct *when it is conceived of as a public rule* reflects **NORM**'s understanding that in making moral judgments we must always implicitly seek others' approval of the kind of conduct in which we propose to engage. To be a moral person is to make this appeal in one's mind. In the **NORM** framework, moral choices and moral judgments are always unavoidably public.

The serious negative impacts of Omicron's implicit rule and the unlikelihood that omnipartial persons would adopt it merely to help one company out of a jam strongly suggest to us that this way of acting is not morally acceptable. But this is not the end of the matter. Step 8 in Box 3.1 tells us that if we have judged a form of conduct to be wrong but there are still good reasons for wanting to permit it, we should consider imaginatively whether there are alternatives to what we propose to do—and whether these alternatives can better meet the test of omnipartial approval. Reviewing the reasons for our discomfort with this proposal, we can see that what makes this conduct so unacceptable is the generalized mistrust in product integrity, the unplanned inconvenience, and the reduced consumer discretion it entails. At the same time, we have reason to want to assist a company in clearing its inventory and to enable some consumers to purchase a lower-quality product at a good price. We can achieve these objectives through the following slightly revised proposed moral rule:

✦

Third Proposed Moral Rule: To avoid layoffs and financial reverses, a company's managers may market products such as defective office copiers as long as they fully inform customers of the nature and extent of the defects involved.

✦

This rule permits customers themselves to decide the trade-offs they are willing to make between price and product reliability. Note that this rule does not require the company to set a fair price for such products since customers—and the market—can determine that. In a world governed by this rule, firms have a way of clearing unwanted inventories of products and no one is unknowingly or involuntarily harmed. Of course, this rule is not perfect. The engineers of a company like Omicron may argue on prudential (as opposed to moral) grounds that selling a defective product will tarnish the company's reputation. This rule also inflicts some harm on Omicron's shareholders and employees since it makes it harder for the firm to market the product. Nevertheless, although we are right to consider these stakeholders, we have seen that any permission for nondisclosure threatens more serious widespread economic harm. This tells us that although ethical conduct will sometimes lead to hardship for some stakeholders, we cannot eliminate that hardship by cutting moral corners.

Compared with our two other methods of moral reasoning, **NORM** can steer us toward a compelling and rationally defensible moral conclusion. Unlike utilitarianism, it does not lead us to believe that only actual consequences count or that cover-ups and concealment can be a legitimate moral strategy. Like deontology, it supports general requirements of truth-telling, honesty, and candor. But it goes beyond this to explicate the rational basis for these requirements, and it helps us understand their applicability in specific circumstances of choice where they may be pitted against other values and requirements. For example, our discussion shows that managers' general obligation to maximize shareholder wealth cannot take priority in cases like this, since a world where Omicron's conduct prevailed would harm everybody in the end, shareholders included. Applied to this case, **NORM** also makes clear to us why, as consumers, we would require firms like Omicron not just to avoid lying but also to maintain a standard of full disclosure of relevant facts about products' performance. Anything less would expose us all to constant uncertainty and inconvenience beyond our control. Where less complex products are involved, where consumers are professionals and can be expected to be knowledgeable about the products they buy, or where the harms of nondisclosure are trivial, we might be willing to hold companies to a lesser standard. What **NORM** affords us, therefore, is clearer insight into the reasoning process that helps us identify, define, and balance the relevant moral rules.

CONCLUSION
✦

In this chapter we have developed and begun to learn how to apply the method of *Neutral, Omnipartial Rule-Making.* In **NORM** we have a guide to judgment derived from basic and widely shared premises. Like utilitarianism, this theory provides a single, high-level procedure for approaching complex decisions. Unlike utilitarianism, it builds publicity into the very heart of the moral reasoning process. In this way it recaptures much of the emphasis on honesty and other publicly important standards associated with deontology. Unlike deontological approaches, however, it equips us with a rational way of addressing complex issues and of balancing rules and rights in conflict.

We have only begun to scratch the surface of **NORM** as a method of moral reasoning. In subsequent chapters, we will repeatedly be called on to apply this method to a series of different cases in organizational and business ethics. This process moves in two directions. On the one hand, we will use **NORM** to shed light on difficult instances of moral decision and to better our understanding of the range of responsibilities managers have to their stakeholders. On the other hand, we will use these cases to deepen and enhance our understanding of the **NORM** method and moral reasoning generally. For this purpose, whenever a theoretically significant point comes up in the course of treating a case, it is signaled by an italicized discussion of the matter. My aim is that, by the end of this volume, we will have an appreciation of ethical matters that transcend specific cases and that crop up again and again in different situations of moral choice.

As we move on to examining cases, it will help to remember that any approach to ethics must stand the test of application and experience. A moral theory tries to explain our most deeply held moral convictions, and it cannot systematically run counter to these convictions. As you ponder the cases ahead, therefore, continue to think as a moral philosopher. Ask yourself how well **NORM** or its competing approaches aid your process of moral decision. Use these cases, as well, to hone your skills of moral analysis and your familiarity with choice in the organizational environment.

Summary

- *Neutral, Omnipartial Rule-Making* (**NORM**) is a new moral theory, with roots in the writings of Immanuel Kant. By rethinking the foundation of our moral judgments, it seeks to capture the best features of deontology and utilitarianism.

- **NORM** defines an action as right *if each of us might reasonably think of it as being accepted by anyone who looked at the matter in an informed and omnipartial way as a moral rule, that is, as an abiding form of conduct known by everyone and open to everyone in similar circumstances.*

- In applying **NORM**, utilitarianism is followed in identifying all stakeholders directly and indirectly affected by a specific mode of conduct and asking how their interests are served or damaged. But we go beyond utilitarianism in identifying the public moral rule implicit in that conduct and asking whether this rule can reasonably be accepted by all those it affects.

- In determining whether a rule can be accepted, we reason omnipartially. That is, we put ourselves in the shoes of each and every stakeholder affected and ask whether, on balance, we would want to live in a world where this rule prevailed.

$\mathcal{N}$OTES

1. Kant's most famous statement of the Categorical Imperative is found in his *Foundations of the Metaphysics of Morals* (1785). Most writings on applied ethics today classify Kant as a deontologist both because of the subordination of happiness to this Imperative and because of a separate matter: his absolutist stance on many specific moral rules. A growing body of literature, however, places Kant in the contract tradition leading to the work of John Rawls. For a fuller discussion, see Ronald M. Green, "The First Formulation of the Categorical Imperative as Literally a 'Legislative' Metaphor," *History of Philosophy Quarterly* 8, no. 2 (April 1991): 163–79.

2. Rawls's leading work is *A Theory of Justice* (Cambridge, Mass.: Harvard University Press, 1971). But the concept of morality as public legislation is better suggested in his earlier article, "Two Concepts of Rules," *The Philosophical Review* 64, no. 1 (January 1955): 3–32. In his books *The Moral Rules* (New York: Harper & Row, 1969) and *Morality* (New York: Oxford University Press, 1988), Bernard Gert has also extensively developed the idea of morality as impartial public legislation.

3. Case developed by John W. Hennessey, Jr. Names have been disguised.

PART TWO

MANAGING STAKEHOLDER RELATIONSHIPS

◆

MANAGERS' OBLIGATIONS

✦

✦AMONG THE STAKEHOLDERS THAT MANAGERS' DECISION MAKING affects, employees have a special status, because most managers, whatever their salary or financial stake in the company, are employees themselves. This puts managers in a dual moral relationship with the corporation. As organizational leaders they have duties to the corporation and must often place the organization's interests ahead of their own or those of their fellow employees. Like other employees, they also have a claim to fair treatment and respect in terms of their material and moral concerns. In Chapters 4 and 5 we look at both sides of the managers' situation. In this chapter we examine the ethical obligations managers have to the firm. We also explore the limits of these obligations and ask when those employed by an organization may legitimately put their personal or moral values ahead of those of the company. In Chapter 5 we look at the corporation's obligations to its employees. Specifically, we examine the array of "employee rights" that many see as part of the legitimate expectations of those who work in modern business organizations.

Case 4.1

✦ ROGER BERG[1] ✦

Sitting alone in his living room, Roger Berg reviewed the conversation he had had earlier that day with Del Leonard when they had met for lunch at a local restaurant.

The conversation had begun with business matters. Roger's company, the Lake Corporation, a real estate development firm, needed an environmental study done in connection with a large resort they were planning in Northern California. As Vice-President of Planning, Roger had to recommend a subcontractor, and he had already decided to give the contract to Ceil Grant. Her small firm had done outstanding work for them in the past, and Roger felt it was in Lake Corporation's interest to develop a competitive field of subcontractors. Del represented another, larger environmental research and consulting firm. As they sat down to lunch Roger knew the contract matter was on Del's mind so he decided to get to the point.

"Like I said on the telephone, I'm going to recommend that we give Ceil Grant the contract."

"Why are you so locked into Grant?"

"Because she's done great work for us in the past."

"We've got twice the experience she has, twice the people she has."

"And you also have two dozen other contracts to keep you fat and happy. Ceil relies on us. It just wouldn't be right."

Del appeared to accept this explanation, and Roger was glad when the conversation turned to other subjects. After the waitress brought them drinks, another more personal matter came up.

"So tell me," Del asked, "how's Linda doing?"

"Well, it's fine really. Considering. I mean she's going to be all right and all that, but she still has to go twice a month for all those awful treatments."

"Twice a month!"

"Yeah, and it's like she's sick for a day afterward. It takes her another day to recover. So it's two or three days each time before she's really up and around again."

"And the kids?"

"The kids are great! They cook, clean up."

"Isn't that something!"

"Yeah. Of course, that's only twice a month, now. The rest of the time it's . . ."

". . . business as usual!"

Later, as Roger and Del walked to their cars, Del returned to the topic of Linda Berg's illness.

"You know about that clinic in Cincinnati?"

"Dr. Neil's?"

"Dr. Neil's, yeah. From what I understand they're having a pretty remarkable success rate."

"Yeah, and they stopped taking names when their waiting list reached *three* years."

"Three years? You're kidding!"

"No. We tried. We couldn't get her in."

"Why didn't you say something? I think I can get her in."

"What?"

"You know, we were one of the subcontractors on the clinic."

"You could get her in?"

"Well, I can sure try."

"Del, that'd be great. You don't know what I would do . . ."

"It would take some doing. I'd have to call in a few markers from out there. Listen, I'm going to be late for that 2:30. We'll talk later. Ciao."

Roger spent the time after dinner turning Del's remarks over in his mind. He knew that Del had not really said whether he would or would not help, only that he could do so. Roger came to the conclusion that the next move was up to him. Picking up the phone, he dialed Del's number.

"Hello?"

"Del? Roger."

"Hi. What's up?"

"What we talked about at lunch today? You know, the clinic?"

"Oh yeah, right."

"Del, if you could pull that off, I don't have to tell you what that would mean to me."

"Like I said. I can't promise anything. But, look, I'll give it my very best. You know that."

"Del, you're the greatest."

"Hey, don't embarrass me now. I'm happy to try."

"By the way, about that resort job . . ."

"Yeah?"

"Well, I'm supposed to run it by the people upstairs tomorrow, and I think I can—you know—give it a little push in your direction."

"Roger, you don't have to do that. But, hey, that's great."

"But I can't do this for you if it's going to cost the company. You know what I mean?"

"Oh sure."

"You have to meet Ceil Grant's price."

"Of course."

"Same schedule. Same money. Same work."

"We'll do *better* work."

"Yeah. You understand that it has to be like that?"

"Of course, Roger. No problem."

"O.K."

As Roger put down the phone, he was already drafting the memo he would send to his boss the next day. In order to "maintain competition among a variety of subcontractors," he would recommend that Del's firm be given the contract.

QUESTIONS TO CONSIDER

1. Does Roger Berg face a moral dilemma? Why or why not?

2. How would a deontologist respond to Roger's conduct? How would a utilitarian?

3. What does **NORM** inform us about Roger's conduct in this case?

THE LEGAL AND MORAL BASES OF MANAGERS' RESPONSIBILITIES

◆

What does a manager owe the company? Over the years, this question has received many different answers. The 1940s and 1950s formed the period of what William H. Whyte dubbed the "organization man," a person for whom loyalty to the company came first on the scale of values, often above his family's welfare or society's needs.[2] During the 1960s and 1970s the general questioning of authority spurred by the Vietnam war eroded this kind of loyalty. In the 1980s, waves of downsizing created by merger and takeover activity or foreign competition led many companies to abandon traditional commitments to their employees, prompting managers and employees to place their interests ahead of the organization. Books with titles like *Pack Your Own Parachute* and *The Death of the Organization Man* signaled the change.

These different "styles" of relationship are important because they affect the way managers and/or employees act within organizations. But our focus in this chapter is less on shifting attitudes toward organizational loyalty and career commitment than on the basic moral norms that govern the behavior of managers in organizations. These norms define what managerial responsibility means and they remain in force whatever the changing styles of employment relationships.

Roger Berg's problem illustrates in a particularly painful form the ethical challenge of managerial responsibility. How do we balance the claims of the company against our own individual needs and responsibilities? Ordinarily, Roger might not consider mixing his business and personal life, but his situation now seems different. He knows that the Lake Corporation has a right to expect that his decisions will be made in a thoroughly professional manner. On this basis, he concluded that Ceil Grant's past performance and the goal of maintaining at least two strong competitive suppliers argue for giving her firm the contract for the environmental impact study. But Roger also knows that Del Leonard's offer may represent a life or death chance for Linda Berg. Emotionally and morally, Roger is not sure that he can live with himself if he fails to do everything possible to save his wife's life.

A good starting place for trying to understand Roger's dilemma—and dilemmas of other employees caught between personal and organizational responsibilities—is business law. In Chapter 2, we saw that although law is not a complete guide to moral responsibility, it provides some direction for ethical decision making in management. Law is related to morality. It comprises those moral norms to which society attaches its most serious penalties, and it can therefore help us identify our clearest and most pressing moral concerns in a particular area. In addition, the methods of legal reasoning, especially the law's focus on public rules of conduct, its emphasis on precedents, and its reliance on omnipartiality in judgment, are the same as those employed by a method of moral reasoning like Neutral, Omnipartial Rule-Making (**NORM**). *This suggests that the patterns of thinking and the norms found in law will often trace the same path as reasoned moral analysis. None of this means that managers can dispense with ethics and make law their sole guide to conduct. Because law concerns itself with only the most serious and punishable moral offenses, it* *omits many important moral concerns. Law also requires interpretation and application to specific cases, something for which moral judgment remains indispensable, whether in the business office or in the courtroom. In helping us think about Roger Berg's problem, therefore, the rules of law do not exhaust the issue, but they can help orient our moral thinking.*

Anglo-American business law regards Roger Berg as an "agent" for the "principal" who employs him, in this case the owners or shareholders of the Lake Corporation. In addition, as a highly placed manager and officer of the firm with responsibility for recommending how contracts should be awarded, Roger would probably also be regarded as a legal "fiduciary" of his firm, someone who stands in a special relationship of trust to his employer. In the law, these roles as agent and fiduciary impose a series of obligations on Roger. They are usually divided into two categories, "duties of service and obedience" and "duties of loyalty."[3] The former requires the manager and/or employee to perform any lawful (and ethical) services for which he or she is employed and to obey the employer's reasonable directions in regard to these services. In doing so, the law tells us, Roger must

- exercise customary and expected care and skill;
- avoid conduct that brings disrepute on his employer or seriously damages the possibility of friendly relations between the employer and employee;
- make reasonable efforts to keep his employer informed of relevant information;
- keep an account of money or goods he receives on the employer's behalf; and
- avoid acting outside the scope of his authority.

In matters related to his employment, Roger's "duties of loyalty" require him to act solely for the benefit of his employer and to refrain from acquiring or acting on interests adverse to his employer's. Specifically in this regard, the law prohibits Roger from

- speaking or acting disloyally in matters connected with his employment;
- taking unfair advantage of his position in the use of information or things acquired by him in the course of his service, even when doing so does not harm the employer in any way;

- entering (without his employer's consent) into business competition with his employer;
- acting (without consent) for persons whose interests conflict with those of his employer; and
- communicating (without consent) confidential information acquired in the course of his employment.

It is not hard to see that the arrangement between Roger and Del Leonard violates a number of Roger's legal duties to his firm. Among the "duties of service and obedience," for example, Roger's conduct threatens to bring disrepute to Lake Corporation by throwing its business procedures open to question and by possibly harming a supplier. As a competent executive, Roger would probably not have come to the point of recommending Ceil Grant's firm for this contract without having made sure that she is able and ready to do the job and thus possibly reinforcing her expectation that she will get it. In view of this, how will Ceil respond to the sudden news that she has lost this important opportunity? Will she perceive a tacit agreement as being violated and hold the Lake Corporation responsible?

Roger's conduct also appears to violate his legal duty of loyalty by taking unfair advantage of his position in the use of information or authority acquired by him in the course of his service. The opportunity to recommend contracts was not given to Roger so that he could promote his own interests. In addition, to ensure that the final price of Del Leonard's bid does not exceed Ceil Grant's, Roger will probably have to offer Del confidential information. On a variety of counts, therefore, Roger's telephone "deal" with Del Leonard threatens to involve him in a series of serious legal violations.

If the law is clear here, from a moral point of view things are more complex. Law may fail to recognize or address important or overriding moral obligations. The evolution of law over time, the tradition of civil disobedience, and the important role of juries and courts in inserting moral concerns into legal judgments show that law and ethics can conflict and that law is frequently in need of ethical correction or reinterpretation. From Roger's point of view, therefore, the question remains whether his moral obligation to Linda creates a situation of this sort. Whatever his immediate legal vulnerability, is Roger morally justified in putting aside his duties to his employer in order to improve his wife's chances of survival? Each of the three leading theories of ethics we explored in previous chapters aims at providing some guidance on this difficult question. Viewing Roger Berg's dilemma within the framework of each of these theories is a good way of further exercising our ability to reason morally and of testing each theory's usefulness in helping us with this difficult problem in moral choice.

The deontological approach leads to several different interpretations in a case like this, but the most obvious ones closely track the concerns we meet with in business law. Viewing Roger in legal terms as an employee who has entered into a contractual relationship and who owes his employer duties of service, obedience, and loyalty, for example, is another way of saying that Roger should not violate some basic moral rules. Of the rules identified by Bernard Gert (see Chapter 2, Box 2.1) Roger's conduct seems to violate his implicit or explicit promise to his employer to act in a professional manner and possibly also any promises made to Ceil Grant about recommending her firm for the contract. In writing a memo to his superiors that misrepresents the facts, Roger engages in deception. Finally, in terms of what we ordinarily think of as a highly placed manager's responsibility, Roger seems to violate Gert's rule that he "must do his duty." Deontologists more attuned to the moral language of rights might say that the Lake Corporation has a right to expect that Roger's decisions will be made professionally and that Roger has no right to divert company resources to his personal use. Both his boss and Ceil Grant may also have a right to fair and honest treatment.

The problem with this approach, of course, is that on virtually any deontological account, Roger faces a conflict of duties. Although he exists in a promissory relationship to his firm, he also made a solemn promise to his wife when he vowed at their wedding to love and support her in sickness and in health. Does this marital vow now require Roger to break his promise to his firm or other persons? Does Linda have a right to protection and care from her husband that takes precedence over his employer's claims?

It would be wrong to suggest that deontologists have no answers to these questions. Commonly, for example, deontologists argue that keeping promises or avoiding harm to persons does not usually permit one to commit unlawful acts or other serious moral wrongs. Yet even deontologists holding this view typically make exceptions to this rule (for example, when they permit the breaking of promises or the unauthorized use of others' property in situations where this is needed to save a human life). The problem, then, is knowing which moral priorities should hold in a case like this. Is this an exceptional instance where, in the name of saving a life, one may suspend ordinary rules of conduct? As in so many cases of conflict between basic moral rules, deontology provides no clear answer to this question.

Utilitarianism, the leading teleological theory, does not share this problem of competing duties. Utilitarianism offers not a series of potentially conflicting moral rules or rights, but a single, unambiguous requirement that we always try to produce "the greatest amount of happiness for the greatest number of persons." For utilitarianism, a practical difficulty arises at the factual level as we try to determine which course of action will most likely maximize human happiness. From Roger's perspective, this is a tough question made even more difficult by his proximity to the issues and the strong emotions coloring his reading of the facts.

On one side, Roger can see possible harms from his conduct. There is potential for injury to Ceil Grant and her firm in losing this contract. If her company was depending on this contract and it founders, the field of competitive suppliers will be narrowed and, as a result, Roger's own firm may suffer. Ultimately, Lake Corporation's shareholders or customers may pay a price for Roger's conduct. Somewhat offsetting this, at least in the short run, is the gain to Del Leonard's firm in winning the contract. Del's behavior may strike us as manipulative and unfair, and his interests as not worthy of consideration, but this is a deontological way of thinking. Within a utilitarian framework, happiness and well-being are relevant, whatever their cause and for whomever they are produced.

Also weighing in on the negative side of the ledger are the series of indirect harms (see Chapter 2, Box 2.3) that may occur if Roger's behavior is discovered. Other suppliers working with Lake Corporation may feel wary from now on about dealing with a firm that allows decisions to be made in this way and that discloses confidential bidding information to competitors. If Roger's superiors learn the reasons for his contract recommendation, they may mistrust his professional advice. Ultimately, Roger may be fired, a serious matter in view of how important his job now is to his family.

Offsetting all this real or potential harm is the enormous benefit involved in saving Linda's life. Her well-being is not important only in itself; as a wife and mother she has people who depend on her practically and emotionally. Of course, some might argue that Del Leonard's means of helping Linda—using his connections and influence to move her to the head of the line for admission to a prestigious medical clinic—raises serious ethical questions because it creates new harms. These include the harm to anyone eligible for treatment who is "bumped" from the line to make room for Linda. If this were to occur, any lifesaving benefit secured by Del and Roger's conduct would be directly offset by the damage done to someone else. Because utilitarianism requires omni-partiality in the assessment of benefits and harms, Roger cannot privilege his wife or family over others unless doing so clearly maximizes overall happiness. Also relevant is what the public reaction would be to the clinic as well as to Roger, Del, and their firms if news of this arrangement were to leak out.

A utilitarian, then, might have good reason for urging Roger to be cautious. He and Del are dealing with matters of potentially far-reaching consequences for others. But it is noteworthy that many of the harms involved in this case occur *only* if Roger's conduct becomes public knowledge. If he can conceal what he plans to do, many of these harms vanish. Then, at no immediate cost to Lake Corporation, Roger gains an enormous benefit for Linda and his children. If we further suppose that Linda will benefit more by obtaining access to the clinic than anyone she bumps from the line—possibly because she's a young woman with an excellent chance of recovery—the utilitarian case for what Roger has done becomes even more compelling.

Although utilitarian analysis provides no clear counsel in this case, it opens the possibility of justifying Roger's act in ways that run counter to legal and deontological-ethical thinking. As long as Roger can effectively conceal his conduct or deceive others about what he is doing, he need only concern himself with the balance of the immediate harms and benefits he creates. Here, we see again that utilitarianism is *theoretically* indifferent to the impact of our behavior on public rules or expectations of conduct. From a utilitarian perspective, Roger's violation of normal business practices and fair medical allocation procedures does not make his conduct wrong. What matters is only the likely harm that will ensue *if* knowledge of these violations becomes public. If Roger can reduce this likelihood by covering up his arrangement with Del, in principle a utilitarian will have no objection.

What does our third moral methodology, **NORM**, say about Roger's conduct in this case? As Box 3.1 shows, this method first requires us accurately to describe what Roger is doing in the form of a public rule of behavior open to all other, similarly situated persons. The immediate outcome of this analysis, based on identifying people directly affected by this conduct, will look very much like the utilitarian one we just reviewed. But **NORM** goes beyond utilitarianism in asking us to assess not just the *direct* impact of this conduct on others, but also to determine whether we can reasonably believe that people who reason neutrally and omnipartially would be willing to accept this behavior as a *rule of conduct* for everyone in similar circumstances.

Formulating one's conduct as a general moral rule is never easy, since behavior can be characterized in many ways. For example, Roger can describe what he is doing as simply "saving my wife's life," whereas someone else might choose to call it "stealing from the company." Clearly, our evaluation of a form of conduct will depend on how we describe it.

*Because **NORM** aims at helping us arrive at a moral evaluation on the basis of a reasoned assessment of patterns of conduct, a suitable description of what Roger is doing should avoid morally charged terms like "stealing" that already contain a moral judgment. Objectively described, Roger's behavior involves the unauthorized use of company resources, and it is up to our final analysis to see whether we want to regard this as the moral wrong of "theft." Since **NORM** also aims at furnishing an evaluation of conduct as a form of behavior open to all persons in similar circumstances, a suitable description should be both general and complete. That is, it should describe all features of Roger's behavior that might affect other persons and in which they might have an interest. For example, in this case the fact that Roger is 37 years old is not relevant to the description of what he is proposing to do since the impact of his behavior on others would be the same whatever his age, whereas the fact that his wife's life is at risk is certainly relevant to why he (or anyone else in his position) would want to violate company policy.*

Developed in this morally neutral, general, and complete way, the following looks like a good candidate for the moral rule implicit in Roger's behavior:

✦

Proposed Moral Rule: Whenever necessary to save a loved one's life and as long as there are no significant increased costs to the company, a manager with the authority to recommend or award contracts may unilaterally and surreptitiously use this authority in ways that violate normal criteria of business decision making and may also breach confidential relationships with suppliers or clients.

✦

According to **NORM** *a type of conduct is morally permissible if we can reasonably imagine neutral, omnipartial persons (who have put themselves in the shoes of all the persons it affects) as accepting it. This involves examining each party's interests and determining whether the rule promotes those interests, thereby providing a reason* for *the rule, or whether it is opposed to them, thus furnishing an argument* against *it. In other words, moral deliberation converts people's interests into arguments for and against a proposal. Since an individual can have several conflicting interests, and because these interests can align with or oppose the interests of other people, there will normally be a series of arguments for or against a proposed moral rule. Reasoning neutrally and omnipartially, our task is to decide where the weight of reasons (i.e., interests) lies.*

What is the likelihood that a neutral, omnipartial person would accept this implicit moral rule? It is not hard to see that there are many good arguments against it. True, this proposed rule benefits Roger, Linda, and, by extension, anyone faced with a similar life-threatening situation. All these people have an interest in "voting for" a rule permitting them to help their loved ones in this way. But we must weigh this gain against the serious harm done to others and to business relationships generally. Many owners, managers, suppliers, and customers will be injured as important contracts come to be awarded on the basis of managers' urgent personal needs rather than on the objective considerations of price and quality. Confidential information, too, will become less secure. Those offering bids will naturally become more hesitant to reveal information they know might be misused or misappropriated. In short, business relationships in a world governed by Roger's implicit moral rule will undergo a fundamental change: success will no longer go to firms and individuals able to compete on price and quality but to people like Del Leonard, skilled at identifying and exploiting others' personal needs and vulnerabilities.

Viewed this way, Roger's moral rule seems to pit the interests of a small number of persons involved in life and death situations of this sort against the interests of virtually everyone else. Since it is not clear how we weigh the urgent needs of the few against the less pressing concerns of the many, it is hard at first to see how we can settle this conflict in our minds. Nevertheless, there is another aspect of this rule that decisively tips our thinking against it. This is the fact that *even those who sometimes wish to appropriate corporate resources for urgent personal needs have a strong interest in the integrity of business practices.* Ironically, the resources and opportunities Roger wishes to use would probably not exist in a world governed by his implicit moral rule. This is true in the general sense that a commercial environment based on bribery and favoritism will probably not be as productive as one based on professional decision making. In such an environment, corrupt organizations will crowd efficient firms out of the marketplace, productivity will decline, and a talented manager like Roger may never reach the position of authority he now wishes to exploit. These resources may also not be available in a very specific sense. If it is permissible for Roger to divert organizational resources to an urgent personal need, then it is also right for his superiors or others within the firm with similar problems to do so. Ironically, in the moral "world" governed by the rule Roger's conduct creates, he may find his recommendations inexplicably overridden by a superior whose own spouse or child has pressing personal or medical needs!

These considerations tell us that a person who had to weigh this conduct and its implicit proposed moral rule from the standpoint of all affected persons would not accept Roger's implicit moral rule, and this means we must judge his conduct as morally wrong. Without analyzing the other features of Roger and Del's arrangement in detail, we can see that they are also morally questionable. For example, neutral, omnipartial persons would surely have trouble if Roger's conduct involved breaking any promises or commitments he had made to Ceil Grant. Depending on how access to the clinic is determined, omnipartial moral rule makers might also have serious objections to Del's use of "connections" to push Linda to the front of the medical line. Assuming that access to the clinic has been determined by a rule of first come, first served among medically eligible candidates, do we want to live in a world where entitlements based on this expectation are suddenly swept aside by someone with more influence? Despite Roger's understandable motives, his conduct thus violates some of our deepest moral convictions about integrity in business organizations and fairness in society.

This analysis of Roger Berg's dilemma confirms the basic norms of business law in this area and provides us deeper insight into their underlying rationale. We saw, for example, that business law prohibits employees from taking unfair advantage of their positions or communicating, without the employer's consent, confidential information acquired in the course of employment. In law, these norms apply *even when violations involve no financial loss to the employer*. In terms of **NORM**, we can understand this feature of business law when we perceive that, apart from the immediate calculus of gain or loss in a particular situation, these basic norms sustain patterns of conduct that benefit us all.

Before leaving Roger Berg to his dilemma, it is worth asking whether, ethically speaking, Roger must abandon his effort to secure Del's assistance in improving Linda's chances of survival. Recall that whenever **NORM** leads us to conclude that a course of conduct is unethical, it also permits us to consider whether there might be other, morally more acceptable ways of achieving our ends. Facing problems of this kind, **NORM** counsels us to focus specifically on the troubling features of a proposed moral rule to see whether these might somehow be altered or eliminated to produce a more acceptable form of conduct. For example, we saw that the unilateral and surreptitious nature of Roger's conduct is troubling from an organizational point of view. Would it change matters if Roger were open about his behavior and sought company support for his contract decision, perhaps by asking his boss's permission for this contract choice? Unfortunately, this would leave intact the basic corruption of the bidding process and the serious violations of confidentiality Roger's conduct implies. It is unlikely that the Lake Corporation would or could give permission for Roger to act in this way.

A more viable alternative is for Roger (or Del) to try to break the morally questionable link between Del's aid and Roger's professional decision making: the quid pro quo of their arrangement. During their fateful evening telephone conversation, Roger might tell Del that, although the decision on this contract has to stand, he wants personally to call on Del for help in improving Linda's chances for survival. He might also offer in the future to try to repay the favor in ways that do not violate his business obligations. This could extend to personal assistance and to business courtesies or favors that do not compromise his duties to the firm or its clients. Applying **NORM**, we can see that a moral rule permitting this kind of personal relationship and exchange of aid between Roger and Del might well pass omnipartial assessment. Personal relationships are unavoidable in business dealings and, by enhancing trust and cooperation between persons, they can sometimes even contribute to good management. Although it is probably wise for managers to avoid excessive personal involvement with suppliers or subcontractors with whom they deal, a moral rule entirely prohibiting such relationships would also involve excessive restraint on personal liberty.

Roger's appeal to Del's friendship and his willingness to reciprocate Del's assistance whenever his professional duties permit does not resolve every moral question—it leaves undiscussed, for example, Del's possible tampering with an established, fair medical procedure (if one exists at the clinic). But it may represent one way a manager like Roger Berg can reconcile his urgent personal responsibilities with his duties to his employer. Roger Berg's dilemma tells us that personal and professional obligations can sometimes seriously conflict. The moral challenge is to recognize these conflicts and handle them in a way we can stand by publicly.

Case 4.2

✦ "LEGAL TENDER"[4] ✦

For over a year, Evan Andrews, a second-year M.B.A. student at a major California business school, had longingly admired Jesse Moore, a fellow student. Jesse is an attractive, outgoing young woman who somehow manages to live extremely well while most of her fellow students scrape by financially.

Evan eventually talks a friend into getting him invited to a poolside party Jesse has at the elegant home she rents. Although Evan and Jesse communicate awkwardly that night, there is a spark between them. Over the next weeks the two fall in love and begin seeing one another regularly. Evan knows that after her father's death Jesse briefly ran the family business, but this does not explain her apparent wealth. One night several weeks into their relationship he asks Jesse how she is able to live so well. At first, Jesse kids him but finally she hints that she has gotten to know one or more local executives in high-tech firms who share useful information with her. This enables her to invest in certain stocks and make considerable short-term profits. Jesse's admission leads Evan to argue with her about the propriety of insider trading, but she dismisses his naiveté. She also suggests that Randco, a fast-growing local firm, would be a good short-term investment for Evan. "It's going through the roof," she says.

Evan soon discovers that Jesse's source of information is Rolf Ingram, a senior executive at Randco whose deft moves have made him a folk hero among the business press and students at the business school. Complicating matters, Evan has just accepted a job at Randco to start after school is out. Maria Peters, the woman Evan will work for at Randco, Jesse's source of inside information reports to Ingram.

One evening, while returning from a local bistro, Evan and Jesse quarrel again about Jesse's behavior. Evan pulls to the side of the road, confronts Jesse, and urges her to give up her insider trading. She refuses, gets out of his car, and says good-bye.

QUESTIONS TO CONSIDER

1. Jesse's conduct apparently violates U.S. securities laws against insider trading. Do you think these laws are ethically justified?
2. Do you believe Jesse's conduct is ethical? Why or why not?
3. Ethically speaking, what should Evan do about Jesse's and Rolf Ingram's behavior? Is he morally obligated to report them to the authorities?

INSIDER TRADING: PERSONAL AND POLICY ISSUES

◆

The problem of insider trading raised here affords us an opportunity to explore some social policy dimensions of managers' obligations to the firm. Initially, at least, the ethical issues in this case seem clear. We know that Rolf Ingram has a legal duty not to share confidential information acquired in the course of his employment. Ingram's passing of inside information to Jesse Moore violates this obligation. Most nations with financial exchanges also prohibit trading based on inside information. In the United States, this prohibition extends to the recipients of such information ("tipees"), whether or not they are employed by the company whose information is involved. This means that Jesse Moore is also violating the law. Since by virtually any account of ethics we have a moral duty to obey the law, this seems reason enough to regard Ingram's and Jesse's conduct as morally wrong.

Nevertheless, taking legal prohibitions in this way as the starting point eclipses other questions of moral importance. One of these is the broader *social policy* question of whether the laws and regulations dealing with insider trading are wise or just. Morally speaking, is this a reasonable, fair, or effective way of handling the matter of sensitive business information, or does it amount to an unwise and morally unjustifiable intrusion on people's liberty? Of course, if the laws governing insider trading are unwise or unjust, it does not follow that Jesse or Ingram are morally right in breaking them. For reasons we can easily understand, citizens are not ordinarily permitted to break laws they do not like. Whenever possible, they are morally required to use legal channels to try to change these laws. Although this policy question thus has little relevance to our evaluation of the conduct of the people in this case, it does raise an important and independent moral question about the larger context in which they act. This is often true in moral dilemmas, where we must evaluate not only our response to situations, but the larger social arrangements that create these dilemmas in the first place.

Jesse's and Rolf Ingram's conduct also raises some very personal moral questions about individual and managerial responsibility within an existing legal framework. What should Evan do with what he has learned? As a prospective employee of Randco, does he have a moral obligation to inform the company of Ingram's behavior? Would this obligation be greater if he had already begun working for the firm? And what are his obligations with respect to Jesse? Is it enough for him to convey to her his views about her conduct? If she refuses to stop, must he report her to the authorities?

Looking first at the policy question of the wisdom and justice of insider trading laws, we encounter the familiar problem that deontological and utilitarian approaches seem to produce conflicting moral conclusions. It is frequently argued on deontological grounds, for example, that insider trading is wrong and should be legally prohibited because it involves the use of fraud and deception in securities transactions. According to this way of thinking, someone who sells a stock which, on the basis of inside information, she knows will soon lose its value is like the sellers of consumer goods—automobiles, food, or pharmaceuticals—whose defects they either fail to disclose or knowingly misrepresent. This interpretation of insider trading laws finds some support in the fact that in the U.S. legal prohibitions in this area initially emerged in the context of laws against securities fraud.[5]

Nevertheless, there is good reason to question whether this interpretation really provides a moral basis for insider trading laws. For one thing, critics of this approach have questioned whether the notion of fraud is really applicable to the kind of impersonal transactions that occur in modern financial markets. In these markets, people trading a stock at a particular price usually do so freely and independently of any information supplied by those who buy or sell it. This impersonal and voluntary aspect of market transactions, critics observe, makes it questionable whether we should think of those who trade on inside information as defrauding or cheating anyone.

Some deontologically inclined defenders of the ban on insider trading point out that regardless of whether buyers or sellers are deceived, there are other clear moral wrongs these laws aim to prevent. For example, those who "own" the information seem to be wronged by insider trading. A company has the right to control access to valuable information it produces. Employees or managers who appropriate this information for personal use are therefore guilty of the moral and legal wrong of breach of confidentiality.[6] However, like the preceding emphasis on fraud, this effort to provide a moral rationale for insider trading laws has problems. For example, it does not entirely explain why, if insider trading primarily represents a breach of an employee's duty to the employer, society has chosen to intervene so actively in this area, going so far as to penalize third party "tipees" who breach no specific duty to an employer when they receive or use inside information.

These difficulties in deontological explanations of insider trading laws make a utilitarian analysis an attractive alternative for those who feel these laws are just. For example, it seems reasonable to argue that financial markets will function most efficiently, allocating resources to the firms most worthy of them, when relevant information is widely shared or at least when this information is accessible to those willing to engage in market research. Insider trading, some argue, causes information to flow only in narrow channels and makes nonrational considerations like people's "connections" or degrees of influence a factor in investment success. However, from a utilitarian perspective there are substantial counterarguments to these claims. Some economists maintain that the flow of market information and the sensitivity of markets to change would actually be enhanced, not reduced, if insider trading were given freer reign. This is because insider trading allows information to impact on stock prices more quickly than if such information could not be used by those who have it.[7] Although no one likes cheaters or those who misappropriate information, within a larger utilitarian framework traders on inside information perform a useful economic function. In the name of everyone's greater happiness, some argue, they should be tolerated, not punished.

What does **NORM** have to say about a policy question like this? As in personal decisions, the test here is which policy neutral, omnipartial, rational persons would be willing to accept as an abiding public rule for their society. In determining whether insider trading should be allowed, the implicit moral rule to which this test is applied looks something like the following:

✦

Proposed Moral Rule: Individuals with access to confidential, inside information about a public company may freely trade for themselves in the stock of that company.

✦

Looked at from a neutral, omnipartial perspective—as though we could be any person in a society governed by it—this proposed moral rule has some benefits and many serious liabilities. On the positive side, it enhances the freedom (and financial standing) of some individuals with access to information of this kind. If the utilitarian economists are right, it may also sometimes expedite the transfer of market information and, through the impact on stock prices, benefit others outside the circle of insiders. Utilitarians are right to stress these benefits, but they are wrong to omit other reasoned concerns that omnipartial persons might have about these practices, especially when we look at these concerns in the context of an open, public choice of policies. One concern is the loss of control that companies will experience with respect to information they produce. In a society governed by this moral rule, where no restraint on insider trading is permitted, corporations will be constantly wary about employees' conduct and will be forced to raise all sorts of barriers to the flow of information within the firm. This is the matter of confidentiality and informational property rights identified by deontological approaches to this issue, but it is not the only or even the deciding concern that omnipartial persons have in assessing a rule of this sort.

Another major worry is the general impact on financial markets when a proposed "rule" of this sort prevails. One of the hallmarks of **NORM** is its focus on the larger behavioral implications of conduct once it is raised to the level of a rule for everyone. Whenever we propose a moral rule, we must think of it as becoming an artifact or item of "moral furniture" in the human environment. As such, it becomes capable of shaping the behavior of others. *In deciding whether we can accept a proposed moral rule, we must also assess these further behavioral implications of the proposed rule. Will our rule encourage or discourage further undesirable forms of conduct?* Because of the inherently public nature of moral reasoning, we must ask this question whether or not other persons actually learn of the proposed rule.

An illustration from the medical realm helps make this key theoretical point clearer. When a patient is diagnosed as having a sexually transmitted disease (STD), physicians are sometimes tempted to breach patient confidentiality and reveal this fact to the patient's sexual partners. On the basis of an immediate utilitarian calculus of benefit and loss this makes sense because these sexual partners can suffer serious injury to their health if they are uninformed, whereas the patient will only be embarrassed by disclosure. But, apart from this immediate calculus, the presence of this practice as an artifact in the human environment can cause serious harm. Imagine this rule as literally an item of furniture in the medical environment, perhaps in the form of a plaque mounted at the entry of every hospital, clinic, or doctor's office saying, "Caution: We disclose cases of STD to your sexual partners." Clearly, many people who see this plaque will become wary of presenting themselves for medical treatment in the first place and the very opportunity physicians have for helping these people or their sexual partners will vanish. This does not mean that the negative implications of this practice as a publicly acknowledged moral rule always weigh decisively against it.

We have to consider the benefits of revealing patient information and we must determine whether patients would actually be deterred from treatment by specific types of disclosure, something societies are doing today for a host of conditions. (As the AIDS epidemic shows, it makes a difference whether the medical community possesses a cure or therapy for a disease, since the availability of treatment is a powerful incentive for people to enter the medical system even at the risk of disclosure.) The point is that in a world where each of our choices must be thought of as creating a morally acceptable practice or "rule" for everyone, we must always consider what the impact of allowing this practice will be on everyone's subsequent behavior and on all our welfare. What further kinds of conduct will our rule encourage? What will they discourage?

It is not hard to see the implications of this insight for a proposed moral rule permitting insider trading. In a financial world where this rule prevails, investor confidence will be seriously eroded and many persons will decide to stay out of the market. This includes not only small investors, who cannot hope to know what forces are shaping the market, but also more skilled analysts and market professionals. Because insider information is by definition not available on the basis of professional skill, these persons, too, will find market behavior increasingly opaque. As a result, the very purpose of stock markets as conduits for the rational economic allocation of capital will suffer. Capital will grow scarcer and the cost of economic innovation will rise. Whatever immediate gains are experienced by inside traders or those who accidentally benefit by their activity are offset by these considerations. Combined with other matters of concern to omnipartial persons—including the heavy burden of information control placed on firms where insider trading laws do not exist—these considerations are strong enough to support a legal ban on this activity and the enforcement of this ban against all parties, whether insiders or not, who violate it. They also suggest why the growth of interdependent financial markets all over the world has led to the extension of these regulations across national and cultural lines.

Just as it does at the policy level, **NORM** helps clarify some of the difficult personal questions raised by this case. One of these is whether Evan should report Jesse to the authorities. Is he morally permitted to do so? Is he required to? To answer these questions, consider the following three proposed moral rules:

✦

First Proposed Moral Rule: A person who, in the course of a personal relationship, learns confidentially from a loved one that he or she is engaged in illegal financial dealings *may or may not* report this conduct to the authorities.

Second Proposed Moral Rule: A person who, in the course of a personal relationship, learns confidentially from a loved one that he or she is engaged in illegal financial dealings *must not* report this conduct to the authorities.

Third Proposed Moral Rule: A person who, in the course of a personal relationship, learns confidentially from a loved one that he or she is engaged in illegal financial dealings *must* report this conduct to the authorities.

✦

The first of these proposed moral rules helps us identify *morally permissible* behavior. If we accept this rule, we are free to report or not report a loved one. The second and third proposed moral rules go beyond this and help us identify conduct that is morally prohibited and conduct that is morally required, respectively. If we accept the second rule, we judge it wrong to report the illegal activities of someone close to us. If we accept the third rule, we are morally required to report this behavior.

Any form of behavior can be assessed in terms of these three possibilities. Figure 4.1 suggests this schematically in terms of a decision tree. It asks us first to look at any proposed form of behavior ("Doing *X*") in terms of its omnipartial acceptability as a rule. Behavior that cannot pass this test is morally wrong; we must not do it. If a proposed form of conduct passes this first test, we must further ask whether we would *require* people to act in the way at issue. This involves reformulating our proposed moral rule in terms of whether someone *must* act this way. In accepting this demanding rule, we conclude that it is wrong for someone to *avoid* acting in this way.

The actual determination of how neutral, omnipartial persons would vote on such matters and whether such conduct is permitted, wrong, or required may be very complex. In considering whether a form of conduct is morally obligatory, for example, we must balance the harms to everyone of not requiring it against the harms imposed on the individual who must act as the rule requires. Judgments of this sort will often be difficult. Our conclusions regarding any specific form of conduct will lie on a continuum like the one depicted in Figure 4.2. As this figure suggests, relatively few acts can be judged as clearly wrong or required. Most will either be permissible or will fall in a shaded area between the extremes. Despite this lack of precision, however, some acts can be clearly located on this spectrum. The decision tree sketched in Figure 4.1 helps organize our thinking about a recurrent problem in ethics.

Against this framework, how do the choices facing Evan look? Is he morally permitted to report Jesse to the authorities (First Proposed Moral Rule)? Is he morally required to do so (Third Proposed Moral Rule)? Surely there are some good arguments for each of these rules. In a society where everyone's relatives, closest friends, or romantic partners are agents of the police, we might apprehend more criminals and deter some illegal conduct. But whatever good these moral rules accomplish is gained at a terrible price. Where even the first (and least rigorous) of these rules prevails, people will become extremely wary about being open with intimates. In a society of this sort, "pillow talk" will become a dangerous activity, possibly leading to criminal prosecution. The nightmare world depicted by George Orwell in *1984* will become a reality. Ironically, as is true of so many seemingly "good" moral ideas that on closer inspection prove unacceptable, both the first and third of these proposed rules are counterproductive. In technical terms, this is so

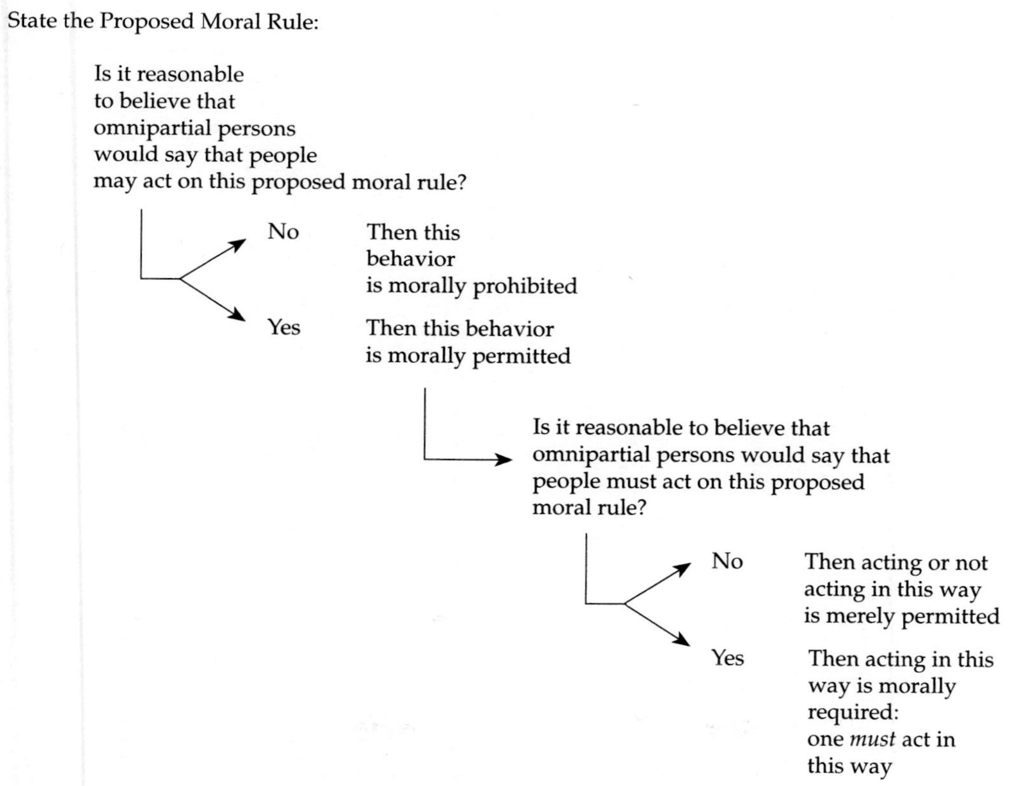

State the Proposed Moral Rule:

Is it reasonable
to believe that
omnipartial persons
would say that people
may act on this proposed moral rule?

No — Then this behavior is morally prohibited

Yes — Then this behavior is morally permitted

Is it reasonable to believe that omnipartial persons would say that people must act on this proposed moral rule?

No — Then acting or not acting in this way is merely permitted

Yes — Then acting in this way is morally required: one *must* act in this way

FIGURE 4.1

A Decision Tree for Assessing Obligations

| Clearly | | Clearly |
| Wrong | Permissible | Required |

FIGURE 4.2
The Spectrum of Moral Judgments

because these rules have "perverse" effects. People living in a world where these rules prevail would hesitate to confide in anyone. As a result, these people will lose the close sources of support and counsel that could help them avoid or halt illegal behavior. Whatever reduction in criminality these rules effect, in other words, may well be offset by their consequence of isolating criminals (or potential criminals) and depriving them of valuable sources of counsel and restraint.

Does this mean that we are *never* permitted to report wrongdoing on the part of those we love? No. The **NORM** method allows us to generate publicly acceptable exceptions (or specific new rules) for every significantly new circumstance we encounter. Exceptions to a moral rule prohibiting the disclosure of intimate conversations are not hard to discover. For example, when people engage in activity that risks their own lives or the lives or health of others, it seems reasonable to subordinate our normal concern to protect the confidentiality of intimate conversations. For cases like this, we can formulate the following rule:

✦

Proposed Moral Rule: A person who, in the course of a personal relationship, learns confidentially from a loved one that he or she is engaged in activities that threaten the life or health of others may report this conduct to the authorities.

✦

Apart from the sheer magnitude of the harms involved here, a further reason for permitting or requiring disclosure in such cases is this rule's different impact on the frankness of intimate conversations. We saw that one major problem with our first proposed moral rule in this area is that it might lead people to avoid the moral counsel and guidance of loved ones. Since matters of law and policy are often very complex, this counsel is important and we are wary of moral rules that would stifle frank discussion of a host of issues. But no one doubts that conduct physically threatening other persons is wrong, so there is less need in such cases for the kind of counsel that intimate conversations afford. Furthermore, by morally permitting (or even requiring) disclosure in cases like this, we provide a way for people to protect their loved ones from embarking on a course of potentially very self-destructive behavior. Indeed, it is hard to imagine that rational people would morally prohibit disclosure in cases like this.

Since Jesse's conduct does not approach this degree of harm, Evan is not morally required to report her conduct and may even be morally forbidden from doing so. In the business context, however, there are fewer concerns with protecting intimacy, which, as we have seen, is our principal reason for disallowing disclosure. There are also very good reasons in a corporate environment for permitting and even requiring employees to report illegal activities (at least, internally, to the company's leadership). Corporations wield enormous power in society. Moral and legal rules impeding the development of criminal conspiracies within companies make good sense. In view of this, if he can do so without harming Jesse, Evan is probably permitted to report Rolf Ingram's insider trading to Randco's higher officers. He may also be morally required to do so. This would most clearly be true if Evan were already working for Randco. As a prospective employee, Evan's obligations to the firm are less clear and more subject to his personal discretion. After all, to require Evan to report Rolf Ingram while Evan is not yet an employee of the firm is to require all of us to report corporate wrongdoing we come across. Not only is this an invitation for uninformed outsiders to meddle in a company's affairs, it also represents a heavy burden of responsibility we might not be willing to impose on one another.

These are not easy matters to assess. Had we pursued a deontological or utilitarian analysis of the hard choices facing Evan, we might well have found ourselves tangled in a web of conflicting duties (the problem of deontology) or drawn to net "social benefit" conclusions that defy our moral common sense (the problem of utilitarianism). In this case, utilitarianism might well counsel Evan to betray Jesse, as long as the benefit to others outweighs any harm done to her. Looking at both the personal and policy dimensions of insider trading from the perspective of **NORM** helps us identify and evaluate the whole range of considerations bearing on these complex issues.

Case 4.3

✦ SUSAN SHAPIRO[8] ✦

Susan Shapiro graduated from Smith College, where she majored in chemistry, in 1970, and from M.I.T., where she received a Master of Science degree, also in chemistry, in 1971. She enrolled in the M.B.A. program at the University of Michigan after working for one year as a research chemist at Parke-Davis and Company in Ann Arbor.

> One of the reasons I came back to get an M.B.A. was that the scientists at Parke-Davis, which is a large drug company with an advanced research division in Ann Arbor, simply weren't ready for women in the laboratory. It got to the stage that there was going to be an armed confrontation the next time some male told me to get his coffee or write up his experiment. Chemistry labs aren't great places for confrontations; there's so much expensive equipment around that can get broken, so I decided that I ought to get either a Ph.D. or an M.B.A. I chose the M.B.A. because most companies seemed to accept women more fully in an administrative role than in a technical capacity.
>
> (Statement of Susan Shapiro)

Susan graduated from Michigan in the lower half of her M.B.A. class. This was partially because she felt that some of her courses, such as marketing, were exploitative; partially because she refused to work or study on Saturday due to religious convictions; but primarily because she returned to the second year of the M.B.A. program seven weeks late.

> I spent the summer of 1973 in Israel, working on a kibbutz in the north, near the Lebanon border. The Yom Kippur War started that fall. I don't think that a good Jew ought to leave Israel just because a war starts, so I stayed and worked as a volunteer in a military hospital until the need was past. Then I came back. Some of my professors understood, but most of them wanted me to make up the missed work, and there

wasn't enough time in the rest of the term. I got three C's that term, and that really pulled my grade average down.

(Statement of Susan Shapiro)

Susan enjoyed the quantitative aspects of finance and economics, and she interviewed with a number of firms for a position as a financial analyst. She found, however, that many of these companies evidently considered the grade point average strongly in their selection procedures for positions in corporate finance, and she received very few invitations for plant visits. Nineteen seventy-four was a recession year, which, of course, reduced the employment opportunities for all the members of her class, but she felt that her job search was more difficult than that of many of her friends, and she thought that this was due to her low class standing.

By 1974, companies had gotten over hiring women despite their sex and were beginning to hire women because of it. So, I don't think being a woman hurt me. And I hope being a Jew didn't hurt me, but you never know. My grades were good, except for the third term and for the marketing course. I explained the reasons to all the interviewers and they would nod their heads, but evidently they did not understand. Two of the interviewers asked if I planned to take vacations in Israel after I started working; what business is that of theirs?

(Statement of Susan Shapiro)

Representatives of two large chemical companies came to Michigan near the end of the interview period; both of them were interested in Susan because of her undergraduate and graduate work in chemistry, and because of her experience with Parke-Davis. Both companies invited her for plant visits; both extended job offers; and Susan accepted the offer from a company with corporate offices in New York City, close to her family and friends. She started the training program with that company in July 1974.

We spent about three weeks in New York City, being told about the structure of the company and the uses of the products, and then they took us down to Baton Rouge, to look at a chemical plant. You realize that most of the M.B.A.'s who go to work for a chemical company have very little knowledge of chemistry. There were 20 of us who started in the training program, and the others generally had undergraduate degrees in engineering or economics. I don't know what you learn by looking at a chemical plant, but they flew us down South, put us up at a Holiday Inn, and took us on a tour of their plant the next day.

(Statement of Susan Shapiro)

During the plant tour, the management trainees were taken to a drying room where an intermediate chemical product was being washed with benzene and then dried. The cake was dumped in a rotating screen and sprayed with benzene, which was then partially recovered by a vacuum box under the screen, but much of the solvent evaporated within the room, and the atmosphere was heavy with benzene fumes.

Benzene is a known carcinogen; there is a direct, statistically valid correlation between benzene and leukemia and birth defects. The federal standard is 10 parts per million, and a lab director would get upset if you let the concentration get near 100 parts for more than a few minutes, but in that drying room it was over 1,000. The air was humid with the vapor, and the eyes of the men who were working in the area were watering. I was glad to get out, and we were only in the drying room for about 5 minutes.

I told the foreman who was showing us around—he was a big, burly man with probably 30 years' experience—that the conditions in the room were dangerous to the health of the men working there, but he told me, "Lady, don't worry about it. That is a sign-on job [a job to which newly hired employees are assigned until they build up their seniority so that they can transfer to more desirable work]; we've all done it, and it hasn't hurt any of us."

That night, back at the motel, I went up to the Director of Personnel who was in charge of the training program and told him about the situation. He was more polite than the foreman, but he said the same thing. "Susan, you can't change the company in the first month. Wait a while; understand the problems, but don't be a trouble-maker right at the start."

I don't want to lose this job, but I don't want to keep it at the expense of those men getting leukemia, or their children having birth defects. What should I do?

(Statement of Susan Shapiro)

QUESTIONS TO CONSIDER

1. Is Susan morally obligated to correct the situation she has found?
2. If you were Susan's friend and she telephoned you for advice, what would you tell her?

WHISTLE BLOWING AND THE LIMITS OF MANAGERIAL LOYALTY

✦

Up to this point we have seen that managers owe duties of obedience, loyalty, and service to their companies and that these can frequently override even the most pressing personal needs. Nevertheless, in both law and ethics there are limits to these obligations. Business law, for example, recognizes that an employee is not required to obey unlawful orders issued by a superior. Many persons also believe that loyalty and obedience do not require us to comply with unethical orders or job requirements.

✦ THE ETHICS OF WHISTLE BLOWING ✦

Possibly the leading area of controversy over the meaning and limits of managerial responsibility and loyalty concerns the practice of "whistle blowing." A whistle blower is an employee who, perceiving an organizational practice that he or she believes to be illegal or unethical, seeks to stop this practice by alerting top management, or, failing that, by notifying authorities outside the organization. Although threats to public safety are among the better-known causes for whistle blowing, whistle blowers may also be motivated to report violations of law or company procedures. Opinions differ radically about the moral character of whistle blowers. Some regard them as "ethical conscientious objectors" who place public good ahead of their own careers, whereas others see them as disloyal and untrustworthy individuals who betray the team they work with. In reality, whistle blowers' motivations are varied. Among people who "blow the whistle" some are mentally disturbed and others are chronic malcontents, but there are also many whistle blowers who are people of integrity genuinely disturbed by practices that violate their own, their community's, or the organization's values.

Studies of whistle blowers show that they are typically motivated by strong personal moral ideals and are committed to the view that individuals must assume responsibility for the conduct of organizations to which they belong.[9] Susan Shapiro fits this description. Her situation gives us an opportunity to look at the personal and organizational factors common in whistle blowing situations. In the past, Susan has shown that she is willing to jeopardize her career in order to act on the moral and religious values she holds. Now, she faces a situation where she believes human life and health are at risk. Susan could take the Director of Personnel's advice and—for the time being at least—let the matter drop. But everything we know about Susan tells us that she will not do that.

Before considering what Susan should do, it is worth asking whether she has any ethical responsibilities in this case. Why must Susan do anything here if it risks jeopardizing her career? After all, each of us frequently encounters situations where human welfare is in peril—from the homeless we meet on the streets of our cities to the problems of disease and starvation in less developed countries around the world. Yet we do not normally feel called upon to put aside our personal pursuits or career goals in order to help the people in these situations. In view of this, why must Susan be her brothers' (or sisters') keeper?

It is tempting to answer this question primarily in terms of Susan's personal moral values. Because *Susan* has the values she does, including her demonstrated concern to put human welfare ahead of her own success, she cannot abandon the problem she has discovered; she has to do something to reduce the harm to the workers and their families. Personal values can sometimes be very demanding, requiring us to act in supererogatory ways beyond the call of duty. When strong values shape our character, as they do Susan's, we cannot ignore them, because we risk losing our self-respect.

Nevertheless, although Susan's values sharpen her dilemma, they are not the main reason she is morally obligated to do something. A moment's reflection suggests that *any* employee of this firm discovering this problem probably has the same degree of moral responsibility to take steps to correct the health hazard that benzene exposure represents. There are features of Susan's situation—her proximity to the problem, her role as an employee or manager of the company, her knowledge of the harms involved, and her seemingly unique ability to take steps to remedy it—that make Susan responsible to do something. To see this, we need only apply **NORM** to this case and consider the following two proposed moral rules that correspond to the issues of moral permissibility and moral requiredness we discussed earlier.

✦

First Proposed Moral Rule: When an employee or manager of a company learns of a condition created by the company that threatens human life or health and that has been missed or neglected by others responsible for correcting it, the employee or manager may take steps outside her or his normal area of authority to report and to try to correct the problem.

Second Proposed Moral Rule: When an employee or manager of a company learns of a condition created by the company that threatens human life or health and that has been missed or neglected by others responsible for correcting it, the employee or manager *must* take steps outside her or his normal area of authority to report and to try to correct the problem—even if doing so could seriously damage her or his career.

✦

The first of these proposed moral rules merely permits an employee or manager to try to remedy a hazardous situation. Since it does not compel anyone to do this, the relevant question is, Why not accept it? What considerations might count against it? One concern is that by permitting employees to "meddle" in matters outside their areas of competence or expertise we might disrupt efficient organizational functioning. But although this may sometimes occur, it seems a small price to pay for the multiple advantages of permitting employee involvement of this sort. For one thing, this permission allows employees to act on their moral concerns and prevents them from having to experience a conflict between their personal values and organizational role. For another, it provides an important monitoring function within organizations to prevent incompetence or malfeasance. An organization where every employee feels morally free to report potentially hazardous situations—whatever their source—is likely to experience fewer hazardous situations. On balance, we can conclude that Susan is at least morally *permitted* to regard this situation as one she may address.

Can we go further than this and say that Susan is actually *required* to do something; that she *must* do something? The answer to this question depends on our response to the second of these two proposed moral rules. In terms of our previous analysis of moral requiredness, we can see that if we reject this moral rule, Susan would not be morally obligated to take further steps to end the benzene hazard. If it is accepted, however, Susan *must* do something and this is true regardless of her personal values and despite the impact on her own career.

The question, then, is whether, reasoning omnipartially, we would choose to live in a world governed by this second rule. There are good reasons for thinking we would. In a world governed by this rule an important internal check exists on dangerous organizational practices. Although rejecting this rule frees us as employees from potential risk to our careers, accepting it helps protect us all as employees, consumers, neighbors, and citizens from the serious harms that large organizations can inflict. Consider how employees at all levels encouraged to act on a rule of this sort might have helped avert the terrible disaster of Bhopal (see Chapter 1, Case 1.1).

From the perspective of those who care about a company, this rule also makes good sense. True, it risks the organizational bother and disruption caused by employees' taking steps beyond their duties to try to correct problems. But business organizations are not just sports teams or military units striving for an immediate goal. They are human organizations whose conduct profoundly affects other persons and whose own long-term survival and success depend on avoiding imposing serious harms on various stakeholders. Requiring all members of an organization to report, and, when necessary, to try to correct problems that risk human life and health (or that seriously violate legal and procedural rules) is a good way of building responsibility into an organization and seeing that the mistakes, failures, or cover-ups of a few do not subvert and destroy the organization as a whole.

Accepting the second of these proposed moral rules tells us that Susan, regardless of her personal values, has a moral obligation to do something about this problem. Neither of these two proposed moral rules specifies what steps Susan should take, but we can subject this question as well to a further **NORM**-type analysis. We can assume that Susan first takes steps to report this matter to her immediate supervisor but makes no headway in this direction. Two options remain. One is for Susan to go outside the firm immediately, reporting these violations to a regulatory agency like the Occupational Safety and Health Administration (OSHA) or to the news media. This course of action implies the following proposed moral rule:

◆

Proposed Moral Rule: Whenever an employee encounters a situation within the company that he or she believes threatens human life or health (or that seriously violates laws or organizational procedures), and his or her immediate supervisor refuses to take corrective action, the employee may then go outside the firm to try to effect change.

◆

This rule has some benefits. Among other things, it seems to increase the chances that a hazardous situation will be corrected as quickly as possible. But it also has some serious drawbacks. In a world where this rule prevails, every employee or manager who perceives a problem of the sort we are describing will feel free to disclose that problem right away to the outside world. Although many informed and responsible managers will act on this rule, so too will a number of malcontents, people with personal axes to grind, or employees simply misinformed about the dangers they think they are reporting. Although the existence of this rule might help deter firms from creating or allowing hazardous situations, it will also lead them to control employees' access to sensitive information out of fear of losing control of such situations or being wrongly accused of misconduct by mistaken or irresponsible employees. In other words, in a world where this rule prevails, employers will come to see all employees as potential informers and as threats to organizational survival. Another unfortunate effect of this proposed rule is that higher management would tend first to learn of problems from hostile outside sources. Instead of responding efficaciously to remedy the problem, they will predictably put their energies into self-protective stratagems and cover-ups that may leave the basic problem unresolved.

Rejecting this rule suggests an alternative that addresses our principal reasoned concerns in this area:

♦

Proposed Moral Rule: Whenever an employee encounters a situation within the company that he or she believes threatens human life or health (or that seriously violates laws or organizational procedures), and an immediate supervisor refuses to take corrective action, the employee must bring this matter to the attention of higher management. *Only once all reasonable internal alternatives have been exhausted* may he or she go outside the firm to try to effect change.

♦

Not only does this rule respect the variety of competing interests we have identified here, it shows us the rational basis of the loyalty that whistle blowing situations demand and the limits of this loyalty when organizations endanger others or seriously violate laws. Putting this proposed moral rule clearly before us also suggests reasonable exceptions to it. For example, where threatened harm is imminent and higher management is unwilling or unavailable to take steps to remedy the problem, immediate recourse to outside authorities or the media might be justified. In the events preceding the space shuttle *Challenger* disaster, the engineer Roger Boisjoly found himself in just such a situation.[10] His repeated warning to Morton-Thiokol and NASA management that the shuttle booster O-ring seals posed a potentially lethal threat were ignored or rationalized away. Boisjoly did not finally choose to alert outsiders to the problem. But this proposed moral rule tells us that he would have been permitted (though not necessarily required) to do so.

Complex whistle blowing decisions remind us that situations are often unique and that moral reasoning always *takes place in context. Even as we form viable moral rules in our mind, we must be prepared to consider possible exceptions to them. But for at least two reasons this contextual quality of moral decision does not mean that every moral decision is only contextual. The* **NORM** *method does not amount to "situation ethics," in the sense of "an ethics without norms" that leaves everything up to actors in the situation informed only by their immediate intuitions of right and wrong. First, many basic moral considerations that crop up in situations recur from situation to situation. In the cases examined here we have repeatedly seen the value of confidentiality and honesty in personal and organizational life. The factors supporting these standards will often appear in new situations. Second, even when situations require us to develop a unique response, what stays the same from situation to situation is the requirement that we think of what we are doing as a public rule acceptable to omnipartial persons. This means that our basic* method *of approach transcends individual situations and applies to all situations. We are not "without norms" in a context and left to vague intuitions or hunches, because we always have the single fundamental norm of omnipartial public choice of rules.* Since we form moral rules or exceptions on the basis of general considerations, our moral conclusions in one instance always apply to all relevantly similar situations. Thus, if we conclude that urgent, life-threatening conditions justify a manager's going outside the company and immediately blowing the whistle to news media, this exception to our normal duty to work our way up the chain of command applies to all similarly urgent situations where the same risks and problems occur. Although it sounds odd to say so, according to **NORM**, moral judgments are, at one and the same time, *specific* to a situation and *universally applicable* to all similar situations.

✦ CORPORATE ETHICS AND WHISTLE BLOWING ✦

So far we have focused primarily on the duties of individual managers or employees in whistle blowing situations, but we should not think of this as the last word on the matter. Managers' ethical responsibilities extend not just to their own personal decision making, but also to shaping the rules and structures of their organization. Alongside matters of personal business ethics, in other words, there is what we might call "corporate" or organizational ethics. Because corporations do not act apart from the individuals within them, "corporate ethics" depends on the ability of managers, directors, and others who run the corporation to maintain moral integrity in the policies, structures, and practices of the organization as a whole.

Where whistle blowing is concerned, corporate ethics involves first of all the maintenance of an environment conducive to the fulfillment of people's moral obligations. This involves promoting positive ethical values and discouraging or punishing forms of unethical behavior. Despite these efforts, however, violations of basic procedures or ethical norms will occur even in the best organizations. Anticipating this, responsible managers must also help shape the organizational environment to make it possible for employees to exercise their duties both to the company and to other constituencies. This is not just a matter of ethics. It is also prudent (in the company's self-interest) to develop rules and procedures for responsibly handling potential whistle blowers, since employees who find their moral concerns ignored by the company will go outside it in ways that can inflict greater harm on the organization.

Specific procedures have either been proposed or put into effect by companies as a way of responding to whistle blowers' concerns. These include telephone hot lines, permitting confidential reporting of harmful practices, easily accessible question boxes with stamped forms available for reporting questionable activities, "ombudsmen" to whom employees can report safety or procedural violations, and standing safety, health, or product liability committees empowered to investigate problems anywhere in the company and to report directly to the board of directors.[11]

As valuable as these procedures may be, however, they are secondary to the essential *moral* attitude that leaders of large organizations must develop in relation to this issue. As the Susan Shapiro case suggests, this attitude involves the understanding that whistle blowing and employee dissent, however they may be abused, are essentially moral activities: employees *are* morally obligated to report harmful practices, and companies are both wise and ethically responsible when they facilitate this obligation by making it possible for employees to do this safely within company channels. Alan Westin, a leading student of whistle blowing, expresses this attitude when he says:

> The single most important element in creating a meaningful internal system to deal with whistle blowing is to have top leadership accept this as a management priority. This means that the chief operating officer and his senior colleagues have to believe that a policy which encourages discussion and dissent, and deals fairly with whistle-blowing claims, is a good and important thing for their company to adopt.[12]

Another way of putting this is to say that top management of companies must understand that managerial and employee loyalty does not mean unquestioning obedience to superiors or mute acceptance of existing practices. Where such a narrow view of loyalty prevails, where loyalty does not include recognition of obligations to wider constituencies and stakeholders, no procedures will ensure that the reporting of harmful practices occurs promptly or stays within the organization. Although sound procedures are indispensable, in other words, their success rests on the creation and maintenance of an appropriate attitude within the organization by the leadership. Potential dissenters or whistle blowers must know that, when blocked, they can jump the chain of command without fear of reprisal and report their concerns to higher-ups in the organization. They also must know that they can do this even if their concerns ultimately prove unwarranted or wrong and that as long as they have acted responsibly they do not have to fear reprisal. Above all, they must have the sense that peers or superiors will not subsequently be permitted to treat them as "traitors" to the organization, rather than as persons who went out of their way to perform a service to the firm and to society.

Susan Shapiro will probably not stay with this company. Her idealism makes her a poor "fit" with an organizational culture in which employee safety is not a top priority. Susan may choose to walk away from both the company and its problem or, more predictably, she will blow the whistle in some public way that damages the company or causes it to "hunker down" and adopt a purely defensive strategy. Whichever way she goes, employees will become unwilling pawns in a legal or regulatory battle. This is unfortunate for Susan, who will have to restart her career. But it is also unfortunate for the company, which, by losing Susan's knowledge and concern, loses a valued asset and, in the process, risks liabilities that may prove very costly.

Susan Shapiro's dilemma recalls a point made earlier: managerial responsibility and loyalty extend in various directions. Managers are individually responsible to their company, to the particular people with whom they have relationships, and to society as a whole whenever their decisions have the capacity to create significant harms. These duties can conflict, as they did for Roger Berg, Evan Andrews, and Susan Shapiro. When conflicts occur, managers must think carefully about the moral rules implicit in their choices and options. At the same time, as heads of companies, divisions, or units, managers also have *organizational* duties to other managers and employees like themselves. These include the ongoing obligation to see that subordinates really are best able to fulfill the multiple and sometimes conflicting moral responsibilities they face. Managers meet this organizational duty when they help create policies, procedures, structures, and attitudes—a corporate "culture" in the fullest sense—that make it possible for individuals to express, discuss, evaluate and, when necessary, act on their moral concerns.

Summary

- Both legally and ethically, managers have duties of service, obedience, and loyalty to their employer. These require them to obey lawful and ethical orders, to exercise reasonable care in the performance of duties, to put the employer's interests ahead of their own in business matters, and not to use organizational resources (including confidential information) for personal gain.

- Managers' duties to their employers go beyond utilitarian considerations of net benefit or loss and hold even when the firm would not be financially damaged by forms of self-dealing or betrayals of confidence. This is because these duties form practices and create expectations that are vital to the successful conduct of organizational life. This becomes clear when we use *Neutral, Omnipartial Rule-Making* (*NORM*) to assess practices of this sort.

- Moral reasoning applies not just to individual choices, but to the broader social policies and laws that shape the context of these choices, including such matters as tax policies or insider trading laws. Since **NORM** is founded on a concern with the omnipartial choice of abiding public rules, its conclusions will anticipate the conclusions of sound public policy.

- How much we should risk ourselves to assist others or to prevent harm from occurring to them is one of the most recurrent and difficult questions of the moral life. In corporations, this question frequently crops up in cases involving whistle blowing. **NORM** suggests a decision tree procedure for looking at these questions. This begins by asking, first, whether we *may* act in the way under review. If this is acceptable, the obligatoriness of the conduct is determined by asking,

"Would neutral, omnipartial persons agree that I *must* act on others' behalf in situations of this kind?"

- Loyalty to larger constituencies or to the long-term interests of the corporation can require employees or managers to engage in forms of ethical dissent and whistle blowing. Managers have an ongoing duty to help structure the organization so that conflicts of this sort are minimized.

Case 4.4

✦ ROSSIN GREENBERG SERONICK & HILL, INC.* ✦

Looking through the latest issue of *Computer Reseller News*, Neal Hill, president of the Boston advertising agency Rossin Greenberg Seronick and Hill (RGS&H), came across a story indicating that Microsoft Corporation was conducting an agency review. Two days later, November 5, 1987, Hill wrote to Martin Taucher at Microsoft, Redmond, Washington, suggesting he consider RGS&H. This was an account the agency was keen to secure.

"OUR AMBITION IS YOUR OPPORTUNITY"

RGS&H was established in 1983. Four years later it had billings of around $25 million and was described in the trade press as the "hottest agency in New England." Yet it was still comparatively small, employing 45 people. Hill would not find it easy to convince the West Coast software company, which had sales of just under $200 million in 1986, that it should transfer its $10 million account to RGS&H. The agency had, however, recently recruited two new creative people, Jamie Mambro and Jay Williams, who had computer industry experience.

In his letter, Hill posed the question: "Why should you even think about an agency in Boston that you've probably never heard of?" He gave four reasons in response:

Copyright © 1989 by the President and Fellows of Harvard College. Harvard Business School case 9-589-124. This case was prepared by Professor N. Craig Smith with the assistance of Professor John A. Quelch as the basis for class discussion rather than to illustrate either effective or ineffective handling of an administrative situation. Reprinted by permission of the Harvard Business School.

1. We turn out a wonderful creative product (which has won much more than its share of national and regional awards) and have a tremendous fund of experience in marketing PC-related products, both hardware and software. (That means we do some great advertising, because it's both on target and creatively powerful. *One specific fact:* I've included the recent Lotus insert because *the creative team which produced it and the rest of Lotus' work over the past year joined this agency last Monday.*)

2. We're just under five years old, and billing just over $25 million annually. (Translation: We're old enough to be "real," and large enough to have terrific resources in creative, marketing, media, and reproduction. It also means that we're young enough and small enough to move quickly and intelligently— to still be *very* hungry to do the kind of work that explodes off the page and screen. Just a note: Lotus' agency is just down the road from us in Providence, R.I., and is the same size we are.)

3. We already handle large national accounts—our clients include Hasbro, Dunkin' Donuts, Fidelity Investments, Clarks of England, and British Telecommunications—and have several concrete ideas for eliminating any problems posed by the (perceived) distance between Redmond and Boston. (This demonstrates that we know how to work with advertising needs on the scale of yours . . . and that we'd love to fly out to show you some of our work and explain some of our logistical approaches.)

4. We are intent on becoming a nationally recognized advertising agency—and doing a bang-up job with one or more Microsoft products would take us a good way down that road. (Which means that our ambition is your opportunity.)

A week later, Hill called Taucher and established that his letter should have been sent to Rob Lebow, director of corporate communications, to whom it had been forwarded. On November 16, Hill wrote to Lebow enclosing further samples of work done by the agency's staff: a Lotus direct mail brochure, an advertisement for Charles River Laboratories, and an advertisement for software by a company no longer active in the U.S. market. His key message was: "We are an awfully good agency, with a great deal of knowledge of

Microsoft's industry, competition, and products. And we would kill to do even one project for you."

Follow-up calls were not returned, so Hill decided to send a further sample of artwork to Microsoft: a 12″ x 9″ brochure promoting RGS&H and containing a plane ticket for a trip to Boston. This specially produced "flier" was mailed by overnight express to Lebow on November 20. On the front, in white letters against a dark background, it simply stated: "You probably haven't thought about talking to an agency in Boston." The interior of the flier is shown in Exhibit 1.

ENCOURAGING NEWS

On November 23, RGS&H received a "no thanks" letter from Lebow. As this was dated November 16, Hill was not too disappointed. A call the following day established that Lebow was out of the office for the next week. On November 30, Hill was told that Lebow "certainly took notice of the mailed piece" and that Hill should call back December 4, when Lebow would be available. Hill wrote a further letter to Lebow expressing his delight at securing some attention with the flyer and explaining that "what we wanted to do was to demonstrate simultaneously our creative approach to messaging and our aggressive approach to marketing—in this case, marketing ourselves." He included an extract from *Adweek* (New England) that discussed RGS&H, its commitment to sophisticated office automation, and how it pitched against New York agencies for the Playskool print account. Hill also explained that the agency would be interested in a single product or limited-term project instead of the entire account: "We just want a chance to show you what we can do for you."

QUESTIONS TO CONSIDER

1. What is your ethical evaluation of RGS&H's effort to woo Microsoft? What ethical issues does the promotion raise?
2. If you were Microsoft's Rob Lebow, how would you respond to RGS&H's pitch?

BUT, SINCE WE KNOW YOUR COMPETITION'S PLANS, ISN'T IT WORTH TAKING A FLIER?

Microsoft is in a terrific position right now. Along with the momentum and success of its other products, the company has a fantastic new product–Excel. It's a product that many people feel is the first real threat to the dominance of Lotus 1-2-3.

Interestingly, the people who most strongly share this opinion are the people who *make* Lotus 1-2-3.

We think this fact alone shows just how big an opportunity you have before you. And it's an opportunity we'd like to talk to you about.

You see, the reason we know so much about Lotus is that some of our newest employees just spent the past year and a half working on the Lotus business at another agency. So they are intimately acquainted with Lotus' thoughts about Microsoft–and their plans to deal with the introduction of Excel.

In addition, the rest of our account service, creative and media departments are up to their ears in high tech experience–hardware, software, retail accounts, you name it. And the only thing they know better than the high tech business is the advertising business.

But don't take our word for it. Take this plane ticket and come out and see for yourself. You've got nothing to lose. And thousands of frequent flier miles to gain.

RGS&H
ROSSIN GREENBERG SERONICK & HILL

EXHIBIT 1

Rossin Greenberg Seronick & Hill flier.

𝒩otes

1. Based on the film case, "The Roger Berg Story," © Salenger Films, 1977.
2. William H. Whyte, *The Organization Man* (New York: Simon & Schuster, 1956).
3. These duties are developed at length in the American Law Institute's *Second Restatement on Torts*, Ch. 13, "Duties and Liabilities of Agent to Principal."
4. Based on Kirk O. Hanson's "Teaching Note" and the video case "Legal Tender," produced by Alan Jacobs and the Media and Arts Club of the Stanford University School of Business, Stanford, Calif. © 1988 by the Board of Trustees of the Leland Stanford Junior University.
5. Current U.S. insider trading regulations derive from the Securities Act of 1933 and the Securities Exchange Act of 1934. These statutes empowered the Securities Exchange Commission to prevent fraud in the issuance, sale or purchase of securities.
6. Gary Lawson, "The Ethics of Insider Trading," *Harvard Journal of Law & Public Policy* 11 (1988): 727.
7. This argument is developed in Henry G. Manne's classic study *Insider Trading and the Stock Market* (New York: Free Press, 1966).
8. Drawn from Larue Tone Hosmer, *The Ethics of Management*, 2d ed. (Homewood, Ill.: Irwin, 1991), pp. 97–99. © 1991 by Larue Tone Hosmer. Reprinted by permission.
9. Myron Peretz and Penina Migdal Glazer, "Whistleblowing," *Psychology Today* (August 1986): 38.
10. For an account of this episode see Richard S. Lewis, *Challenger: The Final Voyage* (New York: Columbia University Press, 1986), pp. 111–17.
11. These approaches are discussed by Kenneth Labich in his article "The New Crisis in Business Ethics," *Fortune* (April 20, 1992): 168–76.
12. Alan E. Westin, ed., *Whistle Blowing* (New York: McGraw-Hill, 1981), pp. 141ff.

EMPLOYEE

RIGHTS

✦

✦CENTRAL TO THE IDEA OF EMPLOYEES AS STAKEHOLDERS IS THE NOTION of employee rights. We can think of these as firmly grounded entitlements to forms of fair treatment or benefits. Possessed by all employees—whether hourly workers, salaried supervisors, or managers—they are not subject to the whims of management or shareholders but they do exert an independent and significant claim on corporate decision making.

In the 1990s, several forces shaping society and business organizations contribute to widespread interest in employee rights. One is the relative decline in union membership. Faced with a weakening of the protections traditionally afforded by unions, employees are asserting their right to fair treatment and are increasingly turning to the courts for support. Legislators, judges, and juries, aware of the vulnerability of individuals within large organizations, are often supporting these appeals. The result has been a series of dramatic changes in legal standards that one commentator has described as a "second civil rights revolution."[1]

Changes within the corporation have also stimulated attention to employee rights. Foremost among these is the broad switch from manufacturing to knowledge-based careers and the increasing reliance on employee decision making at all levels of the organization. For many firms, the adage that "our people are our most important asset" has moved from being a public relations slogan to a belief vital to organizational success. This places new emphasis on firms' ability to attract and retain qualified employees and to provide environments that stimulate high levels of performance.

Employee rights form an important part of this picture. Not only do highly trained or educated employees expect fair treatment and a good work environment, but the enhanced autonomy their assignments require intensifies the need for mutual trust and respect.

Box 5.1 outlines some of the most important employee rights being asserted today. Because rights usually imply corresponding duties, we

---

Box 5.1

SOME COMMONLY ASSERTED EMPLOYEE RIGHTS[2]

- A right to fairness and nondiscrimination in the hiring process
- A right to freedom of speech
- A right to privacy and freedom from intrusions
- A right to freedom in off-hours
- A right to a safe and healthy work environment
- A right to freedom from stress
- A right to freedom from sexual harassment
- A right to information relevant to one's job security and safety
- A right to freedom from propaganda
- A right to participate in essential workplace and employment decisions
- A right to adequate and fairly awarded benefits
- A right to due process in hiring, promotion, disciplinary, or termination decisions
- A right to a reasonable expectation of job security

---

can think of these as a series of obligations incumbent on business firms and their managers. Like all such deontological lists, this one is controversial. Not everyone will agree that all the rights on this list belong there, whereas some would add other rights. Even when there is agreement about what employees' basic rights are, we can expect disagreement about the relative ranking of these rights and their relation to employers' (or other stakeholders') legitimate rights and expectations. The issue of employee drug testing provides an illustration. Although many regard drug testing as a violation of an employee's right to freedom from intrusion, others see it as a natural extension of the other employees' right to a safe workplace, customers' right to adequate service, and the employer's right to a profit.

Such disagreements challenge our skills of moral reasoning and raise a series of important questions. Is it meaningful to speak of employee rights, in the sense of entitlements not subject to management discretion? If so, what is the basis of these rights? How do we justify them? What are their limits? When can organizational needs override these rights?

When the rights of various stakeholders conflict, how do we establish priorities? Rather than looking at these questions in the abstract, we might consider several cases where some of the most controversial rights are a source of dispute.

Case 5.1

✦ LEAN AND MEAN"[3] ✦

Ben Harman said, "Yes Sir," and slowly hung up the phone. He turned from his desk and stared out the window at the lake. Shaking his head, he turned to his credenza, pulled open the bottom drawer, and took out a bottle. Replacing the cap, he made a mental note to pick up another bottle of Maalox on the way home from work. Given his boss's instructions, he was going to be needing the large economy size during the next few weeks.

For several months, his boss, Carl Wilson, had periodically complained to Ben about the job performance of Star Industries' corporate counsel, Bill Willette. In Wilson's opinion, Willette was "just not what Star needs for the future." Wilson, the president and founder of Star, did not mean to suggest that Willette was incompetent or even that he had failed to perform reasonably well on most of his assignments. In his eight years with Star, Willette had burned his share of midnight oil getting documents prepared for Star's string of successful acquisitions. With his nearly twenty years of corporate legal experience in Star's particular industry, most within the company regarded Willette as a real "pro" in his field.

Ben reminded himself, however, that Willette was not without his faults. His reputation for being a procrastinator and for "building a Mercedes, when a Chevrolet would suffice" was legendary within the company. Somehow most managers had always looked beyond these obvious, but annoying, facts to appreciate that Willette's contracts were always complete and correct. Ben had often heard other managers comment on how "tight" Willette's documents were and how confident they were that Bill had covered all the points. However, many were quick to add in jest, "But the contract would have been more effective if it had been signed while the customer still wanted the product."

This penchant for being unnecessarily thorough and slow had long been noticed by Wilson, but he had always suffered through it because Willette was a pleasant, well-mannered employee who rarely rubbed anyone the wrong way. Nonetheless, Wilson had recently given a great deal of thought to the future and strategic direction of the company. He had identified those "high potential employees" (whom he dubbed the "HIPOTS") that he thought would take Star Industries into the next century. Bill Willette was not on the list.

Several months had passed since Wilson first broached the subject of laying off Willette. At the time, Ben had defended him by pointing to Willette's many years of loyal service, his valuable industry experience, and the quality of his work. Wilson had let the subject drop, but pointed out that there were "an awful lot of young, bright attorneys out there whose careers are not riding rockets." Besides, Willette could probably be replaced by someone who was "not only more efficient [i.e., faster], but also cheaper." Recently, however, Wilson's drive to create a "lean and mean" management team to lead the company after his retirement had contributed to an increasing number of criticisms of Willette's work and comments about his future with the company. Clearly, Wilson had made up his mind to replace Willette.

Ben was confident that Willette had no idea about Wilson's feelings. Willette had recently remodeled his home (taking out a new, larger mortgage), his fifteen-year-old son was a freshman in high school, and his wife had returned to graduate school the previous fall to get her teaching certificate. She hoped to supplement the family income while their son was in college. At age forty-seven, Willette was comfortable in his home, his community, and his work . . . or so he thought.

As Ben mentally replayed today's conversation with Wilson, he felt just as queasy about "The Plan" as he did when he had first heard it. Wilson had instructed Ben to begin an active search to replace Willette. There was, however, a twist to the instructions that had caught him off guard. Ben was told to run newspaper ads "blind," with responses to be sent to another city's post office box, and to conduct off-site interviews. This clandestine approach was "just in case" a suitable replacement for Willette was not found. "We wouldn't want to find ourselves with the position unfilled," Wilson had told Ben. To the question of what sort of severance package might be offered Willette should a suitable replacement be found, Wilson had replied "The usual." The usual at Star meant two weeks' notice and a map to the nearest exit.

Ben could not believe it had come to this. Here was an employee who was about to be sacked in the prime of his career, with a student-wife and teenage son soon to be entering college and the employee did not even know it. Even assuming that Willette's personnel file could be quickly "papered" with the requisite legal memoranda documenting an unsatisfactory or, at best, mediocre work performance, how could Ben rationalize this decision to other employees . . . to Willette . . . to himself?

Ben pondered the propriety of giving Willette a warning that "the Big Bang" was coming. If Wilson was correct, terminating Willette might be in the long-term best interest of Star Industries and the welfare of its other 4,000 employees. It was, perhaps, also in the best interest of Ben's career to do it Wilson's way. To get Willette all stirred up by suggesting to him that he might be replaced and, therefore, should start searching for another job might be very counterproductive for everyone. Suppose no suitable replacement was found? Suppose no suitable replacement was found and Willette left anyway simply because Ben had told him he might be replaced?

To tell Bill or not to tell Bill? That was the question worrying Ben. The ad was scheduled to run in the next Sunday's paper.

QUESTIONS TO CONSIDER

1. What do you think of Star Industries' handling of Bill Willette?
2. Would **NORM** lead one to approve of Star's conduct?
3. What advice would you give Ben Harman?

ETHICS AND EMPLOYMENT SECURITY
◆

The choice facing Ben Harman seems to place him and Star Industries at odds with three of the most commonly asserted employee rights today: the right to information relevant to one's job security; the right to due process in hiring, promotion, disciplinary, or termination decisions; and the right to a reasonable expectation of job security. When Bill Willette learns that he is being replaced, he may undertake legal action against the firm, alleging that he is the victim of a wrongful discharge. Would Willette be correct in feeling that he has been wronged? Is he likely to succeed in translating this sense of moral outrage into a successful law-suit?

Until recently, U.S. law provided little support for employees or man-agers like Willette. Unless they were protected by a specific employment contract (or were members of a union that had negotiated such a con-tract), workers and managers were regarded as "at will" employees who could be dismissed without notice and without the employer having to show cause. This doctrine of "at-will" employment stems from the latter part of the nineteenth century and to some extent reflects, both socially and morally, the economic realities of that time. In the minds of many people, economic conditions in a burgeoning economy were too unsettled to lock firms into long-term employment relationships. Not everyone agreed. The rise of unions, with their demands for greater employment security, testified to many people's belief that this turbulent environment made job security even more important for the mass of factory workers. But at the managerial level, at least, the doctrine of at-will employment remained intact and commanded wide support well into the twentieth century.

Recently this has begun to change. In different ways, courts have begun to erode the doctrine of employment at will, and some states have even begun to debate or pass legislation limiting employers' right of discharge. At least three broad exceptions have been introduced into employment law in this area. First, courts have increasingly upheld employees' claims that they were wrongfully discharged for trying to exercise some public duty or for reporting corporate violations of law. This so-called "public policy" exception to the at-will doctrine has been applied to a gamut of issues. Courts have ruled for employees who were dismissed for serving jury duty and for others who were fired in retaliation for having blown the whistle on an illegal or hazardous company practice. A second exception to the at-will doctrine has resulted from cases in which courts have sided with noncontract employees or managers whose companies promised job security and due process in oral statements made at the time of hiring or in company documents like personnel manuals or employee handbooks. These verbal and written statements, courts have ruled, should be regarded as an "implied contract" between the employer and employee. Finally, in a small number of cases, courts have qualified the at-will doctrine by concluding that in discharging an employee an employer has violated a general duty of "good faith and fair dealing." This broad concept provides courts and juries with a way of going beyond the public policy and implied contract exceptions and allows them to express their moral outrage at a particular instance of unfair discharge.[4]

This changing legal environment reflects evolving social attitudes toward employment security. As some commentators have noted, several conditions have worked together to give new meaning to employment security and to strengthen employees' and managers' expectations of fair treatment in the employment process. For one thing, economic power has become increasingly concentrated in the hands of large, impersonal firms. The nature of employment decisions in such organizations renders employees vulnerable to arbitrary decision making and undermines the assumption that employees are free to negotiate the terms of their employment. This power of corporations over their employees also partly explains the "public policy" exception that has come to play an important role in wrongful discharge suits and in legislative initiatives in this area. Permitting a company to discharge an employee who has tried to obey the law or has reported violations of it is an invitation to lawbreaking. In the words of one court ruling upholding the public policy exception, "A different interpretation [of the law] would sanction lawlessness, which law by its very nature is designed to discourage and prevent."[5]

A second important cause of this evolving legal situation is the fact that the work force is no longer predominantly self-employed. Because opportunities for work outside corporate settings are limited, job security has become increasingly important. The connection between employment, health insurance, and retirement benefits makes job security even more important. Finally, employees' expectations of fair treatment and job security in the private sector are heightened by the protections afforded government or union employees. In a competitive modern economy with widespread interaction between various sectors, discrepancies between the rights of private and public, union or nonunion employees become harder to justify or sustain.

This changing legal and social environment tells us that there are solid reasons for affirming employees' basic right to a reasonable expectation of job security, notification, and due process in decisions affecting their employment. If we look at this matter omnipartially, as *Neutral, Omnipartial Rule-Making* (**NORM**) requires, we can see that the importance of job security in all our lives and the relative imbalance in power between the individual and the firm makes it wise to establish moral rules restricting a company's ability to dismiss an employee unnecessarily and arbitrarily. This reasoned judgment provides the rationale for the main rights claimed in this area.

But all rights are limited by competing moral claims and the rights of others. What are the limits here? May an employee's right to job security, information regarding her or his tenure, and due process in termination ever be overridden by organizational needs? And how does the answer to this question bear on Ben Harman's dilemma? It is not hard to see that a company has the right to dismiss employees or managers when this is clearly needed to maintain ongoing profitability and competitiveness. Even massive layoffs or reductions in force (RIFs) are morally permitted when the company's long-term profitability is in jeopardy. A rule prohibiting such reductions would be self-defeating. Forcing a private and profit-making company to maintain a work force beyond its needs or abilities is a prescription for failure, a policy that risks the very jobs it seeks to preserve.

But none of this applies very well to Bill Willette. Terminating his employment is not crucial to company survival or long-term profitability. Willette is not grossly incompetent or engaged in activities (such as theft or bribery) that threaten the company's financial situation or public standing. Is it morally permissible, therefore, for a firm to dismiss a long-standing and diligent employee who no longer meets organizational needs as well as someone else? Consider the following proposed moral rule:

✦

First Proposed Moral Rule: Once a private firm has hired an employee, following a reasonable probationary period it may not dismiss her or him (except for reasons of gross incompetence or malfeasance).

✦

Obviously, there are some good reasons for supporting this rule. Most of us are attracted to the prospect of lifelong job security. Companies acting under this rule also would be encouraged to select employees and managers carefully and would have an incentive to develop employees' potential. They would also be discouraged from dismissing employees merely for reasons of age. Finally, the exception built into this rule against employee incompetence or misconduct protects employers from being held hostage to an employee whose behavior clearly threatens the firm.

This rule might make even more sense if there were further good reasons for supporting it. For example, university professors have enjoyed job security—following a rigorous period of probation—because of society's concern with protecting academic freedom, which would be seriously threatened if private or state institutions could fire teachers espousing unpopular ideas. Most government workers, too, have enjoyed job security, a reflection of the relative stability and predictability of government funding and activities.

But nonacademic employment rarely involves these additional concerns or advantages, and there are some very good reasons for our not accepting this proposed moral rule. For one thing, it would tie the hands of employers by preventing them from undertaking the kinds of downsizing or reassignment of employees often needed for economic success. Since we are all interested in economic efficiency, this counts against accepting this rule. Even affected employees have some reason for voting against this rule. Employees or managers who do not fit well into a company's culture or economic plans are often best advised to seek a better— and happier—situation. If these negative considerations counsel against simply accepting this proposed moral rule, its positive aspects suggest a reasonable compromise, one embodying our most urgent concerns in this area. Such a compromise might take the following form:

✦

Second Proposed Moral Rule: Once a private firm has hired an employee, following a reasonable probationary period it may not dismiss her or him without adequate notification, due process, and, whenever it is economically feasible, enough severance assistance to allow the employee to prepare for and find comparable work.

✦

To the extent that this proposed moral rule identifies and expresses our most important moral concerns in this area, it tells us that Star Industries' treatment of Bill Willette is morally deficient. The behind-the-scenes machinations that Carl Wilson has ordered, and the abrupt and damaging dismissal of an employee who has given many years of service to the firm, constitute a moral wrong that Ben Harman, as an ethical manager, has an obligation to oppose. What should Harman do? An act like secretly informing Willette raises moral questions of its own. In addition to calling for Harman to disobey and deceive Wilson, this strategy puts Willette, whose anger at his boss will be unabated, in a position to damage the firm. It would be far better for Harman to share his concerns directly with Wilson. He might argue, for example, that Willette's long service with the company counsels informing him of the company's plans, giving him adequate notice of termination, and providing a severance package sufficient to allow him to adjust to his new situation. For example, eight months' pay (one month for each year of service) would help Willette and his family prepare personally, economically, and educationally for the transition ahead. As far as Star Industries goes, the cost of this package would soon be offset by savings from the lower salary paid to Willette's younger replacement.

It might be argued that although this generous severance package might not financially harm the company, its extension to other employees would be impossible. This is a relevant concern. **NORM** requires us to act similarly in similar circumstances, and, barring any reasonable differences in situation, if Willette is entitled to such a generous severance, so too are all other Star employees. In fact, this may not be as much of a burden as it appears. For one thing, it is reasonable for a company to proportion benefits to an employee's number of years of service, with the benefits increasing significantly at various watersheds (three years, five years, ten years, and so on) in the employee's career. The assumption is that the longer an employee has been with the company, the more he or she has invested in the firm. Under ordinary circumstances, therefore, paying graded benefits of this sort may not be too much of a hardship, and Willette's dismissal might even afford the company the chance to set a new, more humane policy in this area. Neither does the company have to lock itself into generosity in all circumstances, however different their financial impacts. Future events—a severe recession and the need for massive layoffs—could create a morally different situation and permit a review of the policy begun with Willette.

It might also be argued that notifying Willette and retaining him for any period of time invites him to sabotage the firm or its efforts to replace him. But this risk is reduced if Willette is treated fairly. An added benefit of this approach is that it allows the firm to retain Willette if no adequate replacement is found. Wilson, of course, wants to keep this option open. But his means of doing so almost guarantees that Willette's morale and commitment to Star Industries will be severely damaged. Understanding these issues and arguments, Ben Harman can strengthen his ethical argument by appeal to sound business reasons.

If employers sometimes follow the path that Carl Wilson has embarked on, it is because they seek to minimize organizational risk and expense by the abrupt dismissal of unwanted employees. It is not unusual for employers to ask employees or managers to leave work on the same day that they are laid off, often with only a supervised visit to their desk allowed. This cautious and fearful approach to the treatment of employees is odd because businesspeople pride themselves on their willingness to take risks and to invest in productive opportunities. But because employees are increasingly the major organizational resource, policies that take a risk by *respecting* employees, by trusting them, and by showing a willingness to invest in them can evidence good business judgment. As this case suggests, risk, respect, and trust may be appropriate even when a firm decides that it no longer wants or needs a particular employee.

Case 5.2

✦ WHOSE DESK IS THIS ANYWAY?[6] ✦

In her fourteen years as chief administrator of the Miramar Center, Florence Yukawa had seldom been as troubled as she was today. Spread out on the table in front of her were the contents of the desk and personal files of Dr. William Symington, director of Miramar's residency program. Harry Armstrong, the hospital's medical director, had brought these materials to her office. Among the objects on the table were letters, Valentine's Day cards, and several seminude photographs sent to Dr. Symington over the past few years by various female residents. These objects confirmed Dr. Armstrong's suspicions about Symington's professional misconduct. Yet almost as disturbing to Florence Yukawa as this evidence was Dr. Armstrong's invasion of a colleague's privacy.

Miramar is a twenty-year-old, 200-bed psychiatric facility located on the California coast, north of Santa Barbara. Its patient mix is representative of the middle-class psychiatric population generally, including patients with anxiety disorders, depressive illness, or substance abuse problems. As part of its activities, Miramar runs a medical training program with an average of 15 residents a year. Dr. Symington had graduated from this program ten years earlier and had headed it for six years. He was married and the father of two children.

Symington's duties included the supervision and evaluation of residents' progress through the program. Initially he had managed these duties well, but over the past two years Armstrong had come to question his suitability for the job. Although many of the residents regarded Symington as supportive, a few had complained to Armstrong that Symington's formal and informal evaluations were erratic or biased. They maintained that he sometimes favored specific female residents in the program. Over the past two years there had been several unsubstantiated reports of romantic or sexual involvements between Symington and one or another female resident. There had also been one complaint of sexual harassment from a member of the nursing staff, although the complaint never became a formal charge. During the past two years, Symington's work performance had deteriorated. He sometimes showed up late to work, took an unusually high number of personal days, and was often several days late in completing important patient reports.

Armstrong had met with Symington several times during the past few months to discuss his tardiness in completing reports. During these meetings Armstrong made it clear that he regarded any personal involvement with residents as completely unprofessional and that he viewed sexual harassment as grounds for dismissal. Symington vehemently denied that he was personally involved with any residents or that he had harassed any member of the staff. But, following these meetings, rumors continued among staff and residents. There was even one report that an angry personal quarrel between Symington and a female resident had taken place on the floor.

Several weeks earlier, during a meeting about other matters, Armstrong had told Florence Yukawa that he was "fed up" with Symington's behavior and intended to "get the goods on him." Yukawa did not ask Armstrong what he meant by this, nor did she prohibit him from taking action, although she cautioned him to give Symington a chance to get his life in order.

Now, as she gazed at the materials on the table in front of her, Florence Yukawa realized that Armstrong had taken matters into his own hands. The previous day, after Symington had again failed to show up for work, Armstrong entered his office in search of a patient report he needed. While looking for the report, Armstrong had conducted a thorough search of Symington's desk and files. The objects now on the table in front of them, proof of Symington's involvement with residents in the program, were the results of that search.

Pointing to the cards, letters, and photos, Armstrong said, "This shows what Symington's been doing all along. We have enough evidence here to dismiss him for unprofessional conduct. I won't have a residency director fooling around with the people he's supposed to evaluate or using his position to force anyone into sex."

"You're right about Symington, Harry," Yukawa replied. "But I'm not sure you haven't made matters a lot worse by what you've done."

"What do you mean by that?" Armstrong asked, puzzled.

"I mean, what right do you have to search someone's office in this way? Symington may be out of bounds, but aren't you also behaving unprofessionally by rifling through his personal files and his desk like this?"

"Look," Armstrong objected, "there's nothing personal about this. I had to go into this guy's office to get a report he should have finished days ago. Are you telling me our work here has to come to a standstill because Symington decides to take the day off? Furthermore, this guy is fooling around on the job and keeping stuff in a desk and file cabinet that are on our—the hospital's—premises. He's the one who acted badly by mixing up his personal and professional life. Believe me, we're lucky to have the proof we need to get rid of him."

Florence Yukawa understood Armstrong's point, but she was not sure she agreed. Somehow she felt that Armstrong had worsened a bad situation. She also knew that she now faced a decision. She could cooperate with Armstrong and proceed with the dismissal of Symington, or she could somehow take a stand against what Armstrong had done. Either way, she suspected, a series of tense confrontations lay ahead.

QUESTIONS TO CONSIDER

1. Do you think that Harry Armstrong has acted properly in searching through Dr. Symington's desk and files? Why or why not?

2. What rule or rules are implicit in Armstrong's conduct? What do you think of these rules?

3. To what extent do you believe an employee has a right to privacy in her or his work space, desk, or files?

EMPLOYEES' RIGHT TO PRIVACY

✦

The issue of employee privacy and the right to freedom from intrusion currently appears in many forms. It underlies the issues of drug testing, the use of lie detectors (polygraphs), forms of psychological testing, and the monitoring or surveillance of employees' work spaces, telephone conversations, electronic mail, or computer terminals. Privacy is involved, too, when companies try to control employees' dress, appearance, or off-the-job activities—from smoking to romantic involvements with competitors' employees. Despite the important differences between these issues, they all raise one question: To what extent does an employee working for a firm retain a zone of personal privacy not subject to invasion by the firm because of business necessities? Answering this question requires us to understand the value of employee privacy, the consequences of intrusion upon it, and when, if ever, intrusion might be warranted.

Dr. Armstrong expresses one side of this debate when he insists that the pressing needs of the hospital, including its ongoing need for access to Symington's files and its legal and ethical mandate to protect employees and others from misconduct by a staff physician, come before Dr. Symington's right to privacy in his office. Florence Yukawa's discomfort with Armstrong's behavior reflects an opposing point of view: that even compelling organizational needs do not always justify invasion of employees' privacy on or off the job.

This basic conflict reappears when we look at this issue from a deontological perspective. Although few advocates of employee rights insist that employees' right to privacy is absolute, many regard it as a significant restraint on organizational conduct that demands respect in all but the most urgent circumstances. Those who oppose employee drug testing on privacy grounds, for example, might permit it under designated circumstances where public safety is clearly at risk, but they are less sympathetic to drug testing as a means of reducing business expenses or promoting the goal of a drug-free society. Taking issue with this view are those who insist that the corporation's other stakeholders—owners, customers, communities, or other employees—have rights just as pressing as the individual employee's right to privacy. Some maintain that although the right to privacy usually makes sense off the job, it should not be applied to the essentially public setting of the business firm. Others go further, holding that a company may concern itself with any employee conduct adversely affecting the firm no matter where it occurs. For example, if employees' smoking increases a company's medical costs, this is reason enough for the company to prohibit employee smoking on or off the job. Approached deontologically, in other words, the issue of privacy displays the same kinds of conflicts between competing rights and competing moral priorities that typify deontological arguments generally.

Before looking at this issue—and Florence Yukawa's dilemma—from the perspective of **NORM**, it is useful to consider why privacy is a value worth protecting. Privacy is commonly thought of as a matter of "being left alone," but it also involves people's ability to control others' access to information about them. Someone can be said to enjoy privacy, for example, when she is able to prevent others from monitoring her personal conduct. In other instances, privacy may involve someone's ability to determine who shall have access to her medical records.

To understand the value of privacy, we might ask what it would be like to live in a completely transparent world, where everything we did and all information about us was open to other people's view. Some might think that this would be desirable, since, in such a world, it would be difficult to mislead others about our true nature or intentions. Everything would be out in the open and we could better protect ourselves against others' deceit or wrongdoing. But it is not hard to see that this world would have many inconveniences and would lack some valuable features. For one thing, a world without privacy would not be without deceit. Those who wish to lie to us or to harm us would merely become better able to dissimulate and conceal their intentions. Meanwhile, the rest of us would constantly have to conform our behavior to the expected norms of public conduct or run the risk of being regarded as antisocial or "strange." Because few of us ever entirely live up to these norms, this would demand considerable personal control and would lead us to suppress some activities we value. Singing off-key in the shower would be less likely in such a world, as would more important activities like privately venting built-up anger or hostility. In a transparent world, not only would we lose many psychologically important outlets for self-expression and release, we would also inevitably spend much time and energy in striving to maintain the appearance of conformity to social expectations. If we further consider that some of the most creative aspects of human life initially defy social expectations and standards, the absence of privacy would also deprive us of an "experimental" context in which we could develop and mature new ideas and projects before exposing them to social view.

This suggests that privacy is a value worth protecting. This is doubly true where people have planned their conduct and built their lives around an expectation of privacy. In such cases, the invasion of privacy can cause serious trauma or injury, as aspects of one's life not meant for public scrutiny are suddenly, and sometimes damagingly, exposed.

We can evaluate Dr. Armstrong's conduct against this background of ideas. In fact, Armstrong's behavior is complex and involves more than one argument for its moral acceptability. If we try to sort out these arguments and formulate each in terms of the moral policies implicit in it, we come up with the following two proposed moral rules:

✦

First Proposed Moral Rule: Whenever materials in an employee's desk or files are urgently needed for the proper functioning of the organization and when the employee (or manager) is absent from work or otherwise unable to give permission, a supervisor or fellow employee may conduct a thorough search for those materials.

Second Proposed Moral Rule: Whenever a supervisor suspects an employee (or manager) of serious misconduct that disrupts organizational functioning or violates others' rights, and when materials in the employee's desk or files might help the supervisor to determine the facts, the supervisor may, without the employee's permission or other authorization, conduct a search to obtain these materials.

✦

Although Dr. Armstrong's effort to justify his behavior combines both of these proposed moral rules, they have very different potential implications and we should look at them separately.

The first rule has some costs and some benefits. In a world governed by it, each of us must know that our work space is periodically subject to invasion. Taking this into account, employees will understandably be reluctant to leave personal materials in their work space—from bills or letters they have picked up on the way to work to sensitive memoranda they would not wish to share with others. Some amount of energy will inevitably be spent in the process of self-censorship this requires. At the same time, since this process can never be perfect, and since everyone possesses materials that can be misused if taken without authorization, this policy also involves a certain cost in terms of anxiety. None of this would be true if employees had an absolute right to privacy in their desks or files.

But we also must consider the costs of rejecting this proposed moral rule. Imagine a world where it was regarded as morally wrong for a supervisor or fellow employee to search a desk or files for urgently need-ed business documents. In this world, every unplanned employee absence or illness would impede organizational functioning. An employ-ee's unexpected hospitalization, for example, could hold up work on a major project and bring business to a standstill.

Although there are pros and cons to this proposed rule, a further con-sideration makes it more acceptable. As stated, this rule has what might be called an implicit *limiting principle* built into it that restricts its range of operation. *We can think of a limiting principle as a set of conceptual restraints on the application of a proposed moral rule. Implicitly or explicitly these restraints fall within the definition of the rule. They express its purposes, identi-fy its scope, and suggest what kind of conduct it does or does not permit. To pre-vent misuse of a proposed moral rule, its limiting principle must be clear, even if it is not always spelled out. Those who frame a moral rule must be able to state its limiting principle, and they must be confident that those who try to obey the rule can understand this limiting principle in practice.*

In the case of this first proposed moral rule, the limiting principle permits desk or file searches *for the purpose of securing needed business information.* Nothing else is warranted. No mention is made, for example, of permitting searches for disciplinary purposes or for reasons affecting the employees' status with the firm. The presence of this limiting princi-ple provides an important measure of protection for employees. Although they know that the contents of a desk or files may be subject to periodic examination, they also know that whatever searches are con-ducted will be undertaken only for vital business information and that only that sort of information will be removed. Although this would not eliminate all concerns an employee might have about the misuse or misconstrual of personal materials, in a firm where this proposed moral rule prevailed, and where any searches that were conducted respected it, an employee would not have reason to believe that her or his private space was subject to surveillance for any more threatening organization-al purposes.

These concerns, and the importance of the limiting principle implicit in the first of these proposed moral rules, become even clearer when we examine the second proposed moral rule involved in Dr. Armstrong's conduct. This rule permits supervisors to investigate employees' or man-agers' files whenever they suspect wrongful conduct. Like almost every moral rule that people seriously propose, this one clearly has some posi-tive value. In a world where it prevailed, Miramar Hospital and other organizations would have a powerful tool to help them get rid of troublesome or irresponsible employees. Since such employees can some-times significantly threaten the well-being of others—as Dr. Symington's personal involvement with some residents and possible sexual harass-ment of staff members may be doing—this is an important consideration. But this proposed moral rule also has serious costs.

For one thing, a world governed by this rule would be a place where I must regard every document or object in my work space as possible evidence against me in disciplinary proceedings. Although I may be an honest and trustworthy employee with no sympathy for those whose misconduct makes them subject to discipline, I must realize that suspi-cions or accusations of misconduct can be made against innocent people. In an environment governed by this rule, all employees would suffer anxiety about how their conduct and documentation might be construed and they would constantly have to review their materials with an eye to how they might be used against them in disciplinary proceedings. This imposes a great psychic burden and discomfort on everyone. It also entails organizational costs as employees spend time and effort review-ing and censoring materials in their possession. A further argument against this proposed moral rule, like so many other rules that initially appear attractive, is that, to some extent, it is self-defeating. In a world where employees know their materials are subject to search in this way, dishonest or misbehaving employees will usually take steps to conceal the evidence of their misconduct. Wrongdoers will go unpunished, and only naive and honest employees will be harmed.

A further problem with this second proposed moral rule is that it lacks an adequate limiting principle for its application. As stated, this rule permits invasions of privacy, without any further authorization, whenever a supervisor merely suspects an employee of serious miscon-duct. This allows intrusion for a wide range of reasons, from the most serious violations of public safety to any form of conduct that some supervisor believes might disturb organizational functioning. Because of this proposed rule's reliance on supervisors' judgment, it is not hard to see that in a world where it forms part of the "moral furniture," supervi-sors will predictably intrude on employees' privacy for a host of less-than-pressing or even for self-serving reasons. In Chapter 4 we saw that in evaluating a proposed rule of conduct, we must always take into con-sideration the question of whether the rule's public acceptance in society would encourage further undesirable forms of conduct. This second pro-posed moral rule, with its absence of a limiting principle, illustrates the relevance of this consideration.

The weakness of this proposed moral rule does not mean that employers may never invade the privacy of employees suspected of misconduct. We can easily imagine circumstances where employees act in ways that seriously threaten others' physical safety or the firm's stability. But conduct this harmful usually involves criminal behavior. A moral rule permitting invasion of employees' privacy in such cases could thus incorporate the legal constraints on criminal investigations existing in most democratic societies. For example, it would include the requirements that investigators have "reasonable cause" to believe the law is being broken and that they obtain a warrant for the search from impartial judicial authorities. These constraints form *limiting principles* for legal searches. They are designed to prevent mere suspicions or allegations of misconduct from becoming grounds for uncontrolled and unlimited intrusion on citizens' personal lives. They also make good sense as part of the *moral* restraints on a private organization's invasions of employees' privacy for disciplinary purposes. A viable moral rule in this area would permit an employer to invade an employee's privacy whenever the misconduct involved was serious enough to invoke normal legal procedures for searches and as long as these procedures are respected.

What does this reasoning tell us about Dr. Armstrong's behavior and Florence Yukawa's dilemma? For one thing, it suggests that Armstrong is probably right to think that his search for an urgent report justifies looking through Symington's desk and files. Behavior of this sort, we have seen, is justified by our first proposed moral rule. Armstrong's mistake lies in mixing appeal to this first *acceptable* proposed moral rule with appeal to the second, *unacceptable,* one. Armstrong's conduct in this case illustrates an important moral point: as responsible individuals, we must be careful not to confuse the justification of one aspect of our behavior with all of its related kinds of conduct, especially conduct that differs from it in morally relevant ways. Armstrong's confusion of (permissible) searches for business materials with (impermissible) investigatory forays shows how easy it is to make mistakes of this sort. Confusions like this, whether intended or not, are among the most common sources of immoral behavior.

Even skilled jurists can succumb to these confusions. A 1987 case before the United States Supreme Court, *O'Connor* v. *Ortega,*[7] involved a very similar disciplinary search of a physician's office. The case came under legal review because the physician worked for a public medical facility and the treatment he received thus raised the question of whether hospital authorities had violated his Fourth Amendment right to protection from unreasonable searches and seizures. By a vote of five to four the Court ruled that it did not. Writing for a four-member plurality in that decision,[8] Justice Sandra Day O'Connor presented the case as involving a conflict between an employee's "reasonable expectation of privacy in the workplace" and "government's need for supervision, control and the efficient operation of the workplace."[9] Weighing these interests, Justice O'Connor rejected as "simply unreasonable" the requirement that employers obtain a warrant for work-related searches. Unlike police, who conduct criminal searches solely to obtain evidence for criminal proceedings, she wrote, employers need access to offices and desks for "legitimate work-related reasons" such as retrieval of business files. In a sharp dissent, Justice Harry Blackmun criticized this reasoning for confusing routine business searches with investigatory proceedings against an employee. The result, Blackmun argued, was a standard that "makes reasonable almost any workplace search by a public employer."[10]

O'Connor v. Ortega illustrates how prevailing legal rulings can miss or ignore important moral issues. The plurality's reasoning in this case is like Dr. Armstrong's, whereas Blackmun's dissent raises some of the more complex moral issues we have considered. Because O'Connor v. Ortega involved a public facility, its conclusions have no immediate bearing on the conduct of private employers in the United States. Even if the Court had ruled that legally unauthorized investigatory searches of employees are constitutionally forbidden, this would apply only to governmental employers. Private firms would still be legally free to conduct such searches. Nevertheless, both public and private employers have moral responsibilities that go beyond existing law, and these responsibilities may include a higher standard than the one the courts have set. Given the evolving nature of law and its tendency over time to approximate the conclusions of sound moral reasoning, we would expect future court rulings to sharpen the distinction between routine business and disciplinary searches, to the detriment of those employers who have ignored moral considerations and relied narrowly on the ruling in O'Connor v. Ortega.

This analysis of Dr. Armstrong's conduct shows that, although employee privacy and freedom from intrusion on the job cannot be absolute, they merit respect and should not be simply subordinated to organizational needs. This is so, first, because respect for privacy has intrinsic value. It permits employees a zone of individual expression free from organizational intrusion or scrutiny. When employers trespass on this zone, employees may feel degraded or humiliated. They also lose a sphere in which they can express aspects of themselves they are not willing to share openly with associates. Second, when employers trespass on this zone, employees divert time and energy to protecting themselves from the use or misuse of information not normally subject to scrutiny, and all members of the organization experience anxiety at the thought of what might be done with information gleaned this way. Finally, employers who treat employees as totally subject to organizational surveillance erode an important element of mutual trust. Failure to respect its employees' zone of liberty and privacy places the organization in an adversarial relationship to those who work for it. Ironically, an organization that treats its employees as untrustworthy is likely to make them so.

These basic concerns apply to other issues involving employee privacy today. In the area of drug testing, for example, invasion of employees' private space can be humiliating, as when the supervised collection of urine samples is involved. But even where intrusion is less extreme, the other concerns we have signaled may still be operative. If newer techniques using hair samples as a basis for drug testing prove feasible, employees' concern with the use or misuse of information gained this way will remain. So, too, will the sense that the organization distrusts those who work for it.

In some industries, of course, the threat to public safety caused by employee drug abuse is a major concern—the public transport and nuclear power industries are examples. Yet, even here, there is evidence that employees resent randomized drug testing programs.[11] Because these programs test for metabolic products that may result from off-hour use of drugs or even prescription medications, and because they do not detect alcohol abuse, which many workers regard as a more serious safety threat than drugs, the programs are viewed as unfair and as an excessive invasion of privacy. Faced with these concerns, some human resources experts have argued for greater reliance on performance-based testing in these sensitive industries.[12] Performance testing involves the use of video-game-like devices to measure an employee's reaction and response time. In some trucking companies, for example, employees are required to pass a five-minute test before beginning their day's work. Such testing has several practical and moral advantages. It is directly job-related. It is also more effective than drug testing in identifying safety-related problems, since employees' performance can be impaired by many conditions unrelated to drug use, such as fatigue, emotional stress, or illness. Employees who fail this test are not necessarily guilty of drug abuse. Taken together, these features make performance testing something that employees can perceive as beneficial to themselves as well as those affected by their work. Unlike drug testing, which puts all employees, innocent or guilty, in an adversarial relationship to the company, this approach makes employees and management partners in addressing a common problem.

The issues of drug testing and performance testing illustrate how social concerns and new technologies will continue to shape the area of employee privacy. In some instances emerging problems and technological developments will work together to lead many to believe it is necessary for corporations to diminish the employee's zone of privacy. In other cases, technology may help relieve these pressures. As new issues arise throughout all these changes, however, certain basic moral insights remain applicable. Because the invasion of employees' privacy, on or off the job, erodes trust and mutual respect, it should always be a last resort. Privacy is not an absolute right, but neither can it be overridden by a company's supposition about what would enhance profitability or efficiency. Like other employee rights, privacy may be set aside or reduced only when there are serious evils to be avoided, when no other less intrusive or harmful means are available, and when employees can reasonably be expected to perceive themselves as having a clear stake in the issues involved.

Case 5.3

✦ ENDING THE PENSION PLAN AT HARPER & ROW[13] ✦

In 1981, the management of Harper & Row, the book publishing company, faced a quandary. A major stockholder, the Minneapolis Star & Tribune, which owned 33 percent of the company, wanted out: "The future never looked brighter for Harper & Row," said John Cowles, Jr., the Minneapolis company's president, "but a minority interest in a major publishing company isn't central to our business of newspaper publishing, broadcasting and cable casting."

The fear, among Harper & Row management, was that if the stock were sold on the open market, it would fall into unfriendly hands. The company, with its distinguished publishing history, was concerned about the possible loss of editorial independence.

Harper & Row's answer was to buy out the Minneapolis company's interest. The price was steep. At a time when Harper & Row's stock was selling over-the-counter for about $12 a share,

Harper paid the Minneapolis Star & Tribune $20 a share, or about $20.4 million overall.

"We're paying a premium," Brooks Thomas, president of Harper & Row, told the *Wall Street Journal* at the time, "but we think it's worth it." The Minneapolis company "didn't shop their stock on the outside, but they might have if we hadn't made the offer."

A question arose over how Harper & Row would pay for the stock. The company was not exactly flush with cash at the time. "Funding for the purchase will come from lines of credit, sales of real estate and funds received when the pension plan is terminated," the *Journal* reported. Harper & Row would save $2 million a year by ending its pension and profit-sharing plan, Thomas said. (The company later announced that it would place repurchased shares in trust for employees. This would essentially replace the terminated pension plan.)

A $712 LUMP-SUM PAYOUT

Glen Howard was a publisher in Harper & Row's Professional and Business Publication Division at the time. He recalls receiving a letter. "The letter said simply that they were terminating the pension plan. It didn't tell me why." It said only that he would receive the actuarial equivalent of his accrued pension benefits.

Howard's lump-sum payout amounted to $712. "I said, 'Wait a second. I've been here for thirteen years, I'm a senior executive, fully vested.'"

Howard went to Harper's insurance company, Prudential, to inquire about the cost of replacing his pension plan, which was supposed to pay him about $365 a month at retirement. He learned that it would cost $4,300 to buy an equivalent individual annuity. He went to other insurers. They quoted prices from $5,000 to $7,000 to replace his plan.

How could such a discrepancy arise? Administrative costs are higher for individual than for group annuities, but this accounted for only part of the difference. Howard later learned that Harper's insurer had used a 15 percent interest rate in calculating his lump-sum benefit. In other words, $712 appreciating at 15 percent annually over 25 years would yield approximately the $365 monthly pension benefit Howard had been promised at retirement. Interest rates had skyrocketed at the beginning of the 1980s, so the company had some basis for using this rate. But no other insurer would offer anything approaching 15 percent on a long-term basis. For a long time, Howard was unable to learn from the company how it arrived at the $712 figure.

Howard believed that Harper & Row and its insurer had used actuarial sleight of hand to reduce the lump sum it was required to pay him under federal law. It had artificially created a $3,588 corporate asset (i.e., the difference between $4,300 and $712). And it was this "surplus"—multiplied several thousand times—that enabled Harper & Row management to buy the Minneapolis Star's stock.

Howard saw something wrong in this. "People were not getting what they put into the company. They really hurt the little guys— the guy working in the mailroom for 20 years. He probably got something like $150."

Howard was not alone in his thinking. Ray Harwood, a former Harper & Row chairman, joined Howard in bringing suit against the publishing company and its insurance company. "Harwood," says Howard, "brought suit with me, in part, because he felt the promises he made to people had been breached."

According to Barbara Hufham, Harper & Row's general counsel, employees who stayed with the company did very well under the new employee stock ownership plan (ESOP). "In one sense, terminating the old plan turned out to be of enormous benefit." Because employees owned one-third of Harper's stock, which appreciated dramatically in the years immediately following, "they all got 100 percent better benefits," Hufham maintains. Workers in the company's back office in Scranton, Pennsylvania, "basically feel they were set up for life as a result of the plan."

Of course, no one could have foreseen that at the time, Howard counters. The company, in a sense, was playing casino with the employees' retirement fund. Tying workers' pension benefits to Harper's stock price was extremely risky. Howard acknowledged that employees who stayed with the company made out all right— but only because Rupert Murdoch's News Corporation eventually purchased Harper & Row. "The greatest irony of all is that they ultimately sold out to Rupert Murdoch"—the sort of raider against whom the company said it wanted to defend itself when it repurchased the stock in 1981.

Hufham denies that the company changed the pension rules midgame in 1981. "Our plan said it could be terminated at any time by the board," says Hufham. "That was known by all employees. It was stated in the employee handbook. There was no guarantee that the plan would continue forever." Harper's management also contends that its decision to terminate the pension plan did not violate regulations issued by the Federal Pension Benefit Guaranty Corporation (PBGC). Although the regulations require companies to use money in pension plans exclusively for the benefit of workers and retirees, they also permit companies to terminate plans at any time so long as benefits earned up until that point are paid out to employees. Surplus assets in such plans—assets beyond those needed to pay out promised benefits—can revert to the company.

Nevertheless, some criticize these practices even when the payoff to employees is fairly computed. They contend that what some call a "surplus" in defined-benefit pension plans is often a cushion in case financial markets drop or when inflation threatens retirees' benefits. "From an ethical point of view, any pension plan termination, absent extreme economic distress, is questionable," says Michael S. Gordon, a pension attorney who helped write the Employee Retirement Income Security Act (ERISA), the 1974 law that governs private pension plans. Speaking of the Harper & Row merger, Gordon adds, "It boggles my mind that a company that published Solzhenitsyn would do something like this."

QUESTIONS TO CONSIDER

1. With whom do you agree in the debate over Harper & Row's termination of its pension fund, critic Glen Howard or the company's defender, Barbara Hufham? Why?

2. If you were in Harper & Row's senior management, would you have used the employee pension fund to retain the company's editorial independence? Would you have altered Harper & Row's behavior in any way?

3. Apply **NORM** to the rules of conduct you find in this case. To what extent is the company's conduct defensible in this way? What alternate rules of conduct might you propose?

THE RIGHT TO PARTICIPATE
◆

Do employees have a right to participate in managerial decision making? Developments in the past decade have given this question new importance. Because of the increasing globalization of commerce, for example, European and Japanese companies have challenged American firms to rethink aspects of their labor practices. Complementing this is the growing perception, fostered by popular studies of "excellent" or "vanguard" companies, that older hierarchical or paternalistic styles of management are not suited to motivating a generation of better-educated, more independent employees. Employees who give their best to a company, these studies suggest, also want a say in matters important to them.

The terms *employee participation* and *participative management* cover a host of different approaches involving varying degrees of employee empowerment. At one extreme, participative management can mean a worker cooperative, where employees control all aspects of the organization. Somewhere in the middle, it can signify the German practice of "co-determination," where labor councils or unions are consulted on major decisions affecting workers, including matters like plant closings or overseas expansion. At the other extreme it can involve little more than the use of "quality circles" that give workers some voice in shaping their production environment.

Many factors enter into a company's decision about the degree of its commitment to employee participation. Among these are the firm's economic circumstances and the nature of its business, employees' abilities and expectations, and the competitive advantage afforded by one or another management style. Sometimes, however, employee participation has a clear moral dimension. This appears whenever employees claim that they have a right to be informed about or to have a say in certain decisions that vitally affect their lives.

The conduct of Harper & Row's owners and senior management raises this basic employee rights question. Glen Howard and other employees feel they have been morally wronged by the company's unilateral decision to end their pension plan and replace it with an Employee Stock Option Plan (ESOP). Harper & Row disagrees. It feels it not only made good decisions, but made them in a legally and ethically proper way. Who is right in this matter, and how do we think morally about a complex business decision of this sort?

Approached deontologically, this case displays the sharp conflict of moral rights and rules that so often complicates moral—and legal—reasoning. At the core of the issue are competing notions of property rights, different ideas of what "reasonability" means in financial decision making, and opposing views of what constitutes a promise. Glen Howard and Ray Harwood feel the company took funds rightly belonging to employees. It did this by unilaterally appropriating the "surplus" in the pension plan and by using a formula that set the value of that surplus too high. Harper & Row disagrees. It regards any funds in the pension plan beyond those reasonably needed to meet its annuity obligations as the firm's property, and it feels that its setting of annuity values was fair. The two managers also believe the firm has broken a solemn promise to maintain a pension plan. Harper's general counsel denies that the company broke any promises because the employee handbook made clear that the plan could be terminated at any time. In any case, she adds, no harm was done because employees greatly benefited from the ESOP that management generously set up for them.

These competing claims will eventually be sorted out in the courts on the basis of legal precedent and the diverse, often competing sentiments of judges and juries. The advantage of this approach is that it stays close to people's moral convictions, many of which society has inscribed in its legal norms over time. The disadvantage is that it often depends on fixed legal formulas not suited to changing realities. Whatever the courts decide, we also need independent insight into the rights and wrongs of a case like this.

A utilitarian analysis aims to provide this, and, in contrast to deontological approaches, promises a clear resolution of the issues. From a utilitarian perspective, it is important that no one directly involved was financially harmed and that all Harper & Row stakeholders apparently benefited from this decision. If we add to this the fact that, at least initially, the company was able to preserve its editorial independence, the decision by Harper & Row's board and senior management seems a model of good utilitarian reasoning. True, there are some less measurable indirect harms involved. One is the impact on the morale of Harper's employees made by this kind of unilateral decision making about a matter as important as pension benefits. Will employees suffer anxiety and insecurity in the future now that they see how abruptly and unilaterally management can act? Employees outside the firm also may be adversely affected. Since there is no way that Harper's management can conceal its conduct or prevent others from following its example, these larger negative psychological and social impacts count against this decision. Nevertheless, they weigh in only as conjectural matters, some of which might have occurred whatever Harper did. On balance, they seem relatively less important than the financial and editorial benefits of the plan's termination. A utilitarian analysis, therefore, seems to justify management's conduct in this case.

Neutral, Omnipartial Rule-Making (**NORM**) bypasses deontology's issue of contested rights and rules by asking one question: "How would I or any other omnipartial rational person feel about living in a world governed by the moral rules implicit in Harper's conduct?" Alongside the measurable calculus of economic benefits so important from a utilitarian perspective, it also requires us to consider the human impact on ourselves and others of these forms of conduct as abiding features of our human environment. Of course, utilitarianism does this too, but **NORM** does not confine its analysis to the actual psychological consequences of management's behavior. **NORM** asks us to assume a more basic and enduring perspective. It requires us to conceive of this decision as creating a moral "world" in which we must live. And it asks us to assess that world from the perspective of all the persons who live in it.

We can see that the most basic moral rule implicit in the conduct of Harper's management raises serious and troubling questions. This moral rule might be given the following form:

◆

Proposed Moral Rule: So long as a firm's owners try to preserve the benefits earned by employees and do not deceive or mislead employees about pension entitlements, they may unilaterally terminate existing employee pension plans and use what they regard as surplus assets to pursue important company objectives (such as repelling a threat to a publishing company's editorial independence).

◆

Clearly, there are some good reasons for adopting this rule. The owners of a company have a major stake that they must be reasonably free to protect. Restrictions on owners' liberty are also counterproductive if they discourage investment and reduce business activity and employment. A requirement of consultation with and consent from all affected parties in every major corporate decision does not make sense. It could easily paralyze decision making and threaten a firm's survival. Business firms, which people are relatively free to join or leave and which lack police powers, probably should not be subject to the strict requirements of democratic procedure we impose on political communities.

But if there are good reasons for this proposed moral rule, there are also some good reasons against it. Although restricting the liberty of action of a firm's owners can have adverse affects and be counterproductive, society frequently imposes such restrictions to preserve other important social values. The question is whether such values exist here and morally warrant a limitation of corporate freedom. Obviously, employees' stake in a pension plan represents one good reason for limiting corporate liberty. When employees who had counted on adequate pension benefits lose them, serious evils result. Not only do the employees themselves face the prospect of severe economic hardship at a time in their lives when they are often least able to cope with it, but everyone in society may be forced to step in financially, through programs of government assistance, to ease their suffering. It is a sign of the importance placed by society on preserving people's pensions that many private plans even limit their own participants' liberty of action by forbidding employees to dip into pension assets before retirement.

Against this background, the absence of a *limiting principle* in this proposed moral rule makes it particularly worrisome. By allowing employers unilaterally to terminate a plan and to appropriate what *they regard* as surplus assets, this rule is an invitation to abuse. As it turns out, almost everyone at Harper & Row benefited by the transformation of their pension plan into an ESOP. But in a world where this rule prevails, corporate decisions would sometimes backfire and employees would be left with only a fraction of the resources they counted on for retirement. This argues strongly against giving employers moral carte blanche to use pension funds in this way.

Does this mean that employers may never terminate pension funds or use surplus pension assets (assets beyond those needed to meet their accumulated financial obligations)? We should remember that almost any moral rule has exceptions. Understanding why we have accepted or rejected a proposed moral rule also helps us identify circumstances in which we might come to a different conclusion. We just saw that an employee's economic security in old age is a concern powerful enough to counsel restricting employers' freedom in this area. But economic security in retirement results from many factors, not least of which is the economic viability of the company one spends one's life working for. This suggests that pressing economic needs related to corporate survival might justify a plan's termination, the use of genuinely surplus assets, or a plan's conversion to an ESOP tying future benefits to company stock performance. Attorney Gordon expresses the gist of this view when he suggests that it might be warranted to terminate a plan in cases of "extreme economic distress."

This tempts us to amend the proposed moral rule above to one permitting unilateral decision making when a company faces threats of this magnitude. But no less than the previous proposed moral rule, this would be an invitation to abuse. After all, what firm doesn't periodically face economic hardship, and what managers wouldn't like to have pension moneys at their disposal in economic downturns? Clearly this rule needs some kind of further limiting principle to prevent abuse.

We might go about this matter by continuing to try to specify all the circumstances that would warrant use of pension assets. For example, we could try to incorporate in our proposed moral rule some rough guidelines indicating the degree of financial peril a firm would have to face before using pension resources. We might also try to provide some guidance on how surplus assets might fairly be calculated. The result would be a lengthy moral rule embodying all the specifics of its application, a kind of "pension bill of rights" for employees.

But there is another, more direct way of limiting abusive conduct in this area. *We could simply require employee participation in decision making about these matters.* After all, employees have a large stake in the continuance of their jobs, the flourishing of their company, *and* the availability of their pension assets. By incorporating the requirement that employers seek the advice and consent of employees in matters regarding pension fund termination or conversion, we create a powerful check on misuse of fund assets. A moral rule incorporating this requirement will probably be less specific and more flexible than rules trying to indicate in detail the circumstances warranting employer resort to pension assets. The following proposed moral rule is an example:

✦

Revised Proposed Moral Rule: As long as they elicit the advice and consent of employees, a firm's owners may terminate existing employee pension funds and use surplus assets to pursue important company objectives.

✦

A basic moral rule of this sort leaves many practical questions unanswered. At best, it is only the beginning of moral thinking about the variety of issues that can crop up in any real-life decision making about pension benefits. For one thing, there is the question of what "advice and consent" means. What mechanisms do these words imply for employee involvement in decisions of this sort? Political procedures will surely be needed within a firm to determine employee sentiment on such matters. Since employees will predictably disagree among themselves about policies and decisions, how do we deal fairly with everyone's concerns? What will be the rights of those whose views do not prevail? And since owners and employees will sometimes be at loggerheads about a particular decision, we will also have to think about the norms governing these occasions.

Within a framework establishing the basic moral principle of employee advice and consent in pension matters, each of these questions requires more focused moral analysis. A society that has established this basic principle of employee consent and enacted it into law will normally address these questions in specific decisions by legislatures, courts, or regulatory bodies. We need not anticipate all this thinking here. More important is our grasp of the basic reasoning leading to a high-level moral norm of this sort. Pension matters, we see, are an issue so important to employee welfare that some kind of restraints should exist on company discretion. Employee participation in major decisions regarding the pension plan is one such restraint. *We can think of this requirement as a* procedural limiting principle *on employer conduct in this area.*

Sometimes, we have seen, limiting principles within a moral rule involve concrete descriptions of permissible or impermissible types of conduct. The procedural approach taken here is less specific and achieves its purpose by relying on the informed consent of owners and employees to substantive changes in plan arrangements. It has the advantage of protecting vital interests while leaving considerable room for flexible accommodation to new realities.

This reasoning illuminates the rational basis of claims that employees have a moral "right" to informed consent in basic policy decisions affecting their pension plan and benefits. It also suggests that Harper & Row acted wrongly in its unilateral decision making. With hindsight, we can see that, whatever its legal rights at the time, the company had, at a minimum, the moral obligation to bring this matter before a committee with employee membership. Although such a committee would not be a perfect barometer of employee sentiment, it would be a way for the company to involve employees in a decision that vitally affected them. Use of such a committee and enhanced consultation with employees might have helped avoid some of the sharp resentment and litigation occasioned by the company's decisions.

It might be objected that Harper & Row adequately met its moral responsibility of advice and consent by policy statements regarding pension matters in the employee handbook. This seems to be the view of Harper & Row's general counsel. After all, any prospective employees who disagreed with these policies did not have to join the firm. Those who did presumably consented to these arrangements and the wide latitude they afforded the company. From a moral point of view, however, it is not hard to see that there are serious problems with these assertions. Even if we assume that most employees carefully examine the employee handbook before accepting a job offer, few people are ever in a position to decline an otherwise attractive position because of a single unsatisfactory employment policy. We do not have to explore all the complexities of informed consent to realize that employee handbook pronouncements do not meet the standard of consent this issue merits.

If this reasoning is correct, we might predict that handbook statements will not always protect a firm that violates its employees' moral rights with regard to pensions. It may seem odd that in the area of wrongful discharge, as we saw, courts and juries have relied on statements in employment handbooks to uphold employees' claims of wrongful discharge, whereas in this case they might ignore such statements to rule for employees whose pensions have been placed in jeopardy. But there is really no contradiction here. Underlying these differing surface patterns of reasoning and modes of legal argument is a moral concern to protect employees' most basic rights and to limit companies' unilateral decision making where these rights are concerned.

The idea of a *procedural limiting principle* requiring employee participation extends well beyond the matter of pension plans to a host of other employee rights areas. Changing business realities constantly create new and unexpected areas of conflict between employees and management. Anticipating all the issues that might crop up and developing norms in advance to govern them is impossible. But it is important to see that certain issues so deeply affect employees' welfare that we would find it reasonable to limit employers' liberties with respect to them. We also can see that, when new issues arise, one way of cutting through the thicket of competing moral claims and safeguarding employees' essential concerns is to invoke employee participation in decision making.

The issue of employee monitoring provides a good illustration of this point. With the development of the "electronic office" and the enormous increase in the number of employees who work with computers and video display terminals (VDTs), there has been a corresponding increase in the practice of monitoring employee performance. Employees who perform word processing tasks, for example, often find that their number of keystrokes is recorded and reviewed by supervisors. Telephone service personnel, such as airline ticketing agents and information operators, are often placed under strict time restraints in handling calls, with their performance electronically recorded. Many companies also listen in on calls received by service personnel to maintain performance standards. Employees who fail to meet quantitative or qualitative goals suffer economic penalties and can lose their jobs.

Defenders of these policies maintain that they are merely the electronic equivalent of the supervisor who used to pace the shop floor to see that employees were doing their jobs properly. They point out that computer monitoring has the advantage of offering an objective standard of measurement and is fairer to employees than evaluation procedures relying on human judgment. Although some employees agree with these views, others are sharply critical of aspects of monitoring practices. Some see computer monitoring as little more than an electronic version of the sweatshop or the sped-up assembly line of the past. Others view employer eavesdropping as an unwarranted invasion of privacy and a cause of stress. Critics of these practices point to studies showing increased rates of depression or physical maladies among employees subject to monitoring and surveillance.[14]

Some basic insights developed in this chapter apply to this issue. We have seen, for example, that there are good reasons for respecting employee privacy in the workplace. When privacy is breached, employees lose a valuable sphere of self-expression and can experience anxiety. Although customer relations are not ordinarily something we think of as private, even in the busiest of work environments employees have traditionally been able to preserve a zone of privacy and freedom from immediate scrutiny and supervision. Electronic surveillance and unannounced random monitoring of calls introduces an unprecedented degree of workplace surveillance. In addition, monitoring and electronic eavesdropping threaten to reduce the sense of trust and mutual respect needed to stimulate employees to perform well for their employer. There is anecdotal evidence that employees subject to monitoring often reduce their output to a level needed to just meet numerical goals, and, when they can get away with it, also lower their qualitative performance.[15]

What rights are involved here? Do employees have a "right" to freedom from electronic monitoring or random surveillance? Or do they have a right to the kinds of objective evaluation and review that some kinds of monitoring afford? What of employers' and customers' rights to efficient service? The basic insights developed here can help us begin to think through these complex new questions. To the extent that monitoring can impose serious harm on employee welfare and morale, it may warrant limitations on employer liberty. In balancing the interests at stake, it is also wise to invoke employee participation as a major constraint on companies' conduct.

Participation here can take many forms. At the policy level, it can mean involving employees or their representatives in the design of monitoring systems. Because employees have an interest in objective evaluation and in the company's competitive success, we should not assume that they will oppose monitoring programs that support these objectives. Sometimes, this will result in compromises where each side relinquishes some claims, as when companies agree to confine call surveillance to training programs or to regular, and announced, review periods. In other cases, employee input may help improve monitoring programs by identifying important qualitative factors in customer service. At the level of implementation, participation can mean the use of monitoring in ways that involve individual employees and increase their sense of worth. Some successful programs, for example, use the results of monitoring in nonpunitive ways to help employees improve their performance. Other programs confine monitoring results to the group or unit level, allowing employees to identify and address performance problems among themselves and giving them a role in determining how they can best meet their objectives.

Although participation is no panacea for employee rights issues, its moral value lies in the way it helps us re-create the basic situation of moral choice. That situation requires the free consent of all parties who reason omnipartially and with full information about what basic rules should govern their conduct. In real life, few persons ever reason in a fully informed or omnipartial way. This means that, even when employers and employees freely participate in the effort to settle disputes, they will sometimes fail to resolve their conflicts. In these cases, society eventually has to step in legally or politically to reconcile divergent claims. But although employee participation is an imperfect instrument for identifying or protecting employee rights, it is a useful tool in addressing complex disputes between employers and employees. Participation is more than just one right on a list of employee rights. Because it approximates the basic requirements of moral reasoning, it provides a model for thinking about other employee rights, both those that are well established and those awaiting discovery.

Summary

- Employee rights are firmly grounded entitlements to forms of fair treatment or benefits. Not subject to the whims of management or shareholders, they exert an independent and significant claim on corporate decision making.

- When looked at omnipartially, as **NORM** requires, the relative imbalance in power between the individual and the firm makes it wise to establish moral rules restricting a company's ability to treat employees arbitrarily. This reasoned judgment provides the basis for some of the main employee rights being claimed today, including the right to due process and fair treatment when being dismissed.

- Employees have a right to privacy and freedom from intrusion on or off the job. Privacy is intrinsically valuable and its erosion creates anxiety and mistrust. An organization that treats its employees as untrustworthy by subjecting them to intrusive searches or surveillance is likely to make them so.

- Employee participation in major decisions affecting their lives is among the most important of employee rights. We can think of this right as a *procedural limiting principle* on employer conduct. Rather than spelling out specific criteria for acceptable employer conduct, the right to participate gives employees a say in complex circumstances by moving a company closer to the basic situation of informed, omni-partial choice.

Case 5.4

◆ VIRGINIA RULON-MILLER[16] ◆

Virginia Rulon-Miller started at IBM in 1967 as a receptionist. By 1978, she had worked her way up to the position of marketing manager and her future with the firm looked good. About this time, she began dating Matt Blum. He was an accountant with IBM but soon left the firm to work for a competitor. Ms. Rulon-Miller continued to see Matt.

In 1978, while still in sales in the office products division, she fulfilled her annual sales quota in the fifth month of the year and was given the Golden Circle Award in recognition of her performance. Although Philip Callahan, her supervisor, was aware of her romantic relationship with Blum, he recommended her for promotion.

In 1979 she received a $4,000 merit raise. A week later, Callahan left a message that he wanted to meet with her. According to Ms. Rulon-Miller,

"I walked into Phil's office and he asked me to sit down and he said, 'Are you dating Matt Blum?'

"And I said, 'What?' I was kind of surprised he would ask me and I said: 'Well, what difference does it make if I'm dating Matt Blum?'

. . . "And he said, well, something to the effect: 'I think we have a conflict of interest, or the appearance of a conflict of interest here.'

And I said: 'Well, gee, Phil, you've pointed out to me that there are no problems in the office because I'm dating Matt Blum, and I don't really understand why that would have any, you know, pertinency to my job. You said I'm doing an okay job. I just got a raise.'

"And he said: 'Well, I think we have a conflict of interest . . .'

"He said: 'No' and he said: 'I'll tell you what.' He said: 'I'll give you a couple of days to a week. Think this whole thing over.'

"I said: 'Think what over?'

"And he said: 'You either stop dating Matt Blum or I'm going to take you out of your management job.'

"And I was just kind of overwhelmed."

The next day Callahan called Ms. Rulon-Miller into his office again and told her "I'm making the decision for you." When she protested, he fired her.

QUESTIONS TO CONSIDER

1. Is Philip Callahan right to fire Ms. Rulon-Miller? Why or why not? What is the rule implicit in his conduct? What do you think of this rule?

2. Must a company continue to employ a manager who is married to or has a romantic relationship with someone who holds a senior position at a competing company?

3. When does an employee's or manager's off-the-job life become a legitimate object of a firm's concern? Using **NORM**, formulate and evaluate some relevant rules of conduct in this area.

Case 5.5

✦ ETHICS AT THE BANQUET[17] ✦

On October 18, 1990, Gerry Maleron and Mary Freeland sat beside each other at the annual banquet of the Metropolitan New York Business Council. Both had received their M.B.A.s in 1982 from Cornell's Kellogg School of Management, and in their years of working in Manhattan, they enjoyed this annual event as a way of catching up on what was happening in one another's lives. One part of their conversation dealt with ethics and went something like this:

Gerry: I've been on an ethical kick recently. I decided to swear off cigarettes and actively work to get smoking out of public places. My wife bet me I couldn't do it—that is, give up smoking. We both knew I was addicted. I had smoked since I was 14! My doctor intervened and really scared me. And then my little girl asked me why I smoke. I guess that really did it. So I took one of those stop-smoking courses; and it worked.

Mary: Congratulations. I hope you can stick with it.

Gerry: Oh, I will. It's a matter of honor. Anyway, I don't want to be out of synch in my company. Everything is moving against smoking. It started five years ago when some directors objected to cigar smoking in the boardroom, would you believe that! Our CEO, who has a nice sense of humor, wrote an article about that incident for our company newspaper and asked rhetorically if it wasn't time we do something in other ways. After all, we were one of the first life insurance companies to offer lower premiums to nonsmokers, and we have a lot invested in health.

 Gradually we've ruled out smoking in all but a few parts of our home office building. I'll admit I was beginning to feel guilty about sitting among the dwindling tables for smokers in the executive dining room. I felt I could smoke in my office only when I had no one with me. I began to see myself as some kind of respiratorial leper!

I thought the Personnel Vice-President went too far when he proposed that we stop hiring anyone who smokes. But that proposal has wide support, and I'm told the CEO has bought it. Some of my friends in the legal department think we can't do it—can't ask people if they smoke off the job and can't deprive people of the liberty or pleasure of smoking at work as long as their habit doesn't bother or affect anyone else. The Personnel Vice President says he's willing to go to court—we're right, we're going to become a smokeless society and our company should lead, not follow. We'll get better people if we hire nonsmokers, he says, healthier and with more self-respect and self-control. And we'll lower our health coverage costs to boot.

Before I decided to quit smoking I resented the VP's logic and its implications of second-class citizenship for smokers. I never questioned the matter with the VP directly, but I griped and grumbled like crazy with my peers. Now I go along, and I'm even feeling a bit smug.

Mary: Interesting that you've gone through that, Gerry. We've had some adventures about smoking in my agency, but in a quite different way. Ethics are involved for us, too, and I'm not really satisfied with the way things have worked out.

As you know, we're one of the biggest advertising agencies in the world. We think of ourselves as a first-rate agency, and we were one of the first to adopt a formal code of ethics. Our chairman played a prominent role in creating the industry's 1984 ethical standards statement.

Some years ago we said we wouldn't take a cigarette company as a client; our founding chairman and his wife both felt strongly about it and no one questioned the decision. About 1968 the management committee decided it was wise to change. Tobacco advertising began to be a huge industry all its own, and predictions were it would become the single most potent force in magazine, radio, and TV advertising. So the firm decided to allow each of its agencies to settle the question for itself. Almost immediately our French group took on a large cigarette account and still has it. Many young people in our Paris office have cut their creative teeth on cigarette advertising, to mix images. Over time we took on American companies (we have one of the big four), and the sole consideration was dollar volume and profit. I agree with that.

The ban on TV and radio advertising of cigarettes in 1971 only sharpened the battle lines. Magazines and billboards were the major media and that's a huge business.

Gerry: Haven't you had people objecting inside the firm? How about yourself—don't you think advertising cigarettes raises all sorts of ethical questions and concerns?

Mary: We solved it by saying that no one will be asked to work on tobacco accounts involuntarily. So we have 20 to 30 percent of our people saying, "No, thanks!" And an increasing percentage of new M.B.A.s sign the conscientious objection ballot, proportionately more men than women, to my surprise. So those people make an ethical statement—"Cigarette advertising is wrong, and I don't want any part of it."

Gerry: Really? But they shouldn't be allowed to get away with that! They're taking a top management prerogative unto themselves and no one benefits. The ads still get produced and printed, no questions asked, and those nay-sayers feel better. But they haven't contributed to anything except their own smugness. And they've taken away management's very important right to assign talent to tasks, in the best interests of the shareholders.

Mary: You don't understand ad agencies, especially ones with a really creative aura. You can't force anyone to work on anything they don't want to. So our people can refuse to promote alcohol if they wish or cereal companies that toy with the motivational systems of little kids on Saturday morning TV! If you forced them to those tasks, they'd do a bad job, especially on the creative side of the house. If we became known as an insensitive company, we'd fail to attract the best people we go after.

Gerry: I guess I don't understand. Such a mix of purely personal tastes and business decisions seems to turn the usual organizational imperatives upside down. I would be particularly leery of letting people get away with claiming their preference as an ethical one, because that isn't valid. If you are following an ethical rule by opting out of a cigarette ad campaign, then you have to do more.

Mary: I don't think so. That's like saying that if you feel morally superior (as I think you do) for stopping your own smoking, you have to try to stop others!

Gerry: But how would you reply to R. J. Reynolds (or whoever your account is) if you were courting their business and they asked, "Will you put your best people on our account?" Or even more if they asked for a person by name who was one of your stars and you knew you couldn't produce her because she preferred not to work on tobacco accounts?

Mary: We're strong enough to tell them the truth (tactfully, of course) and take the consequences.

Gerry: Do you let college kids coming for the summer avoid the cigarette account if they have scruples?

Mary: Oh, no. In fact, you aren't given the choices I described until you have three years of service. We're talking about a privilege here and a thoughtful, considered decision.

Gerry: Well, it sounds crazy to me. I think your firm could stand an ethical audit of some sort.

Mary: I've got a feeling anyone who gives into the ethical audit business is going to be very busy, because your firm sure needs a close look at the validity of discriminating against smokers before you even see their smoke! Especially when you probably freely hire people whose addictions or even vices are not so obvious!

[By mutual consent, the conversation then drifted into other topics.]

QUESTIONS TO CONSIDER

1. Do you think a company has a right to refuse to hire smokers? Can it fire workers who will not quit smoking? What general rules are involved here and how well do they withstand omni-partial assessment?

2. Should employees have a right to dissent from participating in company activities—like the advertising or promotion of cigarettes—to which they're morally opposed? Should a company respect this right?

Case 5.6

◆ PARTING WAYS ◆

Sarah Martin's resignation from Carlsson-Brevard's summer intern program was unprecedented. In the more than twenty years that the program had been in operation—with over two hundred M.B.A. students from Harvard, Wharton, Darden, and other top business schools participating—no summer intern had ever quit. By leaving the program early, Sarah passed up several weeks of salary and relinquished the chance for a full-time job with one of Boston's most prestigious consulting firms. She also had to worry about how to explain her resignation if it came up during her job search next year.

Sarah had personally delivered her letter of resignation to William Pauley, a senior partner of the firm and chair of its Personnel Committee. She explained to Pauley that her decision was a response to what she called the "terrifying" behavior of Arthur Comden, another senior partner. She asked Pauley to bring the concerns in her letter to the Personnel Committee "to spare other interns from having to deal with this problem." After Sarah left his office, Pauley read her letter several times. He tried to decide what he would recommend to his colleagues on the committee, and he tried to anticipate what, if anything, they might do.

EXHIBIT 1:

Letter of Sarah Martin to William T. Pauley

August 18, 1991

William T. Pauley
Chair, Personnel Committee
Carlsson-Brevard Associates, Inc.
15 Market Place
Boston, MA 02344

Dear Mr. Pauley:

I am writing to you in your capacity as Chair of the Personnel Committee in hopes that your committee will take prompt action to remedy a problem that has caused me to resign from the summer intern program. In two words, this problem is Arthur Comden. Mr. Comden's abusive and threatening behavior has caused me to fear for my safety and has also alienated other interns in the program.

A few days after I began the internship in June, Mr. Comden demonstrated a pattern that would continue in the coming weeks. During task force meetings, he would sharply rebuke interns for minor errors in reports or tardiness in preparing materials. He called these his "kick ass sessions." His remarks during them were often filled with obscenities and threats of violence. For example, he frequently told male interns that he would "crack their skulls" if they did not meet his standards or quickly perform some task he wanted done. Some of my peers in the program initially excused this behavior as part of Mr. Comden's background in the Marine Corp. But, as time went on, almost everyone in the intern group came to believe that Comden's verbal behavior was excessive and inexcusable.

On one occasion in early July, Comden, who, as you know, is a large individual, ended an argument with a male intern by grabbing the intern's shoulders and pushing him forcibly up against the wall. Following this episode, several of us brought up the matter with other senior partners with whom we were working. Although these partners expressed embarrassment over Comden's behavior, they explained that as one of the highest performing senior partners in the firm, Mr. Comden was "untouchable." They urged us to put up with his "eccentric" style and work around a difficult situation.

Over the past few weeks, Comden extended this pattern of abuse and physical threats to female interns, including me. On one occasion earlier this month, he said that he would "throw me out the window" if I did not immediately correct some data in a report. At that time, I told him that I found such comments unnecessary and frightening. His response to this was to tell me to "lighten up."

Last Wednesday (August 14), during another task force meeting, Comden said that if I did not complete revisions in a report by the end of this week he would "beat the hell out of me." I submitted this report yesterday, but I have been fearful ever since Mr. Comden voiced this threat. I have had difficulty sleeping and have grown increasingly apprehensive about coming to work. From the experience of his dealings with other interns, I feel that Mr. Comden is capable of doing some of the things he threatens. Having seen him use physical force to express his displeasure, I am not confident that I will be safe from these threats even after I leave the firm.

I feel it is my obligation to bring this matter to your attention for the sake of future interns. I hope that you and your committee will promptly take steps to end this pattern of totally unprofessional conduct on his part.

Sincerely yours,

Sarah Martin

QUESTIONS TO CONSIDER

1. Do you believe that Sarah Martin acted in an ethically responsible way in writing to William Pauley? What public moral rule is implicit in her conduct? How would you assess this rule?

2. If you were serving on Carlsson-Brevard's Personnel Committee, what response would you urge to Ms. Martin's letter? Why?

𝒩OTES

1. Quoted in Martha I. Finney, "A Game of Skill or Chance?" *Personnel Administrator* (March 1988): 38–43.
2. In *Workrights* (New York: Dutton, 1983), Robert Ellis Smith lists a number of these rights among his "Fourteen Freedoms in the Workplace."
3. This case was developed by B. H. Turnbull as the basis for class discussion rather than as an illustration of either effective or ineffective handling of an administrative situation. The persons and events described in this case are creations of the author and any similarities to any persons, alive or dead, or to any actual events are purely coincidental.
4. As a legal wrong or "tort," the exception based on "good faith and fair dealing" also goes beyond the sphere of contract law and makes possible punitive damages and other means of legal recovery for the employee. See Jonathan Tompkins, "Legislating the Employment Relationship: Montana's Wrongful Discharge Law," *Employee Relations Law Journal* 14, no. 3 (Winter 1988): 387–98.
5. *Sides* v. *Duke Hospital,* 74 N.C. App. 331, 328 S.E. 2d 818, 821, 826 (1985).
6. This case is derived from the Supreme Court case *O'Connor* v. *Ortega,* 107 S. Ct. 1492 (1987).
7. Ibid.
8. Justice Scalia wrote a separate concurring opinion.
9. Ibid., 1499.
10. Ibid., 1507.
11. Allan Hanson, "What Employees Say about Drug Testing," *Personnel* 67, no. 7 (July 1990): 32–36.
12. Lewis L. Maltby, "Put Performance to the Test," *Personnel* 67, no. 7 (July 1990): 30–31.
13. This case is drawn, with minor revisions, from an article by Andrew W. Singer in *Ethikos* (November/December 1988), pp. 1ff. Reprinted by permission.
14. "Workers Using Computers Find a Supervisor Inside," *New York Times,* 23 December 1990, pp. 1, 18; "Debate Is Brewing over Employees' Right to Privacy," *H R Focus* (February 1993): 1, 4.
15. "Workers Using Computers Find a Supervisor Inside," pp. 1, 18.
16. Based on the case *Rulon-Miller* v. *IBM,* 208 Cal. Reptr. 524 (Cal. App. 1 Dist. 1984).
17. Based on a case developed by John W. Hennessey, Jr.

CUSTOMERS AS STAKEHOLDERS

✦

✦AMONG A CORPORATION'S STAKEHOLDERS, CONSUMERS AND CLIENTS merit respect and constant attention. Customers will not continue to deal with a company unless they are satisfied with its products and services and unless they perceive themselves as being treated fairly. Unfortunately, this self-evident truth is often defied in practice. In the quest for immediate profits, firms often sacrifice customers' interests. Sometimes companies use a dominating market position to dictate the terms of commercial transactions; at other times they exploit consumers' ignorance or vulnerability and sell products or services that are inferior and even harmful. The cigarette industry provides a flagrant example. Critics of the industry point out that in the United States alone smoking contributes to the death of more than four hundred thousand people each year. Yet, despite this constant loss of loyal customers, the industry continues to flourish. By using clever advertising techniques to lure young people into smoking, by relying on the addictive nature of nicotine to maintain the existing consumer base, and by expanding markets to targeted groups at home and abroad, tobacco companies have been able to continue to extract high profits from a product whose promotion (if not sale) defies just about every standard of ethical behavior.

This extreme example shows that clients and customers do not always come first on managers' list of stakeholders. In some cases, the pursuit of profits—with little or no ethical justification—leads managers to ignore customers' claims. In other cases, even morally responsible managers find themselves subordinating customers' needs. Duties to shareholders, superiors, employees, suppliers, or communities may lead managers to engage in questionable sales practices or to compromise product quality or service in ways that harm customers. As a stakeholder group, consumers pose a number of ethical questions for managers. What moral claims or rights do they possess? Is "buyer beware" an adequate standard in sales or advertising, or do managers have an obligation to ensure that customers receive all the information they need to make informed purchasing decisions? To what extent is a firm responsible for the quality of its products? How much must it strive to minimize the harms they cause? And, when a firm's products have injured people, what are its obligations to correct or compensate for the harm that has been done?

REACTING TO CRISIS: THE 1982 TYLENOL POISONING EPISODE

✦

Johnson & Johnson's handling of the Tylenol poisoning episode illustrates an apparently successful response to some of these questions in a situation of extreme pressure. When we look closely at the company's handling of this case we can identify some of the considerations managers should bear in mind as they address consumers' needs and interests. In the immediate aftermath of the poisonings Johnson & Johnson's top managers had to make a series of urgent decisions: What should they do about the vast inventory of Tylenol capsules on the shelves? Should they allow this inventory to clear through sales or should they mount a total recall? What about the brand? Many marketing experts believed that the name Tylenol had become synonymous with death. Should McNeil move quickly to introduce a tamper-resistant line of acetaminophen under a different brand name? Should McNeil continue marketing capsules at all? And, throughout the crisis, what stance should

Text continues on page 222

Case 6.1

✦ THE 1982 TYLENOL POISONING EPISODE[1] ✦

*On one day, every single human being in the country thought that
Tylenol might kill them. I don't think there are enough advertising dol-
lars, enough marketing men, to change that. . . . You'll not see the name
Tylenol in any form within a year.*

> Jerry Della Femina, Della Femina Travisana Partners,
> New York advertising agency Chairman,
> (New York Times, 8 October 1982)

In September 1982, seven people died after taking capsules of
Tylenol that had been contaminated with cyanide. In the days following the deaths, the brand's share of the U.S. analgesic market
fell from 37 percent to almost zero. Many marketing experts felt the
brand was damaged beyond repair. As a result of the poisoning,
executives of McNeil Consumer Products, the maker of Tylenol,
and its parent company Johnson & Johnson, faced a series of difficult decisions. To these executives, the fate of an enormously successful brand, the reputation of a century-old company, and even
human lives depended on how well these decisions were made.

COMPANY BACKGROUND

Johnson & Johnson was founded in 1886 as a manufacturer of anti-
septic surgical dressings. Within decades of its founding the company was a major supplier to the professional and hospital market.
Introduction of the Band-Aid brand line of gauze bandages in 1920
established the company in the field of consumer health care products. By 1982 Johnson & Johnson was a diversified, multinational
health care company with over 82,000 employees, 166 operating
companies in 52 countries, and sales of over $5 billion annually. It
was divided into three key operating segments—consumer products, pharmaceuticals, and medical supplies. Major divisions
included Pharmaceuticals, the Domestic Operating Company (consumer health care and beauty products), Ortho Pharmaceutical
(gynecological and contraceptive products), and McNeil Consumer
Products (consumer analgesic products, including Tylenol).

Robert Wood Johnson, who served as president or chairman from 1932 to 1963, is credited with having had a major influence on the development of Johnson & Johnson's distinctive corporate philosophy. General Johnson (who received the title because of his service during the Second World War) was an outspoken advocate of corporate social responsibility who repeatedly took progressive stands on controversial social issues.[2] In the late 1940s, this philosophy was formalized in what came to be known as the "Johnson & Johnson Credo" (see Exhibit 1 for a recent version of the Credo). General Johnson's successor, James Burke, continued and strengthened this emphasis on corporate values. Under his leadership in the late 1970s, a series of "Credo challenge meetings" was held, during which employees and managers were encouraged to raise sharp questions about the actual role of the Credo in the company's decision making. This "Credo challenge process" resulted in an even greater integration of the Credo into the life of the company. By the late 1970s employees were regularly asked to assess their division's leadership on its success in implementing the Credo's tenets. Framed copies of the Credo, in various translations, decorated the walls of many offices and workstations.

GROWTH OF THE TYLENOL FRANCHISE

Until the mid-1970s, aspirin had dominated the market for the nonprescription treatment of pain, inflammation, and fever. Bayer, a brand owned by Sterling Drug, held the largest share of the market. Bayer subsequently lost share to Tylenol, which contains acetaminophen in place of aspirin. This drug is as effective as aspirin in the relief of pain and fever, although it has no antiinflammatory effect and so is not effective in the treatment of conditions such as arthritis. It does not, however, cause the stomach irritation that some users experience with aspirin.

At the end of 1981, sales of over-the-counter (OTC) analgesics were estimated at $1 billion (see Exhibit 2). The market comprised pain relievers containing aspirin (Bufferin, Bayer, Anacin, and private label brands), brands containing acetaminophen (Tylenol, Anacin-3, and Datril), and one (Excedrin) that contained both.

EXHIBIT 1: THE JOHNSON & JOHNSON CREDO

Our Credo

We believe our first responsibility is to the doctors, nurses and patients,
to mothers and fathers and all others who use our products and services.
In meeting their needs everything we do must be of high quality.
We must constantly strive to reduce our costs
in order to maintain reasonable prices.
Customers' orders must be serviced promptly and accurately.
Our suppliers and distributors must have an opportunity
to make a fair profit.

We are responsible to our employees,
the men and women who work with us throughout the world.
Everyone must be considered as an individual.
We must respect their dignity and recognize their merit.
They must have a sense of security in their jobs.
Compensation must be fair and adequate,
and working conditions clean, orderly and safe.
We must be mindful of ways to help our employees fulfill
their family responsibilities.
Employees must feel free to make suggestions and complaints.
There must be equal opportunity for employment, development,
and advancement for those qualified.
We must provide competent management,
and their actions must be just and ethical.

We are responsible to the communities in which we live and work
and to the world community as well.
We must be good citizens – support good works and charities
and bear our fair share of taxes.
We must encourage civic improvements and better health and education.
We must maintain in good order
the property we are privileged to use,
protecting the environment and natural resources.

Our final responsibility is to our stockholders.
Business must make a sound profit.
We must experiment with new ideas.
Research must be carried on, innovative programs developed
and mistakes paid for.
New equipment must be purchased, new facilities provided
and new products launched.
Reserves must be created to provide for adverse times.
When we operate according to these principles,
the stockholders should realize a fair return.

Johnson & Johnson

EXHIBIT 2: THE U.S. ANALGESIC MARKET, 1981*

Company Sales Revenues ($million)

Tylenol	365	(Johnson & Johnson)
Excedrin	115	(Bristol-Myers)
Anacin	110	(American Home Products)
Bufferin	95	(Bristol-Myers)
Bayer Aspirin	95	(Sterling Drug)
Alka Seltzer	70	(Miles Laboratories)
Arthritis Pain Formula	15	(American Home Products)
Anacin-3	10	(American Home Products)
St. Joseph's Aspirin	10	(Schering-Plough)
Datril	6	(Bristol-Myers)
Other (including private label brands)	109	
TOTAL	1000	

*Source: Dean Witter Reynolds

Tylenol dominated the analgesic market. Its share (37 percent) was four times greater than the next most popular brand, Excedrin. No other nonaspirin product had a significant share.

In 1955 McNeil Laboratories, a small marketer of prescription drugs, launched Tylenol Elixir in liquid form as an alternative to aspirin for children. Johnson & Johnson acquired McNeil Laboratories in 1959 and operated it as one of its many health care interests. In 1960 Johnson & Johnson sought and gained approval for nonprescription sale of Tylenol, but did not advertise it directly to consumers. Instead, McNeil's medical representatives promoted a tablet form of the product to physicians, encouraging them to recommend it when patients suffered allergic reactions to ordinary aspirin. The brand grew slowly but steadily under this program of selective endorsement by physicians. By 1974 it held 10 percent of the analgesic market, with sales of $50 million.

In 1975 Tylenol's success prompted a competitor, Bristol-Myers, to launch its own acetaminophen product under the brand name Datril. The Datril marketing program was built on heavy consumer advertising that emphasized price. The campaign showed Datril at $1.85 beside Tylenol at $2.85 with the slogan, "Why spend more?"

Tylenol responded quickly by reducing its price, and effectively negated Datril's claim. Although the Datril threat was contained, it drew Johnson & Johnson's attention to the possibility that the acetaminophen product category would respond to consumer advertising.

A subsidiary, McNeil Consumer Products Co. (MCP), was formed to market the company's nonprescription drugs. A line extension, Extra-Strength Tylenol in tablet and capsule form, was launched with a national consumer advertising campaign. By 1978 the brand's share had risen to 24 percent. The capsule form contributed to the brand's success. It was easier to swallow than the tablet and seemed to signify potency to consumers. Marketing research had previously shown that many potential consumers regarded Tylenol as somewhat weaker than aspirin. One third of 1982's unit sales were in capsule form.

By 1982 Tylenol had become the largest single brand in the history of health and beauty aids. It was used by 100 million Americans. Worldwide factory sales approached $500 million. A cold remedy named Co-Tylenol had captured 6 percent of the cough/cold market, and a sinus remedy had been launched. It was Johnson & Johnson's most important brand name, contributing 8 percent to sales and 16 to 18 percent to net profit.

Advertising support for Tylenol ran at $40 million in 1982, some 30 percent of all analgesic advertising. Two campaign messages were used. The first, termed the hospital campaign, employed testimonials from people who had been given Tylenol in the hospital and had grown to trust it. The copy concluded, "Trust Tylenol—hospitals do." This element of the campaign received about half the advertising budget. The other half was spent on the Extra-Strength campaign, which used a hidden camera approach. A subject was shown describing a headache, learning about Tylenol, finding it to be effective, and deciding to use it again. Each execution of this theme ended with the slogan, "the most potent pain reliever you can buy without a prescription."

THE CRISIS

On September 30, 1982, James Burke was called out of a morning business meeting to learn of reports that three people in Chicago had died the previous day after taking Tylenol capsules. It took several days more for the scope of the disaster to become clear. Seven people in two Chicago suburbs had died after consuming cyanide that had been inserted into capsules of Tylenol after they had left the factory. It seemed very probable that the problem was confined to one geographic area, that the motive was malicious, and that no blame would attach to the company.

To the public, however, the facts were clouded by rumor and conjecture. Reports (later proved false) implicated Tylenol in deaths in Texas, Pennsylvania, California, Tennessee, and Kansas. Eye drops contaminated with sulfuric acid were reported in California. Many towns and suburbs called off Halloween celebrations for fear of copycat poisoning of trick-or-treat candy. With over 100 million users of Tylenol in the USA, alarm and concern were widespread. The incident was on its way to becoming the most widely reported event since the attempt to assassinate President Reagan a year before.

Marketing experts, polled by the press in the weeks after the deaths, generally agreed that the incident threatened the survival of the brand (see Exhibit 3). Analogies were drawn to Procter and Gamble's experience with Rely tampons, the Firestone 500 tire recall, and the DC-10, Pinto, and Corvair incidents.[3] Few commentators gave the Tylenol name much prospect of recovery.

MANAGEMENT'S RESPONSE

(1) Immediate Postcrisis Actions

The week following the first news of the poisonings was a time of intense activity within both MCP and Johnson & Johnson. In that first week the company issued a worldwide alert to the medical community, set up a 24-hour toll free telephone line, recalled and analyzed sample batches of the product from around the country, briefed the Food and Drug Administration, and publicized a $110,000 reward offer. At the same time the company identified issues in brand policy that, they felt, had to be resolved within a week or two because they determined other choices. Should MCP mount a full product withdrawal or just recall vulnerable batches? If withdrawal, should it plan to return under the Tylenol name or

EXHIBIT 3: COMMENTS BY MARKETING EXPERTS IN THE TWO MONTHS FOLLOWING THE TYLENOL POISONINGS

A flat prediction I'll make is that you will not see the name Tylenol in any form within a year. . . . I don't think they can ever sell another product under that name.

> Jerry Della Femina, Chairman, Della Femina Travisana Partners,
> New York advertising agency (New York Times, 8 October 1982)

Militating against Tylenol is the matter of alternatives. Here you have quite a few alternatives in brands.

> Stephen Greyser, Harvard Business School
> (New York Times, 8 October 1982)

George Fisk, a marketing professor at Syracuse University, feels that the Tylenol brand is irreparably harmed. ". . . death is a strong stimulus."

> (New York Times, 8 October 1982)

I think they might be wise to bring out a product to cannibalize Tylenol before competitors do.

> Ben Lipstein, New York University
> (New York Times, 8 October 1982)

There will be a lot of people who won't touch it with a 10-foot pole. . . . It's just like [Rely] Tampons, some people will never go back to them.

> Buyer for a midwestern dry store chain
> (Business Week, 18 October 1982)

When a brand name is so tarred and feathered, it is difficult or impossible to ever separate the two in consumers' minds.

> David W. Flegal, Oxtoby-Smith,
> New York research and consulting firm
> (U.S. News & World Report, 8 November 1982)

The brand has suffered a mortal wound.

> Ben Lipstein, New York University
> (U.S. News & World Report, 8 November 1982)

Many less expensive brands of acetaminophen are becoming more heavily promoted now that the seemingly impenetrable wall surrounding the Tylenol image has been shattered.

> Larry N. Feinberg, Dean Witter Reynolds
> (New York Times, 17 November 1982)

under a new brand name? Should the capsule be abandoned? Should the distinctive red and white color be changed? What should be done about advertising?

Under Burke's leadership, two independent teams were set up to work in parallel to tackle these decisions. One team comprised five senior Johnson & Johnson officers, including Burke. This team met twice daily at 8 A.M. and 6 P.M. in Burke's office. Meetings sometimes continued throughout the day and night. The second team was made up of five members of the MCP marketing staff. To explore how the crisis might unfold, each team constructed hypothetical scenarios of the future. In the first week, over 150 scenarios were debated.

Many of the scenarios supported the idea of a voluntary withdrawal of all Extra-Strength Tylenol capsules. This would prevent copycat poisonings, protect the public from unanticipated poisoned batches, and—if the product was ever to recover—allow a clean start. On the other hand, the company risked the loss of shelf space to competitors and faced a substantial loss of sales. In each of the management committees, three members voted for withdrawal and two voted against. On October 5, therefore, MCP began repurchasing all trade stocks of Tylenol capsules—31 million bottles with a retail value of $100 million.

The scenario analyses also suggested immediate cessation of all advertising, with communication to the public to be handled by Johnson & Johnson's corporate public relations staff. From the outset the decision was made to share information freely with the press and to be as open as possible in communication with the public.

MCP hired a marketing research firm to track attitudes among consumers of analgesics. One thousand people were screened weekly, at a cost of $40,000 per week. In addition, the Scantrack organization monitored supermarket sales of analgesics in four U.S. markets. The bill for market research for the fourth quarter of 1982 was $1.5 million.

The first market research report, received two weeks after the poisonings, was encouraging. Although awareness of the poisonings was almost universal among analgesic users, they appeared to understand that the problem was confined to capsules, and that no blame attached to the maker:

Knowledge of Tylenol tragedy	95%
Problem involves Tylenol capsules only	90%
Problem could occur for any capsules	93%
Maker not to blame	90%

This result encouraged management to mount its return to the acetaminophen market under the Tylenol name. By the end of the second week, the recovery campaign was under way.

(2) The Recovery Campaign Begins

Management decided that the main element of the recovery would be the reintroduction of Tylenol capsules in some form of tamper-resistant/tamper-evident packaging. However, an interim plan would be needed to protect the brand's franchise while the new package was being developed and the capsules were absent from supermarket shelves. Research indicated that about half of all Tylenol consumers had thrown their capsules away in the wake of the poisonings. These consumers would soon be reentering the market. In the past there had been no reason for them to seek other brands of acetaminophen, but their loyalty could not be relied upon any longer. Management chose a two-part plan to sustain the franchise during this interim period.

The first element of the program was a capsule exchange offer. On October 12, half-page press announcements appeared in 150 major markets across the country that read, "We want you to replace your Tylenol capsules with Tylenol tablets. And we'll help you do it at our expense." The public was invited to mail in bottles of capsules and receive tablets in exchange. Consumer response, however, was poor.

The second component was a brief but intensive television announcement that ran from October 24 to October 28. Management instructed Compton Advertising to meet the following communication goals for the announcement:

Strategy: To convince Tylenol users that they can continue to trust in the safety of Tylenol products and, secondarily, to encourage use of the tablet dosage form until tamper-resistant packaging is available for the capsules.

Support: (1) Localized nature of the tampering incidents,
           (2) Tylenol's heritage of consumer/physician
               confidence,
           (3) voluntary capsule withdrawal,
           (4) tablets not implicated.

The company chose Dr. Thomas N. Gates, the company's medical director, to deliver the message because he rated well on credibility in pretesting. Exhibit 4 records the copy that was selected to achieve the communication goals. It was tested for comprehension and for persuasiveness on previous Tylenol users recruited in shopping malls. Management set very high reach and frequency targets for the announcement. They wanted 85 percent of the market to view the advertisement four times in the four days it ran.

Competitors responded carefully to Tylenol's setback. On one hand, analgesic advertising expenditure rose significantly in the final quarter of 1982. Despite Tylenol's withdrawal of regular advertising, the industry spent 50 percent more during that quarter than during the previous one. None of Tylenol's competitors changed its advertising copy, however. Yale marketing professor Stephen Permut commented to the press, "If you're the competitor to the Titanic when it goes down, what are the right things to say about your ships without being viewed as unfair and in bad taste?" George X. Gikas, a Rockville, Maryland, marketing consultant, said of the competitors, "They were caught off guard. If a strong No. 2 brand had existed, it would have captured the market." The industry seemed to subscribe to the sentiments expressed by a spokesman for American Home Products (maker of Anacin-3) who said his company would not "capitalize unfairly on the misfortunes of competitors" and would not change normal promotional methods. One manufacturer expressed the fear that advertising might invite copycat tampering of his product.

(3) Second Stage of the Recovery Plan: Tamper-Resistant Packaging

As one part of its recovery program, Johnson & Johnson took the lead in coordinating industry and government efforts to develop new standards for tamper-resistant/tamper-evident packaging. A massive effort was involved in establishing these standards and, at

EXHIBIT 4: COPY USED IN CORPORATE SPOKESPERSON CAMPAIGN

You're all aware of recent tragic events in which Extra Strength Tylenol capsules were criminally tampered with in limited areas after they left our factory. This act damages all of us—you the American public because you have made Tylenol a trusted part of your healthcare and we who make Tylenol because we've worked hard to earn that trust. We will now work even harder to keep it. We have voluntarily withdrawn all Tylenol Capsules from the shelf. We will reintroduce capsules in tamper-resistant containers as quickly as possible. Until then, we urge all Tylenol capsule users to use the tablet form and we have offered to replace your capsules with tablets. Tylenol has had the trust of the medical profession and 100 million Americans for over 20 years. We value that trust too much to let any individual tamper with it. We want you to continue to trust Tylenol.

MCP, in readying production of the new packaging. Six weeks after the poisonings, management announced the return of Tylenol capsules to the market in a new triple-seal pack. The announcement was made with a splash. On November 11, James Burke spoke live at a satellite-linked teleconference to 600 news reporters throughout the United States. His announcement of the triple-sealed capsule pack was carried by news media throughout the country.

The effect of this announcement was monitored carefully by MCP. A custom-designed telephone survey over the next five days reported that 79 percent of Tylenol users were aware of the new packaging and that 72 percent could name one or more specific elements of the packaging. The regular marketing tracking study on November 21 found that 73 percent of Tylenol users had heard of the new packaging and that 95 percent of Extra-Strength Capsule users would buy Extra-Strength Capsules in tamper-resistant packaging.

The goal now was to get consumers to try the new capsule packaging. Management debated several methods of building trial: samples in homes, sampling in stores, and couponing by mail or in magazines or newspapers. Coupons redeemable in stores were considerably more expensive than home-delivered samples, because a full retail margin had to be paid on each redemption. They did, however, ensure that retailers would carry shelf stocks and that consumers would have to make some act of commitment to the brand to secure their sample.

Management therefore launched the largest program of couponing in commercial history. The first wave, on November 28, used Sunday newspapers nationwide to distribute sixty million coupons for a free Tylenol product to a limit of $2.50 each. Another twenty million coupons were offered the following Sunday. Samples distributed in this way began to appear in the company's audits of retail sales in four test cities. Share at retail rose by more than ten share points to within six points of predisaster levels.

(4) Return to Advertising

At the end of December 1982, the only television advertising for Tylenol in the three months since the poisonings had been the four-day announcement featuring Dr. Gates. Although couponing was proving very successful in returning previous users of Tylenol to the brand, it was extremely expensive. By December redemption stood at 30 percent of all coupons issued, which generated a charge of $45 million to the brand's budget. In all, it was estimated that up to that point the direct cost of recovery efforts had been about $150 million. Conditions were now stable enough to allow a return to regular advertising support. A month before, Compton Advertising, Inc., had been briefed to develop advertising with the goal:

> To convince Tylenol users that they could continue to use Tylenol with confidence through the testimony of loyal Tylenol users.

As 1982 came to an end, the immediate crisis had been surmounted and MCP and Johnson & Johnson management met to discuss a strategy to return Tylenol to profitability. One year later, the success of their efforts would be clear. In a remarkable recovery, sales of Tylenol were to meet and then exceed their prepoisoning levels.

QUESTIONS TO CONSIDER

1. What are some of the main ethical decisions that Johnson & Johnson executives faced in the wake of the poisoning episode?
2. How would you evaluate Johnson & Johnson's handling of these decisions?
3. What role do you think Johnson & Johnson's "Credo" played in the company's response?

Johnson & Johnson take vis-à-vis media and other public interest groups clamoring for information? Although hindsight makes it appear that the answers to these questions were obvious, they didn't seem so at the time.

The recall decision illustrates this point. The advantages of a total recall were clear: it would remove any remaining tainted product from the shelves and eliminate an invitation to copycat poisonings. This would buy time for the company to fashion its response to the crisis. But there were also some powerful arguments against this strategy. The cost would be enormous—over $100 million. Potentially more important in the long term than the immediate cost was the threatened loss of shelf space. The over-the-counter analgesic business is intensely competitive, with success or failure often measured in the number of inches of space a firm enjoys on a crowded supermarket or pharmacy shelf. Recalling the capsules would forfeit this space to competitors who could then make permanent inroads on Tylenol's market share.

A powerful argument could also be made for refusing to recall the product. Since it was soon determined that the poisoning had been the result of tampering that occurred after the product had left the factory, Johnson & Johnson's management knew that *they* had done nothing to jeopardize consumers. They had manufactured and distributed a product they knew to be safe. Any harm that had resulted had been someone else's doing. Tylenol, Johnson & Johnson, and the whole drug distribution network had also become targets of a form of consumer terrorism. For whatever reason, the person or persons who tampered with the product threatened America's complex system of over-the-counter merchandising. If a company like Johnson & Johnson yielded to this kind of intimidation, where would it stop? During meetings following the disaster, this argument was made to James Burke by William Webster, head of the FBI.[4] Fearing that Halloween would provide an occasion for related forms of product tampering and poisoning, Webster urged Burke not to order a total recall in order to prevent encouragement to those seeking to intimidate other firms and the public by terroristic acts.

That two out of five persons on each of Johnson & Johnson's crisis management committees voted against a total recall shows that these counterarguments carried a good deal of weight. Nevertheless, we can see the moral and business logic in the company's final decision. First, there is the obvious matter of the threat to human life. As long as vulnerable packages of Tylenol capsules remained on the shelves, they invited tampering. True, any deaths that resulted would not directly be Johnson & Johnson's doing. But the company would justifiably be blamed. It is not hard to see that, where life is concerned, anyone who knowingly and unnecessarily creates something that becomes a threat to life bears some responsibility if death occurs. The emphasis here is on the word *unnecessarily*. Many companies manufacture products that threaten human life. Some products are inherently subject to abuse—sharp kitchen knives and caustic drain cleaners are examples of these. Other products, including experimental drugs, are risky in normal use. But in these cases, we assume there is no adequate way for manufacturers to avoid the prospect of injury while still making the product available and meeting legitimate consumer demand. None of this applies to the continued marketing of unsafely packaged Tylenol capsules. Johnson & Johnson would be rightly faulted if any further deaths occurred as a result of their failing to withdraw a still vulnerable product.

Nor does the mammoth cost of a total withdrawal appear to justify such a decision. We can see this if we look at the matter from the perspective of *Neutral, Omnipartial Rule-Making*. Imagine the following proposed moral rule:

✦

Proposed Moral Rule: Whenever needed to avoid major economic losses, a large corporation may knowingly produce and market a product that will needlessly cause death or injury to some unwitting customers.

✦

This rule obviously has a great deal against it. In a world where it prevailed, people who did not consent to a product's risks would find themselves mortally jeopardized by products or processes they believed to be safe. This rule is also a license for corporate negligence, since companies would have less incentive to reduce the dangers of their products. It is true, of course, that, in order to keep costs down, companies sometimes manufacture products that are less safe than they might be. For example, autos could be made far more crash resistant at some significant increase in their cost of manufacture or by reducing their fuel economy. But these cost-saving decisions are different from the one specified by this proposed moral rule because they allow consumers themselves to decide whether and how much they wish to trade off safety for expense. Since we cherish personal freedom, we ordinarily permit people to make their own informed decisions about such things. Free and informed decision making is crucial here. During periods in their history when the auto firms were less competitive and collectively resisted consumer demands for attention to safety, they were often properly blamed for sacrificing lives to profits. As the industry becomes more competitive and offers a genuine choice, we increasingly hold consumers responsible for the consequences of their decisions in this area. But none of this is relevant to Johnson & Johnson's decision. Outside of the unimaginable prospect of a "fire sale" of potentially tainted product, consumers would be unable to engage in trade-off decisions of this sort. Anyone who inadvertently consumed poisoned Tylenol would be regarded as the unwitting victim of a unilateral cost-saving decision by the company. Johnson & Johnson would be seen as acting on a moral rule like the one we just rejected, and its conduct would rightly be condemned.

The argument that Johnson & Johnson must not yield to terrorism raises a separate and intriguing issue. That our thinking about terrorism so often focuses on the *practices* or *precedents* established by our response is a sign that **NORM** taps into a basic mode of our thinking about moral choices. Indeed, we can think of those who counsel resistance to terrorist demands as considering and then *rejecting* something like the following proposed moral rule:

✦

Proposed Moral Rule: When a terrorist or group of terrorists demands money or concessions as the price of preventing them from harming or killing persons under their control, these demands may be met.

✦

We can understand why this proposed moral rule is normally unacceptable if we look at it closely. Although there is one important argument in its favor—the possibility of saving human life—there is a major argument against it. When regarded as an item of "furniture" in our moral environment, as a policy of which everyone is aware and to which they will predictably conform their behavior, this rule can be a major encouragement to future terrorist acts. Like so many other initially appealing but inadequate proposals, it defeats its own purpose. In a world where innocent people become lucrative objects of barter, we can expect terrorism to increase. Lives immediately saved will be offset by casualties as new victims abound. Small wonder, then, that governments frequently refuse to bargain with terrorists even though this policy sometimes places identifiable hostages in peril.

Is our conclusion about this proposed moral rule applicable to Johnson & Johnson's recall decision? Not really. We can see that a major reason for not yielding to terrorism is to avoid encouraging future acts of terrorism. But this factor may not be as important in the situation faced by Johnson & Johnson. If we assume that a small number of persons possess a pathological desire to inflict damage on one or more large corporations, then some of these individuals may be encouraged to repeat terroristic acts if they know that poisoning a product will force companies like Johnson & Johnson to mount costly recalls. But it is an oddity of this case that *refusing* to withdraw capsules might provide a second kind of encouragement to these individuals since the company will also be severely damaged if deaths occur. One way or the other the terrorists will "win." Our reasoning seems finely balanced between these two equally unacceptable outcomes, but several other considerations tip the balance toward a recall. By withdrawing the product, the company can immediately save lives while reducing the force of this second encouragement effect. Furthermore, some who engage in terrorism are motivated not primarily by a desire to damage corporations but by a wish to kill or harm other people. These persons will be discouraged from such conduct if companies promptly withdraw a tainted product. All this suggests that, on close analysis, the antiterrorism argument here works *for* rather than *against* a total recall.

Deciding how to respond to terrorist demands poses some of the most acute challenges to our skills of moral reasoning. Different cases and novel circumstances often make it necessary to qualify the "no bargaining" rule. We will return to the issue of terrorism below, when we examine Johnson & Johnson's public relations efforts on behalf of

Tylenol. For now, it is worth repeating how important it is to analyze complex issues carefully and with a sound theoretical approach. The advantage of reducing moral decisions to the rules implicit within them is that we can thereby identify hidden assumptions and closely assess every implication of our choice.

With the urgent recall decision behind them, Johnson & Johnson's executives had to face a longer-term decision about the brand itself. Would it be wise, as most experts suggested, to make a clean break with the past and use the occasion of a new packaging initiative to introduce a new brand name, perhaps one with its own distinctive colors and logo? Good reasons can be found for and against this course of action. On the side of change was the argument that in the minds of many consumers the name "Tylenol" had come to assume overwhelmingly negative connotations. In the words of one commentator, "death is a strong stimulus." Arguing against change was the fact that Johnson & Johnson had built up enormous "brand equity" in the Tylenol name. It might take years to rebuild a new brand to this level of consumer loyalty.

Putting matters this way makes it appear that this decision rests primarily on the outcome of careful marketing research. Would research show that the continued value of brand recognition and loyalty offset the negative connotations the brand had acquired? But approaching matters this way ignores some very important *moral* issues which, in turn, have a bearing on marketing the product. Not only may scrapping Tylenol underestimate consumer ability to make sound moral judgments about the meaning of the poisoning episode for Tylenol, but the introduction of acetaminophen under a new brand name may signal disrespect for consumers' intelligence.

Some marketing specialists who counseled Johnson & Johnson to abandon Tylenol likened the brand to other defective and lethal products: the Firestone 500 tire that was rendered hazardous by a design defect or Proctor and Gamble's Rely tampon, whose materials and design contributed to toxic shock syndrome. The characteristic feature of these products was that, to one degree or another, their manufacturers were seen to be responsible for developing a defective product and then continuing to sell it after the defects became known. In these cases, consumer confidence in the brand and the company behind it was shattered, and it would have been very hard for the company to relaunch the brand without incurring consumer resistance. But this was not true of Tylenol. Common sense—borne out by Johnson & Johnson's own extensive marketing research—suggests that consumers were able to see that the company had made a good-faith effort to manufacture and distribute a safe product. Unlike the manufacturers of defective products, Johnson & Johnson knew that its efforts to relaunch the brand would not be regarded with suspicion from the outset. The public might be willing to give Tylenol a second chance.

Even more pertinent is the fact that any effort to introduce a line of acetaminophen under a different brand name might generate the kind of suspicion and mistrust that Johnson & Johnson could not afford. To understand this, it helps to keep in mind that human activities convey meanings in subtle ways. By introducing a new line of acetaminophen, Johnson & Johnson would be sending two implicit and interrelated messages: that its previous Tylenol had somehow been defective and that its new product was free of this defect. Both implicit messages create problems for the company. The first message is neither necessary, nor true, and sending it, for whatever reason, could only damage consumer confidence in Johnson & Johnson by implicating the company in the Tylenol deaths. The second message, that the replacement product is "new," is also not true. It might be argued that introduction of tamper-resistant packaging justifies a new product name. But it is not hard to see that changing the name and appearance of a product normally signals that the product itself, and not merely its container, is new. The implicit message would therefore be misleading.

To follow the marketing "experts" here, in other words, would be to squander the single most powerful asset Johnson & Johnson had at its disposal to recover the brand: consumer trust and confidence. The history of Tylenol shows that from the beginning Johnson & Johnson's marketing strategy had been to draw upon its own respected position in hospital-based health care in order to develop consumer confidence in a new and unfamiliar analgesic product. "Hospitals trust Tylenol" was the theme of a fifteen-year effort that built the brand to its current levels. That trust was now threatened by the acts of others. In the weeks and months ahead, Johnson & Johnson would have to rely on millions of individual acts of trust as people dared to buy and use a product that had recently been lethal. Only the confidence that the product, in its new tamper-resistant form, was as safely manufactured and as safely packaged as such a product can be would lead consumers to make these many individual leaps of faith. Anything Johnson & Johnson did in the interval to damage that trust might sink the brand.

These considerations lead us to a truth central to business ethics where customers and clients are concerned: *Trust is at the heart of this stakeholder relationship.* Every time a consumer purchases a product, he or she invests some measure of trust in the seller of that product—trust that the product or service is accurately described and not misrepresented in any way and that its performance will be as claimed. Whatever firms do to undermine trust thus erodes the foundation of commercial transactions generally. Although there are many ways that a firm can damage trust—for example, by deception or by failing to fulfill its part of the sales bargain—there is one less obvious way often missed by marketing specialists. *Trust can be lost when a company fails to respect or trust consumers.* A firm shows its disrespect for consumers and lack of trust in their good sense and judgment when, in its advertising and public relations, it treats them as unintelligent, gullible, and uninformed. It also shows distrust when it regards customers as opponents who must be manipulated, controlled, and outwitted whenever possible.

In Chapter 5 we saw that trust is a key element in a firm's relationships with its employee stakeholder group. I pointed out that a company that treats its employees as untrustworthy—by spying on them and by suspecting the worst of their behavior—is likely to create the very untrustworthiness it fears. Conversely, a company that trusts employees and respects their judgment and opinions can rely on those who work for it to cooperate with reasonable organizational needs and demands and sometimes go "the extra mile" in times of crisis and stress. Now we are seeing this same dynamic at work where consumers are concerned. Johnson & Johnson's handling of the Tylenol crisis shows that a company that trusts its customers can rely on their trust in return. This episode also shows how valuable such trust can be. In many consumer areas—from drugs to food products to automobiles—franchises worth hundreds of millions of dollars year after year draw their worth from trust in the brand or the company's name. Yet, as valuable and as long-lasting as it can be, consumer trust is a delicate phenomenon. It cannot be taken for granted. It is up for grabs every time a customer reads an ad, opens a can or bottle, or turns the key in the ignition. The Tylenol episode shows that Johnson & Johnson's managers understood this central truth. Ignoring those marketing experts whose expertise appears not to have extended to a perception of the moral dimensions of their craft, they acted quickly and effectively to preserve the trust in Johnson & Johnson and Tylenol that their predecessors had taken decades to build.

The important role trust plays in consumer relationships leads to another observation central to this area of business ethics. Where marketing, sales, and advertising are concerned, good business and good ethics often go together. Because moral beliefs and sentiments play an important role in motivating human behavior, ethical insight and fair treatment of customers are not just an add-on but a major contributor to marketing success.

The statement by Dr. Gates that was aired repeatedly during the opening days of the crisis provides a fascinating illustration of this point. Every feature of this statement conveys the moral messages that management knew were critical to brand recovery. For example, a physician was chosen as spokesman because physicians are trusted members of our society. The Gates announcement emphasizes this theme by using the word "trust" five times in connection with the brand.

Interwoven with these obvious moral messages are other points. The public is told to use Tylenol tablets until repackaged Tylenol becomes available. This offers consumers a safe way of exhibiting brand loyalty while serving the company's economic interests (also served by the massive couponing program) in defining Tylenol as the principal acetaminophen alternative. The announcement takes the opportunity to emphasize that the company is free of blame. The poisoned capsules, Gates makes clear, "were criminally tampered with in limited areas after they left our factory."

Finally, in an even more subtle way, the issue of terrorism is invoked—to the company's advantage. According to Dr. Gates, "This act damages all of us—you the American public because you have made Tylenol a trusted part of your health care and we who make Tylenol because we've worked hard to earn that trust." In a narrow sense, of course, a poisoning episode like this one seems to damage only its immediate victims, consumers who still wish to use the product, and the company that makes it. In what sense, then, is "the American public" as a whole injured, as the announcement suggests? This claim makes sense only if we regard the "criminal acts" perpetrated here as a form of terrorism. Just as airline terrorism often aims at harming not just specific passengers or a carrier but a country or the entire air transport system, so this incident can be viewed as an attack on the freedoms enjoyed by all consumers.

This representation of the Tylenol poisonings as an act of terrorism has two moral implications. First, it further distances the company from culpability in the episode, forging bonds of solidarity and shared vulnerability between the company and consumers. "We are victims in this together." Second, it provides a concrete way for consumers to respond to the moral outrage the poisonings represent: they can buy Tylenol. By encouraging many individual acts of courage in purchasing and using the threatened brand, the Gates announcement offers consumers— even those who have never previously taken Tylenol—an opportunity to resist terrorism. This message was particularly important during the early 1980s, when terrorism had recently become an international threat. By skillfully appealing to people's moral sensitivities, therefore, the announcement enlists powerful moral emotions in the brand's recovery.

Viewing Tylenol's public relations and advertising effort this way makes it appear to be some Machiavellian scheme to manipulate consumers for the company's benefit. But this would badly misconstrue the meaning of an analysis of this sort. Appealing to people's moral instincts does not have to be manipulative. It is so when the appeal is dishonest and insincere. But there is no evidence of that here. The Tylenol poisonings can legitimately be seen as terroristic activity threatening the American consumer system, and indeed were viewed that way by top law enforcement officials. We can fully sympathize with Johnson & Johnson for believing that they had done everything within their power to earn consumers' trust, and for also believing that if consumers were to abandon Tylenol, this would only encourage more such incidents in the future. Like any component of a marketing or sales strategy, appeal to the moral instincts of consumers is morally neutral. Whether it is good or bad depends on whether the claims involved are true and whether they are being used for morally legitimate purposes. There is no evidence that Johnson & Johnson's efforts here were otherwise. Rather, they reflected the company's own convictions about its efforts and the nature of the threat this episode represented.[5]

Uneasiness with the suggestion that moral themes can be used for marketing purposes grows out of a far deeper uncertainty in our reaction to the Tylenol case. The great success of the company's efforts seems to put into question the motivations of those who steered the brand recovery. Had Johnson & Johnson, in the name of consumer safety and without further deliberation, withdrawn the capsules at great expense and at a significant loss of market share, we might have an easier time interpreting the company's actions in moral terms. These actions would then have represented a courageous and sacrificial act on behalf of consumer safety. But financial success makes us less sure. Was this a case of exemplary business ethics, or just good marketing? Was ethics a major component of Johnson & Johnson's decision making, or was it just the "wrapping on the box"?

When approaching these questions, it helps to keep two things in mind. One is that it is very hard to sort out human motivations, and the other is that it is not always necessary to do so. As we saw in Chapter 2, questions of motivation are logically separate from questions of right or wrong conduct. We can judge *conduct* as right or wrong without determining the motivations behind it. An individual or company can sometimes do the right thing for a morally deficient reason (as when a company grudgingly recalls a dangerous product just to avoid lawsuits) or do the wrong thing for a good reason (as when a needed recall is delayed in a misguided effort to cushion the impact on distributors). When morally assessing behavior, we preserve our ability to make more nuanced judgments if we distinguish between people's motives and the concrete ways in which they act. This means that, even if we believe that Johnson & Johnson was driven only by business considerations, we can still say that the firm's *conduct* was exemplary and should be followed by other business corporations.

There is a second, and more important, reason for putting aside the question of motivation in assessing a business decision of this sort. When firms attend to their ethical responsibilities, it is very hard to distinguish conduct that benefits the firm—its investors, managers, and employees—from conduct that is also ethically correct. *As we saw in Chapter 4, managers are ethically responsible for structuring their organizations in ways that facilitate others' ethical decision making and that remove incentives to unethical behavior. It is their responsibility to see to it that the organization upholds moral values, that these values are well known by everyone, and they are continually reinforced by an organizational system of rewards and punishments. In an ethically structured firm, individual moral dilemmas should be at a minimum and there should be less need for moral heroism. In such a firm, morally upright conduct is expected of everyone and composes part of what the company defines as "normal" business behavior. Business strategy will also constantly reflect and incorporate stakeholder concerns. To the extent that, over the long term, this way of structuring a company will attract the support of customers and investors, good ethics will also be good business.*

We can see that this description of an ethically structured firm applies to Johnson & Johnson. Over the years, partly as a result of a business strategy and partly as a reflection of the character of the people who led the company, Johnson & Johnson became firmly wedded to the series of stakeholder commitments that the Credo represents. These had been integrated into the life of the company via the "challenge process," reward systems, and training programs. As a result, the Credo became a live document and not merely words pasted on a wall. It provided a set of priorities to guide managers through the poisoning episode. The fact that the Credo begins with a commitment to those "who use our products," and only later mentions profitability to the extent that it is consistent with this and other goals, establishes an order that informed Johnson & Johnson's managers as they approached the decisions facing them. The Credo also imposed a powerful negative constraint on senior managers. Having pledged the company to the primacy of its customers' welfare, they could hardly turn around in the midst of a crisis and renege on this commitment. Johnson & Johnson's response to the Tylenol episode was thus the outcome of several different factors, including a corporate commitment to the ethical treatment of customers as well as shrewd marketing that partly reflected and partly reinforced this stakeholder emphasis. That the company's voice—in Dr. Gates's announcement—reverberates with ethical convictions is not accidental. It reflects the way Johnson & Johnson's management and employees had come to think.

Some might argue that although this interweaving of ethics and marketing makes sense in the health care industry because those firms are especially vulnerable to anything that threatens their reputation for integrity, it is less applicable to companies in other industries. But this ignores the fact that the basic lessons illustrated by the Tylenol episode are being repeated in a range of industries and business sectors. Product quality and attention to consumers are now widely recognized as contributing to the competitive advantage of highly successful companies in a variety of industries.[6] In the recent past, too, product defects and breaches of consumer confidence have threatened the survival of established automobile, airline, financial service, and manufacturing firms. Speaking of the Tylenol episode, James Burke once called the attention given to it a "tragedy" because behavior that should be normal was regarded as exceptional and exemplary. This public attitude may be changing as the need to retain consumer confidence increasingly becomes a part of conventional business wisdom.

Case 6.2

✦ PINNING BLAME[7] ✦

The Alton Club in Louisville, Kentucky, is not the kind of place where people raise their voices. A genteel watering hole for the city's business and professional leaders, its loudest conversations usually revolve around one sports topics or another. But today, at a corner table in the bar, William Connor, a local attorney, and Stephen Tierney, a school administrator, were in the midst of a heated argument. Connor and Tierney were not alone in having strong feelings. A year before, Louisville—and the nation—had been shaken by an accident whose repercussions were only now beginning to work their way through the legal system

At 11 P.M. on Saturday, May 14, 1988, twenty-five young people and two adults were killed on Interstate 71 when the church-owned school bus in which they were riding was hit, head on, by a pickup truck driven by a thirty-four-year-old man who was probably intoxicated. Witnesses later testified that the pickup driver had been tailgating a tractor-trailer on the northbound lane of the highway and had been seen making unauthorized U-turns on the interstate. At the time of the crash, he was driving north in the southbound lane at nearly seventy miles an hour. When he struck the school bus, the gas tank in the bus ruptured and caught fire. The twenty-seven deaths were from smoke inhalation, a result of the fire. A number of other youngsters on the bus were injured. The pickup driver had one previous drunk-driving arrest and conviction. He survived the accident and was charged with twenty-seven counts of murder. The driver of the bus, a church official, died in the collision.

At the time of the accident, the bus was headed back to Radcliff, Kentucky, after an all-day excursion to Kings Island, an amusement park north of Cincinnati. The round-trip distance from Radcliff to Kings Island was 320 miles. The bus was typical of the nearly 350,000 school buses on the nation's roads. It was designed to carry students to and from schools, and not of the type commonly used by commercial passenger carriers for long distance, interstate travel. It had been manufactured in early 1977 by Ford Motor Company and Sheller Globe Corporation (Ford made the chassis and Sheller Globe the body). The Meade County public schools had owned the bus until 1987, when it was sold to the First Assembly of God in Radcliff.

In April 1977, shortly after the bus was manufactured, new federal regulations governing school bus safety had gone into effect. These regulations required, among other things, that all school bus gasoline tanks be protected by a crash-resistant steel cage and that all fuel lines be of metal tubing rather than flexible hose. The regulations, however, applied only to buses manufactured after that date. In 1984 Congress had passed the Motor Carrier Safety Act, which imposed stricter design and performance standards on all private bus carriers, but at the time of the Kentucky accident the Department of Transportation had still not worked out the regulations needed to implement the act.

The bus's sixty-gallon gasoline tank was located under the right side of the bus, just behind the main passenger entrance. It had been filled shortly before the accident. Following the collision, investigators found that the tank had been gashed in the front and pushed about two feet to the rear.

On July 9, 1988, an Associated Press story printed in the *Louisville Courier-Journal* reported that out-of-court settlements amounting to $700,000 per death and $63,000 for each of those injured had been offered by Ford and Sheller Globe to the families of those involved in the accident. Although sixty-four of the sixty-seven families involved had accepted, several felt the offers were too low. One family of a death victim had proposed a $1 settlement, provided that Ford recall and modify its older school buses. It was the settlement offer in this story that had triggered the argument between Connor and Tierney:

Connor: I can't believe that Ford and Sheller Globe would cave in on this one. This is a sign of how crazy liability law has gotten in this country. Look, I agree that the kids and their families got a raw deal. But that's no excuse for blaming innocent people. By settling this thing out of court, Ford and Sheller Globe are encouraging the crazy kinds of lawsuits—from two-bit nuisance suits to some of these wild "class actions"—that are part of the feeding frenzy of unnecessary litigation that's hurting this country.

Tierney: Innocent people? Bill, you've got to be kidding. Ford and Sheller Globe made a bus that wasn't safe. The kids got killed or burned. Who should bear the financial burden of this tragedy? A bunch of injured teenage victims and mourning families, or two huge companies whose product wasn't up to standards?

Connor: Steve, now you're talking law, and I'm the lawyer here. Let's look at the facts. This bus was manufactured in 1977, before new federal regs went into effect. At the time that Ford and Sheller Globe put this bus on the road, it met every federal requirement—*every federal requirement*. Are we going to punish them because the law was changed after that? That seems to me like a violation of the Constitution. Article I, Section 9 of the U.S. Constitution says that you can't pass an ex post facto law. By punishing a company for violating laws passed at a later time, we're doing just that. Beyond this, the accident took place eleven years after the bus was built! How long are you going to hold a company responsible? No, Steve, there *are* some guilty parties in this tragedy. The church shouldn't have been busing kids all over creation in a vehicle made for country roads. And, of course, that drunk driver deserves to fry. But Ford and Sheller Globe didn't do anything wrong. At least not until they agreed to settle this mess. This may get them off the hook and avoid some crazy jury's loading them down with even stiffer penalties. But they did every other manufacturer a disservice by caving in to the mentality that when something goes wrong, the guys with the "deepest pockets" should pay for it. With that way of thinking, there won't be any deep pockets for long.

Tierney: You make a good case, Bill. But I don't see why—even if everything you say is true—Ford and Sheller Globe shouldn't pay up. Someone's got to meet the costs of this accident, and I don't think it should be the families and survivors. The companies carry insurance for this. What's wrong with making them pay? It might even encourage them to make safer buses in the future.

Connor: What's wrong, Steve, is that it's not fair. It's not just. Michael Jackson may be able to pay, too. But he had nothing to do with the accident and it would be a moral outrage if we forced him to subsidize the victims. I'm saying that it's no less an outrage to ask two responsible manufacturers to shoulder the bill for someone else's misfortune. You know, if you're looking for someone to blame, how about the school district that sold that church the bus? How about the government, which didn't pass the right regulations in time? Or the Department of Transportation that failed to implement them? There's plenty of blame to go around here. But I don't see that any of it should be foisted off on Ford and Sheller Globe.

Tierney: I don't know, Bill. I just don't know.

QUESTIONS TO CONSIDER

1. With whom do you side in this debate? Do you agree with William Connor that Ford and Sheller Globe did nothing wrong, or is Stephen Tierney right to believe the companies should be held ethically and legally responsible?

2. How does **NORM** evaluate the implicit rules on which Ford and Sheller Globe acted?

CORPORATE RESPONSIBILITY FOR PRODUCT SAFETY

♦

Over the past two decades a series of legal cases and public controversies has focused attention on the question of a company's responsibilities to consumers for the safety and reliability of its products. Many of these cases have been in the health care and pharmaceutical fields: the deformities and illness experienced by the daughters of women who took the drug DES early in pregnancy[8]; A. H. Robins's disastrous experience with the Dalkon Shield intrauterine device[9]; and, more recently, the controversy surrounding the safety of silicone breast implants.[10] Product safety issues have also caused major legal battles in other industries, including Ford's experience with the Pinto automobile and the unprecedented financial liabilities incurred by Johns-Manville as a result of its mining and sale of asbestos. Although tobacco companies have so far largely escaped legal liability for the harms caused by their products, the industry's continuing high profitability is now threatened by a wave of lawsuits working their way through the courts and by taxing proposals inspired by the health risks created by smoking.

These and a host of less publicized cases raise a series of puzzling questions in ethics and law. What are the extent and limits of a company's responsibilities for the safety of its products? How safe must a product be? May a company ever make and sell a product that it knows to be less than completely safe? Or should its commitment to—and liability for—product safety be absolute? How do changing standards and expectations bear on a manufacturer's responsibilities? Is it enough for a company to do its best—in terms of available information, regulations, and laws—to design and manufacture a safe product? Or must it also bear responsibility for problems that crop up later, whether as a result of field experience, new scientific information, or changing expectations and laws? What are a company's safety obligations when a product's defects become known after it has left the factory and gone into widespread use? May the company assume that the product's current owners can address the problem, should it make reasonable efforts to warn them, or must it actively seek out all who own or use the product and persuade them to correct the problem? Who should pay for repairs or upgrades, the product's owner or the company? And, how responsible is a company for others' misuse or abuse of a product? For example, does this responsibility extend to others' criminal use of the product?

In varying degrees, these questions are raised by all of the major product safety cases that have drawn public attention. We have already touched on these issues by looking at the successful example of Johnson & Johnson's handling of Tylenol. The same issues, in a different form, lie behind William Connor's and Stephen Tierney's argument over moral and legal responsibilities in the Kentucky school bus case.

Once more, the law furnishes a good way of getting into the deeper moral issues raised by this and other product safety cases. Although product safety and liability law does not necessarily identify all the ethical obligations we might wish to recognize in this area, it does raise many of them, and the evolution of the law on this topic sheds light on corporate and managerial ethical responsibilities in this area.

Bill Connor contends that Ford and Sheller Globe should not be held legally responsible for compensating the accident victims or their families, and that any effort to make them responsible would be an inappropriate use of the law. Is he right? To answer this question, it helps to see that over the years product safety law has undergone considerable change and that it continues to evolve. Court decisions in the area of "tort" law (that part of the civil law dealing with "wrongs" between persons) have charted a course through several distinct approaches or "theories" of liability. These theories have tended to emerge in sequence, but traces of each theory can be found throughout legal history right up to the present.

One theory is the doctrine of *caveat emptor*, or "buyer beware." This rule places responsibility for product safety on the purchaser, who must take steps to see that a product meets standards of acceptability and safety. If a product proves defective or harmful, the buyer ordinarily bears the burden. Caveat emptor made sense in the earliest days of legal development, when technology was simple and manufacturers and buyers were on an equal footing to evaluate a product's features. But as these realities changed, this approach quickly came to be supplemented by others that placed more responsibility on sellers of products.

A second approach rested on basic common-law conceptions of *negligence*. Under this theory, manufacturers or retailers of products were held liable if they failed to take "reasonable care" in the preparation of their products for market. For example, an automobile manufacturer who failed to test steering components adequately might be held responsible for injuries and financial costs suffered by someone whose car crashed as a result of a steering failure.

Earlier in this century, the negligence approach came under criticism for a number of reasons. Some criticisms were narrowly legal. For example, at that time negligence law prevented recovery of damages from a manufacturer when the victim had not bought the product directly from the manufacturer. As the sales-distribution system became more complex, with retailers, dealers, and middlemen becoming the major marketing agents for products, this requirement of "privity" was seen as too restrictive. It was eventually modified so that manufacturers tended to be held responsible no matter who finally sold the product.

A more serious problem appeared as it became evident that the financial, legal, and technical imbalances between consumers and manufacturers often made it very difficult for victims in product injury cases to prove that the manufacturer had in some way been negligent in preparing the product for market. For example, if a manufacturer had followed industry standards, this provided a defense against claims of negligence, even though those standards may have been deficient. In such cases, it was often difficult for individual consumers to prove that a widely accepted standard was inadequate.

To address this problem, legal scholars and courts began to introduce a theory of *strict liability* into the law. This third approach holds a manufacturer liable for damages caused by a product that is in a "defective condition" or "unreasonably dangerous" during normal use even if the seller has exercised "all possible care in the preparation and sale" of the product.[11] In other words, strict liability theory eliminates any need to show that the manufacturer was negligent. The focus here is on the product itself. If it can be shown to have a defect (for whatever reason) or if it is judged on some other basis—whether by design or manufacture—to be "unreasonably dangerous" the manufacturer will be held liable for any damages it caused.

Those who favor the strict liability approach typically offer several arguments for it. One is that it relieves plaintiffs in a product liability suit of the difficult, and often impossible, task of proving inadequate care in the design, manufacture, or distribution of the product. Imagine a case in which a driver is injured when her car veers off the road as the result of a defective steering column. Normally, manufacturers subject products and product components to selective quality testing. We can suppose the manufacturer did so in this case by testing, say, one out of three steering columns. To win her case under negligence theory, the crash victim must provide evidence that this one-in-three testing regimen was inadequate, whereas the manufacturer might defend by showing the testing program to be at or above industry standards. Given the technical complexities and cost of mounting such a suit and the powerful support lent the manufacturer by widespread industry practices, the crash victim and her attorneys face a difficult, if not impossible, task. Under strict liability, none of this is necessary. All the victim needs to do is show that the steering column was defective and caused the accident. The company would then be liable, whatever the cause of the defect and however careful or careless it had been. To many, this approach seems to correct an imbalance that favors large and powerful industrial corporations.

Advocates of strict liability point to other benefits. Even though this approach makes manufacturers responsible for defects that crop up despite their best preventive efforts, it does not leave them helpless. Since the rate of unavoidable defects is often statistically predictable, they can insure themselves against this as a cost of doing business. They can also pass these costs along to consumers as part of the price of the product. No one is wronged by this pricing practice because consumers are then paying for the real cost to society of what they buy. Manufacturers can also try to protect themselves by striving to minimize even unavoidable defects. Many defenders of strict liability see this as a real advantage to this approach. Holding manufacturers responsible for the cost of whatever harm is done by their products creates a powerful incentive to improve product safety.

We can best understand a fourth legal approach, *absolute liability*, if we realize that the term "strict liability" is something of a misnomer. Under strict liability manufacturers are not really liable or responsible for every harm their products cause. For one thing, they are responsible only for the harm caused by products that are defective. If a driver misjudges a turn and crashes, the manufacturer need not compensate her. There are some products that are what courts have called "unavoidably unsafe" but that still benefit society—vaccines are a common example. Although they can help the vast majority of people avoid serious disease, there are almost always some who experience an adverse reaction to any drug or medication. Product safety law has not generally concluded that vaccines with this effect are "defective" or "unreasonably dangerous." Finally, strict liability has normally not been applied to products whose defects did not become apparent until well after they had been marketed and that were shown to be dangerous only with the benefit of hindsight. Usually, the judgment of a product as "defective" or "unreasonably dangerous" is applied to the product in light of the best available knowledge at the time the product was manufactured and distributed.

Absolute liability eliminates most of these exceptions. It holds the manufacturer liable for harm caused by a product in its normal use, whatever the cause. Under absolute liability, for example, vaccine makers would have to pay for damages caused by their "unavoidably unsafe" products, and asbestos manufacturers would have to compensate workers whose illness began years or even decades before it was known that asbestos caused lung disease. Those who favor this approach advance many of the reasons put forth for strict liability. They believe it simplifies legal procedures by eliminating arguments about who knew what when. They point out that someone has to pay for the harms caused by a product and that manufacturers are better able to do this than victims. They also believe that absolute liability compels companies to undertake research in order to anticipate and prevent product defects. Finally, advocates of this approach contend that although it may seem unfair to burden manufacturers with liabilities that are sometimes totally beyond their control, this is normal practice in other areas of law, such as worker compensation, where companies are made the insurers of all reported, serious workplace accidents, no matter what the cause.

Critics of both strict and absolute liability question these arguments. They observe that some product defects are unpredictable, rendering it impossible for manufacturers to price their products in a way that covers potential liabilities. This problem becomes especially acute for absolute liability, where some manufacturers, fearing incalculable liabilities, may choose not to develop such socially beneficial products as vaccines and other useful drugs. Critics of strict and absolute liability also point out that in some circumstances, these approaches may even *discourage* manufacturers from investing in product safety. This is most likely to occur when manufacturers see themselves as burdened with liability costs no matter what they do and when preventive efforts, given their cost or limited effectiveness, do not "pay for themselves" by significantly reducing a manufacturer's exposure to accidents. Under negligence theory, it can still be wise for a manufacturer to try to reduce defects in these circumstances in the belief that reasonable, if not totally successful, safety efforts will earn exemption from liability for any mishaps that occur. In contrast, where strict or absolute liability prevails, it may not be cost effective in such cases for manufacturers to invest in safety. Since they face liability no matter what they do, they are better advised to use their resources to pay for whatever judgments are rendered against them rather than for marginally effective safety efforts.[12] This "perverse" effect of strict and absolute liability, critics contend, is a powerful argument against these doctrines.

What can we learn from these legal debates? First, we might note how closely legal thinking tracks the path of moral reasoning identified by **NORM.** *Note how, in considering each legal approach, theorists weigh the beneficial and harmful aspects of each policy (or legal proposal) when it is raised to the status of a public rule. Note, too, how important are the predictable impacts of each proposal on people's behavior and on the factoring of these impacts into the overall assessment of the approach. For example, it is critically important to determine the most likely outcome of each theory in terms of the social goal of encouraging companies to manufacture safe products. As in ethics, proposals prove unacceptable if they end up defeating their own most important purposes. As in ethics, too, the full ramifications of each proposal are not always immediately clear, since determining these often requires us to understand the psychology and decision making of many actors in an imagined environment where a proposal has become a public moral rule.*

A second implication of these debates is that product safety law is obviously in a state of flux. Good reasons exist for several competing legal theories, and each theory crops up as the law is applied to new and changing circumstances. This suggests that in his argument with Tierney over the Kentucky school bus case, Attorney Connor is probably wrong when he states that Ford and Sheller Globe do not (and should not) bear any legal responsibility for this accident. It is true that the U.S. Constitution, like most legal systems, prohibits retroactive legislation where criminal conduct is involved. This follows from the criminal law's basic purpose of influencing and shaping people's behavior by the use of clear and harsh state-imposed penalties, something that would be impossible if those ruled by the law were unable to know what it requires. But we have just seen that, in an area like product safety, civil law, which applies to disputes between private individuals or groups, has multiple objectives. Apart from encouraging manufacturers to produce safe products, it aims at compensating accident victims and minimizing the difficulties or inequities of lawsuits. Product safety law pursues these multiple objectives by sometimes adhering to a theory of absolute liability or even a seemingly impossible requirement of "hindsight" knowledge. For example, in asbestos liability cases, in order to cut off endless debate about when appropriate knowledge became available and in order to channel needed financial assistance to thousands of injured workers, courts have sometimes held manufacturers responsible for injuries they could not reasonably have foreseen at the time of manufacture.[13] This suggests that in the Kentucky school bus case, where great human suffering is involved and where the risks involved in the product (an unprotected gas tank) were probably far more predictable than were the risks of asbestos during the earliest years of its production, it is likely that courts and juries will hold the manufacturers to the most rigorous interpretation of strict liability or even to a standard of absolute liability. Ford and Sheller Globe probably did well to seek an out-of-court settlement.

Some may object that in this case, although this may all be true of law, it says nothing about the manufacturers' moral responsibilities. But the point here is moral. It tells us that, contrary to Attorney Connor's contention, neither Ford nor Sheller Globe would necessarily be wronged were they to be held liable for damages in this accident. Because law has multiple objectives, it sometimes chooses to ignore important individual features of our moral thinking without necessarily being unjust. Normally, we believe that people should be penalized only for behavior they can reasonably avoid. But when legislation has other objectives—such as the quick and efficient compensation of people injured in acci-

dents—we can choose to set aside this single feature of our moral judgment. The fact that worker compensation, no-fault auto insurance, and some forms of strict product liability are widely accepted shows that specific forms of unfairness do not necessarily render a law as a whole unjust. Incidentally, this same logic applies to ethics. Sometimes in the name of morally desirable objectives, we override otherwise important features of our moral judgment. For example, parents faced with a squabble between their own children and those of a guest may choose to refrain from determining who caused the fracas and merely punish all the youngsters. Although this may seem unfair to some of the children, the parents know that determining blame in such cases can be extraordinarily difficult and that they risk the appearance of bias if they rule for their own children even if their children are in the right. Although this example is trivial, it illustrates how, in weightier instances of choice, competing moral objectives can sometimes lead us to suspend fairness or other ordinarily important moral concerns. Despite what deontologists think, moral judgments do not always rest on such specific considerations as fairness. Instead, they represent the outcome of complex "balancing" decisions where multiple objectives, including fairness, play a role.

It may not be unjust, therefore, to hold Ford and Sheller Globe responsible for compensating victims' families and survivors in this case even if the companies adequately fulfilled their moral responsibilities at the time the bus was made and sold and thus were neither legally nor morally negligent. But the justice of these penalties would be even clearer had the two companies actually failed in their moral obligations at the time they built and marketed the bus. This returns us to a central question in this case: Do manufacturers have moral responsibilities for the safety of their products beyond those imposed by law or regulation? Did Ford and Sheller Globe act blamelessly in their sale of this product?

A way of answering this is to examine the following proposed moral rule and to ask whether, if we were any (and all) the parties in this case, we would want to live in a world ruled by it:

◆

First Proposed Moral Rule: A manufacturer who builds and markets a school bus during a time when the need for significant safety improvements has been recognized and is being debated for enactment into law may ignore this debate and, at least until the law is changed, sell the bus *as is* to willing buyers.

◆

The advantages of this rule are obvious. It protects manufacturers from having to identify and implement product changes during every twist and turn of legislative debate and it provides a definitive moment—legal enactment—when new standards become obligatory. It also prevents a manufacturer from having to add to product cost and from losing sales to less scrupulous competitors. But the disadvantages of this rule are equally obvious. A buyer unaware of the intricacies of school bus safety or unfamiliar with the status of legislative debate may inadvertently purchase a vehicle whose safety features are inadequate in terms of the best current technological knowledge. The fact that this vehicle will transport many children during its long lifetime compounds the potential harm of this moral proposal.

These powerful negative considerations counsel us to try to amend this proposed rule to minimize its potential harm without creating serious new hardships. The following rule looks like a good candidate:

✦

Second Proposed Moral Rule: A manufacturer who builds and markets a school bus during a time when the need for significant safety improvements has been recognized and is being debated for enactment must take steps to see that potential buyers are adequately informed of pending changes.

✦

We can see that this rule removes some of the significant harms of its predecessor while imposing a minimum burden on vehicle manufacturers. Among other things, it allows buyers to determine whether they are willing to pay for needed safety improvements and retrofits. Overall, it seems a reasonable means of balancing the competing interests here. By extension, we can see that the logic of this proposal probably also extends to the postsale relationship between manufacturer and owner of a product like school buses. Sometimes the need for safety becomes apparent only after the product is out of the manufacturer's control. Do manufacturers have a continuing responsibility to warn owners of product defects? This proposed moral rule rests on the presumption that there is a normal imbalance in information possessed by manufacturers and buyers that we all have an interest in correcting. Manufacturers are most familiar with the safety issues related to their product, are a natural "funnel" for information regarding changing technological standards and product improvements, and provide a centralized location where registries of owners can be maintained. All this suggests that it is not unreasonable to hold manufacturers ethically responsible for active efforts to inform and warn owners—including those who have purchased the vehicles from others—of relevant product safety standards.

Complexities abound. For example, we might want to adjust this proposed moral rule to the special problems of other product categories. It makes sense to place narrower limits on manufacturers' moral responsibility for products (such as lawnmowers or small electrical appliances) that are far more difficult to keep track of once they enter the marketplace. It would probably be absurd to hold a manufacturer morally responsible for constantly maintaining up-to-date ownership records on bicycles it has sold—although, even here, it might be prudent for a wise and responsible manufacturer to make strenuous efforts (including advertising) to alert owners when serious defects come to light.[14]

Who should pay to correct postsale product defects? Arguments can be made on both sides. Requiring the manufacturer to pay might expedite product repair, although it creates a major and unpredictable cost of business not easily passed along in future products. Opinions about this issue might vary with the nature of the product involved. Many automobile owners, for example, might not present their vehicles if they had to pay for the costs of repair or upgrades. Bus owners, however, would probably face legal liability should they fail to repair or upgrade a vehicle, providing them with a powerful incentive to comply with manufacturers' warnings. This suggests that, at least where a safety upgrade is concerned, school bus manufacturers may not be morally required to pay for product improvements that were not legally required at the time of sale.

From the point of view of ethics, then, there is no set point at which manufacturers can declare themselves free from the responsibility of seeing to it that a product is safe. This responsibility is independent of the state of the law. It comes into being when the product is being designed, manufactured, and marketed, and it continues for an indefinite period after that, depending on the nature of the product and the risks involved. It imposes a minimum requirement of product registration and of warnings whenever possible. In some cases it may go further, requiring recalls and product repairs at the manufacturer's expense.

These ethical guidelines are obviously not separate from the law. As our review of product liability shows, civil law also tends to perceive an ongoing duty of manufacturers beyond the letter of existing statutory requirements. Here, ethics and law mutually inform one another and reinforce the incentives good managers have for understanding and paying careful attention to their moral obligations in this crucial area. This point has been made by Tom Stephens, who served as president & CEO of Johns-Manville in the wake of the series of product liability suits that nearly destroyed this asbestos manufacturer and saddled it with unprecedented liability obligations. Stephens sums up a key insight that illustrates the importance of business ethics for business law: When large firms think about product liability, he observes, "the key to survival in today's climate is to live by tomorrow's law."

Case 6.3

◆ CASHING IN ON CASHING OUT[15] ◆

Participants in a week-long continuing education program for insurance agents were asked to prepare memos on experiences that had caused them ethical problems. An agent employed by an independent agency submitted the following case for discussion.

TO: Colleagues in the Advanced Sales Seminar
FROM: Joanne Smith, Blackburn Life & Casualty
RE: Ethics Problem

I don't know about other people, but I have found it hard to handle sales situations where it seemed to me that commission considerations confused matters. There was a time, two or three years ago, when I faced a particularly difficult decision. My primary company has a variable annuity product offered in two forms. The single premium form requires an immediate payment into the annuity with no future payments in allowed. The flexible premium form permits continuing contributions. Each type of annuity has the following schedule of surrender fees, payable if the policy is cashed in early:

Year	Single Premium	Flexible Premium
1	5%	8%
2	4	8
3	3	7
4	2	6
5	1	5
6	0	4
7		3
8		2
9		1
10		0
Commission Schedule	3%	4½%

I had a client who was going to roll over approximately $300,000 from a pension plan with a previous employer into one of these contracts. He was investing this money for his retirement and intended to make continuing contributions. Each annuity contract carries an annual fee of $35. If the client chose the single premium annuity, he would have to purchase a second, flexible premium annuity, for the continuing contributions. The client didn't like the idea of multiple contracts due to the $35 fee. He asked for my recommendation.

My commission would have been as follows:

Single Premium	Flexible Premium
$9,000.00	$13,500.00

The client was age 46, and said that he did not intend to take money out of the plan until the normal retirement age of 65.

The difference in commissions would have made a difference in my "club status" with the company. This was a few weeks from year end for commission credit.

This was my dilemma: Were my interests in conflict with my client's best interest? If the commissions were the same, what would I recommend? What would you have done in my shoes?

I struggled for several days until our scheduled appointment. I decided to handle the meeting as follows:

Disclosure

1. I meticulously reviewed the relevant prospectus differences between the two contracts, including commission implications.

Do unto others . . .

2. I recommended the single premium contract. If I were in the client's shoes, that is what I would take. I calculated the annual fee for the second contract to accept ongoing contributions as a percentage of total assets (.01%), and advised the client that this should *not* be an issue.

QUESTIONS TO CONSIDER

1. What obligations does someone who sells complex financial products or services owe the customer or client?
2. In your view, has Joanne Smith properly exercised this sales responsibility? Why or why not?
3. What do you think of Smith's decision to reveal commission details to her client? Would **NORM** require this kind of conduct?

ETHICS IN SALES
✦

All sales and marketing activities raise basic ethical questions about the extent of our moral obligations to assist and inform the consumer. Personal sales, face-to-face encounters between a buyer and a seller, pose some of the most difficult dilemmas. Whether the product is a vacuum cleaner, real estate, mutual funds, or insurance, several factors contribute to ethical corner-cutting in this area. Those engaged in personal sales typically work on their own, without supervision. They often earn the bulk of their pay through commissions, and this generates pressure to "close" sales prospects by any means. In addition, there is often a disparity of information between buyer and seller, creating an opportunity for exaggeration, misrepresentation, or outright deception.

Insurance agents like Joanne Smith, along with brokers and others who sell financial products or services, face a further problem. The complex nature of the product makes clients particularly dependent on the salesperson's expert knowledge and advice. Rightly or wrongly, this leads clients to view agents and brokers as "fiduciaries." Like doctors or lawyers, they are regarded as ethically committed to meeting the client's needs and to placing the client's interests above their own. The training that agents and brokers receive tends to reinforce this perception. It is a commonplace of all personal sales training that a salesperson's ability to demonstrate trustworthiness is a necessary condition for closing sales.[16] Training literature often encourages trainees to go out of their way to earn and cultivate the client's trust: "People want more than just a product or service," says one leading training manual. "They want you to be concerned about their needs; they want you to inspire confidence and trust and to communicate that you are strongly committed to their welfare."[17] Yet, even though trust is a key component of sales, agents and brokers are not fiduciaries in a legal or moral sense. As salespeople, their primary loyalty lies with the firm that employs them and their foremost personal and professional goal is to maximize sales revenue.

These tensions and strains underlie the dilemma faced by Joanne Smith. Like any salesperson, she wants to earn a commission that will enhance her personal income and professional status. But she is in a situation where the client has, expectedly, come to view her as a source of reliable counsel and advice. In this instance, Smith sees these dual aspects of her role as opposing one another. She can either enhance her commission by failing to make clear to the client the drawbacks of the single-policy flexible premium alternative (because of its high surrender fees) and by concealing her vested interest in selling this annuity, or she can be entirely up-front, sacrifice the higher commission, and strive to persuade the client to purchase the policy she believes is best for him.

On the surface, Smith's resolution of her dilemma seems ethically commendable. To see this, consider the following moral rule, which she has implicitly rejected by her choice:

✦

Proposed Moral Rule: Whenever insurance agents can substantially increase their commission by doing so, they may use the client's trust in their financial advice to sell a service or product they believe not to be in the client's best interest.

✦

Clearly, this is a self-defeating policy. If salespeople in quasi-fiduciary roles acted on it, they would destroy the very trust they seek to exploit. Indeed, the significant decline in public esteem experienced by both insurance agents and insurance companies over the past few decades shows how abuses of trust caused by an excessive emphasis on short-term profits can erode the moral standing of an entire industry.

Faced with this unacceptable alternative, Smith opts for its opposite: she actively recommends the annuity she believes will benefit the client and simultaneously tries to remove the possibility of conflict of interest by disclosing her financial stake in the sale. But before we conclude that her choice is the only moral one available, we might ask whether—apart from the risk of reducing her commission—there are any considerations that argue against this course of action. At first sight, this may seem to be an odd question. What can possibly be wrong with a salesperson's striving to benefit a customer who has given her his trust? But the question makes sense if we look more closely at what "benefit" means in a sales context.

Smith believes she benefits the client when she recommends the annuity package, which, at a small cost in additional annual fees, has the least punitive schedule of surrender fees. But is this necessarily to the client's benefit? The answer will depend very much on what the client's needs and expectations are. If it is the case, for example, that the client has a firm expectation that he will have no need to cash in the annuity early, the surrender fees are irrelevant; the fees will have ended by year ten. It might be argued that no one can be sure he will not be forced by some emergency to cash in an annuity, and this may justify Smith's conviction that she must recommend the single premium policy. But who should make a decision about a matter like this—the salesperson or the client himself?

The point is that our interest as customers or clients is in seeing to it that our own most important needs are met. Because it is difficult for anyone to know those needs better than ourselves, this means that, unless we acknowledge our incapacity to make an informed decision and expressly put matters in an advisor's hands, we do not want others to make decisions for us, but rather to provide us with all the relevant information we need to make the decisions ourselves. In view of this, the course Smith should follow to benefit her client takes on a slightly different character. "Listening" takes priority over "recommending." Above all, the salesperson must determine just what the needs, wishes, plans, and expectations of the client are, and she must ask questions based on her own familiarity with the products and customer experience. In this instance, for example, it may be less appropriate for Smith to recommend a particular policy than to review with the client, after drawing his attention to the different surrender fees, such matters as his employment situation, educational expenses, and health care needs, so that he can determine what the likelihood is that he will have to call on his pension savings prematurely.

Joanne Smith is right, then, to believe that she must respect the trust the client has placed in her and must not allow her own interests to color her advice. But she may be wrong in thinking that this requires her to make decisions *for* the customer. There is a third and intermediate position in ethical sales relationships between the extremes of caveat emptor and the kind of paternalistic decision making in which the seller usurps the buyer's right to decide (or to make decisions the seller believes are unwise or foolish). This intermediate position stresses the buyer's right to make a fully informed decision. Where the seller is concerned, this position requires a salesperson, no matter what his or her personal stake in the sale might be, to inform customers fully about a product or service, to disclose all relevant information, and to avoid any kind of evasiveness or misrepresentation. It is not up to the salesperson to impose her or his tastes or preferences on the customer. If asked, a salesperson may volunteer opinions about a product, but respect for others' freedom implies allowing them to make the decision they believe best meets their needs. Obviously, the duties imposed by this intermediate position are always proportional to the nature of the product involved and the degree of expertise of the potential buyer. A positive obligation to inform the customer fully becomes especially important when complex products or services are involved and when customers' expertise is limited. It is less important when sales involve well-informed professionals or businesspeople.

What does this tell us about Joanne Smith's decision to reveal commission details to her client? Her motives for doing so are laudable. Morally uncomfortable about a possible conflict of interest, she acts to neutralize this consideration by informing her client of this factor in her thinking. Must she do this? One way of answering this is to look closely at the moral rule implicit in her decision:

◆

Proposed Moral Rule: Whenever it is likely that commission considerations will color or distort the information or advice that will be offered to a customer, a salesperson must reveal commission details to the customer.

◆

At first sight, this rule makes good sense. Although it may be undesirable from the salespeople's point of view—since it requires them to reveal private compensation matters and since it may have a negative effect on customers unfamiliar with the complex pay and incentives aspects of the sales process—these concerns do not seem overwhelming where commissions are customary, fair, and reasonable. As customers, we all want information relevant to our purchase decision, and this kind of information—with its impact on the salesperson's reliability and credibility—may be valuable. But before adopting this rule, let us look closely at its opening phrase: "Whenever it is likely that commission considerations will color or distort the information. . . ." What assumptions lie behind this rule? For one thing, this rule assumes that a salesperson cannot be relied on to act professionally to meet the customer's needs. This means that, for Joanne Smith, to act on this rule by revealing commission details in this case is an admission that she cannot be counted on to act in a fully professional manner by exercising the kind of objectivity needed to inform and educate the customer. This may be true, but it is an admission of professional failure.

This suggests that salespeople's obligation in selling need not extend to revealing personal matters of commission or compensation. Their primary obligation is to ensure that the client or customer receives (and properly understands) all the information needed to make an informed purchase decision. However, spelling out this requirement also points us toward circumstances where revealing commission information might be desirable. For example, it makes sense as a matter of practice for a company or for an industry as a whole to reveal commission details in literature and brochures whenever there is reason to believe that a commission structure might tempt salespeople to act in a less than ethical manner.

The area of sales is one of the most ethically complicated and trying in business ethics. It is an area filled with tensions and apparent contradictions. If omnipartiality and objectivity are hallmarks of moral reasoning, this is an area where businesspeople commonly experience conflicts between their own interests and the needs of clients, and where omnipartiality is constantly being threatened by powerful economic motives. It is an area where the cultivation of personal trust between buyer and seller is often a key to success, but where there is always the temptation to exploit this trust for short-term gain or personal advantage. The sorry record of sale practices and the widespread scorn for salespeople attest to these problems. The used car salesperson has become a virtual icon of ethical sleaze and laws have proliferated to protect customers and buyers. But these are not the only realities salespeople need accept. Salespeople serve at the interface of a firm's relationship with its consumer stakeholders. They educate the organization about the consumer's needs and they educate the consumer about the company's products and services. By understanding and respecting the ethical rules governing their role, salespeople can earn a living commensurate with their talents while retaining their own and others' respect.

Summary

- Trust is crucial in a company's relationship with customers and clients. There are many ways that firms can damage trust—by deception or by failing to fulfill their part of the sales bargain—but trust can also be lost when a company fails to respect or trust consumers or when it treats them as opponents who must be manipulated, controlled, and outwitted.

- Johnson & Johnson's handling of the Tylenol poisoning episode illustrates how good business and good ethics sometimes go together. Because moral beliefs and sentiments play an important role in motivating human behavior, ethical insight and fair treatment of customers can be a major contributor to marketing success.

- When firms attend to their ethical responsibilities, it is hard to distinguish conduct that benefits the firm from conduct that is also ethically right. By fostering an ethical culture and by structuring incentives to reduce unethical behavior, managers limit the need for moral heroism and integrate ethics into ordinary decision making.

- Ethical reflection suggests that some features of product liability and safety law, including strict liability and a requirement of hindsight knowledge, are not necessarily unjust. Manufacturers have a continuing responsibility to ensure that their products are safe. This responsibility comes into being when the product is being designed, manufactured, and sold, and it continues for an indefinite period, depending on the nature of the product and the risks involved.

- In sales, a governing moral consideration is the buyer's right to make a fully informed decision. Although its meaning will depend on the nature of the products and the expertise of the parties in a sales transaction, this right rules out misrepresentation and requires full disclosure of relevant information.

Case 6.4

✦ CLOSING THE DEAL[18] ✦

Now that she had to, Jean McGuire wasn't sure she could. Not that she didn't understand what to do. Wright Boazman, sales director for Sunrise Land Developers, had made the step clear enough when he had described a variety of other effective "deal-closing techniques."

As Wright explained it, very often people actually want to buy a lot, but at the last minute they're filled with self-doubt and uncertainty. The inexperienced salesperson can misinterpret this as a lack of interest in a property. "But," as Wright pointed out, "in most cases it's just an expression of the normal reservations everyone shows when the time comes to sign our names on the dotted line."

In Wright's view, the job of a land salesperson was "to help the prospect make the decision to buy." This didn't mean that salespeople should misrepresent a piece of property or in any way mislead people about what they were purchasing. "Law prohibits this," he pointed out, "and personally I find such behavior repugnant. What I'm talking about is helping them buy a lot they genuinely want and which you're convinced will be compatible with their needs and interests." For Wright Boazman, salespeople should serve as motivators, people who could provide whatever impulse was needed for prospects to close the deal.

In Wright's experience one of the most effective closing techniques was what he termed "the other party." It went something like this.

Suppose someone like Jean McGuire had a "hot" prospect, someone who was exhibiting a real interest in a lot but who was having trouble deciding. To motivate the prospect into buying, Jean ought to tell the person that she wasn't even sure the lot was still available, since there were a number of other salespeople showing the same lot, and they could already have closed a deal on it. As Wright put it, "This first ploy generally has the effect of increasing the prospect's interest in the property, and, more important to us, in closing the deal *pronto*."

Next, Jean should say something like, "Why don't we go back to the office and I'll call headquarters to find out the status of the lot?" Wright indicated that such a suggestion ordinarily "whets their appetite" even more. In addition, it turns prospects away from wondering whether they should purchase the land and toward hoping that it's still available.

When they return to the office, Jean should make a call in the presence of the prospect. The call, of course, would not be to "headquarters" but to a private office only yards from where she and the prospect sit. Wright or someone else would receive the call, and Jean should fake a conversation about the property's availability, punctuating her comments with enough contagious excitement about its desirability. When she hangs up, she should breathe a sigh of relief that the lot's still available—but barely. At any minute, Jean should explain anxiously, the lot could be "green-tagged," which means that headquarters is expecting a call from another salesperson who's about to close a deal and will remove the lot from open stock. (An effective variation of this, Wright had pointed out, would have Jean abruptly excuse herself upon hanging up and dart over to another sales representative with whom she'd engage in a heated, though staged, debate about the availability of the property, loud enough, of course, for the prospect to hear. The intended effect, according to Wright, would place the prospect in the "now or never" frame of mind.)

When Jean first heard about this and other closing techniques, she felt uneasy. Even though the property was everything it was represented to be, and the law allowed purchasers ten days to change their minds after closing the deal, she instinctively objected to the use of psychological manipulation. Nevertheless, Jean never expressed her reservations to anyone, primarily because she didn't want to endanger her job. She desperately needed it owing to the recent and unexpected death of her husband, which left her as the sole support of herself and three young children. Besides, Jean had convinced herself that she could deal with closures more respectably than Wright and other salespeople might. But the truth was that after six months of selling land for Sunrise, Jean's sales lagged far behind those of the other sales representatives. Whether she liked it or not, Jean had to admit that she was losing a considerable number of sales because she couldn't close. And she couldn't close because, in Wright Boazman's words, she lacked technique. She wasn't employing psychological closing devices that he and others had found so successful.

Now as she drove back to the office with two "hot prospects" in hand, she wondered what to do.

QUESTIONS TO CONSIDER

1. How would you morally evaluate the practices Wright Boazman recommends to Jean McGuire?

2. Are there ethical and effective ways that McGuire can accomplish her sales objectives? What advice would you offer her?

𝒩OTES

1. This case is substantially based on "McNeil Consumer Products Company: Tylenol," prepared by John Deighton, Associate Professor of Marketing, Graduate School of Business, University of Chicago.
2. See the Harvard case by Richard S. Tedlow and Wendy K. Smith, "James Burke: A Career in American Business (A)," no. 9–389–177 (Boston: Harvard Business School, 1989), pp. 6–7.
3. "When a Brand Name Gets Hit by Bad News," *U.S. News and World Report*, 8 November 1982, p. 71.

4. These aspects of the episode are mentioned in "James Burke: A Career in American Business (B)," no. 9–390–030, p. 3.

5. Johnson & Johnson CEO James Burke publicly voiced his perception of the Tylenol episode as a terroristic act which, within the framework of its other obligations, the company had a moral obligation to resist. See the Harvard video presentation, "James Burke: A Career in Business," no. 890–513 (Boston: Harvard Business School, 1989).

6. See Chapter 10.

7. This case is based on Numan A. Williams and Howard M. Hammer's discussion of "The Case of the Kentucky Church Bus," in *CPCU Journal* (December 1988): 196–206. Additional materials have been drawn from articles in the *New York Times* and the *Wall Street Journal*, 16, 17, and 18 May and 5 and 9 July 1988.

8. "Granddaughter's DES Suit Raises Liability Concerns," *Business Insurance*, 14 January 1991, pp. 2, 4.

9. Nicole Grant, *The Selling of Contraception: The Dalkon Shield Case, Sexuality, and Women's Autonomy* (Columbus: Ohio State University Press, 1992).

10. "Legal Breast Implants: What Did the Industry Know, and When?" *Business Week,* 10 June 1991, pp. 94–95; Tatiana Pouschine, "The Survivors," *Forbes,* 7 December 1992, p. 148.

11. *Restatement (Second) of the Law of Torts* (Washington, D.C.: American Law Institute, 1965), section 402A.

12. David P. Griffith, "Product Liability—Negligence Presumed: An Evolution, *Texas Law Review* 67 (1989): 877.

13. *Beshada* v. *Johns-Manville Products Corp.* 90 N.J. 191, 447 A2d. 539 (1982).

14. See the Harvard case by N. C. Smith, "Black & Decker Corp.: Spacemaker Plus Coffeemaker (A) and (B)," nos. 590–099 and 599–100 (Boston: Harvard Business School, 1991, 1992).

15. Written for Robbin Derry by Pamela A. Newman, Graduate Residency, the American College, June 1991.

16. G. Oakes, "The Sales Process and the Paradoxes of Trust," *Journal of Business Ethics* 9 (1990): 671–79.

17. Ibid, 673, quoting C. Millar, *Prudential Training Program: The Financial Security Selling System,* Book 1 (Newark, N.J.: PruPress, 1986), p. 15.

18. This case is drawn from Vincent Barry, *Moral Issues in Business,* 3rd ed. (Belmont, CA: Wadsworth Publishing Company, 1986), pp. 441–42. Reprinted by permission.

COMPETITORS AND SUPPLIERS AS CORPORATE STAKEHOLDERS

◆

◆"ALL'S FAIR IN LOVE, WAR—AND BUSINESS COMPETITION." TO MANY people, this slightly modified old adage is an obvious truth. Although they may be willing to admit that employees and customers deserve to be respected as stakeholders of a business organization, they have a far harder time thinking that competitors merit moral respect. Like Albert Carr or Milton Friedman, they recognize the obligation to obey laws governing business competition. But outside this framework they believe that business is all about tough, no-holds-barred competition, with rewards going to the shrewdest and most aggressive players. Although somewhat less common, the same attitude is often applied to a company's suppliers and vendors. In a highly competitive environment, suppliers are regarded as lucky to get a company's business, making them subject to the wishes—or the whims—of the buyer. Here, the motto is "Who pays the piper plays the tune."

This chapter challenges these conventional views of competitor–supplier relationships. Both groups, we shall see, are corporate stakeholders with a claim to fair treatment. Not "everything goes" where competitors are concerned. Although vigorous competition usually best serves the public interest, some things done in the name of competition are primarily destructive in nature. Among these are practices that create short-term advantages for one firm by imposing new burdens on everyone else in the marketplace or that promote one firm's products while discrediting an industry as a whole. When destructive practices like these become commonplace, they invite legal regulation. Fairness and mutual respect have an even more obvious place in relationships with suppliers and vendors. In an era of reduced inventories and "just-in-time" manufacture, collaborative relationships with suppliers—including a willingness on both sides to go the extra mile—are being seen as a key factor in business success. In the cases in this chapter, we will look at some of the ways that competitive pressures place stress on the relationships with competitors and suppliers, and we will try to determine when the drive to compete should be tempered by ethical considerations.

Case 7.1

✦ CHILD WORLD SAYS RIVAL CHEATS TOYS "R" US ANSWERS: "GROW UP"[1] ✦

Wall Street Journal, September 19, 1991—Where does Toys "R" Us Inc., the giant toy retailer, buy some of the goods that line its shelves? Down the street at Child World Inc. stores, one of its biggest rivals.

Strange as it seems, that's what Child World claims—and Toys "R" Us isn't denying it.

Child World, which says it is considering legal action against its competitor, contends that Toys "R" Us is "systematically abusing" a Child World promotion that specifically excludes dealers, wholesalers, and retailers. The promotion gives customers gift certificates valued at $25 on purchases in October when they buy $100 of products now, with smaller certificates given for smaller purchases.

Child World, based in Avon, Mass., alleges that Toys "R" Us managers and employees, under the guise of being regular customers, are "making large purchases of items that Child World sells at close to cost—particularly diapers, baby food, and formula—receiving the dollars-off coupons and reselling the Child World goods as Toys "R" Us inventory.

Toys "R" Us wouldn't dispute the allegations and said the practice is common in the industry. "It's not an unusual thing for one retailer to buy merchandise from another. I'm sure that we have. We know that [Child World] has done it to us," said Angela Bourdon, a spokeswoman for the Rochelle Park, N.J., retailer. A spokesman for Child World denied that the discount retailer has purchased goods in bulk from Toys "R" Us. . . .

This isn't the first incidence of rivalry between the two retailers. Earlier this year, troubled Child World launched an industrywide price war by slashing its prices in an attempt to pump up sales and raise cash. Toys "R" Us, as well as other retailers, was forced to follow suit. Profit margins were hurt as a result.

Child World said it was first alerted to the practice last week, when someone claiming to be a Toys "R" Us manager gave an anonymous tip to Child World. "The manager said Toys "R" Us was making him do it," said John Devine, Child World's chief executive officer and a former executive vice-president of Toys "R" Us.

But why would Toys "R" Us, with all the buying power of a large corporation, go to that trouble?

Mr. Devine responds that because Child World is selling its promotional fare at manufacturers' prices, "Toys "R" Us would initially pay no more [than it already pays the manufacturer] and, in addition, it would be gathering [our] gift certificate."

Child World said it has received reports of suspected daily Toys "R" Us purchases at "many" of its 153 stores nationwide. It estimates, via the number of "suspicious" customers visiting its stores every day, that its competitor has bought up to $1.5 million of Child World's goods and has received as much as $375,000 of gift certificates.

Mr. Devine contends that in some cases, when confronted, "customers" making big purchases have acknowledged that they work for Toys "R" Us. In other cases, Child World's managers have followed in their cars those customers "right back to Toys "R" Us later and [have] seen the customer there working," he added.

... Sean McGowan, an analyst at Gerard Klauer Mattison & Co., New York, said the announcement may be a public relations stunt by Child World, which has had major financial problems and was acquired earlier this year by its bank and an investor group that includes Mr. Devine.

QUESTIONS TO CONSIDER

1. What is your estimate of Toys "R" Us's conduct? Is it acting within the bounds of ethically permissible competition, or has it exceeded these bounds?
2. What would **NORM** tell us about Toys "R" Us's conduct?

OBLIGATIONS TO COMPETITORS

✦

Over the years, most free-market economies have imposed various legal restraints on competitive practices. Antitrust laws and rules against price fixing or product "dumping" aim at preventing abuses of economic power that would impede market entry, drive out smaller firms, or otherwise limit consumer choice. Regulations like those prohibiting preferential prices for favored customers seek to maintain a level playing field for all competitors in an industry, whereas other laws aim at protecting consumers against competitive practices not adequately controlled by the normal dynamics of the market. In the United States, for example, the Federal Trade Commission has established a complex series of regulations to prevent firms from gaining competitive advantage by deceptive or misleading advertising. The underlying moral logic of all these legal interventions is not hard to understand. Since the value of the marketplace derives from vigorous competition and informed consumer choice, practices that pose serious threats to either are morally questionable.

Sometimes competitors engage in conduct that fits none of these categories and that forces us to rethink the nature and limits of fair competition. The dispute between Child World and Toys "R" Us is an example of this. Are we dealing with a normal and accepted competitive practice, as Toys "R" Us argues, or with a form of conduct that is morally reprehensible, as Child World contends? In fact, two different questions are raised by this episode. One is whether the kind of raid on a competitor's sales stock of which Toys "R" Us is accused is in itself a legitimate competitive practice, one that we can think of as having a place in normal business activity. The second question is more complex. It assumes a negative answer to the first question and also concedes Toys "R" Us's claim that conduct like this is commonplace. Does the fact that an undesirable or wrongful practice is widespread in a competitive environment make a difference in our moral estimate of it? Does "Everyone's doing it" ever make something that is wrong morally right?

Our first question about the legitimacy of "raiding" of this sort seems to be answered by the observation that Toys "R" Us's conduct could involve lying and deception. Normally, firms that mount special sales and promotion efforts try to protect themselves against raids by retailers or competitors by limiting the number of units a customer can buy. "One to a customer" or "five per family" are common tag lines in sales advertisements or coupon promotions. If Child World had imposed such restrictions on the purchase of its own sales and bonus merchandise, Toys "R" Us employees would have had either to lie or to misrepresent themselves. We have no trouble seeing that this is ethically wrong.

Child World may not have imposed such limits. Does this remove the moral problems with Toys "R" Us's behavior? Not entirely, because emphasizing the possible element of deception in this case misses the deeper issue of why it is necessary for a company to impose this kind of control on its promotional efforts in the first place. Purchase limits are a hardship for the small number of customers who can benefit from the availability of cheap promotional goods, and they impose a burden on retailers who must go out of their way to see that the limits are not being circumvented. In a sense, they represent an unfortunate but necessary policing function designed to prevent the massive purchase of promotional goods by competitors. If these restrictions make sense, it must be because there is good reason to prevent overbuying by retailers or competitors. This returns us to the question of why such conduct is undesirable.

To find the answer we might look briefly at the ethics of sales campaigns in general. In ethical terms, promotions have a valid place in business life. Consumers clearly benefit from them, and, retailers, too, use sales to advantage. By boosting traffic through a store and familiarizing customers with its offerings, promotions make sense even when selected merchandise is sold at or below cost. The normal working of the markets prevents a firm from unfairly damaging competitors by these promotions, since, unless it enjoys a potentially monopolistic position (the problem of "dumping"), no firm can long sell goods unprofitably. These valid aspects of promotions also help us identify the most obvious abuses. Loss-leader campaigns where only a few of the sale items are available and prices are increased before sales are obvious abuses of consumer trust. They discredit sales campaigns as a whole and increase consumer resistance.

Against this background, we can see that the kind of conduct alleged of Toys "R" Us in this case is morally unacceptable, even apart from the evasion of stated limits on retailers' purchases. Imagine a world where every retailer felt free to avail itself of the reduced prices and bonuses offered in competitors' sales promotions. Such a world would be governed by something like the following moral rule:

✦

Proposed Moral Rule: Whenever a firm mounts a sales promotion that offers goods at or below cost, a competitor may use its purchasing power to buy up large quantities of those goods.

✦

In a world where this is an acceptable competitive practice, it would be far more difficult to mount sales campaigns. Consumers and retailers would lose the benefits of sales. Blocked from using sales to promote themselves, retailers would also have to devote energies to breaking up others' sales campaigns in order to prevent them from gaining competitive advantage. In short, the practice embodied in this proposed moral rule is destructive in every way. Although in the short run it may benefit one merchandiser, it contributes nothing to the welfare of buyers or sellers. Small wonder that firms are driven to prevent it by imposing quotas or other restrictions on buyers. But deceitful evasion of these restrictions is not the primary wrong here. Rather, it is the behavior that calls them forth: the effort by one firm to benefit itself in a way that damages every other actor in the marketplace and that ultimately undermines the practice (sales campaigns) it would exploit.

"EVERYONE'S DOING IT"

✦

Would it make a difference to Toys "R" Us's moral defense of its position if this kind of conduct were widely practiced in the industry? Situations in which a morally undesirable form of behavior is widespread and a firm that fails to engage in it loses a competitive edge crop up frequently in business (and in other highly competitive activities such as war or athletics). In these circumstances, people often use the phrase "everyone's doing it" as a moral justification for conduct that they know to be less than ideal or even morally wrong. Large beer companies, for example, have been known to justify their promotional efforts on college campuses by pointing to competitive realities. Although it would be best that nobody glamorize or market alcoholic beverages to young people, any company that refused to do so would lose a foothold in an important market segment and might eventually be driven out of business by less scrupulous competitors. Similarly, Toys "R" Us spokespersons suggest that the prevalence of "raids" on sales campaigns is a reason for their acceptability. Of course, it is often not true that "everyone's doing it." This justification is sometimes used by people in situations where they are the only ones breaking a moral rule. In this case, there is no evidence of any previous effort by Child World or others to disrupt Toys "R" Us's campaigns. But although the facts in this case do not really support the claim, the spokesperson's remarks show how common it is for people to argue that widespread wrongdoing sometimes justifies an individual's adapting to lowered standards of behavior.

Does the fact that "everyone's doing it" ever morally justify otherwise unethical conduct? Many say it does not. Two or more wrongs, they insist, do not make a right. We should not accommodate to widespread wrongdoing, but resist it. Those who hold this view have powerful arguments on their side. There are obvious circumstances where others' misbehavior clearly does not justify our following their lead. The fact that some businessmen sexually harass female colleagues surely provides no moral justification for others' doing so. If peers are cheating on an examination, I may or may not be required to inform on them, but I myself am not morally entitled to cheat. Nevertheless, we have all encountered situations where a widespread pattern of undesirable or wrongful conduct forces us to act in similar ways and even seems to make it permissible to do so. Many businessmen and businesswomen believe that overstatement and exaggeration by the opposing side in contract negotiations justify one's being less than candid in statements of one's own negotiating position. In Olympic athletics, the widespread abuse of "amateur" status by some nations is seen by many as justifying similar "defensive" evasions by other national teams.

Neutral, Omnipartial Rule-Making *helps us think about this issue by reminding us that all moral conduct is inherently public and subject to the omnipartial approval of everyone it affects. It further reminds us that we have to assess anything we propose to do in terms of the impact our proposal will have on people's conduct once it has been raised to the status of a moral rule. This means that we must look not only at our proposal's immediate effects, but also at the behaviors it will predictably produce once it becomes an artifact—or item of "furniture"—in everyone's moral environment. We have seen repeatedly that conduct that initially seems to make good sense sometimes becomes self-defeating when raised to the status of a public rule.*

Applying this insight to the question of whether a pattern of widespread wrongdoing justifies our joining in misconduct, we can see that permitting people to act in morally undesirable ways just because others are doing so is a recipe for moral chaos. Allowing people to cheat or lie because competitors have done so, for example, will produce a cascade of wrongdoing as one wrong leads to another. The problem is worsened by the fact that, where this policy prevails, every person will be quick to interpret any sign of misconduct by others as a license to lower standards. To prevent these "cascade" effects, we ordinarily prohibit people from engaging in wrongful behavior just because others are doing so. Each of us is required to act as a bulwark against moral compromise by upholding high standards of conduct even in morally corrupt environments.

Like any moral rule, this one has exceptions, and its underlying logic helps point them out. Since the purpose of prohibiting moral compromise is to prevent a slide into wrongdoing or even to move behavior back to a higher level, we might be less willing to insist on high standards when it is clear that our conduct is not likely to have either of these effects: when no stand against corruption is likely to *prevent* or *minimize* its occurrence or when going along with corrupt practices is not likely in any way to *increase* their incidence. We will be even more willing to permit compromise in such circumstances when maintaining standards proves very harmful, either to those upholding the standards or to innocent third parties who might be affected. The literature of business ethics and public policy provides many examples of instances where some believe these conditions are met. Many businesspeople, for example, believe that it is morally acceptable to pay small-scale bribes or "facilitating" payments overseas in contexts where failing to do so makes doing business impossible. Those who favor paying minor "baksheesh" of this sort point out that refusing to do so is a pointless exercise in moral purity because it has no effect on the commercial environment and because it only drives away companies that might otherwise play a positive role in helping nations develop. Here at home, some people have justified government's involvement in legalized gambling—through state-sponsored lotteries or numbers games—on similar grounds. Although advocates of legalization often agree that gambling has many undesirable consequences, they point out that if government holds itself aloof from this activity, people will still gamble and the whole sphere will be turned over to criminal elements. Moral purity is thus achieved at the cost of lost revenues, increased criminality, and violence. The facts advanced in these various arguments are not necessarily correct, of course. Sometimes there are positive effects of a company's resisting involvement in bribery even in places where it is widespread, and state-supported gambling may, on balance, prove more harmful than its defenders admit. But the point is that in very special circumstances, a prevalent pattern of misconduct or corruption can sometimes permit (though not necessarily encourage) involvement in similar less-than-ideal behavior. Three conditions seem to govern when this is so:

(1) Where the misconduct is publicly acknowledged and is clearly an accepted fact of life;

(2) Where resistance to it is *clearly* morally pointless; and

(3) Where resistance is sure to produce more harm than good.

Situations that meet these conditions are not likely to be common. When these conditions are not met, the fact that "everyone's doing it" will not justify complicity in less-than-ideal or wrongful behavior. Even when these conditions are met and the adoption of lowered standards is permitted, such behavior is not morally required. Individuals may still freely choose to resist "going along" and may be morally praiseworthy for doing so. In addition, this concession to wrongdoing does not relieve morally responsible firms or individuals from pursuing effective ways of improving conduct. Where bribery is commonplace, for example, ethically responsible people can still struggle to see better laws passed and stricter codes of conduct adopted. The idea of "mutual restraint mutually agreed upon" makes sense whenever individual heroism is pointless and destructive.

Are these three conditions met in the Toys "R" Us case? Is this behavior really so common as to be virtually accepted as a fact of business life? Is Toys "R" Us able to show that its refusal to engage in raiding activities is pointless and will have no impact on the prevalence of others doing so? And will Toys "R" Us or other parties be seriously injured should Toys "R" Us refuse to participate in this conduct? It is easy to see that none of these conditions is met in this case. Not only is this conduct not widespread and acceptable to many people, but if Toys "R" Us were to join in a practice of sales raiding, it is very likely that its example will lead other firms—including those who presently refuse to engage in this practice—to follow suit. Alternatively, if Toys "R" Us were to take a stand against such practices, it might help prevent an erosion of industry standards. This tells us that Toys "R" Us's resistance to this practice would by no means be pointless. Nor is there any evidence that Toys "R" Us or others will suffer serious harm if the company refuses to engage in this pattern of behavior. Certainly a company like this does not need to pilfer other retailers' merchandise in order to survive, and its refusal to do so will not somehow open the way to serious harm for other parties.

Competitive pressures are a distinguishing feature of the business environment. Although other professions, like law or medicine, have their unique ethical problems, the dilemmas created by competition are not foremost among them. Success for businesspeople, however, often requires defeating competitors. This emphasis on competition creates ethical problems in several ways. It can lead businessmen and businesswomen to violate the rules needed to maintain fair competition. It sometimes prompts them to introduce practices that make matters worse for everyone. Or it can prompt them to take advantage of others' wrongdoings to hasten the slide toward lowered standards. All these tendencies, we can now see, should be resisted. As important as competition itself are the moral commitments needed to direct competition toward the matters that justify it—price, quality, and service—and away from practices that damage the marketplace for everyone.

Case 7.2

✦ MADISON-WARNER [2] ✦

"How did it go?"

Rob Solomon eased himself into a chair and looked glumly across at the sofa where his fiancée, Pat Kogin, was sitting.

"Not too good," Rob replied.

"What's the matter?" Pat asked. "Were the recruiter's questions too tough? Was he unsympathetic?"

Rob's mind wandered over the events of the hour-long interview he had had that afternoon in the Career Services Center with Kevin Lochner, a partner of Madison-Warner, one of the country's top management consulting firms. Rob had gone into the interview feeling confident. A month before, during a visit to the firm's Washington office, he had conversed with another partner. The talk gave Rob reason to believe he was the kind of person Madison-Warner might want. His previous experience in consulting was an asset, as was his high academic standing in Virginia's MBA program. In fact, Rob had come to think that the on-campus interview with Lochner was just a formality—until the question about ethics came up.

Rob explained, "We got to talking about my work at Ericson. I started the whole thing by volunteering how much I liked working for the company because of its value system."

"What exactly did you say?" Pat asked.

"Well, I told him about my assignment gathering competitive marketing information for one of our clients, a major auto supply chain that was thinking about expanding into the southwest. I pointed out that many consulting firms involved in this kind of research actually encourage employees to lie or misrepresent themselves when approaching competitors. For example, they tell employees to pretend that they're graduate students gathering information for theses or something like that. Not Ericson. All of us were told that we had to be 'up-front' with the companies we contacted."

"I always thought you were," Pat interjected. "Did you ever break that rule?"

"No, not at all," Rob continued. "I mentioned that, one time, I phoned a small company that was known to have plans for expansion in the southwest. I explained to the woman who answered the phone that I worked for Ericson, a consulting firm, and that we were conducting research for a large auto supply chain that was seeking to gather information on other companies' expansion plans in the southwest. I asked to be connected with someone who could give me that information.

"The woman I was speaking to told me she could help me herself. She asked whether I had a fax machine. I said I did, and she told me that she would send me a copy of the company's expansion plans for the southwest region. I thanked her very much for the assistance. One hour later I had the information I needed. It was complete and supported by other data I had gotten from public sources."

"I don't see anything wrong in what you did," Pat said.

"Neither did I," Rob replied. "But you wouldn't believe how Lochner jumped on me. He said that what I did was outrageous, that it violated the most basic rules of ethics."

"Why did he say that?" Pat asked.

"He said that it was wrong of me to just accept that information. He said that I had a moral responsibility to find out whether the person who offered the information was authorized to do so—that I should have checked with her superiors. He said that what I did amounts to theft. And he added that I bear personal responsibility if she's fired."

"What did you say to him?" Pat asked.

"I repeated to him that nothing I did was dishonest in any way, I made my identity and my purpose very clear, and asked to speak with someone who could provide me with this information. I also pointed out that firms sometimes want to give out information like this in order to discourage other companies from entering areas where they plan to be."

"Did that satisfy him?"

"No," said Rob. "He kept on saying that he couldn't understand how I could be so ethically obtuse. Then we turned to other matters. But I left the interview with a really bad taste in my mouth. I still don't think I did anything that was wrong or compromised my own values. But I'm very confused."

"So am I," said Pat.

QUESTIONS TO CONSIDER

1. Do you agree with Kevin Lochner's criticism of Rob Solomon's behavior? Why or why not?
2. What do you think are the moral constraints that should apply to ethical competitor intelligence gathering? What would NORM-type reasoning suggest in this case?

THE ETHICS OF COMPETITOR INTELLIGENCE GATHERING

◆

The phrase "competitor intelligence gathering" brings to mind images of a spy-versus-spy world of industrial espionage, where corporate or governmental sleuths wage sinister battles with one another over high-tech information. This picture is not altogether false. In the increasingly competitive world of global business, industrial espionage undertaken by firms and governments is on the rise.[3] But "corporate intelligence gathering" also describes a more familiar and benign set of activities. As firms take seriously the need to secure competitive advantage, they find that information about the markets in which they function and what their competitors are doing or planning to do is essential for success. This places a premium on careful and systematic attention to industry publications, attendance at trade expositions, and market research—all activities that come under the heading of "competitor intelligence."

There are signs that competitor intelligence gathering is becoming a more widely accepted and more important part of business life. A survey of more than three hundred marketing, sales, and planning managers recently showed that nearly all believed that monitoring competitors' activities is important to their business.[4] In 1986, the Society of Competitor Intelligence Professionals (SCIP) was formed, and it now counts more than sixteen hundred members.[5] With this growth in intelligence-gathering activity, ethical questions have abounded. Few persons would hesitate to judge theft of a competitor's materials as morally and legally wrong. But what about direct observation of his plant under secret conditions? Or hiring away of employees who might have access to useful information?

In many cases, corporate intelligence-gathering activities are business students' first experience with questions of business ethics. Many consulting firms, it seems, regard information gathering as a useful training exercise for their newest employees or summer interns. Since it is also common for competitive information gathering to take place under the guise of students' "thesis research," many summer interns or trainees soon find themselves in the thick of ethically questionable intelligence-gathering practices.

In this context, Rob Solomon's quandary is somewhat unique. The most common questionable practices involve lying or misrepresentation, and it is not difficult to see what is wrong with this. Someone who gathers sensitive competitor information by passing herself off as a graduate student doing research, for example, muddies the waters for every real student who follows. No matter how valid or valuable a project, researchers who follow her will encounter suspicion and limited cooperation. Since morality is inherently public, this is true whether or not one is found out: the practice itself cannot be advocated as a public moral rule without undermining its own basis. Fortunately, Rob understands this and he is proud to report that he has been entirely honest with his informant. But he is amazed to learn that Lochner believes that honesty is not enough. Lochner insists that Rob has an affirmative obligation to make sure that his informant is fully authorized to share the information with him. Having failed to do this, Rob is responsible for any damage that results.

Is Lochner right? And how do we think ethically about an activity so basic to relationships among competitors? One way of answering these questions is to adopt a deontological approach. In a discussion of this issue, ethicist Lynn Sharp Paine identifies four basic rules or principles she believes should govern competitor intelligence gathering. According to Paine, ethical intelligence gathering must not involve:

- theft of documents and other tangible property;
- deceit or some form of misrepresentation;
- attempts to influence the judgment of persons entrusted with confidential information (particularly the offering of inducements to reveal such information); and
- covert or unconsented-to surveillance.[6]

These are sensible and ethically understandable rules. They also appear to provide a basis for evaluating Rob's conduct. Since he stole no documents, did not misrepresent himself in any way, and offered no induce-ments to his informant, Rob's own judgment seems to be confirmed: he did nothing wrong.

Nevertheless, the uncertainty remains. How do we know that Paine's list is the right one? Lochner clearly does not agree; he believes that in certain circumstances we must add a rule specifying an affirmative obliga-tion to seek proper authorization for information. Paine's list also raises questions of interpretation. For example, what exactly does the phrase "covert or unconsented-to surveillance" mean? Illegal wiretaps and elec-tronic bugs probably qualify here, but what about visual surveillance of public spaces? Is it ethically wrong for a manufacturer to count the num-ber of trucks entering a competitor's factory in order to determine his business plans? What if a manager overhears a competitor's employees discussing sensitive business information in the cocktail lounge of a con-vention hotel? Is it wrong to use information picked up in this way? Paine's fourth rule does not tell us. As is true of all deontological approaches, in other words, Paine's four rules raise further questions regarding their derivation and application.

NORM offers an alternative approach. It asks us to put Rob's conduct and Lochner's alternative proposal in the form of proposed moral rules or general rules of practice. It asks us to evaluate each proposal omnipar-tially from the perspective of all the affected parties, and then to make a reasoned judgment about each proposed rule in terms of its benefits and harms. We can easily state the two competing rules in this case:

✦

Rob's Proposed Moral Rule: A consultant or manager seeking sensi-tive information from a competitor for an employer must be honest about her or his identity and purpose and must avoid misrepresen-tation, but need not take pains to determine whether informants are properly authorized to release that information.

Lochner's Proposed Moral Rule: A consultant or manager seeking sensitive information from a competitor for an employer must be honest about her or his identity and purpose, must avoid misrepre-sentation, and must take pains to determine whether informants are properly authorized to release that information.

✦

Rob's rule has several obvious advantages. Its requirement of honesty protects firms from deceptive inquiries they could not easily detect and spares them the effort of investigating every inquiry they receive. Since it would be enormously difficult to verify each caller's credentials, if such honesty was not required many firms would release little or no information to the public, handicapping everyone's access to information. This explains, of course, why Paine's rule of honesty is so important. By limiting researchers to honesty, however, Rob's proposed rule has additional advantages. It minimizes the burden on them and facilitates their access to valuable information.

Of course, Rob's rule also exposes companies to the accidental or careless release of sensitive information. From the perspective of firms, it would be convenient to have the enhanced protection that Lochner's stronger requirement provides. In a world governed by Lochner's proposed rule, if a secretary, receptionist, or lower echelon employee mistakenly offered valuable confidential information to an outsider, the firm could count on that person's verifying whether the information was properly released.

But there is also a "down side" to Lochner's proposed rule. For one thing, it would increase the difficulty of gathering information from large corporations. Consider the effort implied, for example, by the phrase "must take pains to determine whether informants are properly authorized to release the information." What does this mean? If I am a student, researcher, or journalist, how do I make sure my informant is "properly authorized" to release information, and how far must I go? Is it enough just to ask, and may I then rely on whatever answer I receive from my (possibly naive) informant? Or must I acquaint myself fully with the company's organization chart? Must I track down the appropriate person, even if he or she is out of town? Is an outsider even in a good position to fulfill these obligations? What about the implied rebuke involved in second-guessing informants? Will this offend them, and will raising the issue of authorization cause all lower echelon people to "freeze up" in the face of every inquiry? Looked at closely, Lochner's proposal threatens to make it far more difficult to gather information from large organizations. In a world where such organizations are already very self-protective but wield great power to affect everyone's lives, is this chilling effect desirable?

In view of the difficulties outsiders face in understanding or determining the control of information inside a large organization, the objective of preventing the inadvertent release of information is probably better met by holding firms responsible for establishing procedures for

information security and for properly training personnel in these procedures. This places the moral burden on firms themselves. When they fail
in their duties, we need not ordinarily hold outsiders morally responsible for correcting their mistakes. Doing so might even encourage firms to
be careless in their handling of sensitive information. This suggests that
if there is moral failure in this case, it lies either with an employee who
has knowingly violated her obligations (and who probably deserves to
be fired as a result), or with a firm that has not properly trained its
employees in information security and should not hold anyone responsible but itself. Of course, it may well be that no mistake was made here,
that Rob's informant was well trained and was authorized to release
information as she did. Whatever the facts, Rob Solomon is probably
right to feel that he behaved properly. Lochner's age and position do not
necessarily mean that he is ethically wiser than the young MBA.

This analysis tells us that in matters of information gathering moral
reasoning requires a complex "balancing judgment" regarding the benefits and burdens of various rules of conduct. Of course, this is true of any
moral judgment, but it becomes especially pertinent where something
like information is involved. Unlike tangible property, information can
be taken without depriving its initial "owner" of its use and often without that owner even knowing that something has been taken. It can even
be acquired by someone not intending to gather it. Handling, protecting,
and preserving sensitive information therefore can be a difficult task. A
central question is, on whom should this burden fall? And why?

We can see that, in the context of corporate information gathering, it
makes sense to impose much of the burden of security on firms themselves. In specific cases, however, we might modify this judgment.
Surveillance activities provide an illustration. It is now technically possible to eavesdrop on private conversations inside a building by beaming
laser light on a window and recording vibrations made by the sound
waves within. Is it ethical for someone to gather information in this way?
The burden placed on individuals and firms to protect themselves
against this would be enormous and communication as we know it
would be seriously impaired. It is advisable, therefore, to regard eavesdropping of this sort as morally unacceptable and to blame those who
engage in it—perhaps to the point of legally prohibiting activities of this
sort. What about conversations overheard in train stations, airports, or
on the street? Suppose in this way I accidentally overhear a discussion
about a competitor's valuable marketing plan? Am I morally obliged not
to use this information? Here again, we must ask where the burden is
best imposed. Obviously, I cannot go through public spaces wearing ear-

muffs and blinders, nor will it be easy for me to "forget" valuable information I have accidentally picked up. It would be better to hold people responsible for being discrete about sensitive matters in public spaces and ethically to impose a general rule of "finders keepers, losers weepers" on information acquired in this way.

The exact shape of our ethical obligations with respect to competitive information gathering will depend upon the nature of the information and the context and means of its release or acquisition. Behavior that will be morally right in one situation (overhearing a conversation and then using the information) will be wrong in others (seeking to "overhear" normally private conversations by means of sophisticated technology in order to use the acquired information). Does this mean that ethical judgments in this area are relative and situational? Yes and no. "Yes," because the facts of the matter and the particular burden a rule imposes will shape our thinking and lead to different conclusions in different cases. "No," because there are some abiding ethical requirements above and beyond contexts. We are always required to identify and omnipartially assess the public rule implicit in the conduct we are examining. In looking at different ways of apportioning praise and blame for conduct, we must first ask who is affected by a particular rule and in what ways they are benefited or harmed. Thinking from the standpoint of any and all of these people, we must ask ourselves whether we would find it reasonable to accept the burdens the rule imposes. By adhering to these abiding requirements we can make ethical headway through a realm of competitor relations that is increasingly challenging businesspeople at all levels, from CEOs to summer interns.

Case 7.3

✦ SAATCHI & SAATCHI[7] ✦

The scene is the crowded cabin of a commercial airliner. A voice-over announces that beginning April 23, 1988, smoking will no longer be permitted on domestic Northwest Airlines flights. All but one of the passengers applaud and cheer.

The executives at the advertising agency of Saatchi & Saatchi DFS Compton who developed this spot for Northwest Airlines had reason to be proud of their work. They were supporting a bold initiative by one of their firm's leading clients. But whatever reasons the Saatchi & Saatchi people had for self-congratulations soon evaporated. Within days of the ad's initial appearance on March 24, RJR Nabisco, another major Saatchi & Saatchi client, abruptly expressed its displeasure at Saatchi & Saatchi's role in the anti-smoking campaign. Claiming "philosophical differences," RJR terminated its eighteen-year relationship with the agency. The cost to Saatchi & Saatchi: approximately $80 million in annual RJR Nabisco billings or about 7% of the agency's U.S. revenues.

The events leading up to RJR Nabisco's withdrawal from Saatchi & Saatchi began with a decision by executives at Northwest to seek competitive advantage in an impending federal ban, set to go into effect on April 23, against smoking on all domestic flights of under two hours duration. Studies by the airline had shown that 9 out of 10 passengers requested nonsmoking seats and surveys showed that many smokers would support a policy prohibiting all in-flight smoking. Armed with this information, Northwest officials decided on the total ban and turned to Saatchi & Saatchi to help them carry the message.

Because Northwest officials wanted to get the jump on their competition, they asked Peter McSpadden, president of Saatchi & Saatchi DFS and the individual responsible for the $55-million airline account, to keep information about the campaign strictly confidential. McSpadden agreed. Inside the agency, information was distributed only on a need-to-know basis. The campaign was not even discussed at the agency's regular Monday morning management meetings.

Agency executives were aware that their Northwest involvement might disturb other agency clients. A particular source of concern was Lorillard, whose True brand of cigarettes Saatchi & Saatchi handled. As a result, on the day the first Northwest ad appeared, Saatchi & Saatchi executives called their counterparts at Lorillard. As they expected, the Lorillard people were not happy with the campaign or the agency's role in it, but they stated that they valued their relationship with Saatchi & Saatchi and had no intention of moving their account.

It did not occur to anyone at Saatchi & Saatchi to call RJR Nabisco. In the words of one executive, "Nabisco is our food client." Although agency people had become accustomed to reviewing campaigns for potential conflicts between different clients, these reviews had largely been confined to product categories. Agency executives knew that Nabisco had been acquired three years before by the large Reynolds tobacco firm, but in their thinking Nabisco meant products like Oreo and Chips Ahoy cookies, Life Savers candies, and CareFree gum—not cigarettes. The fact that Nabisco, following its acquisition by Reynolds, had not objected to their continued handling of Lorillard only confirmed agency executives in this assumption.

However, to top executives at RJR Nabisco and particularly to R. J. Reynolds Tobacco Co.'s chairman-CEO, Edward Horrigan, this neglect of RJR Nabisco's interests was a serious and unforgivable mistake. Like many other tobacco executives, Horrigan felt himself at the head of an embattled industry. Antismoking forces were pressing in on all sides and the recent smoking ban on short-haul flights was just another lost skirmish in this war. Like other firms, RJR had countermoves of its own. The acquisition of Nabisco was itself part of a strategy of diversification meant to help the firm survive possible legislative or legal assaults ahead. But the industry's defensive posture went beyond this. It led to an attitude of broad hostility to antitobacco efforts and a willingness to use a variety of aggressive means to combat them. "If we're attacked, we're not going to roll over and play dead," said Walker Merryman, vice-president of the Tobacco Institute, an industry trade organization. "The sooner our adversaries, friendly or otherwise, learn that, the less difficulty they're going to find themselves in."

In the minds of RJR executives, Northwest's campaign made not only the airline their enemy but Saatchi & Saatchi as well. Morgan Hunter, a former president of Reynolds Tobacco, summed up his colleagues' view of the issue when he said, "This isn't about conflicts of interest, it's about loyalty. Any agency that is getting a lot of company money and doing an ad gloating over a no-smoking policy is going to be perceived as disloyal."

RJR's displeasure at Saatchi & Saatchi's involvement was compounded by the secrecy and lack of notification. In the words of one insider to the decision, RJR executives' view was that "you don't blindside a partner." According to this informant, RJR did not expect to be told any secrets about Northwest. But they objected to the fact that the agency "never even had the decency to pick up the phone [and say] 'We are involved in something confidential and it could be an embarrassment to both of us.'"

Others in the advertising industry agreed. Stanley Katz, chairman-CEO of FCB/Leber Katz Partners, an RJR Tobacco Co. agency, said Saatchi & Saatchi had been "insensitive" and "arrogant" in its failure to anticipate the client's concerns in this matter. He went on to attribute the episode, in part, to the merger and acquisition frenzy that helped fashion the large conglomerates that both RJR Nabisco and Saatchi & Saatchi had become. The incident, he said, "was another by-product of megamergers, of [people] not seeing faces when they look at the issues." All Saatchi & Saatchi had to do, Katz concluded, "was be up-front."

Saatchi & Saatchi's executives vehemently disagreed with these assessments of their conduct. The understanding with Northwest, they maintained, represented a commitment they could not compromise. They were convinced that RJR Nabisco had overreacted to the incident and responded out of emotion rather than reason.

Others in the industry agreed. John Bowen, chairman-CEO of D'Arcy Masius Benton & Bowles said about the concerns of the merged clients: "It's one of the biggest examples of an overreaction I've ever seen. It's not fair." Bowen also defended the agency for respecting its agreement of confidentiality and for avoiding any kind of disclosure to RJR. "You can't sneak around the corner. That's not playing the game fairly," he said. Norman Campbell, president of BBDO Worldwide, added, "Part of the underpinnings of client/agency relationships is confidentiality. To . . . breach that confidence would be wrong."

Whether a defense of principle or a bad mistake, Saatchi & Saatchi's actions were costly to the agency. With 110 staffers on Nabisco business, loss of the RJR account meant substantial layoffs. Beyond Saatchi & Saatchi, however, RJR's conduct raised important new issues for the advertising industry. Other ad agency executives worried about the extension of conflict-of-interest guidelines the episode portended. Existing guidelines already severely limited an agency's growth. For example, it had become an accepted principle that an agency could not take on a product competing with one of an existing client. But RJR's action carried this kind of ban to the entire product line of huge, diversified companies and to the philosophical commitments each product might represent.

The chairman of one international advertising firm summed up the views of many other advertising executives when he said, "This is typical of a trend. We've gone from a product conflict to a company conflict to a category conflict. It's a sweeping extension of the conflict principle. It has to do with the huge size of some clients.

They feel they can set the rules. I think it was wrong for RJR to take the step."

QUESTIONS TO CONSIDER

1. In your view, did Saatchi & Saatchi wrong its client RJR Nabisco in its handling of this episode?
2. How would you evaluate RJR Nabisco's response to Saatchi & Saatchi?
3. What does **NORM** tell us about the rule(s) implicit in Saatchi & Saatchi's and RJR Nabisco's conduct?

FAIRNESS AND RESPECT IN SUPPLIER RELATIONSHIPS

◆

Relationships between a company and its suppliers are often charged with ethical tension. Because smaller suppliers or vendors are dependent on contracts from larger companies, they sometimes resort to unethical or illegal behavior as a way of winning business. Purchasing managers, the individuals within manufacturing firms who deal closely with suppliers, report that among their most frequent ethical problems are offers of gifts and other inducements by suppliers' salespeople. They also complain about finding that their department has been bypassed by suppliers trying to build support for their product or service within other divisions of the firm. But suppliers are not the only ones who create ethical problems. This same dependency makes them vulnerable to pressure for unethical behavior arising from their customer-firms. In the 1970s, for example, the H. J. Heinz company embroiled several of the advertising agencies serving its business in a pattern of income transfer practices that violated both law and generally accepted accounting practices. We look closely at this episode in Chapter 9. Among their practices, Heinz managers apparently applied pressure to the agencies to furnish misdated invoices that would aid the Heinz managers in meeting their bonus objectives. As one agency executive put it, cooperation with these questionable practices became "a cost of doing business" with Heinz.[8]

Key ethical norms in this area are reasonably clear. Honesty and respect for promises are basic. So, too, is respect for confidentiality. Companies and their suppliers are a little like married people; they often share important details of one another's life. Confidential information is inevitably communicated in the course of bidding and performing a job, and breaches of confidentiality disturb this whole relationship. Against the framework of these norms, we can easily assess some aspects of Saatchi & Saatchi's encounter with RJR Nabisco. Having guaranteed confidentiality to Northwest, for example, Saatchi could not ethically inform RJR Nabisco of what it was doing. "Being up-front" with RJR Nabisco, despite its forthright and honest sound, is really an act of betrayal.

But to say that Saatchi could not breach confidentiality only scratches the surface of this case. On a deeper level, we can ask whether Saatchi should ever have entered into an agreement that would end by pitting it against RJR Nabisco's perception of its interests. Was this "business as usual," as the agency affirms, or an act of disloyalty that justified the tobacco company's abrupt termination of their relationship? Deeper still is the question of what kinds of moral allegiance an ad agency owes its clients. What is "conflict of interest" in a supplier relationship of this sort, and when is it legitimate to say that an ad agency must maintain exclusivity in certain product or industry categories? Finally, when things go wrong, when a firm or supplier has violated the other's expectations, what does it owe its former partner? If a firm's relationship with its suppliers is like a marriage, how should they ethically conduct the divorce?

A way of getting into these questions is to consider whether the avoidance of product conflicts is a legitimate expectation by a company of its ad agency. Consider the following proposed moral rule:

◆

First Proposed Moral Rule: While holding a client's account, an advertising agency may not take on competing products without the client's express consent.

◆

From the point of view of advertising agencies, this proposal is not attractive since it limits the agency's freedom and business opportunities—especially its ability to develop and market its expertise within product categories. But from the client's point of view, this rule makes good sense. It protects against loss of confidential competitive information within the agency, without having to impose the cumbersome and uncertain device of "Chinese walls" to keep creative groups apart. It also guarantees the client the agency's undivided attention and prevents an intra-agency "bidding war" for creative talent or ideas. These considerations are so overwhelming that it is hard to see how an omnipartial person could fail to side with the client perspective on this issue. The alternative of internal divisions, competitive pressures, and breaches of confidentiality is so clearly unacceptable, that we can imagine this rule being a normal expectation, even where these matters were not expressly discussed and agreed on in advance by agencies and their clients.

Against the background of this rule, let us consider the one that RJR Nabisco would replace it with:

✦

Second Proposed Moral Rule: While holding a client's account and without that client's express consent, an advertising agency may not take on competing products, nor must it represent *other* non-competing lines of products marketed by firms otherwise in competition with its client *or* take on promotional campaigns or social causes that its client is likely to regard as opposed to its interests.

✦

In fact, there are three different rules present here, and it is worthwhile separating them. The first is the rule we just looked at. The second rule prohibits an agency from taking on any products that might compete with those handled by its client, even though they do not form a part of the agency's own business with the client. Like its predecessor, this rule has one argument in its favor: it guarantees a firm the absolutely undivided loyalty of its advertising agency. But this loyalty is bought at an enormous price. Not only must an agency refuse business from any possible competitor of a large and diversified company it represents, it also must devote considerable energies to knowing when, in an environment of highly diversified companies, such conflicts are likely to arise. In a world where this rule prevailed, today's untroubled client–agency relationship could be seriously disrupted by tomorrow's corporate acquisition, whether or not the divisions and products involved were represented by the agency. These burdens might be justified if they were necessary.

But what possible purpose is served by prohibiting agencies from taking on accounts in noncompeting product lines? Except in very special circumstances no confidential competitive information is involved, and the creative energies, talents, and objectives of an agency are not pitted against one another.

The third rule contained within RJR Nabisco's proposed moral rule is even more troubling. This prohibits an agency from supporting promotional campaigns or causes that its client is likely to regard as "philosophically" opposed to its interests. As expressed, this rule has an immediate problem: it is vague and lacks a "limiting principle" defining its application. In its present form, this rule would permit a company to abruptly fire an ad agency whenever the agency did anything the company disliked. In a world governed by such an imprecise principle, agencies would be wary of undertaking any professional activity that might conceivably antagonize a client.

We can reduce this problem by giving this third rule more precise formulation. Consider the following alternative:

♦

Third Proposed Moral Rule: While holding a client's account, and without that client's express consent, an advertising agency must not take on promotional campaigns or social causes that are *clearly* critical of and have as their targets product lines or activities of the client firm or its industry partners.

♦

Like all seriously proposed moral rules, this one has a rational basis. In an environment where entire product categories—tobacco, alcohol, firearms, entertainment media featuring themes of violence or erotica, and so on—are under criticism by segments of society, an advertiser will understandably be concerned if its agency is also a voice for the opposition. A tobacco company, for example, might wonder whether an agency can really enthusiastically service its business if it also works for antismoking causes or campaigns. Nevertheless, whenever moral issues are under analysis, it helps to look closely at the factual premises and the implications of an argument. For example, is it really the case that an agency cannot simultaneously handle a product line as well as campaigns that may be critical of that product? Since society is currently divided over such issues as smoking and smokers' rights, these divisions also inevitably exist within the advertising world. An agency might, therefore, have two different pools of talent willing to apply their skills to "philosophically" opposed issues, without any more conflicts than already surround us in our homes, schools, or businesses. Indeed, by permitting people to express their different convictions in this way, agencies can effectively harness the energies of these different viewpoints and put them at the service of their clients.

There is also at least one good reason for *not* adopting this proposed rule: it would permit companies or industries to use their economic power to control others' access to advertising. Some have noted—and criticized—a related effect in the publishing industry, where tobacco companies, by virtue of their large advertising expenditures, have been able to reduce the number of antismoking articles in popular magazines.

These considerations suggest to us that even in the clearest of cases—for example, where an agency that handles tobacco advertising also takes on an antismoking campaign by the American Heart Association—we might be reluctant to adopt this proposed moral rule. But the Saatchi–RJR Nabisco episode does not begin to approach this degree of clarity, and its conduct is better described in terms of our second, and unacceptable, moral rule, which prohibits an agency from undertaking anything a firm is likely to regard as opposed to its interests. Northwest's promotion, after all, is primarily directed against competing airlines, not smoking. Although we can easily understand why besieged tobacco executives might react emotionally to anything that casts their product in a bad light, RJR Nabisco is acting on a rule that would badly complicate agency–client relationships.

Taken together, these considerations suggest that RJR Nabisco was probably not morally justified in venting its anger at Saatchi & Saatchi in this way, and the Saatchi executives are right to feel that they were treated unfairly. In effect, by its conduct RJR Nabisco unilaterally imposed on the industry a rule of warfare: "Whoever's not with me is against me." If this rule is sometimes inappropriate in war, it is even less appropriate in business. In general, suppliers and vendors owe each other mutual respect even when their interests diverge and their behavior causes discomfort to one another. RJR Nabisco's abrupt retaliatory firing of Saatchi & Saatchi may have achieved some immediate short-term objectives. It punished Saatchi and put other agencies on notice that tobacco clients will henceforth require total and unswerving loyalty. But it won these gains at a substantial price. By imposing an unreasonable rule, and by doing so without warning, RJR Nabisco appeared to play the role of a bully, earning resentment in the advertising industry and perhaps increasing public mistrust of tobacco companies.

From the point of view of both firms, this episode was a disaster. RJR tarnished its public image and Saatchi lost an $80-million account. Could this outcome have been avoided, and are there lessons here for company–supplier relations generally? On its side, RJR Nabisco might have taken the high road. Respecting the complex moral issues involved, it could have applied to Saatchi the kind of tolerance it had previously shown with regard to the agency's handling of competing tobacco accounts. If it wished to make the point that it found its agency's affiliation with antismoking campaigns of any sort unacceptable, it could have communicated this in a less destructive fashion—either before the episode ever occurred or in its aftermath. Although the expectation of such absolute loyalty may be unreasonable, the perception that RJR acted improperly is intensified by the abrupt, unilateral, and harmful way this expectation was communicated. Arrogant displays of power are rarely justified in human relationships, and they are particularly inappropriate in a context where close and cooperative relationships should prevail.

Could Saatchi, on its side, have done anything to avert or ease the crisis? We have already seen that the agency could not ethically breach the confidentiality of its relationship with Northwest. Making veiled hints at its Northwest involvement, as some industry spokespersons suggested, is no solution, since this invites RJR to coax Saatchi into a full ethical violation. Despite these prohibitions, Saatchi could have been more aware of the context in which it was working and more alert to Nabisco's concerns. "Putting yourself in the other person's shoes," a basic requirement of morality, might have been good business here if it led Saatchi's senior executives to consider the impact of the Northwest campaign on *all* its clients' interests. This may not have led them to agree that there was an ethical conflict of interest here, as RJR Nabisco believed, but it could have helped Saatchi anticipate the tobacco company's adverse reaction and, without violating any ethical norms, to moderate this reaction by thoughtful attention to the client's needs on the morning the Northwest campaign began. Ethical integrity and a willingness to stand on principle are always in order, but they do not preclude—and sometimes even require—sensitivity and courtesy to those affected by one's principled stands. In different ways, but with the same dismal results, in this instance both Nabisco and Saatchi missed this point.

Summary

- Vigorous competition usually best serves the public interest, but some things done in the name of competition are unethical. These include practices that create short-term advantages for one firm by imposing new burdens on everyone else or that discredit an industry as a whole.

- When three conditions are met, it may be permissible to participate in a widespread pattern of otherwise morally undesirable conduct: (1) The conduct must be a publicly accepted fact of life; (2) resistance to it must clearly be morally pointless; and (3) such resistance must be likely to produce more harm than good. These conditions are not easily met, and even where they are, other efforts to reduce the incidence of such wrongdoing may still be required.

- Competitor intelligence gathering is on the rise. Unethical conduct in this area includes theft, deception, attempts to influence the judgment of persons entrusted with confidential information, and covert or unconsented-to surveillance. When issues are less clear, an important question is who should bear the primary burden for information security.

Case 7.4

✦ THE WOLVERINE FASTENER COMPANY[9] ✦

(This case was written by Lance Edson while he was a student at the Amos Tuck School of Business Administration, Dartmouth College. Prior to coming to Tuck, Mr. Edson had worked for three years as a sales engineer and technical representative at NCR Corporation in Dayton, Ohio. He had graduated from Purdue University in electrical engineering in June 1980. The case was based on a summer employment experience with the Wolverine Fastener Company. Names have been disguised.)

The Wolverine Fastener Company was founded twenty years ago by Roger Gordon and Edwin Andrews in Detroit, Michigan. Wolverine's early years were relatively unstable, and the company was on the verge of bankruptcy on more than one occasion. By 1983, however, Wolverine had blossomed into one of the most prosperous manufacturers' representative firms in the state of Michigan, with annual orders of over $10 million. The majority of the company's business was centered around Detroit's automobile industry. Wolverine represented, in addition to many smaller product lines, a major fastener corporation based in Chicago, Illinois. In its manufacture, every automobile requires hundreds of fasteners (screws, bolts, clips, latches, and customized metal and/or plastic connectors).

Both Roger Gordon and Edwin Andrews had come from well-to-do Michigan families. Each attended a different Big Ten university from which he graduated with honors. Soon after their graduation, both men were married in the same year to women who were sisters. Thus, their relationship began as brothers-in-law. About a year later, the two men, both manufacturers' representatives, decided to form a partnership they called The Wolverine Fastener Company.

Gordon gave the impression of being a dynamic businessman. Always in a hurry, Roger consistently tried to get fourteen hours of work into his ten-hour day. This often created a large sense of disorganization and bedlam in the office. He had an uncanny ability to get things done just under the wire. He was what is often called a "doer," never refusing a potential money-making venture because he lacked the time to give it the attention it deserved. Somehow he managed to get everything done.

Edwin Andrews was Roger's working partner in the company, and they shared equally in its profits. The two men made all corporate decisions together, yet each was responsible for his own accounts. Thus, in day-to-day work they went their own way and seemed quite independent of each other.

As the company reached its most prosperous point in 1976, the automotive industry began to drop off rapidly and Wolverine and others followed the downward track. After about two years of steadily dropping profits, Roger Gordon realized that he must gain an edge over the many other vendors competing for the limited business of the automotive industry in order to survive. Because one of the "Big Three" automakers (which we will call Genchryford or GCF) accounted for the majority of the company orders, he decided to concentrate in that area.

Roger examined the process by which he obtained orders from the individual fastener buyer at GCF, Robert Jacobs. It had long been GCF's practice to accept only closed quotations (i.e., all quotes were privately submitted and the lowest group got a percentage of the order for that part). Gordon knew that if he could find out the exact price or even a range of the quotations, he would have the advantage he desired. He was sure that the fastener buyer himself, Jacobs, would not disclose this type of information. However, his secretary, Mary Swoboda, who was responsible for opening all the quotes, seemed a possible source of help. During 1979, Roger began to get to know her better.

Mary Swoboda was a pleasant woman in her mid-twenties. She was unmarried but had a steady boyfriend. Mary was very sharp and always interested in helping to take care of any "problems" that might arise in her area. She was very quiet, and from a lower-middle-class, suburban Detroit background.

Roger Gordon began a very extensive yet subtle implementation of his "plan," as he told it to me. He started by taking Mary to lunch at frequent intervals. As this became an accepted practice, Roger began to take her out to dinner at the poshest of Detroit's establishments. Next, he offered her various presents such as paintings and plane rides (Gordon flew his own plane). The relationship, however, remained purely platonic to the best of anyone's knowledge. Roger said that whenever he took Mary out for dinner, he invariably included his wife in the plans. The Gordons were obviously a happily married couple. Once during the summer of 1983, Roger included me in a dinner with Mary and Mrs. Gordon at the Grosse Pointe Country Club, and we all had a cordial time together.

The results of this process were remarkable. After a short time, Mary began to tell Roger if his quotes were "warm or cold." That helped, but Roger realized that his profits would be maximized if he knew the exact price he must beat. As his program to "win over" Mary Swoboda continued, he eventually realized his goal. Gordon could be observed late in the afternoon when a quote was due calling Mary to receive the lowest price of the quotes that she had to date. Then he would call Chicago to determine if he could undercut that price. If he found that he could, he would type his quotation and take it over to GCF for submission. Two weeks later he would receive an order for that part, which could amount to as much as $750,000. It is important to note that not every quote he submitted was the lowest. Often Wolverine was not able to supply a particular product at a competitive price, due to many market factors. As a result, no suspicion ever arose from Gordon's practices, as far as I could tell.

I had intended to work in New York for Citicorp between my two MBA years at Tuck School, but a family illness required my being home for the summer. So, it was in June of 1983 that I came to Wolverine Fastener as an assistant to Gordon, who was a close friend of our family and a good friend of mine. My primary responsibilities were to handle a number of the company's smaller product accounts, thus allowing Gordon to devote more time and energy to his larger customers, the "Big Three" automakers. Within a few days of arriving at Wolverine, I could see the special relationship between Gordon and Mary Swoboda and could understand its importance. During my summer at Wolverine, the number of part orders from GCF more than doubled. The reason for this seemed clearly to be the tremendous help Gordon received from Mary. Edwin Andrews, Roger Gordon's partner, seemed to be well aware of the situation and, although he never utilized Mary's help, never expressed concern or objection to the situation. What was part of Edwin's straightforward, mind-your-own-business approach surely played a major role in his personal success.

One Friday afternoon, late in August 1983, I returned from my lunch hour to find a memo from Gordon on my desk. The gist of the memo was quite clear. Due to circumstances beyond his control, Roger was unable to return to the office for the rest of the day. I was instructed to submit a very important quote ("in the rough neighborhood of $125,000 . . .") to GCF by four o'clock that afternoon. As I read on, I discovered that Gordon wanted me to do what he had done so often prior to submitting a major quotation: "Call Mary, find out the lowest quote she has received, call Chicago to get their O.K. for a slightly lower price, then type our quote and deliver it to Mary's office."

When I had finished reading the memo I sat back in my chair and looked out the window. Many different thoughts ran through my head. Was what I had been instructed to do ethical? Fair? I thought about the other vendors that were going to suffer because of the advantage we had. It seemed to be, in effect, cheating the system. If I did carry out my orders, was I responsible for my actions? I wondered why our system never seemed so bad in the past, but now. . . . I also tried to diagnose why Mary Swoboda had chosen to supply Gordon with this important information. Surely other vendors must have tried to get this kind of help. Perhaps the economic difficulty of the times had forced Mary to rely on Roger's help. Maybe she just liked him; after all, he was an extremely likable man. In addition, Roger did not come across as a cutthroat vendor, the way many others did, and Mary seemed to appreciate this courtesy.

I also thought about what Roger had told me about his arrangement with Mary—that it was not uncommon in business, that it broke no laws even if it violated GCF standard practice, and that if he hadn't "gotten the edge," a competitor would have. "After all," he told me one day, "I have had a lot of experience, and I really worked to get this advantage in bidding. The system owed that to me."

But there I was, an MBA candidate who thought of himself as a responsible, professional person, and I was unsure what to do in a fairly simple summer job. The irony was that I was confident in discussing much more important ethical cases in my MBA courses. Yet, I felt really paralyzed by the dilemma. What should I do? I did not have anymore time to think.

QUESTIONS TO CONSIDER

1. What is your estimate of Wolverine's business practices in this case? Do you agree with Roger Gordon's claim that the system "owes him" the competitive advantage he has developed by cultivating Mary Swoboda?

2. How should Lance Edson respond to the memo Gordon has given him? What are his responsibilities to Gordon, Wolverine, and society as a whole?

3. What does **NORM** tell us about the various options facing Lance?

𝒩OTES

1. Based on a story by Suzanne Alexander, *Wall Street Journal*, 19 September 1991, pp. B1, B6.
2. © 1992 by Ronald M. Green. This case was prepared for class discussion at the Amos Tuck School of Business Administration. Names have been changed.
3. For a recent discussion of the range of activities in this area, see Douglas Waller, "The Open Barn Door: U.S. Firms Face a Wave of Foreign Espionage," *Newsweek*, 4 May 1992, pp. 58–60.
4. The Conference Board Study, *Competitive Intelligence*, Research Report No. 913 (New York: The Conference Board, 1988).
5. For more information on SCIP, write to them at 818 18th St. N.W., Washington, DC 20006; telephone (202) 223–5885.
6. "Corporate Policy and the Ethics of Competitor Intelligence Gathering," *Journal of Business Ethics* 10 (1991): 426.
7. © 1988 by Ronald M. Green. This case was prepared for class discussion at the Amos Tuck School of Business Administration. Sources used include articles by Philip H. Dougherty, *New York Times*, 6 April 1988; Jon LaFayette, *Advertising Age*, 11 April 1988; and Larry Collins, *Adweek*, 11 April 1988.
8. See Chapter 9, pp. 332–358.
9. This case was developed by John W. Hennessey, Jr. Reprinted by permission.

BUSINESS ETHICS IN A GLOBAL CONTEXT

✦

✦GLOBAL BUSINESS IS NOT NEW. CENTURIES AGO, MERCHANTS PLIED international trade routes, and large banking firms—some of which are still doing business—got their start as financiers of international commerce. In our day, global business activity has increased enormously, with multinational corporations becoming major actors on the world economic stage. If we define a multinational as "a national company in two or more countries operating in association, with one controlling the other in whole or in part,"[1] it is fair to say that many companies that only a few years ago were national firms are now multinationals. Among the factors that make the multinational the dominant form of large business organizations are improved communication and transportation systems, the need to control labor costs, and the existence of competitive pressures forcing companies to take advantage of ever larger economies of scale.

Multinational business poses an ethical challenge to companies and their managers for several reasons. One is the matter of sheer size. It is difficult enough to monitor and control the behavior of managers and employees within a national firm that is large and diversified, and the challenge increases enormously when a firm's divisions and branches are separated by oceans or continents. This problem is compounded by the diversity of cultural values that international business brings with it. In Chapter 2 we saw that ethical relativism, the view that right or wrong depends solely on the teachings of each society, is a logically and ethically incoherent position. Beginning as an effort to promote at least *one* objective and enduring moral value—tolerance—ethical relativism ends by having to accept militant intolerance as "right" so long as it is defended by some social group. We also saw that it is not clear that the obvious fact of ethical diversity really implies *fundamental* differences in basic moral norms. Beneath their surface disagreements people and cultures share some very basic moral values. But to criticize ethical relativism philosophically is not to deny that some moral values and beliefs differ from society to society. Cultural diversity is an undeniable fact, one that frequently forces managers of multinational companies to find themselves operating on unfamiliar moral terrain when they do business abroad.

A final challenge to ethical business conduct in international contexts is the absence of clear or enforceable legal rules. Although value differences exist within an individual country like the United States or Great Britain, they are muted by common legal standards that set limits on what companies or managers can do. This is one reason why business managers are so attracted to the idea that law is their only necessary guide to conduct. But in the international environment the legal limits are far less clear. Multinational firms often engage in activities in the spaces between legal jurisdictions that are not well regulated by the laws of one nation or another. Sometimes the laws are explicit but, because of poverty or corruption, they go unenforced. In Chapter 1 we saw that an uncertain legal and regulatory environment contributed to the Bhopal disaster.

Besides organizational size, moral diversity, and unclear legal standards that intensify the difficulty of decision making in the international setting, there are specific practices common in multinational business that tend to provide opportunities or pressures for unethical conduct. Surveys of multinational firms consistently turn up a list of practices that pose the most frequent problems for managers working overseas.[2] This includes the following categories:

- Small-scale bribery: payment of small sums of money to a foreign official or business employee in order to induce the official to violate some official duty or responsibility or to speed up routine actions (sometimes referred to as grease payments, kickbacks, or baksheesh).

- Large-scale bribery: significant payments made directly or indirectly to government or corporate officials to induce a violation of the law or to influence policy directly or indirectly (these payments are sometimes misleadingly labeled "political contributions" or "agent's commissions").

- Gifts, favors, or entertainment: can include lavish gifts or entertainment, call girls, or expensive travel paid for at the company's expense.

- Pricing: pricing practices that favor selected customers, questionable or deceptive invoicing, dumping products at prices well below those in the home country, and legal or illegal forms of price fixing and bid-rigging.

- Products/technology: the export and sale of products or technologies that are banned for use in the home country but legal in the host country or that, whether legal or not, are unsuitable or inappropriate for use by the people of the host country.

- Tax evasion practices/financial misdealing: includes the use of "tax havens," evasive forms of transfer pricing (prices or interest paid between affiliates and/or a parent company that are adjusted to minimize tax liabilities), or the transfer of currency in violation of host or home country laws.

- Employee rights violations in the host country: practices such as maintaining unsafe working conditions or participating in forms of racial, religious, or sex discrimination normally prohibited by home country values and laws.

- Environmental abuses: taking advantage of a host nation's reduced vigilance or legal standards to pollute the environment or to dispose of toxic wastes.

- Violations of intellectual property rights: involvement in or toleration of product or technology copying in contexts where the protection of patents, trade names, or trademarks is not well enforced.

- Political influence by multinationals: includes tampering with voting or other political processes, as well as illegal technology transfers or involvement in marketing activities when either home or host country is at war or under international controls.

Where some of these practices and categories are concerned, U.S. law has intervened in ways that simplify managerial decision making. For example, in the wake of a series of major international bribery scandals, Congress passed the Foreign Corrupt Practices Act (FCPA) of 1977. This forbids managers of U.S. corporations to pay bribes, directly or indirectly, to foreign political officials. The law does not prohibit all kinds of bribes—for example, those paid to managers of private companies—nor does it rule out modest "facilitating" payments or "baksheesh." Critics of the law have argued that it disadvantages U.S. firms in competition with foreign companies, although empirical studies have tended not to support these claims.[3] We will return to the role of law and international codes below, when we look more closely at the bribery issue.

But even where laws exist, managers face acute dilemmas as they try to do business overseas. Lax enforcement, competitive pressures, the perception that "everyone's doing it," and, most puzzling of all, the sense that a practice may not be morally wrong because it is firmly rooted in local cultural values complicate moral decision making. In this chapter, we examine several selected issues in international business ethics through the lens of *Neutral, Omnipartial Rule-Making*. As we do so, it helps to keep in mind several key features of this method. First of all, as a contextual and situational approach to moral reasoning, it requires us always to take into account the specific facts of a case, including such matters as local beliefs, preferences, and values. These are morally relevant because they shape people's interests. As omnipartial evaluators, we have good reason to want to respect the interests of people we could be. This concern to respect local customs and interests explains the valid moral element in ethical relativism. But there are limits to this respect for localized values, and they show us why relativism cannot be the final word on ethical responsibility. For one thing, members of a local culture or society are not always in agreement about what their values are. In some cases, so-called local values conceal violence or oppression. Disagreements like these force us to decide how we wish to relate to each instance of value conflict, and this, in turn, requires an independent determination of which values merit respect. In addition, individuals or firms operating in foreign environments have values of their own. These shape their interests, and, when conflicts occur, these values must be factored into omnipartial moral choice.

It is not enough, therefore, to say, "When in Rome, do as the Romans do." First of all, we must determine what it is the Romans really "do"—what they are committed to as free and informed members of a society, as opposed to what are merely the practices of some unrepresentative majority or minority. We must also ask what we—as U.S., Canadian, French, or German citizens—owe ourselves and what we are owed by the Romans as we live and work in their midst. Like all instances of moral tension, in other words, value conflict in the international environment cannot be settled by appeal to some overarching relativistic or absolutist rule, but must be adjudicated, rationally and omnipartially, on a case-by-case, issue-by-issue basis.

Case 8.1

✦ THE OIL RIG[4] ✦

This description focuses on one of the three exploratory rigs that have been drilling for several years along the coast of Angola, under contract to a major U.S. multinational oil company. All three rigs are owned and operated by a large U.S. drilling company.

The rig *Explorer IV* is a relatively small jack-up (i.e., with legs) with dimensions of approximately 200 ft. by 100 ft. which houses a crew of 150 men. The crew comprises laborers, roustabouts (unskilled laborers), and maintenance staff, and 30 expatriate workers who work as roughnecks, as drillers, or in administrative or technical positions. The top administrator on the *Explorer IV* is the "tool pusher," an American expatriate, who wields almost absolute authority over matters pertaining to life on the rig.

The crew quarters on the *Explorer IV* were modified for operations in Angola. A second galley was installed on the lower level and cabins on this level were enlarged to permit a dormitory-style arrangement of 16 persons per room. This lower level is the "Angolan section" of the rig, where the 120 local workers eat, sleep, and socialize during their twenty-eight-day "hitch."

The upper level houses the 30 expatriates in an area equal in square footage to that of the Angolan section. The expatriate section's quarters are semiprivate with baths, and this section boasts its own galley, game room, and movie room. Although it is nowhere explicitly written, a tacit regulation exists prohibiting Angolan workers from entering the expatriate section of the rig except in emergencies. The only Angolans exempt from this regulation are those assigned to the highly valued positions of cleaning or galley staff in the expatriate section. These few positions are highly valued because of the potential for receiving gifts or recovering discarded razors, etc. from the expatriates.

The separation of Angolan workers from expatriates is reinforced by several other rig policies. Angolan laborers travel to and from the rig by boat (an eighteen-hour trip), whereas the expatriates are transported by helicopter. Also, medical attention is dispensed to the expatriates by the British R.N. throughout the day, but, except in emergencies, only during shift changes for the Angolans. When there are serious injuries, the response is different for the two groups. If, for example, a finger is severed, expatriates are rushed to Luanda for reconstructive surgery, whereas Angolan workers have an amputation operation performed on the rig by a medic.

Angolan workers are issued gray coveralls and expatriates receive red coveralls. Meals in the two galleys are vastly different; they are virtually gourmet in the expatriate galley and somewhat more proletarian in the Angolan section. The budgets for the two galleys are nearly equal despite the gross disparity in numbers served.

Communication between expatriates and Angolans is notable by its absence. This is principally because none of the expatriates speaks Portuguese and none of the Angolans speaks more than a few words of English. Only the chef of the Portuguese catering company speaks both English and Portuguese and, consequently, he is required to act as interpreter in all emergency situations. In the working environment, training and coordination of effort is accomplished via sign language or repetition of example.

From time to time an entourage of Angolan government officials visits the *Explorer IV*. These visits normally last only for an hour or so, but invariably, the officials dine with the expatriates and take a brief tour of the equipment before returning to shore via helicopter. Never has an entourage expressed concern about the disparity in living conditions on the rig, nor have the officials bothered to speak with the Angolan workers. Observers comment that the officials seem uninterested in the situation of the Angolan workers, most of whom are from outside of the capital city.

The rig's segregated environment is little affected by the presence of an American black. The American black is assigned to the expatriate section and is, of course, permitted to partake of all expatriate privileges. Nevertheless, it should be noted that there are few American blacks in the international drilling business and those few are frequently less than completely welcomed into the rig's social activities.

QUESTIONS TO CONSIDER

1. Which features of the living/working arrangements on the rig strike you as morally acceptable? Why?
2. Which features strike you as morally unacceptable? Why?
3. If you were put in charge of the rig, what changes would you make? Why?

EMPLOYEE RIGHTS IN THE MULTINATIONAL SETTING
✦

How should firms treat their foreign employees working in overseas branches or divisions? At one extreme is the view that local laws and expectations should apply to matters of pay, employee safety, or rules governing nondiscrimination. This permits companies to act like "moral chameleons," taking on the coloration of their surrounding environment. Opposing this is the view that a firm must apply the laws and values of its home country wherever it operates, whatever the local conditions. Somewhere in the middle are views allowing a measure of accommodation to local situations, or that permit adjusting some standards but not others.

The oil company in this case seems to have opted for the chameleon position. Each deck of the rig physically embodies the value of the separate home and host country cultures. The upper deck is presumably no different from the living quarters in a rig stationed off the Louisiana or Scottish coast. Its thirty expatriates enjoy semiprivate accommodations, recreational facilities, excellent food, and prompt attention to their medical needs. One deck below, Angolan workers live in an environment reflecting the poverty and backwardness of their country. Four times the number of workers share the same amount of space and resources as thirty expatriates. Transportation and medical care are markedly inferior.

Although this situation may first strike us as grossly unfair, an ethical argument can be made for at least some of the differences in treatment. A key to this argument is the insistence that these conditions reflect economic realities. Presumably, the superior conditions provided for the expatriates are needed to attract skilled workers to this job. As for the Angolans, their wages and working conditions are good enough to attract 120 of them to the rig. Although we know little about them, it appears that no one has forced them to accept these conditions. They come from a poor region of a poor country. If we assume the Angolans value their jobs, requiring the employer to spend more on food or amenities might actually worsen the workers' lot. To keep the enterprise profitable, money spent on improved working conditions might have to come out of salaries or even a reduced level of employment, and we have no reason to believe that the Angolan workers want these trade-offs.

Economic arguments like these have great force. They reflect the value we place on freedom and they bring to light facts that moral reasoning cannot ignore. We have repeatedly seen how proposed moral rules that initially seem like good ideas sometimes prove unacceptable because, once they are acted on, they encourage behaviors whose consequences undermine or destroy the rules themselves. Similarly, economic arguments like these are moral arguments to the extent that they call into question some good moral intentions in this area. They remind us that it can be self-defeating to insist on strictly equal job conditions for everyone in a firm when this erodes the incentives needed to keep the company productive and competitive. In the less-developed world, economics warn us against insisting on equalized pay or working conditions in contexts where the lesser costs of doing business are a major incentive to productive investment in the first place.

Like all sound moral argumentation, this way of thinking implicitly appeals to omnipartiality and objectivity. Those who argue on economic grounds against more equal treatment of third-world employees would presumably do so even if they found themselves in the shoes of these employees, because it is the nature of their argument that the policies they criticize harm even the workers. *But there is a difference between the token use of omnipartiality for the sake of making a moral point or defending a moral prejudice, and the strenuous and sincere examination of a decision in terms of all its factual presuppositions and its real-life consequences for all those it affects. Rationalization differs from sincere moral reasoning because it involves the use of token argumentation to justify morally unsustainable conclusions. Moral sincerity requires a detailed and honest encounter with the facts of a case.*

Applying this more rigorous standard to conditions on the oil rig, what do we learn? To begin with, we probably want to know more about the economic and human facts of this situation. To what extent, for example, are the extreme differentials we see here really necessary for the economic viability of this exploratory operation? Would the rig's owners really be compelled to reduce salaries or lay off Angolan workers in order to improve the food and other job conditions? And what about the Angolans? Have they in fact freely accepted these working conditions, or are they victims of misinformation or duress (including the pressures of extreme poverty they may be trying to escape)? Would they really refuse to make trade-offs of one sort or another for an improved work environment? Although we do not have the answers to these questions, their importance alerts us to something about the rig that is morally awry: the nearly total absence of communication between the Angolan workers and the expatriates. Not only does this absence of communication—exhibited by the lack of workers with appropriate language skills and the company's apparent indifference to hiring or training them— erode our confidence in the workers' informed consent to these job conditions; failure to maintain good communications is itself a moral wrong in an environment where a natural disaster or industrial accident can occur at any time.

In my earlier discussion of employee rights (Chapter 5), I mentioned the importance of employee participation as a surrogate for the standpoint of moral choice. I pointed out that sometimes it is impossible, outside a particular work environment, to know what omnipartial persons would advocate in making the difficult trade-offs imposed by business realities. But I also pointed out that participative decision making—active involvement of all those affected by a decision—is a way of overcoming these difficulties and of modeling the situation of free, informed, and omnipartial choice that morality requires. This point applies here. We would feel more comfortable with the differences in working conditions on this rig if we had reason to believe that they were acceptable to the Angolans themselves. The absence of communication makes us doubt whether the matter of working conditions has ever been considered.

Reasoning omnipartially, even without a detailed knowledge of the economic realities, we are also led to question other aspects of life on the rig. It is not clear that compelling economic realities can justify all the inequalities we see here. Some may be acceptable, but others may not. Not knowing whether we are Angolans or expatriates, for example, we might be willing to put up with the existing differences in food. Assuming that the Angolans' diet is more basic, relying heavily on vegetable products, its lower cost might represent no real difference in nutritional value and its familiarity to the workers might recommend it. (Given what is currently known about nutrition, it is even possible that the Angolans' diet is healthier than the expatriates.) But we cannot say the same thing for the differences in medical care. A worker threatened with a permanent handicap because of the lack of prompt medical attention or hospitalization is seriously harmed whether he is an Angolan or an expatriate. Different expectations about care may make the Angolans more willing to put up with these inequities, but the harm following an accident has the same lifelong implications. What could justify such differences of treatment? Not only do we lack convincing evidence that it would be too expensive to provide helicopter evacuation and hospital care for all seriously injured workers, but, even if this were true, it is not clear that this would justify these differences in treatment. After all, Angolan workers accept work on the rig in the hopes of improving their life conditions. They may be willing to put up with several years of work under relatively harsh conditions in order to save up the "grubstake" they need for future prosperity. But even in such circumstances, the bargain is changed and seriously worsened by the prospect of unnecessary death or permanent physical impairment. Reasonable and informed people would hesitate to accept these trade-offs.

We must not confuse the reasoning of informed people under conditions of omnipartiality with the actual thinking of the Angolan workers themselves. In moral reasoning we can sometimes confine our inquiries only to what the actual people touched by a decision want. As rational and omnipartial persons, we do not need to actively correct every illusion that people harbor or every mistake they make. But, where serious issues of life, health, and the capacity to function are concerned, we must be prepared to go beyond people's immediate judgments and to arrive at a fuller and more objective assessment of the impact of our decisions on them. Uninformed of the alternatives, perhaps naively hoping that the worst will not happen to them, the Angolan workers may never think of questioning the medical arrangements that threaten them with death or impairment. But *because moral reasoning requires us to consider that we could be them—experiencing both their naiveté and their suffering—we must protect ourselves against the most grievous outcomes we face. Just as we sometimes rationally decide to override our own liberty to protect ourselves against thoughtlessly incurred harm—for example, by voting for laws that mandate the use of seat belts or motorcycle helmets—so we sometimes rationally and omnipartially choose to override the preferences and wishes of others when we know these preferences to be ill-considered and dangerous to them. This is the meaning of paternalism, and it is sometimes justifiable.* In this instance it would be paternalism in the best sense of the word to insist on better health-care arrangements, even if the workers themselves did not voice or support this demand.

This same rigorous standard of informed omnipartiality raises a question about another feature of life on the rig: the pervasive appearance of racial discrimination. The key word here is "appearance," since there is some evidence that these patterns of discrimination are not so much intentional as the result of history and circumstance. The fact that the rig is stationed off Angola and employs unskilled workers is a guarantee that the lowest echelon will be black. The paucity of blacks among skilled expatriate oil-rig workers—something that itself may be the result of a previous history of discrimination in the industry—accounts for the largely white upper deck, although the presence of one black is a sign that, at least officially, the company does not discriminate. Assuming that there is no corporate intent to discriminate here, we are still left with an interesting, and odd, moral question: What is a company's responsibility when its policies unintentionally produce what seem to be discriminatory employment patterns? Are *appearances* grounds for moral concern and action?

To answer this question, it helps to understand why racial discrimination is wrong. To be discriminated against because of the color of one's skin is not only evil in itself, because it denies one access to valued opportunities, but it has long-term and devastating psychological impacts on its victims in terms of reduced social standing and self-esteem. Human beings do not live by bread alone. Status and self-respect are goods we all pursue—sometimes at the cost of life itself—and any practice that erodes them can be as evil as direct physical injury.[5] Against this background we can see that the situation on the rig, even if it does not result from intentional discrimination and does not represent an effort to block access to more desirable jobs, still reinforces the psychological attitudes that accompany racial discrimination. By perpetuating racial stereotypes, it threatens to foster racial prejudices among the expatriates and to undermine the self-respect of the Angolans. Intended or not, this situation is vicious.

How can a responsible company address this problem? One response is to do everything possible to reduce the appearance of racial divisions on the rig. Some steps are easy to take: providing identical uniforms to all workers is one way of symbolizing their equal dignity. (Indeed, the present color differences in the uniforms may represent a particularly dangerous kind of discrimination, since it is easier to locate a worker who falls into the sea when he is wearing red.) Ending the virtual apartheid that governs the access to different areas of the rig is another step. If theft is a consideration, there are better ways to prevent it, such as locks on the doors of individual rooms. A sustained effort to bring more black workers into the expatriate group, whether by promoting qualified Angolans or by bringing in additional black expatriates, would also be strongly advisable. Not only would this break up the pattern of racial stereotyping, it would provide the Angolans with new role models and opportunities. In this case, the *Explorer IV*, like multinational corporations at their best, would become not just an economic opportunity for Angola but a valuable educational and cultural resource as well.

This evaluation of human relations and policies on the oil rig furnishes us with some insight into the complexities of doing business in the international environment. Not every difference in treatment of foreign employees is morally objectionable. Pay and work-condition differences can be morally acceptable if they are a condition of the economic viability of an enterprise overseas, and if they do not impose serious risks to the health, lives, and self-esteem of workers. If we think back to the Bhopal case described in Chapter 1, we can see that Union Carbide made a mistake by compromising on those aspects of its plant operations that reduced the safety of workers to below the level in its equivalent U.S. plants. **NORM** provides a key insight here. If we allow developed-nation companies to engage in life-threatening or other similarly dangerous practices in third-world nations, practices that are normally forbidden to them in their home countries, we create a rule of practice that invites abuse. In such a moral world, rather than obeying tough home country laws, companies will predictably export their most dangerous jobs and practices overseas. Since poor nations desperately need employment and investment, we can even imagine a bidding war resulting between developed and third-world nations that will drive down workplace standards everywhere. Although omnipartial persons may allow some degree of lowered standards of pay or other less consequential matters across national or regional lines, it is hard to imagine that they would invite or encourage an invidious competition of this sort.

Another lesson of the oil rig is that appearances count. Firms should strive to avoid employment practices that reinforce discriminatory stereotypes or make it seem as though the enterprise supports racism or other forms of oppression (even when this is not true). Responsible multinational companies will lean over backward, possibly at the expense of short-term profits, in order to set a standard of behavior that affirms the dignity of all who work for it. By adopting this stance, multinationals can make a positive cultural and economic contribution to their host countries and earn the long-term goodwill on which their continued presence in the host country depends.

COPING WITH BRIBERY AND EXTORTION

◆

Bribery is one of the most common and troubling problems faced by international managers. Offering bribes is a type of involvement in corruption that managers often deeply resent, and yet in some nations it appears to be a condition of doing business. Resisting involvement in bribery can even seem futile: the company that refuses to go along with requests for bribes may jeopardize its business while less honest competitors stand by, ready to jump in to keep the corrupt practice alive.

Looking at this issue, a few definitions and distinctions are in order. It is important, for example, to recognize the difference between small-scale and large-scale bribery. "Baksheesh" and "grease" payments are undeniably common and even openly accepted in many less-developed countries. In some cases, they represent the way that poorly paid government officials supplement their income. Large-scale bribery aimed at high government officials is another matter. Bribes of this magnitude are always concealed from public view. Even in societies where high-level corruption is said to be common, the disclosure of large bribes to public figures can result in political turmoil and the unseating of a minister or a government. Since businessmen and businesswomen sometimes try to justify complicity in bribery by pointing to its prevalence, it is important to ask what kind of bribes they are talking about. Widespread baksheesh, for example, does not necessarily provide a license for involvement in political corruption.

It is also important to distinguish between bribery and extortion. Bribery involves the payment of money or other valuable goods to a

Case 8.2

◆ ALEXANDER GAVIN'S DILEMMA[6] ◆

The following letter was sent by Alexander Gavin to his former instructor in a summer executive education program.

April 10, 1983

Dear Professor _____ ,

I have not talked with you since my participation in the Executive Program in the summer of 1978. Many times I've hoped I might come back to visit but my life has been one surprise after the other, and I have been too busy to take any vacations in recent years.

I want to tell you about a situation that happened to me recently. I know you will be interested in it, and if you have time I'd like you to tell me what you would have done had you been in my position.

As I think you know, I am Senior Project Manager for the El Sahd Construction Company in Kuwait. The company is a prosperous one, with an excellent reputation for producing in a timely and cost effective way on major construction projects in the Middle East. The Chairman and Chief Executive Officer is a well-known Kuwaiti and my direct boss is another American expatriate who is Senior Vice-President for urban construction projects.

Two months ago we put in a bid to be the principal subcontractor on a project in Iran. Our bid was $30 million, and we expected to bargain with Ajax, Ltd., the British-based company that was asking for the bids. We had built a heavy profit into the $30 million.

I was asked to go to Tehran on March 3rd to talk with the Ajax manager of the major project. That manager told me that we were going to get the job. I was delighted. The job meant a lot to us. We had put a great deal of planning into it, and it was exactly the kind of work that we do best.

Then came the surprise. I was told our bid had to be $33 million. My response was that we can always raise our price, but I would like to know why we were being asked to do so. The reply was, "Our way of doing business requires that because $1 million will go directly to the Managing Director of our Company in London, I will get $1 million, and you, Alexander, will get $1 million in a numbered Swiss account." "Why me?" I asked. "Because we need to have you on the hook as insurance that you will never talk about this with anybody else."

I went back to Kuwait to ponder the matter. I was particularly disturbed because I had heard of cases like this where if the bidder failed to cooperate the next message was that physical harm might be part of the exchange. I had been involved in "pay-offs" before. They are a common part of doing business in the Middle East, but I had never been in a situation where I was being coerced into taking a "cut" myself. I didn't like that. It went against my ethics.

At that point I really didn't know what to do. I thought, among other things, how helpful it would have been to put my dilemma before one of your classes and listen to the discussion.

Sincerely,

Alexander Gavin

QUESTIONS TO CONSIDER

1. In your view, does Alexander Gavin face a moral dilemma? Why or why not?

2. What does **NORM** tell you about aspects of the decision facing Gavin?

3. If Gavin asked you for advice, what would you recommend that he do?

private or public official in order to get that official to breach a duty to his or her organization. Bribery is usually wrong because we normally expect people to fulfill their duties.[7] In contrast, extortion involves the use of force or other unacceptable forms of pressure to elicit money or to cause someone to breach a duty to his or her organization. Many people feel that acquiescence to extortion is less blameworthy than bribery since it is not freely undertaken but results from coercion.

It is not hard to see that bribery and extortion are both unfortunate aspects of economic and political life. When economic systems work properly, decisions by consumers or governments are supposed to be made on the basis of such rational criteria as price, quality, and service. Bribery and extortion seriously upset this process. In terms of **NORM**, we can see that the act of bribing a corporate agent or public official creates a moral world in which power, deviousness, and the potential for private gain become the basis of corporate and political decision making. It is important to understand the pernicious effect of bribes, since some of the terminology in this area tends to obscure it. For example, use of the term "grease" suggests that certain small-scale payments made to customs agents or other government officials lubricate the administrative process, and in a certain sense this is true. In some foreign countries, businessmen or businesswomen often find it impossible to get the simplest official task done until a payment has been made. But grease payments really do not expedite the process. They unblock obstacles deliberately placed in the way in order to elicit the payments, and the more these payments are made, the more the obstacles appear. As we have seen repeatedly, policies or practices are never isolated; they form a system of conduct where one person's actions generate further behaviors and expectations on the part of other people. Those who use grease encourage the behavior that necessitates it. In this sense, within a system of behavior, grease is better thought of as "grit."

It is also important to see the destructive implications of even small-scale bribery. Many students of less-developed societies point to the widespread presence of corruption as one of their most serious obstacles to development. Some years ago, Gunnar and Alva Myrdal argued in their classic study *Asian Drama* that the best foreign assistance which developed societies can provide to underdeveloped ones is the systematic refusal to engage in bribery or to yield to extortion. By helping to break down the practices that hobble these societies and frustrate rational decision making, the Myrdals argued, this stance could make a more positive contribution to economic development than outright grants or foreign aid.[8]

Undoubtedly, many businesspeople agree with these ideas. Nevertheless, they still feel hamstrung by the seemingly omnipresent and inescapable pressure of extortion to pay bribes. Faced with the prospect of a valuable piece of computer or medical equipment sitting indefinitely on a dock exposed to the elements, is it reasonable to refuse to pay a small "fee" to a customs agent? What is one to do when a large contract affecting the welfare of many corporate stakeholders seems to hinge on the payment of a bribe demanded by a government minister? Moral scruples are fine, but do they make sense when they lead to the loss of valuable business and when competitors with even fewer scruples are ready to take one's place?

These questions are on Alexander Gavin's mind as he writes to his former teacher. Alexander is no stranger to bribery. Operating in the Mideast, he is familiar with the system of "agents' commissions" that is used to cloak bribes to political figures or influential members of royal families. Alexander admits he has been involved in "payoffs" before, but now he faces a situation that strikes him as different. He is troubled by the fact that he is the one who is the recipient of a bribe, and he fears physical harm if he refuses to comply. In this sense, Alexander is a victim of extortion: he sees himself as being pressured, bribed, and even physically threatened by the Ajax managers to violate duties to his firm.

Is Alexander right to think this situation differs from the payoffs he had previously been involved in, or is this just a belated awakening to moral issues he had been ignoring? Like many managers, Alexander excused his previous involvement in corruption on the grounds that what he was doing was "in the best interests of the company." This is a common excuse for managerial wrongdoing, and it is not without moral force.[9] Each of us has moral obligations to our firms. Managerial wrongdoing done in the name of the company at least fulfills some of these duties, whereas receiving bribes represents a betrayal of the firm, of society, and of our own moral integrity. Of course, even in this case Alexander could see receiving a bribe as "in the company's interests," although there is the new element of personal gain for Alexander that makes this whole affair particularly troubling to him. Gavin has some reason, then, to see the Ajax deal as representing for him a new level of involvement in corruption, but he is probably wrong to think that his previous deeds were morally blameless.

The element of extortion further complicates matters. On one level, there is the possibility of a direct threat to Alexander and his family. It is not clear whether this threat is real or a product of Alexander's imagination, but surely if such a threat were present it would affect our thinking about his dilemma. On another level, the extortion reaches to Alexander's duties to his firm. Implicit in the Ajax "offer" is the threat to withhold the contract if Alexander does not go along with the deal. Alexander thus finds himself at the center of a vortex where personal financial gain, managerial responsibility, and his personal and familial interests all conspire to force him into conduct he ordinarily believes is wrong.

What can we say to Alexander Gavin? To begin with, we can help him by identifying *all* the stakeholders his decision affects and itemizing each stakeholder's interest in the outcome. *This is a necessary discipline in every instance of moral choice, but it is particularly important in a complex case like this one, where it is easy to overlook important actors in the situation. To do this, it helps to begin an analysis by carefully itemizing—literally writing down on a sheet of paper—all the stakeholders involved.* In Alexander's situation, this discipline initially yields the following list:

- Alexander Gavin (and his family)
- El Sahd Construction Company (and its stakeholders)
- Ajax, Ltd. (and its stakeholders)
- The Ajax project manager
- The Ajax managing director
- Others doing business in the Mideast, including U.S. managers in this part of the world
- The Iranian customer (and its stakeholders)

Some of these stakeholders have multiple and even mutually conflicting interests. Alexander, for example, has duties to his firm and his family. As an individual he is not averse to receiving a million dollars, but he is also concerned about not becoming involved in corruption. If Alexander were working for a U.S. company, he would have a specific interest in obeying the law, since behavior of this sort violates various U.S. statutes, including the FCPA. But his firm is Kuwaiti, and it is not clear which Kuwaiti, British, or other national laws apply in this setting.

The El Sahd Construction Company's stake partly overlaps Alexander's. Its owners and employees have an interest in winning a valued contract. At the same time, a company does not want to risk its integrity or reputation by involvement in an illegal or corrupt deal. A very specific interest of the firm is in ensuring that its managers deal openly and honestly with it. The deal threatens this interest since the Ajax managers are paying Alexander to keep quiet and even to deceive his firm about the source and object of the additional funds in the bid. It is not clear how these managers expect Alexander to tap the $3 million he is being asked to charge, but getting this money may require Alexander to falsify the invoices that he submits to his firm.

The Ajax project director and managing director have an obvious stake. They each want to earn $1 million and keep alive a scam that has been lucrative for them in the past. This pits them against the interests of their employer. If Ajax's bid is attractive enough to allow an overcharge of this sort, the money belongs to the owners of the English firm, who alone have the right to determine what should be done with it. In simple terms, the two Ajax managers are embezzling, and their company has an obvious interest in preventing this.

Other businessmen and businesswomen receive no significant benefit from the Ajax scam. To the extent that this behavior spreads to other firms, it brings the usual checkered array of gains and harms typical of business corruption. In general, only individual managers or companies that feel adept at corruption can benefit from practices of this sort, whereas hardworking and honest firms are harmed, along with investors and consumers generally.

What of the Iranian customer and its stakeholders? We do not know much about this actor in the case, apart from the fact that it is an organization large enough to fund a project costing tens of millions, perhaps hundreds of millions, of dollars. This suggests government involvement. If the customer is the Iranian government, the Ajax scam will cost it— and Iranian taxpayers—at least $3 million. We might also ask what the source is of a government's willingness to overpay on a presumably competitive bid. Perhaps the quality of Ajax's work merits the overcharge. If so, the Iranians have an interest in anything that threatens the stability or reputation of a valued contractor. Alternatively, it is not out of the question that the Ajax managers have won this plush contract by resorting to their usual underhanded methods: by bribing some important government officials. If so, excluding those receiving the bribes— who are beneficiaries of the deal—the government has an important interest in halting practices that needlessly drain its funds and corrupt its functionaries. If we consider that Gavin is writing in 1983, at the height of the Iranian Islamic revolution, and when Iran's relations with the United States and with other Western governments were strained beyond the breaking point, this governmental stakeholder is an important one indeed.

The possible political background of this deal reminds us of another stakeholder or set of stakeholders we failed to include on our initial list: the U.S. government and its citizens. As an American, Gavin represents his nation. Even though he works for a foreign company, in this volatile environment his involvement in corruption may unleash retaliation against U.S. citizens in Iran or elsewhere. Alexander may find himself at the center of a major international incident. This illustrates how important it is to be as inclusive as possible in identifying the individuals affected by our moral choices.

Merely identifying and listing the stakeholders affected by Gavin's decision provides a cautionary note in approaching his decision. Alexander may be right in saying that payoffs are common in this environment, but we are not dealing here with ordinary baksheesh. Without knowing all the details, this looks more like full-scale bribery of the political officials of a sensitive regime, compounded by acts of embezzlement and possible thuggery. On purely prudential grounds, does Alexander Gavin really want to become involved in a scheme of this sort?

The possible threat of violence is a matter of moral concern. When do threats morally justify our going along with immoral practices? Assume for the moment that Alexander's fears have a basis. Does the threat of violence justify his complicity in this deal? Consider the following moral rule:

◆

Proposed Moral Rule: A businessman who is threatened with physical violence unless he becomes a party to fraud and embezzlement may participate in these activities to the extent needed to ward off the threat.

◆

This rule has the advantage of offering a means of self-protection to those threatened in these ways, but the problems with the rule are also obvious. As always, it is important to see what kinds of expectations and behaviors our proposals are likely to encourage. In a world governed by this rule, the work of extortionists will be made easier. Those they threaten will feel morally justified in acquiescing. As a result, this rule enhances the power of extortionists and widens the circle of those engaged in these destructive practices. Conversely, if we conclude that threats do not ordinarily justify complicity in criminal activities like these, and if we back up this moral judgment with penalties for such cooperation, we place a major obstacle in the way of those who would use other people as tools for wrongdoing. We also strongly encourage people threatened in this way to find *other* means of working themselves out of their dilemma, such as reporting the threats to the authorities and seeking police protection.

All this suggests that, on the grounds of morality and prudence, ethics and self-interest, Alexander is well advised to stay away from this scheme. Bribery and embezzlement on this scale are nowhere widely acceptable practices, nor can they be. In Chapter 7 we saw that some businesspeople have sought to justify involvement in small-scale bribery by claiming that "everyone's doing it." Behind this claim lies the argument that in very special circumstances, when *three* conditions are met, involvement in a pattern of widespread misconduct such as small scale bribery can be morally justified. Recalling our previous discussion, the following conditions permit such involvement:

(1) Where the misconduct is publicly acknowledged and is clearly an accepted fact of life;

(2) Where resistance to it is *clearly* morally pointless; and

(3) Where resistance is sure to produce more harm than good.

Although these conditions are not commonly met, they probably apply to the kinds of low-level facilitating payments we have discussed. This explains why even the fairly rigorous standards of the FCPA exempt these kinds of payoffs from criminal penalties. However, the behavior engaged in by the Ajax managers and being forced on Alexander is in a different league altogether. The secrecy demanded by the Ajax manager shows that the first of these conditions is not being met and suggests that conditions two and three are not, either.

All this tells us that it would be morally wrong and probably unwise for Alexander to become involved in this scheme. What, then, should he do? One key to answering this question lies in the recognition that Alexander has important duties here to his company. El Sahd is a major stakeholder that Alexander's action will seriously affect no matter what he decides to do. El Sahd's possible involvement, along with the counsel, support, and protection that the company can provide, also make it a natural ally for Alexander in this situation. As a first resort, Alexander should probably talk the Ajax offer over with his direct boss, a fellow American. If he has reason to be dissatisfied with his boss's advice or response, he can always proceed higher up in the firm, to the Kuwaiti chairman-CEO or to the Board of Directors. Because his own safety may be on the line, Alexander should insist on confidentiality and a right to participate in decision making at every step.

This course of action raises an odd moral question. Let us assume that in the course of dealing with the Ajax manager, Alexander, apprehensive and uncertain about what to do, had agreed to keep their conversations to himself. Does Alexander now have a moral duty of confidentiality? Deontologists commonly answer such questions with the observation that our duties of truth-telling, promise-keeping, and confidentiality do not extend to wrongdoers. Legal systems support this view by declaring agreements to break laws "unconscionable" and nonbinding. **NORM** confirms and helps further explain these judgments. If we were to insist that people respect agreements to commit legal and moral wrongs, we would greatly extend the reach of wrongdoers. The same is true if we conclude that people must adhere to agreements elicited by force or guile. Rules relieving people of responsibility to uphold these kinds of agreements send a clear message to wrongdoers that the ability to appeal to others' sense of moral obligation is not a weapon in their criminal arsenal.

There is one important objection to this line of reasoning. A rule dissolving promises or agreements in coercive or illegal situations to some extent annihilates itself. In a world where wrongdoers know that collaborators will not feel compelled to tell the truth or to keep promises, malefactors will be wary about trusting anything said to them. In such circumstances, promises and veracity will cease to exist and we may lose moral practices that are sometimes valuable in extreme situations.[10] For example, people like Alexander Gavin would lose the ability to "play along" with the Ajax conspirators as a way of buying time to rethink their decision. This objection is important, but there are responses to it. For one thing, this loss must be weighed against the obvious dangers of allowing wrongdoers to think they can morally obligate others to cooperate in their misconduct. For another, we may not totally lose the benefits of these valuable moral practices in such circumstances. A rule suspending obligations of promise-keeping or truth-telling in situations where one must lie or speak untruthfully in order to escape from threatening circumstances is not entirely self-defeating. Victims of extortion and others in similar danger can still *try* to persuade extortionists or terrorists that they are telling the truth or that they intend to keep their promises. This is admittedly dishonest, but we have already seen that special circumstances can suspend features of our ordinary moral judgment such as fairness or honesty. Certainly wrongdoers who use force, ruse, or guile cannot morally complain when these are turned against them.

Alexander, then, both may and should discuss this matter with his employer. But this does not eliminate all the features of his dilemma. We still have the question of what El Sahd should do. What are a company's obligations in the face of corrupt practices like these? May El Sahd cooperate with the Ajax managers, depositing the $1 million bribe into company coffers, or must it resist complicity in this scheme? Most of the issues we have discussed—the harms that bribery and embezzlement impose on various stakeholders—persist even when a corporation is the agent. No less than an individual, a company has an obligation to resist corruption of this sort. Like an individual, a company will sometimes suffer for this stance by losing a valuable sale or contract. But large companies have a greater range of options available to them than individuals. They can use their economic power and the attractiveness of their products to go over the heads of corrupt officials and appeal directly to potential corporate or government clients. They can impose strict internal codes of conduct and audit procedures that make it hard for employees to cheat and that deter outsiders from trying to induce them into cheating. If El Sahd had previously done this, it might have reinforced Gavin's ability to resist these extortionary pressures.

Companies can also strive for tough industry-wide codes of conduct or laws that reduce the pressures to comply with extortion or to engage in bribery. The FCPA is one example of a ruling that, in overseas markets where U.S. firms have been the principal competitors, has given honest managers a credible means by which to resist the approaches of corrupt officials and has prevented these officials from pitting firm against firm in a bidding war of corruption. The FCPA is far from being a perfect solution to this problem. American managers complain that it handicaps them in some situations where non-U.S. competitors are involved. Although statistical evidence suggests that U.S. firms have not lost market share in countries or regions where the FCPA has changed U.S. practices, no one can doubt that the extension of such legislation to other countries and competitors is desirable. Tougher laws in other countries and new and enforced international initiatives such as the proposed United Nations Code of Conduct on Transnational Corporations are needed for a long-term reduction of bribery and corruption.[11] In Chapter 7, I noted that even when the three conditions that make it permissible to participate in otherwise undesirable conduct are met, responsible firms and individuals must still to try to eliminate the unsavory conduct involved. This means seeking laws or industry-wide codes of practice that encourage mutual restraint by all parties, what one writer has called "mutual restraint mutually agreed upon."[12] Instead of accepting the blanket claim that "everyone's doing it," therefore, a responsible company like El Sahd can take the lead in Kuwait and elsewhere in encouraging the development of higher business standards.

Although his company's involvement relieves Alexander of the burden of deceiving and cheating his employer, he will still have to decide whether he can accept its final decision in this matter. If El Sahd chooses to go along with this deal and takes no steps to correct these practices, Alexander will have to ask whether he wants to continue working in such a corrupt environment. The requirements of personal integrity and the sense that individuals must always resist organizational wrongdoing tell us that Alexander cannot ever hand his conscience over to a company or a culture.

DONALDSON'S ETHICAL ALGORITHM

✦

"The Oil Rig" and "Alexander Gavin's Dilemma" illustrate a recurrent problem faced by managers of global firms. The values, practices, or standards of certain host countries seem to permit or even encourage conduct that would not be allowed in the home country. When such value conflicts occur, how can they be resolved? Which standards should prevail? **NORM** tells us that in such cases we must try to formulate the moral rule implicit in our decision, whether this involves accepting or rejecting the host country's standards. Then, putting ourselves in the shoes of every party that this practice affects, whether in the home country, host country, or elsewhere, and taking *their* interests as our own, we must see whether we are prepared to live under the rule we create.

In his book *The Ethics of International Business,* the philosopher-business ethicist Thomas Donaldson takes another, more deontologically inclined approach to these questions.[13] He begins by developing a list of "fundamental international rights" that he believes everyone possesses (see Box 8.1). According to Donaldson, since rights imply duties, all moral agents, whether they are individuals, corporations, or governments, have duties not to deprive people of these rights. In some cases, he maintains, agents also have the more demanding duties of *preventing* people from being deprived of these rights and even of *aiding* those who have been so deprived.[14]

Box 8.1

DONALDSON'S FUNDAMENTAL INTERNATIONAL RIGHTS

1. The right to freedom of physical movement
2. The right to ownership of property
3. The right to freedom from torture
4. The right to a fair trial
5. The right to nondiscriminatory treatment (freedom from discrimination on the basis of such characteristics as race and sex)
6. The right to physical security
7. The right to freedom of speech and association
8. The right to minimal education
9. The right to political participation
10. The right to subsistence

With this list as background, Donaldson then proposes a moral decision procedure that we can apply to perplexing cases where the values extant in a multinational's home country conflict with more permissive (or "lower") host country standards. He calls this procedure an "ethical algorithm," and it takes us through a series of steps in reasoning. First, says Donaldson, we must determine whether the moral reasons underlying the host country's more permissive practices relate to that country's relative level of economic development or whether they are independent of economic factors. Donaldson calls problems having to do with relative levels of economic development "type 1" conflicts. An example of this type is a poor country's toleration of higher levels of thermal pollution in its waterways than are permitted in a multinational's home country. Typically, poor countries that permit this sort of pollution do so either because they lack the economic and regulatory means to maintain higher standards or because the higher standards would increase the cost of their products and reduce their competitiveness in a global market.

Where type 1 conflicts occur, Donaldson offers a test for the practice at issue. We can accept or adopt a practice, he says, "if and only if the members of the home country would, under conditions of economic development relevantly similar to those of the host country, regard the practice as permissible."[15] Since many developed nations permitted higher levels of pollution when they were initially industrializing, practices of this sort will frequently pass this test.

In some cases, the reasons for a practice are independent of a country's relative level of economic development. Donaldson calls these "type 2" conflicts. Examples of these include many of the forms of bribery and corruption that occur in overseas environments. These practices are not the result of a lack of means or resources. Not only do they occur in some already developed nations but they tend to remain part of the culture as poorer nations advance economically. In a different domain, South Africa's apartheid system is another example of a type 2 conflict. In this case, the conflict is related to deeply rooted local values that persist despite economic realities and that are not simply related to difficult economic trade-offs.

When faced with type 2 conflicts, Donaldson's algorithm instructs us to ask, in order, the following questions:

1. Is it possible to conduct business successfully in the host country without undertaking the practice?
2. Is the practice a clear violation of a fundamental international right?

If the answer to the first question is "yes," according to Donaldson, then our problem is resolved. We need not go on to the second question. We are morally obligated to maintain the "higher" home country standards. For example, according to this provision of the algorithm, as long as a firm can refuse to cooperate with apartheid and its business can still remain financially viable in the host country, it should not adopt any of the practices associated with the system of segregation. This is true even if "doing business" in this way entails higher costs, as when a company must arrange for transportation from distant localities for its nonwhite workers as a way of resisting the impact of residential segregation on the makeup of its work force. Only if it is financially or legally impossible to do business without participating in the local practice—if the answer to this first question is "no"—do we move on to the second question.

Here, the critical question is whether the practice at issue violates any fundamental international rights. If the answer to this is also "no," then the practice is morally permissible. If the answer is "yes," a company may not involve itself in the practice, even if this means that it must cease doing business in the country. Italian tax mores offer an example of the first possibility. It is well known that in Italy taxable income is often routinely and massively underreported by firms and individuals. A company that honestly reports its income will find itself exposed to ruinous levels of taxation. Should a U.S. company try to avoid major financial penalties by adopting these deceptive practices? Since underreporting income does not appear to violate any of Donaldson's fundamental international human rights, a firm may presumably adhere to a reduced standard of honesty if it must do so to remain competitive. In contrast, applying this second question to the matter of whether a firm should cooperate with apartheid by refusing to hire or promote black workers produces a negative evaluation. Such practices *do* violate a fundamental international right (the right to nondiscriminatory treatment) and hence are morally impermissible.

Like similar deontologically-inclined approaches that rely on a set of moral rules or rights (and associated priority rules), Donaldson's algorithm seems attractive initially. The rules and priorities here make moral sense, since they reflect deeply held moral judgments, and the procedure as a whole seems to organize our thinking and helps us proceed systematically through some complex and puzzling dilemmas. Nevertheless, on closer inspection, as the algorithm is applied to difficult cases, this apparent applicability fades. For one thing, as with all deontological approaches, there is the question of whether this is a complete set of rules or rights, and whether the rights that have been identified have been adequately defined. Consider Alexander Gavin's dilemma. Whose fundamental rights are violated if Alexander chooses to cooperate with the Ajax managers' scam? In cooperating, Alexander certainly does not discriminate against or expose anyone to physical risk; if someone is physically endangered by this practice, it is Alexander himself by refusing to go along. But perceiving the Ajax managers' ethical violations does not help us understand *Alexander's* obligations.

It might be argued that by cooperating, Alexander violates the fundamental international "right to ownership of property" of various people. After all, he would be helping the Ajax managers both to steal from their company and to defraud Iranian taxpayers. However, if we interpret this right as applicable to this case, what are we to say of tax evasion and similar fiscal chicanery in the Italian context, which reduces government revenues and forces some people to pay more than their fair share for public services? As discussed above, this kind of tax evasion seemed illustrative of the kind of conduct that could pass the test of Donaldson's algorithm. Once again, we see that it is often extraordinarily difficult to determine whether a deontological rule really has been violated—or whether it even applies—in a concrete instance of moral choice.

"The Oil Rig" offers a more favorable illustration of the application of Donaldson's algorithm, although serious problems crop up even for this case. Some of the practices on the rig may be type 1 conflicts, since the lower standards of treatment given to the Angolan workers reflect the country's relative level of economic development. Among these conflicts, the cheaper food served to the Angolans might be morally acceptable on the grounds that home country citizens would accept this diet if they were at the Angolans' level. But what about the very different medical treatment? If we feel this to be wrong, must we add to our list of fundamental international rights a right to high-quality emergency medical care? Or is the problem one of discrimination (a violation of the fifth right on Donaldson's list)? And if it is, why is it discriminatory to deny employees equal medical care but not discriminatory to deny them an equal diet? How do we think about such matters?

In fairness to Donaldson, we should note that in developing and applying his approach, he utilizes some very basic tools of moral reasoning. The fundamental rights he identifies result from a careful assessment of the interests that rational persons hold and would find rational to protect. In balancing these rights in instances of conflict, Donaldson also repeatedly invokes ideas of reciprocity and omnipartiality. Thus, his type 1 conflicts are resolved by asking the question of what we, as citizens of more developed nations, would be prepared to accept were we in the shoes of citizens of a less developed country where lower standards prevail. This suggests that underlying Donaldson's approach is the more basic mode of moral reasoning associated with **NORM**. In developing his list of rights, and in weighing them in conflict cases, Donaldson actually seems to ask a more basic question: "What would I or anyone reasoning omnipartially accept as a general and public rule of practice in cases of this sort?

If we keep this in mind, we can appreciate Donaldson's approach without succumbing to its potential weaknesses. To the extent that it reflects our deeper modes of reasoning, an algorithm of this sort is a useful guide to thinking through tough cases. But we must not be seduced by its apparent precision into believing that the rights it identifies are the only ones applicable to a case or that its priority rules will eliminate the need for a more precise moral analysis. When using a quasi-deontological method of this sort, we must always be ready to invoke **NORM**-type reasoning and look at any resultant rule of conduct at which we arrive in terms of its (omnipartial) acceptability as an abiding public rule of conduct. Thus, we need not describe the *appearance* of racism on the oil rig as a violation of an international right to see that in this case even appearance is wrong. Reasoning omnipartially, we have good reasons for wishing to eliminate or improve this vicious and unnecessary situation. Similarly, whether or not there is a fundamental right to high-quality emergency medical care in *all* cases, given the resources available to this company, there is good reason for not tolerating the double standard of care that prevails on the rig. By allowing us to consider our choices in all their contextuality and complexity, **NORM** permits us to develop moral conclusions tailored to cases like these. Deontological lists of rights and their related priority rules are usually the crystallized results of previous **NORM**-type reasoning. This explains their usefulness. But we must not lose sight of the underlying reasoning that leads to these lists and priorities. We must also always be ready to test the specific moral advice offered by a deontological approach by looking at the resulting conduct in terms of its acceptability as an abiding public rule.

International business raises a host of difficult moral issues. In this chapter, we have touched upon only a few of these. At the heart of many of the problems of global ethics, however, is the question of when and how one may accommodate to local or host country standards different from one's own. The key to thinking about this is to recognize that, depending on the circumstances, *both* accommodation to local values and the maintenance of home country standards may be allowable. Which is so is a function of what general rules of practice, for all actors in the international community, it is reasonable to adopt from an omnipartial standpoint.

Summary

- Global business is on the rise. Cultural diversity and conflicting or nonexistent laws pose an ethical challenge for managers working in this environment. A variety of specific issues cause moral problems. These include small- and large-scale bribery; problems related to products and technology; pricing practices; tax evasion and financial misdealing; employee rights; environmental abuses; and corporate interference in local politics.

- Multinational companies are not morally required to eliminate all differences in their treatment of employees in different foreign contexts. Careful reasoning can help identify acceptable inequalities between branches of multinational firms. Despite this, multinationals can play a positive role in global business by maintaining and communicating their own highest and most defensible moral values.

- Although it is commonly claimed that bribery is accepted in foreign environments, this often is not the case. Large-scale bribery, in particular, shows its unacceptability by the secretive and covert way in which it is conducted. Careful stakeholder analysis reveals the prudential and moral dangers of involvement in practices like these and underscores the companies' responsibility for pursuing collective and legal action to minimize their occurrence.

- When—if ever—may multinational managers adopt more permissive (or "lower") host country standards? This question crops up frequently in global business ethics and has prompted efforts to provide a systematic way of resolving it. Decision rules like Donaldson's "ethical algorithm" can help, but every instance of accommodation to the lower standards of a host country must finally be tested in terms of its acceptability as an abiding public rule of conduct.

Case 8.3

✦ FOREIGN ASSIGNMENT[16] ✦

Sara Strong graduated with an MBA from UCLA four years ago. She immediately took a job in the correspondent bank section of the Security Bank of the American Continent and was assigned to work on issues pertaining to relationships with correspondent banks in Latin America. She rose rapidly in the section and received three good promotions in three years. She consistently got high ratings from her superiors and received particularly high marks for her professional demeanor.

In her initial position with the bank, Sara was required to travel to Mexico on several occasions. She was always accompanied by a male colleague even though she generally handled similar business by herself on trips within the United States. During her trips to Mexico she observed that Mexican bankers seemed more aware of her being a woman and were personally solicitous to her, but she did not discern any major problems. The final decisions on the work that she did were handled by male representatives of the bank stationed in Mexico.

A successful foreign assignment was an important step for those on the "fast track" at the bank. Sara applied for a position in Central or South America and was delighted when she was assigned to the bank's office in Mexico City. The office had about twenty bank employees and was headed by William Vitam. The Mexico City office was seen as a preferred assignment by young executives at the bank.

After a month, Sara began to encounter problems. She found it difficult to be effective in dealing with Mexican bankers—the clients. They appeared reluctant to accept her authority and would often bypass her in important matters. The problem was exacerbated by Vitam's compliance in her being bypassed. When she asked that the clients be referred back to her, Vitam replied, "Of course that is not really practical." Vitam made matters worse by patronizing her in front of clients and by referring to her as "my cute assistant" and "our lady banker." Vitam never did this when only Americans were present, and in fact treated her professionally and with respect in internal situations.

Sara finally complained to Vitam that he was undermining her authority and effectiveness; she asked him in as positive a manner as possible to help her. Vitam listened carefully to Sara's complaints, then replied, "I'm glad that you brought this up, because I've been meaning to sit down and talk to you about my little game-playing in front of the clients. Let me be frank with you. Our clients think you're great, but they just don't understand a woman in authority, and you and I aren't going to be able to change their attitudes overnight. As long as the clients see you as my assistant and deferring to me, they can do business with you. I'm willing to give you as much responsibility as they can handle your having. I *know* you can handle it. But we just have to tread carefully. You and I know that my remarks in front of clients don't mean anything. They're just a way of playing the game Latin style. I know it's frustrating for you, but I really need you to support me on this. It's not going to affect your promotions. You just have to act like it's my responsibility." Sara replied that she would try to cooperate, but that basically she found her role demeaning.

As time went on, Sara found that the patronizing actions in front of clients bothered her more and more. She spoke to Vitam again, but he was firm in his position, and urged her to try to be a little more flexible, even a little more "feminine."

Sara also had a problem with Vitam over policy. The Mexico City office had five younger women who worked as receptionists and secretaries. They were all situated at workstations at the entrance of the office. They were required to wear standard uniforms that were colorful and slightly sexy. Sara protested the requirement that uniforms be worn because (1) they were inconsistent with the image of the banking business and (2) they were demeaning to the women who had to wear them. Vitam just curtly replied that he had received a lot of favorable comments about the uniforms from clients of the bank.

Several months later, Sara had what she thought would be a good opportunity to deal with the problem. Tom Fried, an executive vice-president who had been a mentor to her since she had begun her work at the bank, was coming to Mexico City. She arranged a private conference with him, during which she described her problems and explained that she was not able to be effective in this environment and that she was worried that it would have a negative effect on her chance of promotion within the bank. Fried was very careful in his response. He spoke of certain "realities" that the bank had to respect and urged her to "see it through" even though he could understand how she would feel that things were not fair.

Sara found herself becoming more aggressive and defensive during her meetings with Vitam and her clients. Several clients asked that other bank personnel handle their transactions. Sara has just received an Average rating, which notes "the beginnings of a negative attitude about the bank and its policies."

QUESTIONS TO CONSIDER

1. How do you think William Vitam regards the ethical issues in this case? How does Sara Strong?

2. What would the approach taken by Thomas Donaldson say about the conduct of Vitam and Sara?

3. Applying **NORM** to this case, what recommendations would you make to the parties involved?

Case 8.4

✦ GLOBAL ADVERTISING, INC.[17] ✦

A lot had changed in Scott Andrews' life since the day, six months earlier, when the President-CEO of Global Advertising, Inc., Howard Caulfield, had summoned him to his office. Scott had not known what to expect at that meeting, and in fact had come prepared to answer any questions Mr. Caulfield might ask him about the Chicago office that Scott ran for Global.

But that had not been Mr. Caulfield's reason for wanting to see him. Instead, it had been to tell Scott that he was promoting him to become Regional Vice-President for Northern Europe.

"You've done a great job of turning around the Chicago office, Scott," Caulfield had said, "and you've done it faster than we had expected. While it may be early to pull you out—just when things are beginning to go well—we have a bigger need and bigger challenge for you now elsewhere. In Europe. Responsible, in fact, for all of our offices in Northern Europe. You'll be replacing Charlie Stevens, who we are promoting to become President-International, replacing Finlay, who will be retiring at the end of this year.

"Charlie will become a member of the Executive Committee of the Board. It's a big and well-deserved promotion for him. He's done an outstanding job. He's made some excellent acquisitions for us in Europe, hired several very talented new people to run our local operations, and the impressive result is that we're finally a major, profitable factor in Northern Europe now.

"You'll be reporting to Charlie, and I'm sure you'll like it and learn a lot from him. You also should benefit from the things he's done to build a strong base for us in Northern Europe. Your challenge next year will be to nearly double our pre-tax profits there from $16 million to $26 million—no easy task, but we really need it to offset our heavy investments in our developing Far East agencies. To do that, you're going to have to keep your General Managers there highly motivated and to significantly build revenue by winning a lot of new accounts. There's probably not too much you can do on the expense side, as Charlie has pretty much pared costs there to the bone.

"We're depending on you, Scott. If you do well in this assignment I'll be bringing you back here in a top executive capacity."

* * * *

The next few months were hectic for Scott as he disengaged from Chicago. However, Nancy and their two sons were excited with the prospect of living in Europe, so it seemed like only a matter of weeks before they were on the 747 flight for London.

Scott had had several phone conversations with Charlie Stevens about the Northern European operations, but it was not until he landed in London that the two men had a chance to review all the offices in detail. Scott was impressed with Charlie as a tough manager who demanded loyalty and results, but who also allowed the local general managers considerable independence as to how they ran their offices.

At one point in their discussions Charlie had told him:

"It's a totally different world doing business in Europe, Scott, and *you* have to adapt to it. It won't adapt to you. You've got to be a more flexible, more entrepreneurial manager than you probably were in Chicago. You've also got to understand that doing business in one European country is usually very different from doing business in another European country. It took me about a year to learn this, but when I did it made a helluva difference in our results. So forget a lot of what you learned in Chicago.

"Of course you'll be reporting to me. Even though I'll be based in New York, I'll be able to give you advice along the way. But don't feel you need to change everything. It's going well now and morale is up. Besides, first you'll need to build up some experience working over here anyway."

* * * *

Global Advertising is the fourth largest advertising company in the world, with offices in thirty-eight countries and with a prestigious group of blue chip multinational clients. Its core operations consist of full-service advertising agencies in each country.

Moreover, Global is a "private" company. All of its stock is held by about thirty key managers of the company—none of whom individually own more than 10 percent, but all of whom have to sell back their stock to the company when they leave the company due to retirement, resignation, or termination. Being privately held is a big and highly motivating advantage for Global because it means that (a) management can invest, when necessary, and does not have to worry about the pressures of achieving earnings growth every single quarter or about appeasing malcontent outside shareholders; (b) the company is protected from outside "takeover"; and (c) the company's actual financial results and dealings are kept secret. The only disadvantage of being "private" is that Global cannot raise large sums of capital via public share offerings, as can most of its competitors, and this makes it imperative that Global achieve high earnings and a very favorable cash flow to afford major investments in expansion and acquisitions.

Achieving high earnings, however, had become an increasingly difficult task for all advertising companies, including Global, because:

1. Media spending by advertisers (clients) was showing no growth in most countries due to the rapid decline in inflation and the pressure to achieve global advertising efficiencies.

2. Compensation costs, which account for about 70 percent of an advertising company's costs ("its assets go up and down the elevator each day"), were increasing by about 10 percent annually due to the shortage of top talent, principally creative people, and the consequent fierce competition between agencies to attract (steal?) and keep them. These compensation costs consist of (a) salaries and bonuses, (b) an incremental 100 percent of salaries and bonuses for social security contributions, payroll taxes, etc., and (c) fringe benefits.

3. Other costs, such as rent, had been soaring, too, due to the desire of advertising companies to be located in the fashionable center of cities—for reasons of image and also to enable them to be located close to the media, suppliers, and some clients. As a result, the "average" profit margin (profit before tax as a percent of revenue) had been about 20 percent for the industry as a whole. Global's worldwide profit margin was 16 percent.

* * * *

Scott's Northern Europe region consisted of the Scandinavian countries (Norway, Sweden, Finland, Denmark), Germany, Austria, and Switzerland. Its profit margin was currently 17 percent—up from break-even under Charlie Steven's leadership but still considerably below the Global average.

Scott's first couple of months on the job had been relatively "easy"—orientations, briefings, etc. He immediately found it stimulating to be involved in such diverse cultural and business environments and, as Charlie had prophesied, he started learning a new modus operandi fairly quickly.

Soon, however, as he pressed for ideas to improve Global's profitability and revenues in Northern Europe, Scott was faced with a number of ethical/business issues. Two of these troubled him a great deal:

Sweden—Jan Anderssen, General Manager of Global's Swedish subsidiary, came to Scott with a request to change the method of compensation in a way that would benefit the key managers of the subsidiary *and* its profitability.

Specifically, Anderssen proposed that the ten key managers no longer be paid via straight salary and year-end bonus in Sweden, but instead at least partially via a consultancy arrangement in the U.K. Anderssen pointed out these key managers currently paid personal income taxes in Sweden of about 80 to 85 percent of their Swedish income—just about the highest rate in the world, but necessitated by the huge "welfare state" that Sweden had built over the years.

Anderssen pointed out that this meant that at a salary-plus-bonus level of about $125,000, a key Global manager paid taxes of $103,000, leaving only $22,000 net for himself. If part of that $125,000, say $50,000, could be paid in London to the key Swedish managers as "consulting" fees, they could keep most or all of it depending on whether or not they declared it on their Swedish income tax forms. This new method of compensation would be a great motivator to the key managers, he argued, and would also save Global money because they would not have to pay Swedish social security or payroll taxes to the government on it (a 50 percent savings).

Scott calculated that a Swedish employee earning, say, $125,000 a year actually cost the company $250,000 (including related government social security and taxes). Therefore, if the company paid $50,000 in London to each of the ten Swedish managers, Global would save a nifty $500,000. Besides, he reasoned, Global would not be guilty of helping these managers purposely and illegally avoid paying Swedish income taxes on the money because, "How can the company know what income a person declares on her or his income tax form? That's a private matter."

Scott also knew, however, that this proposed new method of compensation was not entirely legal because there was no real "consulting" service being rendered by these ten managers and that the corporation would be in effect "sheltering" the money from taxation. He knew the managers would never declare this income. So he hesitated to approve the idea.

That is when Anderssen looked surprised and told Scott, "Hell, this is exactly the same compensation arrangement that I've got now—except that mine is for $65,000—and Charlie Stevens expressly approved it."

Scott deliberated. Should he approve the proposal, especially since an apparently acceptable precedent had been set? After all, it would quickly help him take a big step toward reaching his assigned objective of improved profitability in Northern Europe. And it already had the blessing of Charlie, his boss. Scott also deliberated whether, if he approved the Swedish proposal, he should extend the same idea to other high-tax countries in Northern Europe.

Or should he call Charlie and take a stand against it—one that was likely to cost Anderssen his compensation deal (how could the company be inconsistent in applying ethical judgments?) and might also provoke Charlie's fury and Anderssen's resignation?

Or should he go directly to Mr. Caulfield and expose what had already been done in Sweden (i.e., what Charlie had approved)?

Denmark—Jan Lindstrom, the Denmark General Manager, called Scott one day very excited about a major new client prospect that Lindstrom had been pursuing for many months. This was National Brands, a blue chip multinational advertiser that had large media budgets and would be a "plum" account for Global to win in Denmark. Besides, if Global did good work for National Brands in Denmark, the client might subsequently want to use Global in other countries as well.

Scott was thrilled by this news. He realized that National Brands would help build his Danish company's revenues signifi-cantly, and hopefully would go on to build those of other Global offices in Europe. It was a big opportunity—one of those leverage opportunities that came around only rarely. So he encouraged Lindstrom to do everything he could to get it.

Scott knew that, if successful, the win of a prestigious and potentially huge account like National Brands would reflect well on him too; it would be his first big piece of news to pass on to Caulfield and Stevens and would give his region momentum and notoriety.

Two weeks later Lindstrom called back to say Global-Denmark had won the National Brands account. Scott congratulated him, sent several cases of champagne to everyone at his Danish compa-ny, and faxed the good news to Caulfield and Stevens. Both men then called Scott to congratulate him personally on the news. Caulfield said, "I knew you'd be successful in Northern Europe, Scott, and you've proven me right. You're off to an even faster start than Charlie."

It was not until three months later, when Scott was visiting his company in Denmark, that he learned what had really cemented the local deal with National Brands. Lindstrom revealed that Nils Carsten, the Managing Director of National Brands, had made the award of the Denmark account to Global *contingent* on Lindstrom's agreeing to kick back 1 percent of the 15 percent media commission to Carsten (personally), a deal Carsten said he had been getting for the last two years from his previous advertising agency. Lindstrom had agreed to Carsten's condition, and together they concocted a "dummy invoice" scheme (directed to a relative of Carsten's who owned a production company) as the vehicle for the kickback. Lindstrom figured the dummy invoices would be sufficient to keep the Danish tax inspectors from noticing the irregularity—if they ever checked—and Scott agreed he was probably right. Scott also knew Global would still make a hefty profit on the account, even at 14 percent.

But now Scott was faced with a difficult decision. Should he allow the scheme to continue? (It had already begun.) If so, should he tell anyone else (e.g., Charlie) about it or let sleeping dogs lie (after all, it would certainly diminish the luster of the "win," and thus the praise)? Scott knew that if he overruled the win it would greatly upset Lindstrom, whom he had urged to go full bore after it.

Scott also figured that if he overruled Lindstrom, he would have to tell Charlie, which might get Lindstrom in trouble.

And one final decision: If Scott nixed the deal, should he or someone else at Global tell the National Brands corporate management in New York what their Danish Managing Director (Carsten) had been doing illegally? Certainly they would not have known about it and would be very disturbed.

* * * *

It had been an eventful six months for Scott. His eyes had been opened wide and he figured that he had become a lot more experienced during that time. But as he faced all these difficult ethical/business decisions he wondered whether he had become a better manager or merely a more "street savvy" one.

The words of advice from Charlie still stuck in his mind: "It's a totally different world doing business in Europe, Scott, and *you* have to adapt to it."

It was time to look in the mirror now and determine where he stood on the issues. One way or another, his career might depend on what he decided to do.

QUESTIONS TO CONSIDER

1. What are the ethical issues raised by each of the decisions facing Scott Andrews?
2. What would Donaldson's "ethical algorithm" counsel Andrews about these decisions?
3. Applying **NORM** to this case, what recommendations would you make to Andrews and other parties involved?

$\mathcal{N}$OTES

1. J. Coates, "Toward a Code of Conduct for Multinationals," *Personnel Management* 10 (April 1978): 41. Quoted in Thomas Donaldson, *The Ethics of International Business* (New York: Oxford University Press, 1989), p. 3.
2. See, for example, Robert W. Armstrong, "An Empirical Investigation of International Marketing Ethics: Problems Encountered by Australian Firms," *Journal of Business Ethics* 11 (1992): 161–71, and Michael A. Mayo, "Ethical Problems Encountered by U.S. Small Businesses in Marketing," *Journal of Small Business Management* 29, no. 2 (1991): 51–59.
3. See, for example, Kate Gillespie, "Middle East Response to the U.S. Foreign Corrupt Practices Act," *California Management Review*, 29, no. 4 (1987): 19–20, and John L. Graham, "The Foreign Corrupt Practices Act: A New Perspective," *Journal of International Business Studies* 15, no. 3 (1984): 107–21.
4. This case was developed by Joanne Ciulla. © 1990. Reprinted by permission.
5. For a discussion of the moral importance of self-respect, see John Rawls, *A Theory of Justice* (Cambridge, Mass.: Harvard University Press, 1971), § 67.
6. Most names have been disguised. This case was prepared for instructional purposes by John W. Hennessey, Jr., The Amos Tuck School of Business Administration, Dartmouth College. © 1983.
7. In some rare cases, such as the bribing of a Nazi concentration camp guard to save a life, the duties themselves may be morally evil and the bribe may not be wrong. For a fuller discussion of this, see Kendall D'Andrade, Jr., "Bribery," *Journal of Business Ethics* 4, no. 4 (1985): 239–48.
8. Gunnar and Alva Myrdal, *Asian Drama* (New York: Pantheon Books, 1968), vol. 2, pp. 943, 958.
9. Saul W. Gellerman, "Why 'Good' Managers Make Bad Ethical Choices," *Harvard Business Review*, 64, no. 4 (1986): 85–90.
10. This brief argument furnishes a response to the position developed by Immanuel Kant in his provocative essay, "On a Supposed Right to Lie from

Altruistic Motives," in *Critique of Practical Reason and Other Writings in Moral Philosophy*, trans. and ed. Lewis White Beck (Chicago: University of Chicago Press, 1949), pp. 346–350.

11. G. R. Bassiry, "Business Ethics and the United Nations: A Code of Conduct," *Advanced Management Journal* 55, no. 4 (Autumn 1990): 38–41.

12. Garrett Hardin, "The Tragedy of the Commons," *Science* 162 (1968): 1243–48.

13. New York: Oxford University Press, 1989.

14. Ibid., pp. 83–86.

15. Ibid., p. 103.

16. This case was developed by Thomas Dunfee and Diana Robertson, The Wharton School. Reprinted by permission.

17. Names have been disguised. This case was prepared for John W. Hennessey, Jr., for instructional purposes only. © 1988.

OPERATIONALIZING ETHICS IN ORGANIZATIONS

✦

✦HOW CAN BUSINESSES BE ENCOURAGED TO OPERATE ETHICALLY? IN previous chapters we looked at a series of cases and challenges facing individual managers and tried to develop and apply a method for reasoning about tough moral choices. This focus on individual decision making suggests that we can achieve higher levels of ethical conduct in business by helping managers think more clearly about their moral responsibilities This is true, to an extent. Individual conscience is the bedrock of morality. The best-designed organizations will founder if individuals repeatedly fail to act ethically, whether through ignorance, selfishness, or ill will.

But human beings rarely act in isolation. We are social creatures, shaped by the people around us. This means that organizational design and culture play an important role in encouraging moral or immoral behavior. In this chapter we look at some of the organizational issues that are crucial to business ethics. The approach is initially negative, since the extended organizational cases in this chapter portray instances of moral failure, in which individuals' worst impulses were reinforced by their surroundings. Toward the end of the chapter I set forth a more comprehensive vision of the course managers can follow and the pitfalls they must avoid if they are to operationalize ethics in the business environment. An extended positive example of organizational ethics is explored in Chapter 10.

As we make the transition from moral reasoning to organizational analysis, it is important to note that an understanding of ethical theory provides insight into the challenge facing those who would design and sustain ethical organizations. *Theory tells us that even those with the best intentions are occasionally prone to behave in unethical or less-than-ethical ways. Morality involves acting on the rules we would adopt were we to look at the choices before us in an informed, rational, and omnipartial way. This is the key idea of* Neutral, Omnipartial Rule-Making (**NORM**) *as a method of moral reasoning.* However, we often act without full information. Even worse, we rarely achieve the degree of omnipartiality needed for flawless moral reasoning. In some cases we cannot "put ourselves into the shoes" of others affected by our decisions because they have experiences and values different from our own. We are responsible for making as strenuous an effort to do this as we can—by learning more about the people we affect and by using every means at our disposal to understand their perspectives—but we all predictably fall short of the degree of empathy needed. Sometimes we *willfully* avoid adopting the omnipartial moral point of view. When our own interests are threatened, we sometimes openly reject the task of thinking omnipartially. More commonly, we engage in subtle strategies of self-deception, clothing self-interest in the appearance of omnipartial reasoning. We deceive ourselves into believing that a self-interested course of conduct would be approved by other, neutral people, or we develop elaborate rationalizations, sometimes based on blatant falsehoods, to lend rational support to our pretensions. Human history is littered with rationalizations of this sort, from the kind of "God is with us" thinking that fosters violence between nations to the smug self-satisfaction of those who use perverted forms of moral reasoning and unsupported prejudices to justify economic injustice, racism, or sexism.

Keeping these threats to moral reasoning in mind can help orient managers as they strive to operationalize ethics in organizations. Managers' task is to hinder the rationalization of misconduct in the name of morality and to reduce the tension between partial and omnipartial interests. They can accomplish the first of these goals by educating the members of their organization in proper values and by challenging evasion and deceit. They can achieve the second by minimizing organizational incentives for wrongdoing and by enhancing those aspects of organizational life that encourage moral responsibility. In the cases discussed in this chapter, dealing with H. J. Heinz Company and Volvo, respectively, we will see how difficult this task can sometimes be in competitive business environments.

Case 9.1 (A)

✦ H. J. HEINZ COMPANY:
THE ADMINISTRATION OF POLICY* ✦

April is the cruelest month.
T. S. Eliot

In April 1979 James Cunningham, H. J. Heinz Company's president and chief operating officer, learned that since 1972 certain Heinz divisions had allegedly engaged in improper income transferal practices. Payments had been made to certain vendors in a particular fiscal year, then repaid or exchanged for services in the succeeding fiscal year.[1]

These allegations came out during the investigation of an unrelated antitrust matter. Apparent improprieties were discovered in the records of the Heinz USA division's relationship with one of its advertising agencies. Joseph Stangerson—senior vice-president, secretary, and general counsel for Heinz—asked the advertising agency about the alleged practices. Not only had the agency personnel confirmed the allegation about Heinz USA, it indicated that similar practices had been used by Star-Kist Foods, another Heinz division. The divisions allegedly solicited improper invoices from the advertising agency in fiscal year (FY) 1974 so that they could transfer income to FY 1975. While the invoices were paid in FY 1974, the services described on the invoices were not rendered until some time during FY 1975. Rather than capitalizing the amount as a prepaid expense, the amount was charged as an expense in FY 1974. The result was an understatement of FY 1974 income and an equivalent overstatement of FY 1975 income.

Stangerson reported the problem to John Bailey, vice-chairman and chief executive officer; to Robert Kelly, senior vice-president finance and treasurer; and to Cunningham. Bailey, CEO since 1966, had presided over 13 uninterrupted years of earnings growth. He was scheduled to retire as vice-chairman and CEO on July 1 and would remain as a member of the board of directors. James Cunningham, who had been president and chief operating officer since 1972, was to become chief executive officer on July 1, 1979.

Subsequent reports indicate that neither the scope of the practice nor the amounts involved were known. There was no apparent reason to believe that the amounts involved would have had a material effect on Heinz's reported earnings during the time period, including earnings for FY 1979 ending May 2. (Heinz reported financial results on the basis of a 52–53-week fiscal year ending on the Wednesday closest to April 30.) Stangerson was not prepared to say whether the alleged practices were legal or illegal. "This thing could be something terrible or it could be merely a department head using conservative accounting practices; we don't know," one Heinz senior official stated to the press.[2]

BACKGROUND

Henry J. Heinz, on founding the company in 1869 in Pittsburgh, Pennsylvania, said: "This is my goal—to bring home-cooking standards into canned foods, making them so altogether wholesome and delicious and at the same time so reasonable that people everywhere will enjoy them in abundance."[3] The company's involvement in food products never changed, and in 1979 Heinz operated some 30 companies with products reaching 150 countries. Heinz reported sales of over $2.2 billion and net income of $99.1 million in FY 1978.

After a sluggish period in the early 1960s, a reorganization was undertaken to position Heinz for growth. Under the guidance of

John Bailey and James Cunningham, Heinz prospered through a major recession, government price controls, and major currency fluctuations. The 1978 annual report reflected management's pride in Heinz's remarkably consistent growth:

> Fiscal 1978 went into the books as the fifteenth consecutive year of record results for Heinz. Earnings rose to another new high.
>
> Sales reached more than $2 billion only six years after we had passed the $1 billion mark for the first time in our century-long history. We are determined to maintain the financial integrity of our enterprise and support its future growth toward ever-higher levels. [Exhibit 1 presents a financial summary of fiscal years 1972–1978.]

Although Heinz was a multinational firm, domestic operations accounted for 62 percent of sales and 67 percent of earnings in FY 1978. Five major divisions operated in the United States in 1979.

Throughout the 1970s Heinz's major objective was consistent growth in earnings. While Heinz management did not consider acquisitions to be crucial to continuing growth, it looked favorably on purchase opportunities in areas where Heinz had demonstrated capabilities. Bailey and Cunningham stressed profit increases through the elimination of marginally profitable products. Increased advertising of successful traditional products and new product development efforts also contributed to Heinz's growth. Heinz's commitment to decentralized authority as an organizational principle aided the management of internal growth as well as acquisitions.

ORGANIZATION

In 1979 Heinz was organized on two primary levels. The corporate world headquarters, located in Pittsburgh, consisted of the principal corporate officers and historically small staffs (management described the world headquarters as lean). World headquarters had the responsibility for "the decentralized coordination and control needed to set overall standards and ensure performance in accordance with them."[4] Some Heinz operating divisions reported directly to the president; others reported through senior vice-presidents who were designated area directors (see Exhibit 2). World headquarters officers worked with division senior managers in areas such as planning, product and market development, and capital programs.

Heinz's divisions were largely autonomous operating companies. Division managers were directly responsible for the division's products and services, and they operated their own research and development, manufacturing, and marketing facilities. Division staff reported directly to division managers and had neither formal reporting nor dotted-line relationships with corporate staff.

World headquarters officers monitored division performance through conventional business budgets and financial reports. If reported performance was in line with corporate financial goals, little inquiry into the details of division operation was made. On the other hand, variations from planned performance drew a great deal of attention from world headquarters; then, divisions were pressured to improve results. A review was held near the end of the third fiscal quarter to discuss expected year-end results. If shortfalls were apparent, other divisions were often encouraged to improve their performance. The aim was to meet projected consolidated earnings and goals. Predictability was a watchword and surprises were to be avoided.[5] A consistent growth in earnings attended this management philosophy.

MANAGEMENT INCENTIVE PLAN

Designed by a prominent management consulting firm, the management incentive plan (MIP) was regarded as a prime management tool used to achieve corporate goals.[6] MIP comprised roughly 225 employees, including corporate officers, senior world headquarters personnel, and senior personnel of most divisions. Incentive compensation was awarded on the basis of an earned number of MIP points and in some cases reached 40 percent of total compensation.

MIP points could be earned through the achievement of personal goals. These goals were established at the beginning of each fiscal year in consultation with the participant's immediate supervisor. Points were awarded by the supervisor at the end of the year, based on goal achievement. In practice, personal goal point awards fell out on a curve, with few individuals receiving very high or very low awards.

MIP points were also awarded based on net profit after-tax (NPAT) goals. (On occasion, other goals such as increased inventory turnover or improved cash flow were included in MIP goals.) Corporate NPAT goals were set at the beginning of the fiscal year by the management development and compensation committee (MDC) of the board of directors. The chief executive officer, the chief operating officer, the senior vice-president of finance, and the senior vice-president of corporate development then set MIP goals for each division, with the aggregate of division goals usually exceeding the corporate goal. Two goals were set: a fair goal, which was consistently higher than the preceding year's NPAT, and a higher outstanding goal. The full number of MIP points was earned by achieving the outstanding goal.

Senior corporate managers were responsible for executing the system. While divisional input was not uncommon, division NPAT goals were set unilaterally and did not necessarily reflect a division's budgeted profits. Once set, goals were seldom changed during the year. The officers who set the goals awarded MIP points at the end of the fiscal year. No points were awarded to personnel in a division that failed to achieve its fair goal, and points were weighted to favor results at or near the outstanding goal. One or more bonus points might be awarded if the outstanding goal was exceeded. Corporate officers also had the authority to make adjustments or award arbitrary points in special circumstances. The basis for these adjustments was not discussed with division personnel.

MIP points for consolidated corporate performance were awarded by the MDC committee of the board. Corporate points were credited to all MIP participants except those in a division that did not achieve its fair goal. The MDC committee could also award company bonus points.

Heinz also had a long-term incentive plan based on a revolving three-year cycle. Participation was limited to senior corporate management and division presidents or managing directors for a total of nineteen persons.

CORPORATE ETHICAL POLICY

Heinz had an explicit corporate ethical policy that was adopted in May 1976.[7] Among other things, it stated that no division should:

1. have any form of unrecorded assets or false entries on its books or records;
2. make or approve any payment with the intention or understanding that any part of such payment was to be used for any purpose other than that described by the documents supporting the payment;
3. make political contributions;
4. make payments or gifts to public officials or customers; or
5. accept gifts or payments of more than a nominal amount.

Each year the president or managing director and the chief financial officer of each division were required to sign a representation letter which, among other things, confirmed compliance with the corporate Code of Ethics.

APRIL 1979

Heinz itself had originated the antitrust proceedings that led to the discovery of the alleged practices. In 1976 Heinz filed a private antitrust suit against the Campbell Soup Company, accusing Campbell of monopolistic practices in the canned soup market. Campbell promptly countersued, charging that Heinz monopolized the ketchup market.[8] Campbell attorneys, preparing for court action, subpoenaed Heinz documents reflecting its financial relationships with one of its advertising agencies. In April 1979, while taking a deposition from Arthur West, president of the Heinz USA division, Campbell attorneys asked about flows of funds, "certain items which can be called off-book accounts." West refused to answer, claiming Fifth Amendment protection from self-incrimination.[9] Stangerson then spoke with the advertising agency and received confirmation of the invoicing practices.

EXHIBIT 1. FINANCIAL SUMMARY, FISCAL YEARS 1972–1978 ($ THOUSANDS EXCEPT PER SHARE DATA)

	1978	1977	1976	1975	1974	1973	1972
Summary of Operations							
Sales	$2,150,027	$1,868,820	$1,749,691	$1,564,930	$1,349,091	$1,116,551	$1,020,958
Cost of products sold	1,439,249	1,262,260	1,228,229	1,097,093	939,565	772,525	700,530
Interest expense	18,859	16,332	22,909	31,027	21,077	13,813	11,463
Provision for income taxes	69,561	71,119	53,675	49,958	36,730	30,913	30,702
Income from continuing operations	99,171	83,816	73,960	66,567	55,520	50,082	44,679
Loss from discontinued and expropriated operations	—	—	—	—	—	3,530	2,392
Income before extraordinary items	99,171	83,816	73,960	66,567	55,520	46,552	42,287
Extraordinary items	—	—	—	—	8,800	(25,000)	—
Net income	99,171	83,816	73,960	66,567	64,320	21,552	42,287
Per Common Share Amounts							
Income from continuing operations	4.25	3.55	3.21	2.93	2.45	2.21	1.98
Loss from discontinued and expropriated operations	—	—	—	—	—	.16	.11
Income before extraordinary items	4.25	3.55	3.21	2.93	2.45	2.05	1.87
Extraordinary items	—	—	—	—	.39	(1.10)	—
Net income	4.25	3.55	3.21	2.93	2.84	.95	1.87

Other Data

Dividends paid							
Common, per share	1.42	1.06%	.86%	.77%	.72%	.70	.67%
Common, total	32,143	24,260	19,671	17,502	16,427	15,814	15,718
Preferred, total	3,147	3,166	1,024	139	146	165	184
Capital expenditures	95,408	53,679	34,682	57,219	44,096	48,322	28,067
Depreciation	31,564	29,697	27,900	25,090	22,535	20,950	20,143
Shareholders' equity	702,736	655,480	598,613	502,796	447,434	399,607	394,519
Total debt	228,002	220,779	219,387	295,051	266,617	249,161	196,309
Average number of common shares outstanding	22,609,613	22,743,233	22,696,484	22,633,115	22,604,720	22,591,287	22,538,309
Book value per common share	28.96	26.27	23.79	22.04	19.61	17.50	17.26
Price range of common stock							
High	40	34%	38	34%	34%	30%	31%
Low	28%	26%	28%	18	24%	25%	25%
Sales (%)							
Domestic	62	62	59	58	59	58	57
Foreign	38	38	41	42	41	42	43
Income (%)							
Domestic	67	78	66	71	57	53	54
Foreign	33	22	34	29	43	47	46

Source: Company records.

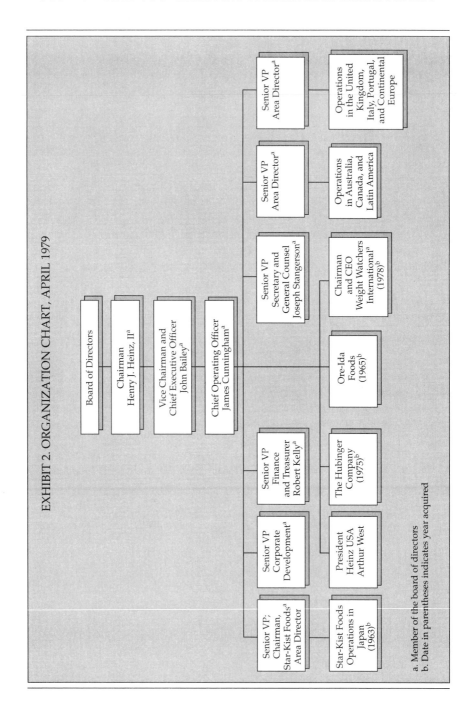

EXHIBIT 2. ORGANIZATION CHART, APRIL 1979

a. Member of the board of directors
b. Date in parentheses indicates year acquired

Case 9.1 (B)

✦ H. J. HEINZ COMPANY:
THE ADMINISTRATION OF POLICY ✦

In April 1979 Heinz's senior management learned of improper practices concerning the transfer of an undetermined amount of reported income from one fiscal year to the next. At two of the Heinz operating divisions, payments had been made to vendors in one fiscal year, then repaid or exchanged for services in the succeeding fiscal year. The scope of the practice and the amounts involved were not then known.

Aware that the practice might have affected the company's reported income over the past seven fiscal years, management consulted an outside legal firm for an opinion on the seriousness of the problem. Based on that opinion, John Bailey, Heinz's chief executive officer, notified the Audit Committee of the board of directors. Composed entirely of outside directors, this committee was responsible for working with internal auditors and financial officers and with the firm's outside auditors, thus preserving the integrity of financial information published by Heinz.

The Audit Committee held a special meeting on April 26, 1979. After hearing from outside counsel and from Joseph Stangerson (Heinz's general counsel) about the practices, the committee adopted a resolution retaining an outside law firm and independent public accountants to assist in a full investigation of the matter.[10]

An attorney from Cravath, Swaine & Moore, the outside law firm, accompanied Stangerson to Washington to advise the Securities and Exchange Commission of the information available and of the investigation then under way. (An excerpt from form 8-K filed with the SEC is attached as Exhibit 1.) The two also informed the IRS of possible tax consequences of the practice.

On April 27, 1979, Heinz publicly announced its investigation. "At this stage," the formal statement said, "It isn't possible to determine the scope of the practice or the total amounts involved." It also stated that there "isn't any reason to believe there will be any material effect on the company's reported earnings for any fiscal year including the current fiscal year." While the investigation would cover the period from 1972 to 1979, Heinz would not identify

EXHIBIT 1. FORM 8-K EXCERPT, APRIL 27, 1979

Item 5: Other Materially Important Events

On April 27, 1979, the registrant announced that it had become aware that since 1972 in certain of its divisions or subsidiaries payments have been made to certain of its vendors in a particular fiscal year, which were repaid or exchanged for services by such vendors in the succeeding fiscal year.

The registrant stated that at this stage it was not possible to determine the scope of the practice or the total amounts involved, but that there was no reason to believe there would be any material effect on the registrant's reported earnings for any fiscal year including the fiscal year ending May 2, 1979.

The Audit Committee of the registrant's board of directors has retained the law firm of Cravath, Swaine & Moore, independent outside counsel, to conduct a full inquiry of the practice. Cravath, Swaine & Moore will retain independent public accountants to assist in the investigation.

The registrant has heretofore advised the Securities and Exchange Commission and the Internal Revenue Service of the foregoing. At this time the registrant is unable to estimate the extent of any adjustments which may be necessary for tax purposes.

---

the divisions or vendors involved. Stangerson stated: "We aren't prepared to say whether [the practices] were legal or illegal." He added that the company had informed the SEC and the IRS.[11]

THE INVESTIGATION

The Audit Committee supervised the conduct of the investigation. Teams composed of lawyers and accountants from the two outside firms interviewed present and former company and vendor personnel about possible improprieties. The investigators focused on the following areas:

1. practices that affected the accuracy of company accounts or the security of company assets;
2. practices in violation of the company's Code of Ethics;

3. illegal political contributions;
4. illegal, improper, or otherwise questionable payments; and
5. factors contributing to the existence, continuance, or nondisclosure of any of the above.

The investigating teams interviewed over 325 Heinz employees, many of them more than once. The teams also interviewed personnel employed by many of Heinz's vendors, including advertising agencies. Accounting records, correspondence, and other files were examined. The board of directors at its regular May meeting asked for the cooperation of all officers and employees.[12]

On May 10, 1979, Heinz announced that a settlement had been reached in its private antitrust suit against the Campbell Soup Company. The settlement resulted in the dismissal of Heinz's action against Campbell, which had been brought in 1976, and of Campbell's counterclaim against Heinz. The court ordered the record of the suit sealed and kept secret.[13]

On June 29, 1979, Heinz disclosed a preliminary figure of $5.5 million of after-tax income associated with the income transferal practices. Stressing that this was a "very soft number," the company indicated that it was delaying release of audited results for FY 1979 (ended May 2, 1979) and that its annual meeting, scheduled for September 12, would be postponed until the investigation (which could continue well into the fall) was completed. The preliminary unaudited figures released by Heinz showed net income of $113.4 million ($4.95 per share) on sales of $2.4 billion, after the $5.5 million deduction. Press reports indicated the investigation was being broadened to include Heinz's foreign units.[14]

On September 13, 1979, it was reported that the preliminary figure had grown to $8.5 million. Heinz's statement, filed with its first quarter FY 1980 earnings report, also stated FY 1979 income as $110.4 million or $4.80 per share. Most of the $3 million growth was attributed to the discovery of improper treatment of sales in addition to the improper treatment of prepaid expenses discovered earlier.[15]

Heinz's 1979 annual report contained audited financial statements for FY 1979 and restated financial statements for FY 1978. The report contained an unqualified opinion from Peat, Marwick, Mitchell & Company, Heinz's auditors, dated November 14, 1979. In Note 2 to the 1979 financial statements, the report also contained a restatement and reconciliation of sales, net income, and earnings per share for the previous eight fiscal years. (The 1979 results are shown in Exhibit 2. The restatement of FY 1971–FY 1978 is shown in Exhibit 3.) This information was filed with the Securities and Exchange Commission on November 20, 1979.[16]

In February 1980 Heinz reorganized its top management structure (see Exhibit 4). Arthur West, formerly president of Heinz USA, was promoted to world headquarters as area director. He assumed responsibility for the Hubinger Company and Weight Watchers International, both of which had previously reported directly to James Cunningham, Heinz's president and new CEO. West was also to be responsible for Heinz's Canadian subsidiary. Heinz USA would now report through Kevin Voight, senior vice-president, rather than directly to Cunningham. Unlike other area directors, West would be neither a senior vice-president nor a member of the board of directors.[17]

In April 1980 Doyle Dane Bernbach, the only publicly held firm among the advertising and consulting firms included in the Audit Committee's investigation, admitted in an SEC filing that it had participated in the income-juggling practices by prebilling and issuing bills that did not accurately describe the services provided.[18]

On May 7, 1980, the Audit Committee presented its report to the Heinz board of directors. The eighty-page report was filed on form 8-K with the SEC on May 9, 1980. (The remainder of this case is derived substantially from the Audit Committee's report.)

THE FINDINGS

The Audit Committee reported widespread use of improper billing, accounting, and reporting procedures at Heinz's divisions including Heinz USA, Ore-Ida, Star-Kist, and a number of Heinz's foreign operations. The two major areas of impropriety were:

1. *Improper recognition of expenses:* These were most often advertising and market research expenses, improperly recorded in the current fiscal period when in fact the services were performed or goods were delivered in a later fiscal period. This treatment resulted in an overstatement of expenses (and understatement of income) in one period and a comparable understatement of expenses (and overstatement of income) in a later fiscal period.

Text continues on p. 350

EXHIBIT 2. FINANCIAL SUMMARY, 1979 ($ IN THOUSANDS EXCEPT PER SHARE DATA)

	1979	1978[a]	Change
Sales	$2,470,883	$2,159,436	14.4%
Operating income	214,735	187,062	14.8
Net income	110,430	99,946	10.5
Per common share amounts			
Net income	$4.80	$4.28	12.1%
Net income (fully diluted)	4.64	4.17	11.3
Dividends	1.85	1.42	30.3
Book value	32.29	29.33	10.1
Capital expenditures	$118,156	$95,408	23.8%
Depreciation expense	38,317	31,564	21.4
Net property	481,688	412,334	16.8
Cash and short-term investments	$122,281	$84,044	45.5%
Working capital	401,169	453,517	(11.5)
Total debt	342,918	228,002	50.4
Shareholders' equity	778,397	711,126	9.5
Average number of common shares outstanding	22,330	22,610	
Current ratio	1.70	2.14	
Debt/invested capital	30.9%	24.7%	
Pretax return on average invested capital	20.7%	20.7%	
Return on average shareholders' equity	14.8%	14.5%	

Source: 1979 annual report.
[a] As restated

EXHIBIT 3. RESTATED FINANCIAL DATA, 1971–1978

Change in Sales, Net Income and Earnings per Share

In Thousands Except for Per-share Amounts	1971	1972	1973	1974	1975	1976	1977	1978
Sales as previously reported	$876,451	$1,020,958	$1,116,551	$1,349,091	$1,564,930	$1,749,691	$1,868,820	$2,150,027
Net increase (decrease) resulting from restatement to correct improper treatment of sales	—	—	14,821	(1,777)	(4,747)	4,725	8,480	9,409
Sales as restated	$876,451	$1,020,958	$1,131,372	$1,347,314	$1,560,183	$1,754,416	$1,877,300	$2,159,436
Net income as previously reported	$37,668*	$42,287*	$21,552*	$64,320*	$66,567	$73,960	$83,816	$99,171
Net increase (decrease) in income before income taxes resulting from restatement:								
Correct improper treatment of sales, net of related costs	—	—	1,968	309	(1,527)	1,815	1,294	2,872
Correct improper recognition of income/expense	1,290	512	1,813	5,615	(1,861)	(684)	3,822	(1,417)
	1,290	512	3,781	5,924	(3,388)	1,131	5,116	1,455
Income tax effect	(671)	(263)	(1,566)	(2,698)	1,254	(604)	(2,203)	(680)
Net adjustments	619	249	2,215	3,226	(2,134)	527	2,913	775

Net income as restated	$38,287	$42,536	$23,767	$67,546	$64,433	$74,487	$86,729	$99,946
Income per common share amounts:								
Income from continuing operations as previously reported	$1.71	$1.98	$2.21	$2.45	$2.93	$3.21	$3.55	$4.25
Net increase (decrease) from restatement	.02	.01	.09	.14	(.09)	.03	.12	.03
Income from continuing operations as restated	1.73	1.99	2.30	2.59	2.84	3.24	3.67	4.28
Loss from discontinued and expropriated operations	.02	.11	.16	—	—	—	—	—
Income before extraordinary items	1.71	1.88	2.14	2.59	2.84	3.24	3.67	4.28
Extraordinary items	—	—	(1.10)	.39	—	—	—	—
Net income	$1.71	$1.88	$1.04	$2.98	$2.84	$3.24	$3.67	$4.28

In Thousands	Income from Continuing Operations	Loss from Discontinued and Expropriated Operations	Extraordinary Items	Net Income as Previously Reported
1971	$38,171	$ (503)	$ —	$37,668
1972	44,679	(2,392)	—	42,287
1973	50,082	(3,530)	(25,000)	21,552
1974	55,520	—	8,800	64,320

The following table presents the as-reported and as-stated interim results, which are unaudited, for 1978 and 1979

In Thousands Except Per-share Amounts	Sales		Gross Profit		Net Income		Earnings per Share	
	As Reported	As Restated	As Reported	As Restated	As Reported	As Restated	As Reported	As Restated
1978								
First Quarter	$ 491,469	$ 472,955	$156,538	$152,639	$19,645	$ 17,621	$ .83	$ .74
Second Quarter	520,051	525,440	169,476	170,348	23,613	22,676	1.00	.96
Third Quarter	523,640	517,738	170,621	169,001	19,901	20,208	.85	.86
Fourth Quarter	614,867	643,303	214,143	221,992	36,012	39,441	1.57	1.72
Total	$2,150,027	$2,159,436	$710,778	$713,980	$99,171	$ 99,946	$4.25	$4.28
1979								
First Quarter	$ 555,558	$ 536,301	$178,250	$171,330	$21,161	$ 16,783	$ .91	$ .72
Second Quarter	620,230	619,627	203,708	203,964	28,204	26,026	1.23	1.13
Third Quarter	575,410	566,747	202,171	199,497	23,301	21,192	1.01	.91
Fourth Quarter	—	748,208**	—	267,584**	—	46,429**	—	2.04**
Total	$—	$2,470,883**	$—	$842,375**	$ —	$110,430**	$—	$4.80**

*Net income as previously reported above includes losses from discontinued and expropriated operations and extraordinary items as shown.
**Not previously reported.
Source: 1979 annual report.

EXHIBIT 4. ORGANIZATION CHART, FEBRUARY 1980

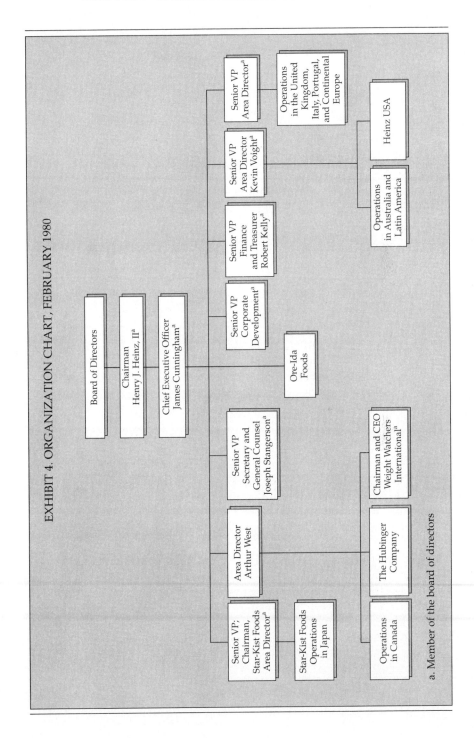

a. Member of the board of directors

2. *Improper recognition of sales:* Sales were recorded in a fiscal period other than that in which those sales should have been
recorded under generally accepted accounting principles.

Table A indicates the amounts involved. The accumulated effects of
such practices on shareholders' equity and working capital did not
exceed 2 percent.

TABLE A. INCREASE (DECREASE) OF CONSOLIDATED INCOME
BEFORE TAX, NET OF RECOVERIES ($ THOUSANDS)

	Improper Recognition			*Net Income Before Tax*		
FY	*Expenses*	*Sales*	*Other Practices*	*Increase (Decrease)*	*Total After Restate- ment*	*% Effects of Restate- ment*
1972	$(513)	—	—	$(513)	$75,894	(.7)
1973	(1,814)	$(1,968)	—	(3,782)	84,777	(4.5)
1974	(4,250)	(309)	$(1,364)	(5,923)	98,173	(6.0)
1975	2,476	1,527	(615)	3,388	113,137	3.0
1976	(111)	(1,815)	877	(1,049)	128,682	(.8)
1977	(4,139)	(1,294)	268	(5,165)	160,101	(3.2)
1978	734	(2,872)	671	(1,467)	170,198	(.9)
1979	8,888	7,085	396	16,369	183,178	8.9
1980	76	(354)	(233)	(511)	—	—

The Audit Committee indicated that these income transferal
practices were designed to adjust the income reported by divisions
to corporate headquarters and were motivated primarily by a
desire to meet the constantly increasing profit objectives set by
world headquarters. While division management supported the
publicly announced goal of steadily increasing profits, the committee reported that the management incentive program (MIP) under
which the goals were administered created significant pressures.
Aside from obvious personal financial considerations, many divi-
sion-level personnel reportedly viewed the achievement of MIP
goals as the key to advancement at Heinz. One manager told the

committee that failure to achieve these goals constituted a "mortal sin."

The Heinz principle of decentralized authority extended to financial reporting and internal control procedures. Division financial officers were not responsible to corporate headquarters but to their division president or managing director. The MIP goal pressures provided the incentive, and autonomous control the opportunity, for adopting the improper practices being reported.

One reason for using such reporting techniques was explained to the committee:

> If this fiscal year's goal is, say, $20 million net profit after tax (NPAT), it can be anticipated that next year's goal will be, say, 15 percent higher, or $23 million NPAT. This year seems to be a good one and it is anticipated that earnings will be $24 million NPAT. But, if that figure is reported to world headquarters, it is likely that next year's goal will be about 15 percent higher than the $24 million NPAT, or approximately $27 million NPAT. Of course, there is no assurance that there will not be some unforeseen disaster next year. Thus, if it is possible to mislead world headquarters as to the true state of the earnings of the [division] and report only the $20 million NPAT, which is the current fiscal year's goal, and have the additional $4 million NPAT carried forward into next year, the [division] will have a good start toward achieving its expected $23 million NPAT goal next year and will not have to reach $27 million NPAT.

Explanations for accepting these practices at lower levels included job security and the desire to impress superiors.

The committee's report stated: "There is no evidence that any employee of the company sought or obtained any direct personal gain in connection with any of the transactions or practices described in this report. Nor did the investigation find any evidence that any officer or personnel at world headquarters participated in any of the income transferal practices described in this report." The report went on to describe activities at each division in greater detail.

DIVISION INCOME TRANSFER PRACTICES

Heinz USA

Income transfer at Heinz USA started late in FY 1974 when world headquarters realized that Heinz USA might report profits in excess of those allowed by the wage and price controls in effect at the time. World headquarters sought to have Heinz USA report lower profits, although no evidence indicates that any world headquarters personnel intended GAAP to be violated. After some commodity transactions lowered expected profits, there was a reluctance in Heinz USA to reduce its expected profits further. Nevertheless, to accomplish the further reduction, $2 million in invoices for services that would not be performed were obtained from an advertising agency and recorded as an expense in FY 1974.

Heinz USA reported a FY 1974 NPAT of $4,614,000. NPAT goals for the year were $4.9 million (fair) and $5.5 million (outstanding). In calculating NPAT for MIP purposes, world headquarters allowed an adjustment of $2 million ($1 million after tax) for advertising. This adjustment resulted in Heinz USA achieving its outstanding goal for FY 1974. The division also received a bonus point. The use of improper invoices to manage reported income continued after FY 1974 at Heinz USA, although there was no evidence that world headquarters personnel knew about these transactions.

Beginning in FY 1977, additional income transfer methods were developed. Distribution centers were instructed to stop shipments for the last few days of the fiscal year to allow the recording of sales in the subsequent year. These instructions presented practical difficulties and some of the shipments were not held up. Without the authorization of division senior management, paperwork was apparently altered or misdated to record the sales as desired.

Vendors' credits were often deferred and processed in the subsequent fiscal year to assist the income management program. Detailed schedules were privately maintained that served as the basis for discussions on income management. One employee had the job of maintaining private records to ensure the recovery (in subsequent fiscal years) of amounts paid to vendors on improper invoices.

The use of improper invoices spread to the departmental level as well. Individual department managers used either prepaid billing or delayed billing, as required, to ensure complete use of their departmental budget without overspending. This practice provided protection against future budget cuts during those periods when the full budget would not otherwise have been spent. Division management actively discouraged these transactions.

Vendor cooperation was not difficult to obtain. One Heinz manager described it as "the price of doing business with us." During the period in question, ten vendors participated in improper invoicing at Heinz USA, and eight participated at the department level. Most vendors' fiscal years did not coincide with Heinz's.

In FY 1975 a sugar inventory write-down was used to transfer income. Sugar inventory, valued at an average cost of 37 cents per pound, was written down to 25 cents per pound. This adjustment, which amounted to an increase in FY 1975 expense of $1,390,360, was justified on the basis of an expected decline in price early in the next fiscal year. This would result in lower selling prices in FY 1976 for some division products. The lower NPAT figure that resulted was used for establishing FY 1976 goals, but when FY 1975 performance was evaluated, world headquarters adjusted Heinz USA's income up by the amount of the sugar writedown. The anticipated price decline did not occur.

At other times, inflated accruals, inventory adjustments, commodity transactions, and at least one customer rebate were used to report income other than that required by GAAP.

Ore-Ida

Improper invoices to transfer income were also used at Ore-Ida during that period, and the issue of obtaining these invoices was discussed at meetings of Ore-Ida's management board. Even though the invoices contained descriptions of services that were generic or had no correlation to the actual services to be rendered, members of the management board believed the practice was appropriate because comparable services would have been purchased at some point. During two fiscal years Ore-Ida received interest payments from an advertising agency in connection with the payment of these invoices.

Ore-Ida's management believed that members of world head-quarters' management were aware of the income transfer practices, but raised no objections to them. Documents submitted to world headquarters by Ore-Ida contained references to special media billing, prebills, year-end media billing, special billing adjustments, and advertising and promotion prebilling. Some documents indicated that these items actually applied to the fiscal year following that of expense recognition. The amount of these expenses was indicated each year to world headquarters' management (in one year, the amount was understated). In FY 1974 corporate management increased Ore-Ida's income before tax by the amount of the prebilled advertising expense for MIP award purposes. Ore-Ida's management did not know if world headquarters' management appreciated the fact that this practice did not conform to GAAP.

Star-Kist

Both improper expense recognition and improper sales recognition were used to adjust reported income at Star-Kist. Improper invoices were solicited from vendors to accumulate an advertising savings account. Sales during the last month of a fiscal year were recorded during the first month of the next fiscal year by preventing selected documents from entering the sales accounting system. These practices were apparently present only in Star-Kist's marketing department.

Similar practices were also discovered at some of Heinz's foreign subsidiaries.

OTHER IMPROPER PRACTICES

Although it focused primarily on income transferal practices, the investigation uncovered a number of other practices. Again, the committee stated that no member of world headquarters' management appeared to have any knowledge of these practices, and no employee sought or obtained any personal financial gain. All of these transactions took place outside the United States. None of the countries in which the transactions took place were identified by the committee.

In one country six questionable payments totaling $80,000 were made during FY 1978 and FY 1979. Two were made to lower-level government employees in connection with alleged violations of import regulations. One was made to a lower-level government employee in connection with the settlement of a labor dispute. Municipal employees received one payment in connection with real estate assessments. Labor union officials received the remaining two payments. In January 1979 three of these payments were reported by division management to world headquarters. A brief investigation ensued and the board of directors reprimanded certain officers of the division.

Star-Kist was involved in several transactions listed in the following section of the report:

1. In one country the payment of interest to nonresidents was prohibited. Star-Kist collected interest on its loans to fishing fleets through the falsification of invoices indicating the purchase by Star-Kist of supplies for the fleets.

2. In another country Star-Kist acted as a conduit through which funds flowed to facilitate a fish purchase involving two other companies. Letters of credit requiring the approval of the exchange authorities were used.

3. In a third country Star-Kist received checks from a fish supplier and endorsed those checks to a wholly owned U.S. subsidiary of the supplier. These transactions were not recorded in Star-Kist's accounts.

The Heinz operating company in yet another country made payments for goods to individual or designated bank accounts rather than to the supplier involved. These payments were not made through the normal cash disbursement procedure; rather, the division was acting at the supplier's request.

CONTRIBUTING FACTORS

The Audit Committee reported that only a small part of the failure to detect these practices could be attributed to weakness in

Heinz's internal controls. In most cases, those controls were circumvented by or with the concurrence of division management. With the autonomy enjoyed by division management, it would have been difficult for world headquarters personnel to detect these practices.

The committee attributed part of the problem to a lack of control consciousness throughout the corporation. *Control consciousness* referred to the atmosphere in which accounting controls existed and it reflected senior management attitudes about the importance of such controls. Clearly, control consciousness was not then present in most Heinz divisions. The committee blamed world headquarters' senior management for creating an environment that was seen as endorsing poor control consciousness:

> If world headquarters' senior management had established a satisfactory control consciousness, internal accounting controls that were cost/benefit justified should have been able to survive reasonable pressures to meet or exceed the defined economic goals. In establishing this atmosphere, world headquarters' senior management apparently did not consider the effect on individuals in the [divisions] of the pressures to which they were subjected.

Other factors cited by the committee included:

- corporate internal auditing personnel report to their respective division managers and not to the director-corporate audit;
- the lack of an effective Code of Ethics compliance procedure;
- the lack of standardized accounting and reporting procedures for all Heinz divisions;
- the lack of an effective budget review and monitoring process;
- the lack of enough competent financial personnel at world headquarters and at the divisions; and
- the lack of a world headquarters electronic data processing manager responsible for the control procedures of the divisions' EDP departments.

CONCLUSIONS OF THE AUDIT COMMITTEE

1. The amounts involved in the income transferal practices were not material to the consolidated net income or shareholder's equity of the company in the aggregate during the investigatory period (FY 1972–FY 1978).

2. The income transferal practices were achieved primarily through circumvention of existing internal controls by division personnel who should have exercised responsibility in the enforcement of such controls. Such practices were also assisted by certain inadequacies in the internal control systems of the divisions.

3. Although world headquarters' personnel did not authorize or participate in the income transferal practices, their continuance was facilitated by the company's philosophy of decentralized management and the role played by world headquarters' financial personnel in reviewing the financial reports from divisions.

4. No individual employee obtained any direct financial benefit from the practices uncovered in the investigation.

5. Perceived or de facto pressures for achievement of MIP goals contributed to the divisions' desirability of providing a cushion against future business uncertainties.

6. The income transferal practices did not serve any valid corporate need.

7. The income transferal practices and other questionable practices described in this report [of the Audit Committee] indicate the lack of sufficient control consciousness within the corporate structure; that is, an understanding throughout the company and the divisions that responsible and ethical practices are required in connection with all transactions.

8. The entrepreneurial spirit of the divisions fostered by the philosophy of decentralized autonomy should be continued for the good of the company and its shareholders.

9. World headquarters did not have the number of competent financial personnel needed to fulfill its role.

10. The continuance of the income transferal practices was aided by the independence of division financial personnel from world headquarters.

11. The continuance of the income transferal practices was aided by the reporting relationships of the internal audit staffs within the company.

12. The administration of the MIP and the goal-setting process thereunder did not result in adequate dialogue between senior world headquarters management and managements of the divisions.

13. The board of directors and management of the company have the duty to take all steps practicable to ensure safeguarding the assets of the company and that all transactions are properly recorded on the books, records, and accounts of the company.

QUESTIONS TO CONSIDER

1. How would you morally evaluate the income transfer practices discovered at Heinz? What—if anything—is morally wrong with them?

2. On a scale ranging from "trivially wrong" and "moderately wrong" to "very seriously wrong," indicate how unethical you think these practices are.

3. As comprehensively as you can, identify the factors that *caused* these practices at Heinz.

4. What do you think of the Audit Committee's report? If you were a member of this committee, what recommendations would you have made?

ORGANIZATIONAL FACTORS IN INDIVIDUAL WRONGDOING
✦

The Heinz case illustrates a dynamic all too common in large organizations. Practices or policies designed to achieve valid organizational goals somehow go awry and lead to unethical behavior. In some cases, bad organizational dynamics provide an occasion for unethical individuals to step forward and take control. In other cases, even people with good intentions find that pressures within the organization make it hard for them to maintain their integrity. Good people end up doing things they regret.

✦ MORAL ISSUES ✦

Before looking at the organizational dynamics at work in the Heinz company, it is important to take our moral bearings on the income transfer practices that were uncovered. On the surface, these practices may not seem particularly significant ethical violations. For one thing, within the context of Heinz's revenues, they did not amount to a great deal of money. Although not exactly "peanuts," as one insider would later say, the sums involved would not have greatly affected Heinz's tax liabilities or estimates of the company's financial situation by potential shareholders. Beyond this, various manipulations of revenues and expenditures— what some call "massaging the numbers"—are commonplace in business as well as in not-for-profit organizations. Anyone who has managed a budget is familiar with the end-of-fiscal-year race to use up unspent funds to avoid losing them or having next year's budget proportionately reduced. Among older managers, the term "building up the coal pile" designates a practice of increasing inventory near the end of a good year to offset possible future financial reverses.

Since some degree of "income management" is almost inevitable in business, are the practices at Heinz really of concern? To answer this question, it is important to see that ethics is frequently about drawing lines. Although certain questionable practices may be acceptable, at some point a line is crossed into wrongful conduct. Moral reasoning involves determining where that line is. Not every income management practice crosses the line. For example, it is hard to fault managers who, in order to improve their department's year-end sales picture, labor to get a shipment out the factory door on December 28 rather than January 2. Applying **NORM** to this conduct, we can see that a moral rule condemning such practices would probably not be acceptable to omnipartial rational people. Such a rule would require considerable second-guessing of managers' activities. How can we determine whether a shipment on December 28 was motivated by income concerns, whereas one on December 23 was part of the year's normal business? Beyond this, such a rule might frustrate the kinds of energy and initiative that often serve valid organizational purposes.

But the practices at Heinz go well beyond benign "income management" of this sort. They involve direct violations of GAAP and relevant laws, falsification of invoices, and, in some cases, maintenance of two sets of books. Many Heinz employees were not only lying to the outside world, they were also lying to members of their own company. To this we can add such moral wrongs as cheating—since employees who were willing to cut ethical corners got a competitive edge over more honest peers—and extortion. When Heinz managers instructed ad agencies to submit false invoices they were using economic pressure to force other managers into unethical conduct. Some overseas practices of Heinz's managers also may have violated the Foreign Corrupt Practices Act, a major set of legal requirements governing the conduct of international business by U.S. firms. We can see that proposed moral rules involving any of these types of behavior would meet serious resistance from omnipartial persons. No one wants to permit large companies to engage in systematic deception, the moral corruption of supplier or vendor firms, and lawbreaking.

In prudential terms, from the point of view of the Heinz Company's long-term welfare, these practices were also perilous. A large corporation is something like a steamship, the navigation of which depends on reliable information regarding the vessel's course and speed. However, because of these practices at Heinz, the instrument dials on Heinz's control panel were giving erroneous readings. It is anyone's guess how dangerous such faulty information might be for senior management or Heinz's owners—the board and the shareholders they represent—but the prospect for serious strategic and financial misdirection was there, especially if these practices became so ingrained that they widened and deepened over time. Even more serious damage might occur if ethical corner-cutting reached Heinz's core food business. A manager at Heinz USA who tried to protect his division's NPAT points by failing to replace defective machinery or by falsifying quality and assurance reports regarding food sterilization could contribute to the shipment of tainted product. Heinz's name could be associated with a major food poisoning episode in a way that could jeopardize the company's survival. Much of the equity of a century-old company like Heinz lies not in its capital resources or even its personnel, but in the established brand name under which it does business. Conduct that threatens public trust in this brand represents an incalculable business loss. Anyone who doubts this might recall the experience of Beechnut Foods, where public outrage over the sale of adulterated infant juice nearly destroyed the firm,[19] or Sears Roebuck, where the exposure of unethical sales practices in the auto repair business not only cost millions of dollars in fines and lost sales, but crippled the company during a perilous moment of restructuring.[20]

◆ IDENTIFYING THE CAUSES ◆

The moral and financial seriousness of these income transfer practices makes it all the more important to ask why they occurred. Which specific features in Heinz's corporate culture and business environment caused so many managers to follow a course that jeopardized their own integrity and the firm's reputation? Certainly, the MIP played a major role. On the one hand, by threatening a manager with the loss of up to 40 percent of annual compensation as well as serious career reverses, it severely penalized anyone who failed to meet NPAT goals. Heinz's emphasis on divisional performance also meant that a manager whose performance was lacking came under intense pressure from associates. Returning to the ship metaphor for a moment, we can see that Heinz's MIP made each division into something like the crew of a Roman galley depicted in old Hollywood films. Chained in place, oarsmen would have to row furiously to prevent the ship from being rammed and to prevent themselves from going down with it.

But if the MIP severely penalized failure, it also placed no premium on excellence. There were no points for exceeding one's goals. Really high performers at Heinz would be prudent not to excel, but instead to "bank" their excess revenues and put their productive energies into self-protective and evasive strategies. Ethical misconduct in business is often a way of avoiding the hard work of competitive endeavor, but at Heinz the MIP actually penalized performance and encouraged misconduct. The fact that personal and divisional objectives were unilaterally set from "on high," that they were inflexible, and that they took little account of year-to-year fluctuations or special business circumstances only compounded the pressure on employees to manage the environment to their advantage.

These unfortunate effects of the MIP raise the question of why it was adopted in the first place. We cannot entirely blame this on the consultants who devised the plan, since they undoubtedly worked under broad guidelines supplied by senior management or the board. But why would Heinz's top leadership want a plan of this sort? The answer to this question probably lies in the phrase "constant earnings growth" that crops up again and again in Heinz's corporate literature. Steady and predictable earnings growth is something investors in blue chip firms like Heinz value. Senior managers sensitive to "the Street" neglect this concern at their peril. The challenge before John Bailey, James Cunningham, and other top managers at Heinz was to come up with an incentive scheme that allowed them to achieve this objective. By creating pressure for managers to meet fixed annual objectives set by headquarters, Heinz's MIP was designed to minimize year-to-year spikes and dips in earnings and to produce the smooth 15 percent annual increases valued by financial analysts and some investors. The unethical practices the plan fostered were a foreseeable side effect of this human engineering.

Heinz's organizational structure also played a role. Decentralization meant that independent business units were free to develop subcultures that ran counter to the company's own long-standing values. Placing financial audit responsibilities entirely within divisions and having auditors report to division managers almost guaranteed that reporting integrity would be subordinated to divisional financial goals. In "closed roof" reporting schemes of this sort, auditors find it hard to maintain an independent stance with regard to their superiors. How to decentralize a large and complex corporation is one of the most important management questions. Although decentralization can unleash enormous energies by giving each unit a sense of "us against the world," it can also lead to the existence of private cultures that undermine organizational cohesion and integrity. The trick is to identify those activities that are properly decentralized and distinguish them from those that must remain in central control. Heinz learned to its distress that financial accounting is one function that cannot be left to affiliates.

Up to this point, everything we have said makes it seem as though the organizational and ethical failures of Heinz's top managers were largely sins of omission. By not paying enough attention to what was going on in the divisions and by failing to examine the unintended side effects of their incentive plan and decentralized structure, these managers allowed unethical practices to flourish. Although partly true, this picture ignores senior management's active role in setting the example for what happened at Heinz. As the case makes clear, income management at Heinz started in 1974, when world headquarters instructed Heinz USA to ask its advertising agencies to submit invoices for work not performed in that fiscal year. Having showed what could be done, senior management then ignored the spread of practices it helped create. World headquarters, in other words, was not just a passive or negligent contributor to wrongdoing. Leadership set the example.

The role of top managers in encouraging income transfer at Heinz partly explains why these practices flourished despite a corporate Code of Ethics that explicitly prohibited them. In organizational ethics, it is not what leaders *say* but what they *do* that counts. We can put this in more technical terms by observing that it is important to distinguish between an organization's *espoused* and its *operative* ethical values.[21] Espoused values are those that an organization publicly declares as its own. They are the ones mentioned in formal speeches by senior managers, in public relations documents, annual reports, ethical "credos" and codes. Operative values are the ones that actually govern organizational life. The two sets of values may not be the same. Operative values are rarely written down. Instead, they are reflected in organizational policies, practices, and structures. They may also reveal themselves in a company's "informal culture": in the kinds of "war stories" that are told, the people who are labeled "heroes," or even in the kinds of jokes that are regarded as funny. For example, an organization may be publicly committed to equal opportunity and inclusive hiring regardless of race and sex, and this forms part of its espoused value system. But if it consistently recruits key employees from an "old boy" network, if it tolerates racist or sexist humor at business meetings and social events, its operative value system actually encourages discrimination and exclusion.

Since operative values are crucially reflected in policies governing hiring, compensation, promotion, or termination, they have a more powerful influence on employees' behavior than do espoused values. This means that fostering ethics in organizations requires an emphasis on operative values. Codes and credos can be important, but they must be part of a total effort to bring an organization's operative value system into line with its espoused commitments. Looking at Heinz, we can see that in important ways this consistency in values was not achieved. In some respects Heinz was a schizophrenic organization, with two value systems pointing in opposite directions. One stressed the need for integrity in financial reporting; the other said that failure to "hit your numbers" was the mortal sin. Not surprisingly, for many managers, the latter took priority.

✦ HEINZ'S RESPONSE ✦

The ethically questionable practices uncovered at Heinz stemmed from a variety of organizational factors, including a faulty incentive system, excessive decentralization, management neglect, and poor examples. None of this excuses individual employees who chose to lie and cheat.

People must act responsibly and resist wrongdoing even where the circumstances are not conducive to doing so. But understanding the complex mix of personal and organizational failures involved here shows us how important organizational factors can be in promoting ethical or unethical conduct in business organizations. It also complicates the task of deciding how the Heinz company should respond to the discovery of wrongdoing in its midst.

The choices are not easy. How does one change the direction of an organization when so much momentum has been built up carrying it in a wrong direction? Heinz's Audit Committee's apparent answers to this question are straightforward, but they seem to address only superficial aspects of the problem. Some remarks in the report are directed at the MIP and the inattention to the code, but the report places its greatest emphasis on the need to establish proper financial controls and a more pervasive control consciousness in the company. A central problem at Heinz, the committee seems to conclude, was inadequate policing. This ignores pervasive features of the organizational culture that encouraged circumventing controls and that placed a relatively low value on the integrity of financial information, fairness to peers, or other stakeholders. A key question for Heinz—and really for any human group—is whether "laws" and "police" are the best way to prevent misconduct. Isn't it at least as important to develop habits of honesty, rectitude, and a commitment to sound organizational values? Earlier, in our discussion of the Tylenol case, we saw that Johnson & Johnson was able to surmount a potential organizational disaster by drawing on habits of ethical response developed over many years and reinforced by the "Credo process." Such "habits" or "instincts" often guide people through complex situations in ways that specific rules cannot. But if these habits are important, how can managers go about developing them in a complex corporate culture? And how can Heinz now do this in the wake of a trauma in its corporate life?

In some ways the Audit Committee report is a missed opportunity. Instead of major cultural reform, the report recommends a series of "technical fixes." In the wake of a crisis in Heinz's corporate life that revealed aspects of Heinz's culture that were getting dangerously out of line with its century-old commitments, the report in some ways reinforces the moral attitudes that led to the crisis in the first place. Of course, the task before those who would reform Heinz is daunting. Later in this chapter I examine comprehensively some of the considerations managers and companies should keep in mind as they try to avoid the trouble Heinz experienced.

Case 9.2 (A)

VOLVO'S CRUSHING BLOW[22]

The title card reads "June 12, 1990 Austin, Texas." Visuals move between crowd shots and views of a giant pickup truck with 6-foot-high tires identified as "Bear Foot." The truck drives over a line of cars, leaving only a Volvo station wagon intact. "There's one car still standing out there," says an announcer over the public address system. A voice-over adds, "Apparently, not everyone appreciates the strength of a Volvo."

In October 1990, executives at Volvo and their advertising agency Scali, McCabe, Sloves were pleased. Their "Bear Foot" spots were adding a sly touch of humor to Volvo's tradition of promoting the safety and reliability of its cars. The ads, first broadcast early in the month on several cable channels, and appearing in print versions in *Forbes* and *Car & Driver*, were also drawing critical praise. In a review of car advertising, *USA Today* described the "Bear Foot" spots as one of the most effective television promotions of the 1991 model year.

But by the end of the month "Bear Foot" had turned into a nightmare for Volvo and Scali. Late in October, James Mattox, attorney general of Texas, announced that he was pressing charges against Volvo North America Corporation, the car maker's American arm. In a lawsuit, Mattox charged that the ads had been shot after production people had reinforced the Volvos and sawed through the pillars on the competing cars. The ads, he told the press, were "a hoax and a sham."

Volvo reacted quickly. Within a week of Mattox's public announcement, the firm withdrew the spots and began running corrective ads explaining its decision in 19 Texas newspapers, *USA Today*, and the *Wall Street Journal*. Volvo also agreed to reimburse the attorney general's office $316,250 for investigative costs and legal fees.

Volvo's corrective ads took the form of a letter "to all interested consumers" from Joseph L. Nicolato, company president-CEO. The letter stated that the advertising "inaccurately characterized the event as a car-crushing exhibition when in fact it was a dramatization of the actual event in Vermont."

The letter continued:

> On Oct. 30 Volvo management learned for the first time that the film production team had apparently made modifications to two of the vehicles. There were two reasons for the modifications: first, to enable the filming to be done without threatening the safety of the production crew, and second, to allow the demonstration Volvo to withstand the number of runs by the "monster truck" required for filming.

As Volvo issued its statement it was still unclear who had authorized the modifications. Perretti Productions, New York, had handled production of the commercial for Scali, but Jim Perretti, the spot's director, was unavailable for comment.

In a separate statement to the press, Volvo's manager of public relations, Bob Austin, said that an investigation was under way to determine what caused the mistake. He explained that Milt Gravatt, the importer's marketing services manager, had been in Austin during the shoot but had not been on site at every moment during the 15 to 18 hours over two days it took to film the commercial.

"[Mr. Gravatt] assured us he did not see anything improper," said Austin. "We normally go down to a shoot to be nearby in case we can do anything to facilitate the production, but our basic attitude is to let the professionals do it. At this point, it is unclear what happened when, and who authorized it."

Executives at Scali expressed confusion and dismay. Agency chairman-CEO Marvin Sloves told reporters, "The agency never authorized any alterations of any vehicles at the shoot. We knew of no alterations made to create any misleading impression. I am just overwhelmed and shocked by the whole thing."

Sloves insisted that the agency creative team on site had not seen the alterations being made. "They say, and I believe them, that we had no idea they were doing anything to alter the cars to create a misleading impression." Although the spot itself was a dramatization, Sloves added, "This was a real live thing we had documentation for."

Stephanie Frawley, a development specialist at the Arthritis Foundation of Vermont, supported the claim that the ads were based on fact. The Foundation, she said, had sponsored a "monster truck" event at the fairgrounds in Essex, Vermont, two years earlier and, of the four cars that participated, a Volvo was the only one that was not crushed. "From other people who were there and from photos we have, it was obvious," she said. "Volvo is telling the truth."

Specialists in advertising law disagreed over the legal norms relevant to the "Bear Foot" spots. Felix Kent, an advertising lawyer with Hall, Dickler, Lawler, Kent & Friedman, said that a U.S. Supreme Court decision in the 1970s clearly established that demonstration ads could not use "any form of mock-ups or deception." But Rick Kunit, a partner at Frankfurt, Garbus, Klein & Selz, said that "for the past 10 years or so we've been able to be fairly free about not putting in 'dramatization' and 'recreation' and similar supers, basically because a lot of the time you get enough in the context of the commercial that people know it's a dramatization."

As November wore on, Volvo weighed the course of its future advertising. Speaking for the company, Bob Austin insisted that Volvo had no intention of backing off from its emphasis on safety, which has been featured in advertising virtually since the company entered the U.S. market in 1956. "Volvo was built around a solid set of basic values: safety, reliability, and longevity," Austin said. "We will have to allow the public to decide whether they believe in Volvo."

As for Scali's future on the $40 million account, "We will establish what happened and take appropriate corrective action," said Austin, who acknowledged that some outsiders had suggested Volvo fire the agency.

"Any conversation of that type would be premature," Austin added. "We have resisted the temptation to throw a body out there for the media."

Some advertising industry professionals saw major damage to the industry in the "Bear Foot" incident. DeWitt Helm, president of the Association of National Advertisers, said the episode "feeds the fuel of activists and overly zealous regulators. It's giving all advertising and business a tarnish and black eye we don't deserve."

But not every consumer agreed. Donna Gates, a Chicago public relations executive, said the flap over the ads would not have changed her mind about the car. "As a Volvo owner, I think it's a wonderful car," she said. "It feels like a little tank. I feel very safe in it."

Case 9.2 (B)

✦ VOLVO'S CRUSHING BLOW ✦

On November 18, 1990, in the wake of a highly publicized scandal involving its "Bear Foot" commercial, Scali, McCabe, Sloves ended a twenty-three-year relationship by resigning the Volvo account. Loss of its oldest, largest, flagship account was estimated to cost the agency $40 million in revenues and to require the layoff of thirty-five to fifty staffers.

"I'm devastated by it," said Marvin Sloves, the chairman and chief executive of the agency he had founded twenty-three years earlier with Sam Scali and Ed McCabe. Resigning the account, he said, "was the right thing to do. The executives at Volvo deserve a chance to put this thing behind them."

According to William Hoover, the senior vice-president of marketing for Volvo Cars of North America, an investigation showed that the production company hired by Scali apparently knew the demonstration was a fake. "The agency had to accept responsibility and the only thing to do was to resign," said Hoover.

Despite the resignation, questions remained over who had authorized and who knew of the product rigging that took place at the production shoot June 12 in Austin.

In an interview in October, before Volvo had been contacted by the Texas attorney general's office, Dean Stefanides, Scali executive vice-president and group creative director, explained that the idea for the spot initially came from an account executive at the agency who learned from a friend that a real monster truck exhibition in Vermont had used a Volvo in a lineup of other cars. In that event, the Volvo was the only car uncrushed. Engineering personnel at Volvo confirmed that Volvo's roof supports were theoretically strong enough to sustain the 11,000-pound weight of a monster truck.

"We looked into it and substantiated it. We thought the Volvo audience would find it funny or campy, even though they might not go to those events," Stefanides said. He added that it was simply a fresh and creative way to continue Volvo's long-running safety demonstration spots. Scali subsequently hired Perretti Productions to oversee production of the commercial.

Perretti, in turn, handed the re-creation of the Vermont event to International Productions, a company based in Phoenix, Arizona, that specializes in the promotion and production of motor sports events.

Jesse Spindler, promotion director of International Productions, said that his company did not have any advertising responsibility during the shoot. "Our understanding was that we were to recreate that event." The issue of bracing the Volvos came up during the contract negotiation stage with Perretti, said Spindler, but "they elected not to because of the cost factor."

According to Spindler, the first of the three Volvos used in the shoot was not reinforced and was crushed early in the day by the monster truck. Once that car was crushed, work to brace the remaining two Volvos immediately got under way. Wooden supports were added to the second Volvo, and the third was reinforced with steel. "The decision was also made to weaken the structures of competing cars by cutting their roof supports."

Those at the scene had included Jim Perretti; John Slaven, Scali executive vice-president and management representative; Dean Stefanides; and Larry Hempel, another Scali executive vice-president and group creative director. An initial Volvo inquiry revealed that a Volvo management representative, Milt Gravatt, had been at the site from early morning until about 6:30 P.M. At that point, the shooting was declared a wrap and Volvo and top Scali management left the scene. Apparently some filming continued after that using one or more modified Volvos.

Sources reported that before the airing of the spots, Scali submitted to the TV networks a producer's report vouching for the accuracy of the commercial and stating that no special effects or techniques had been used.

Whatever its causes, the episode marked a serious setback for an agency whose creativity had long been the envy of others in the industry. Over the years, Scali had put Perdue and its foul-faced chairman on the map and had held kosher Hebrew National franks accountable to "a higher authority."

Mark Messing, a Scali senior vice-president, noted that the agency could have avoided the fiasco by labeling the ad a "reenactment."

"Rookie error," he said.

QUESTIONS TO CONSIDER

1. Do you think that there was anything ethically wrong with Volvo's "Bear Foot" campaign? Why or why not?
2. What factors contributed to this episode?
3. Do you agree with the judgment that this was a "rookie error," a simple misstep by an otherwise professional organization?

"THE SEDUCTION OF THE CREATIVE IDEA"

✦

Splashed across the front pages of newspapers and trade magazines, aired and re-aired on news broadcasts, Volvo's "Bear Foot" campaign swiftly became one of the most discussed episodes of advertising ethics. Some would say that the ethical issues here were blown out of proportion by a local politician seeking to build his career and by a public that is always amused when one of the "mighty"—in this case a staid manufacturer of solid family cars—takes a fall. From the point of view of Volvo and its advertising agency, Scali, McCabe, Sloves, however, this was no tempest in a teapot. It cost the advertiser one of its most valued accounts and it came close to damaging a reputation that Volvo had taken decades to build. How could this come about? What led a group of skilled professionals to misstep so badly?

✦ MORAL ISSUES ✦

The legal and ethical norms that the "Bear Foot" campaign appeared to violate provide a context for the episode. In the United States and many other countries, advertisers are held to strict standards of accuracy and honesty that are enforced both by the government and by self-regulating industry boards like the National Advertising Division of the Better Business Bureaus. In keeping with these standards, product claims must be truthful and, where necessary, based on supporting documentation and studies. Disputed advertisements are assessed not only in terms of *what they say* but also of *what they are normally interpreted as saying* by viewers. Advertisers must be prepared to test product claims and audience responses to them, and they can be called to account for subtle or unintentional misrepresentations. Laws forbid any alterations in products used in visual representations that have the tendency to mislead the public about product attributes.[23]

It is not hard to understand the moral basis of these laws. We all have a stake in the accuracy and truthfulness of advertising because it provides us with much of the information we need about products. Deceptive or misleading ads subvert advertising's informational role. Of course, we also have an interest in the truthfulness of political, ideological, or religious expression, but we do not normally try to ensure this by government regulation. Instead, we allow statements to be tested in the "free marketplace of ideas." Why not do the same with advertising? Why not permit any sort of advertising claims and let consumer experience and competitive pressures sort out truth from falsehood? Part of the answer is that advertising, as a form of "commercial speech," deals with issues that are less central to the conduct of public or personal life than are political or religious opinions. More important, even though we would like to ban falsehood and prejudice from the public sphere, we know that we cannot safely rely on governments to do this. Government officials are often the target of these ideas and are predictably self-protective. In contrast, qualified government regulators can be counted on to establish the truth or falsity of advertising claims. As in so many other moral judgments, therefore, not one criterion but a multiplicity of criteria work together to explain our willingness to give governments an important role in monitoring the truthfulness of advertising.

How does the "Bear Foot" campaign measure up against these legal and ethical standards? U.S. law requires that dramatizations or reenactments be labeled as such unless the fact that they are so is clearly evident to viewers. No one would say that Volvo's ads were self-evident dramatizations. But, in view of the fact that the "Bear Foot" ads were based on a real event in which a production Volvo actually survived repeated passes by an identical monster truck, were viewers misled in any way?

In responding to these questions, we should keep in mind that we all have a stake in advertisers' respecting the requirement that dramatizations or reenactments be explicitly labeled. A world *without* such labeling, where advertisers are free to present dramatized events as real as long as they believe the dramatizations are rooted in reality, is one where we literally cannot trust our eyes. Like so many other types of deceptive practices, the implicit rule of conduct here casts its shadow on truthful representations, with the result that we may come to regard even presentations we normally think of as real as reconstructions of events. Since this rule of conduct lacks an obvious limiting principle stipulating how much basis in reality a dramatization must have, it also leads to a world where advertisers have license to alter presentations visually in ways that can wander unpredictably from truth and accuracy.

The "Bear Foot" campaign illustrates this point. The ads reproduced an earlier Vermont event. But the very fact of reproduction subtly alters the information being conveyed. Those who witnessed the earlier event may have been impressed by the Volvo's durability, but they also might have reasonably wondered whether the episode was just a fluke, a result of the positioning of the Volvo or the other cars. They might also have wondered whether what they saw was repeatable: Will Volvos consistently resist abuse of this sort? Volvo might have been within its rights in airing videos of the original Vermont event, but in doing so it would have had to avoid conveying any unsubstantiated claims about the strength of its cars. With the "Bear Foot" campaign, however, these complexities are swept away. Now the singular becomes the general, both through the implication that Volvos "regularly" survive punishment of this sort and by visuals enhancing every feature of the episode. Can Volvos really withstand repeated pounding on their roofs? For some of us, it is important to know. We go out of our way and spend extra money to buy a vehicle that will stay intact in a serious accident, and we do not want to be misled into basing our purchasing decision on ads with such tenuous links to reality.

✦ IDENTIFYING THE CAUSES ✦

If both law and ethics issue a negative judgment on the "Bear Foot" ads, how can we understand Scali's and Volvo's missteps in this incident? Is it a "rookie error," as one Scali executive suggested, a simple technical mistake by an otherwise professional organization, or does it point to more basic organizational problems? One telling aspect of the episode is the fact that someone at Scali signed a producer's report vouching for the accuracy of the commercial and stating that no special effects or techniques had been used. Whether intentional or not, this deception indicates serious problems in Scali's handling of its ethical responsibilities.

Either one or more persons at the agency knowingly chose to deceive the networks, or there was serious negligence regarding the preparation of an important legal document. Either way, the agency bears responsibility for not having clearly communicated and enforced its standards.

Similar disorganization and neglect appear to crop up in earlier stages of the episode. In the development of the campaign, responsibility was variously parceled out between Volvo, Scali, Perretti Productions, and the Phoenix-based company that actually staged the event. Nowhere in this process does there appear to have been explicit discussion of relevant ethical and legal norms, nor did anybody take responsibility for this aspect of the campaign. It may be that Volvo managers assumed that Scali would assume this responsibility. But Scali managers, perhaps distracted by immediate production problems, dropped the ball. In ethics, as in any other area of management, success depends on good leadership that shows itself willing to be accountable. In this case, diffused authority, indecision, and buck-passing replaced both leadership and accountability.

Paradoxically, the "Bear Foot" incident also suggests that there can sometimes be *too much* trust in stakeholder relationships. We have repeatedly seen that trust is central to ethical business relationships. It is also a key component of business success in an era when corporations are increasingly being called on to flatten management structures, delegate more authority to fewer people, decentralize operations, and give an enhanced role in production to suppliers or other stakeholders. Yet the "Bear Foot" episode shows that companies must back up trust by clearly enunciating and periodically reinforcing standards. With twenty-three years of successful collaboration between them, Volvo and Scali had come to trust one another too much. This led Volvo to assume that the agency would attend to its duties, even though Volvo would be the first to be harmed by any breach of integrity. It may also have led managers at Scali to believe that their interests and those of their client were the same. This produced a campaign that, although it initially won advertising industry accolades, took the client's reputation out over uncharted terrain.

We might finally point to the very ingenuity of the "Bear Foot" campaign as part of the problem. Not that cleverness and creativity are bad; they make a vital contribution to all human activities and are a driving force in advertising. But sometimes highly motivated professionals find themselves being carried away by their own ideas. Immediate objectives loom ahead, and more ordinary considerations, including ethical norms, are pushed aside. In advertising, goal obsession of this sort often takes the form of "the seduction of the creative idea." Here it was Scali's managers' fascination with the premise of the "Bear Foot" campaign and the challenge of moving from idea to visualization. In other industries it may not be an idea or campaign that creates the excitement so much as a new product line or financial objectives. Whatever the case, managers are at peril when they become obsessed with immediate goals, when, rather than owning the goal, the "goal owns them." In such instances, crucial considerations that make the goal worthwhile can be pushed aside and larger objectives within which the immediate goal fits can be lost. In the drive to create a campaign that would dramatically exhibit the product's structural integrity, Scali and others lost the account and almost destroyed their client's reputation for moral integrity.

WHY DO "GOOD" PEOPLE DO "BAD" THINGS?

♦

In 1982 a Wall Street investment banker named Bowen H. ("Buzz") McCoy took a six-month sabbatical leave from his firm and decided to spend it hiking in Nepal. In the course of that trip, Buzz had a disturbing experience that he eventually wrote up in an article for the *Harvard Business Review* entitled "The Parable of the Sadhu."[24]

Three months into his trek, Buzz and his party were ascending to a mountain pass at 18,000 feet. Their goal was the holy city of Muklinath. The group included Buzz, an American anthropologist named Stephen, and several Sherpa guides and porters. In order to get to Muklinath they had to rise early and cross a series of snow steps that would melt later in the day as the sun rose. Buzz was already suffering from the altitude sickness that had caused him to experience pulmonary edema on a trip some years before.

As the group ascended to the summit of the pass, they were met by a New Zealander from a party ahead of theirs. He came down toward them carrying a sadhu, an Indian holy man, whom his group had found, barefoot and almost naked, lying unconscious in the snow. The New Zealander handed the sadhu over to Buzz and his companions, saying, "Look, I've done what I can. You have porters and Sherpa guides. You care for him. We're going on."

In a few minutes, the sadhu revived, but he was unable to walk or to explain what he was doing at those heights without shoes and clad only in a skimpy garment. The sadhu was soon clad in warm clothing, but

Buzz and Stephen were unsure of what to do. Below them, they spotted a Japanese party with a horse. Buzz told Stephen that he was concerned about the altitude and wanted to cross the pass. Without much thought, he took off after some of the porters who had gone ahead.

Several hours later, Stephen rejoined Buzz at the summit. Stephen was angry. He explained that the Japanese had refused to take the sadhu. The guides wanted to get across the pass. At Stephen's urging, the Sherpas carried the sadhu down to a rock in the sun 500 feet below and pointed to a hut another 500 feet below. To this day neither Stephen or Buzz knows what happened to the sadhu.

Buzz McCoy apparently wrote up this episode as an act of contrition. He wished to extract from this experience a moral lesson of broader import. As an active layman in the Presbyterian Church, McCoy came to believe that he had somehow unwittingly violated his own deepest values. He had read the "Parable of the Good Samaritan" many times in his life, but when it came time for him to act as a good Samaritan, he missed the opportunity. In McCoy's view, what happened to him and his companions also occurs in business organizations. In moments of stress and because of complex group dynamics, good men and women, "nice" people with solid values, end up doing things they morally regret.

Box 9.1

FACTORS CONTRIBUTING TO ORGANIZATIONAL MISCONDUCT

- Stress
- Teleopathy (goal obsession)
    Fixation
    Rationalization
    Detachment
- Failures of leadership
    Value conflicts
    Buck passing
    Decision making by technicians
- Bad examples
- Alien cultural environments
- Blaming the victim
- Failures of individual moral responsibility

If we use Buzz's experience as a touchstone and review the events that contributed to Heinz's income transfer practices and Volvo–Scali's "Bear Foot" disaster, we can identify some of the key organizational and personal factors that contribute to ethical misconduct in business. These factors are summarized in Box 9.1. By understanding these factors in depth and by aggressively taking steps to avoid or minimize them, managers can help ensure the ethical integrity of their company and the people who work for it.

✦ STRESS ✦

Stress can take many forms. For Buzz McCoy, it was experienced in the hypoxia of 16,000 feet and the reduced physical and mental functioning it causes. For the managers at Heinz, stress was financial and psychological: the keen awareness that failure to hit your numbers was "a mortal sin" that could endanger your own and your division's future. For executives at Scali and Perretti Productions, it was the pressure to complete a complex shoot in time and on budget—when, just a few hours into the filming, with the first of three Volvo cars crushed and hundreds of extras and personnel standing by, pressures built to rig the remaining vehicles.

Of course stress is unavoidable in the competitive, goal-oriented environment of organizational life. But it is important to recognize that stress usually degrades the quality of decision making. Under stress, a kind of myopia ensues that magnifies near and immediate objects and eclipses what seem to be peripheral concerns. Since ethical decision making often concerns longer-term objectives and less obvious stakeholders, it is poorly served by decisions made under stress. Two hundred extras on a set have a claim, as do financial officers who want an ad to come in on budget; but they are dwarfed by Volvo's other managers and shareholders or by the buying public that expects honest advertising.

Since stress is unavoidable, but since it is also so dangerous, managers seeking to enhance the ethical quality of organizational decision making *must plan for ethical stress.* Several things are involved here. First, wherever possible, managers and their firms must try to avoid or minimize the things that cause stress. Particularly relevant are organizational policies that encourage ethical evasion. The Heinz case offers several examples. Heinz's decentralization of its audit structure—the "closed roof" arrangement that required division auditors to report to division managers—made misreporting or cover-ups more likely. Heinz's MIP also created unnecessary pressures on managers. The emphasis placed on the plan, its inflexibility, and the way it penalized excellence created an environment for the misconduct that ensued. Heinz's MIP had been "engineered" to produce a specific result. But those who designed it and those who implemented it failed to include foreseeable human and ethical outcomes. Like a motor run at too high a speed, Heinz's MIP met some of its performance expectations (smooth, consistent growth), but it broke down in ways its managerial "engineers" should have anticipated and tried to prevent.

Incentive schemes, methods of hiring, promoting, and firing employees are among the policies that most affect ethical performance in organizations. This is because they are among the greatest generators of stress. Managers must always scrutinize policies of this sort, policies that form the *operative* as opposed to the *espoused* values of an organization, for their full impact on employee conduct and morale. If they neglect this task, no code of conduct or admonitions to ethical behavior will do the job.

Managers must not only seek to reduce the sources of ethical stress, they must also plan for its inevitable occurrence. Nothing will prevent situations from arising where individuals find themselves pressured to abandon their moral values, but, as Buzz's experience shows, once stress occurs, it is often too late to think through complex decisions. Someone at 16,000 feet suffering altitude sickness cannot easily determine which course to follow. Similarly, managers faced with a problem such as cars that collapse during a shoot cannot invent organizational values on the spot. This has to be done in advance, *before* the stress hits.

In Buzz's case, group discussion of "the rules of the mountain" before the hikers took to the heights might have helped steer them through the decision. Of course, these rules, which require halting an expedition when life is in peril, do not say anything about sadhus. But they lay down a basic set of priorities that might have helped Buzz and his companions better perceive the moral issues the sadhu's presence raised for them. Thinking back a moment to the Tylenol case described in Chapter 6, we can see how the clear organizational priorities identified and constantly reinforced by Johnson & Johnson's "Credo Process" helped steer that company successfully through what, at the time, was an extraordinarily stressful organizational crisis.

✦ TELEOPATHY ✦

The word "teleopathy," a compound of the Greek words for "goal" (*telos*) and "sickness" (*pathos*), was coined by business ethicist Kenneth Goodpaster to describe the kind of *goal obsession* that is a major contributor to ethical wrongdoing in organizations.[25] As a rule, professionals are goal-driven people, and the organizations they serve thrive by identifying and pursuing objectives. But teleopathy is more than the normal pursuit of objectives. It occurs when the goal becomes so overwhelmingly important that it eclipses all other considerations. Teleopathy is present when the "goal owns you" instead of "you owning the goal."

According to Goodpaster, teleopathy has several characteristic features. One is a quality of almost hypnotic *fixation*. Like a magnetic field, this fixation becomes stronger as the goal is neared. When the objective is almost in hand, when time and energy have been invested in it, reaching the goal can seem to be the most important thing in the world. At this point, anything that opposes the goal will be shunted aside or argued away. *Rationalization* takes over. Reasons are found why the goal must come first, and falsehoods or careless moral reasoning are used to support the goal. In business organizations, it is often easy to find justifications for doing the wrong thing because organizational needs can cloak or mask self-interest. Managers can tell themselves that what they are doing is really in the company's best interests, even when they know that the behavior is unacceptable to society at large.[26] In Chapter 8, we saw that Alexander Gavin was relatively untroubled by payoffs and bribes as long as he could justify them as benefiting the company rather than himself.

If achieving the goal means harming people, a third feature comes into play: *emotional detachment*. Those damaged by the pursuit of the goal are objectified or dehumanized so as to make their neglect or abandonment morally tolerable. In an extreme case, as we will see below, this kind of detachment fuses with rationalization and leads to blaming victims for the wrongs done to them.

Managers should always be on the lookout for signs of teleopathy in themselves and in others in their organization. They should prepare those they work with for ethical stress by imparting organizational values and priorities as an ongoing process. And, when goals loom in importance and put people on a collision course with ethical requirements, everyone involved should step back and look more carefully at the impending conflict. The great danger of teleopathy is that it can lead people to pursue immediate goals while causing them to lose sight utterly of the larger objectives that these goals are meant to serve. Consider Buzz McCoy. Why did he go to Nepal? To get away from his daily business environment? To collect his thoughts? To exercise new skills? To put himself to the test and, perhaps, through this, to learn more about himself and his own most basic values? On the mountainside all these valid objectives became equated with "getting to Muklinath." But by putting aside this immediate *goal*, by turning around and bringing the sadhu back down to safety, Buzz might have far better achieved his larger *objectives*. He would have managed truly to test himself by exercising not just physical courage but the moral courage of being able to put aside a lesser goal to save a human life. As is, the mountainside taught Buzz something about himself. But because he had developed an acute case of teleopathy, this was probably not what he had hoped to learn.

◆ FAILURES OF LEADERSHIP ◆

Leaders play a crucial role in fostering ethical conduct in organizations. It is their job to identify the group's key ethical values, to convey those values by personal example, and to reinforce them by establishing appropriate organizational policies. When leaders abdicate this responsibility, dynamics take over that can cause ethical failure. Without control or coordination, the values of individual members push them in opposite directions and the resulting *value conflict* can lead either to indecision or to impulsive, harmful action. With no one holding people accountable, *buck passing* becomes common and individuals are led to adopt self-protective strategies that can damage the organization. Finally, as critical decisions are forfeited to lower levels of the organization, authority to make decisions often comes to depend on the possession of narrow expertise in one specialized area or another. *Decision making by technicians* replaces leadership on behalf of larger group values or goals.

The experience of Buzz and his companions vividly illustrates these dynamics. Confronted with the sadhu, no one stepped forward to direct a common effort, and the group literally went to pieces. Individual decision making replaced group resolve. The tendency to buck passing, already established by the New Zealanders, became pronounced. Even though the climbing party had been formed by Buzz and Stephen for their own purposes, at this critical juncture the Americans deferred to their guides and porters, who, unaware of their employers' larger objectives, steered the group toward the goal for which they were paid: crossing the mountain pass.

Failures of leadership can also isolate individuals with good intentions and make their decisions even harder. Stephen's experience illustrates this. Having struck out on his own to aid the sadhu, Stephen soon faced a new and acute moral question. Should he remain with the sadhu and see him down to safety? This could risk abandoning Buzz and the others to dangers high on the mountain. Or should he rejoin his group and leave the sadhu to an uncertain fate? Had the group worked together to solve this problem in the first place, no one would have had to face a life-for-life choice of this sort. When there are no leaders to coordinate a single group response, the full burden of choice falls on individuals, and serious moral dilemmas arise where none need exist.

We can perceive these same dynamics at work in Volvo's "Bear Foot" fiasco and Heinz's embarrassing income transfer episode. Despite the existence of an ethics code at Heinz, extreme decentralization and a "see no evil, hear no evil" attitude on the part of top management allowed individuals lower in the organization to follow their own course. Organizational policy became a function of divisional and personal needs. In the "Bear Foot" campaign, uncertain lines of authority among various managers in different organizations and the fact that no one was in charge permitted neglect of key ethical and legal matters. In this case, managers lacking direction from above permitted lower-echelon specialists with only immediate technical concerns—"How can we get this shoot done well and on budget?"—to take over. In the end, someone at Scali, McCabe, Sloves, faced with the tough choice of halting the momentum of the campaign or falsifying a legal document for the networks, chose to lie. Failures of leadership may have thus intensified an individual's moral dilemma, just as they did for Stephen on the mountainside.

✦ BAD EXAMPLES ✦

Human beings are social creatures. As much as we like to think of ourselves as autonomous, decision-making adults, we are greatly influenced throughout our lives by the same group dynamics that caused us anguish in the schoolyard or at the high school social event. In organizations, peer pressure and peer modeling have a very real bearing on the creation of ethical or unethical conduct. Examples set by top management and other influential actors in the organization play a major role in forming the operative, as opposed to the espoused values of the group. This is also why "war stories" and formal and informal reward systems ("Who's being promoted? Who's invited to play golf?") have such importance in organizational life. By identifying organizational winners and losers in this way, organizations model forms of desirable or undesirable conduct.

We are often unaware of how powerfully examples shape our response to ethical challenges. Buzz and his companions paid little attention to the conduct of the New Zealander, who came and went in an instant. Nevertheless, his example proved decisive. He established the pattern of buck (or sadhu) passing that led Buzz's group to think in terms of how they, too, could pass the sadhu on. At Heinz, the income transfer practice, established in 1974 by world headquarters in response to Nixon administration wage and price guidelines, got the ball rolling. It is no accident that these practices later flourished at Heinz USA, the division most influenced by these early examples.

We should never underestimate the power of examples in forming organizational ethics. Managers must watch, not just what they say, but what they do. They must also be prepared to set a proper example by punishing those who have violated organizational norms.

People today are generally averse to punishment, believing that positive educational efforts can replace harsh treatment in most circumstances. This may be true. But there are times when leaders must make it clear that certain forms of conduct will not be tolerated. The starkest way of doing this is to discipline or fire people who have misbehaved or failed in their duties. One of the ironies of Heinz's handling of its income management embarrassment is that no senior managers were ever singled out for serious punishment. This, of course, reinforces the message that got Heinz into trouble in the first place: that cutting ethical corners will be overlooked so long as you "hit your numbers."

✦ ALIEN CULTURAL ENVIRONMENTS
AND BLAMING THE VICTIM ✦

The need to operate in a strange or alien cultural environment can also compromise the quality of ethical decision making. It is often hard enough to determine one's ethical responsibility without adding the burden of unfamiliar surroundings or stakeholders whose values we do not understand. In such circumstances, rationalization easily takes over. Because it is sometimes true that we must *accommodate* to local values, we can wrongly conclude that a prevalent pattern of misconduct justifies our *doing* the same. "Everyone's doing it," becomes a catch-all excuse. Ignorance or prejudice can lead us to underestimate the impact of our behavior on some stakeholders, and we can even blame those we injure for the harm we cause them.

"The Parable of the Sadhu" provides illustrations of these dynamics. Faced with the nuisance and burden of an unconscious, ill-clad holy man, it was natural for Buzz and his colleagues to try to shift the problem in his direction. "What's someone so poorly prepared doing at these heights? What right does he have to interrupt our trek? Maybe he wants to be up here? Is he possibly involved in some kind of religious test or act of suicide?" These are natural questions, but it is not hard to see that in this situation they have no bearing on the decision facing Buzz and the others. So long as the sadhu was unable to explain his behavior, something had to be done to get him to safety. In the end, rationalization also took over. Confronted with Stephen's accusation that he may have contributed to the death of a fellow human being, Buzz initially replied by insisting that "everyone had done his bit." In this way, he sought to represent buck passing and evasions of responsibility as a well-thought-out collaborative effort.

One need not go halfway around the world to be in an alien cultural environment. Volvo and Scali both entered uncharted territory when they embarked on the "Bear Foot" campaign. In previous efforts, the companies had operated in a more familiar, engineering-oriented advertising environment. Volvos would be shown supporting the weight of a truck or several stacked autos on their roofs. Beguiled by the Vermont "Bear Foot" event and intrigued by the prospect of adding a touch of humor to their campaign, Volvo and Scali ventured out onto the unfamiliar terrain of rodeos and auto demolitions. In the process, they left behind the world of demonstrated engineering claims. Finally, rationalization took over. As vehicles failed to stand up, managers on the spot excused modifications as "technical changes" needed to adapt truthful claims to the production demands of this unfamiliar environment.

Should companies avoid novelty or refuse to do business in places where they have not operated before? Of course not. Business is all about risk and innovation. But it is also about *managing* these. This suggests that, as companies embark on new ventures or enter culturally unfamiliar terrain, they must take ethical precautions. They should make sure that organizational values are clear and that managers feel free to seek help with problems. They must also strive to minimize rationalization and victim-blaming by educating managers about the realities of the new issues and new environments they will face.

✦ FAILURES OF INDIVIDUAL MORAL RESPONSIBILITY ✦

Up to this point, we have explored some of the major situational and organizational factors that can lead to moral failure. But the best structures and the most comprehensive organizational policies and planning will go by the board if individuals choose to abandon their moral responsibilities. Nor are bad systems and a poor ethical culture an excuse for misconduct. Individuals are always called on to rise above group pressures and to act with integrity no matter how unsupportive the environment. All the cases of ethical failure explored in this chapter provide instances of simple failures of moral responsibility. Buzz's charging off up the mountainside leaving Stephen to shoulder the weight of the sadhu is one example. So, too, is the behavior of the managers at Heinz who accepted, apparently without questioning, the income transfer practices, or of the account managers in Heinz's advertising agencies who quickly succumbed to pressure to falsify invoices. And, in the Volvo episode, whatever combination of poor management practices and neglect may have led to a campaign that violated legal and ethical standards, those who knowingly falsified documents or chose to deceive others about what went on that day in Austin bear moral responsibility for their decisions.

Does this mean that organizational factors are unimportant? Just the opposite. In these and other cases throughout this book, we have seen that careful attention to organizational policies can help spare managers from being faced with acute or agonizing moral dilemmas. Furthermore, managers' individual moral responsibilities extend to the decisions they make—whether in the examples they set or in the policies they select—that shape and mold the organization's culture. Organizational ethics and individual ethical striving are not alternatives but mutually reinforcing aspects of business ethics.

SUMMARY

- Organizational design and culture play an important role in encouraging moral or immoral behavior. Managers must strive to implement and monitor organizational policies so as to reduce the pressures that lead to wrongdoing.

- Among features of organizational life that are particularly important in fostering ethical or unethical conduct are the examples set by the company's top leadership, the company's systems of rewards and punishments, and its operative, as opposed to its espoused, value system.

- Organizations predictably break down ethically and good people succumb to moral compromise when the members of the group are under stress and prone to teleopathy, when leadership is lacking, when instances of misconduct proliferate and go unpunished, and when unfamiliar or alien environments generate moral confusion. Ethical managers should be alert to these problems and should constantly strive to minimize them.

NOTES

1. H. J. Heinz Company, form 8-K, April 27, 1979, p. 2.
2. "Heinz to Probe Prepayments to Suppliers by Using Outside Lawyers, Accountants," *Wall Street Journal*, 30 April 1979, p. 5.
3. H. J. Heinz Company, annual report, 1976.
4. "Report of the Audit Committee to the Board of Directors: Income Transferal and Other Practices," H. J. Heinz Company, form 8-K, May 7, 1980, p. 7.
5. Ibid, p. 8.
6. Ibid, pp. 10–12.
7. Ibid, p. 12.
8. "Heinz Slow Growth Behind Juggling Tactic?" *Advertising Age*, 24 March 1980, p. 88.
9. "Results in Probe of Heinz Income Juggling Expected to Be Announced by Early April," *Wall Street Journal*, 18 March 1980, p. 7.
10. H. J. Heinz Company, form 8-K, May 7, 1980.
11. "Results in Probe of Heinz Income Juggling Expected to Be Announced by Early April," *Wall Street Journal*, 18 March 1980, p. 7.
12. H. J. Heinz Company, form 8-K, May 7, 1980, p. 4.

13. H. J. Heinz Company, form 8-K, May 10, 1979, p. 2; *Wall Street Journal*, 18 March 1980, p. 7.

14. "Initial Study of Some Heinz Units Finds $5.5 Million in Profit Juggling Practices," *Wall Street Journal*, 2 July 1979, p. 8.

15. "Heinz Discloses Profit Switching at Units Was Much Broader Than First Realized," *Wall Street Journal*, 13 September 1979, p. 15.

16. H. J. Heinz Company, form 8-K, May 7, 1980, p. 2.

17. "H. J. Heinz Realigns Its Senior Management in Consolidation Move," *Wall Street Journal*, 19 February 1980.

18. "DDB Admits Heinz Role," *Advertising Age*, 28 April 1980, pp. 1, 88.

19. James Traub, "Into the Mouths of Babes," *New York Times Magazine*, 24 July 1988, p. 18.

20. "California Accuses Sears of Bilking Auto Service Customers," *National Petroleum News*, August 1992, pp. 21–22.

21. I owe this distinction, in part, to Kenneth E. Goodpaster's distinction between espoused values and "values in action."

22. This case was prepared by Ronald M. Green for class discussion at the Amos Tuck School of Business Administration. Sources used include articles by Barry Meier and Kim Foltz in the *New York Times* (6 November 1990, pp. D1, D7, and 14 November 1990, pp. D1, D7); Raymond Serafin, Jennifer Lawrence, Jan Lafayette, and Gary Lovin in *Advertising Age* (12 November 1990, pp. 1, 76, 77, and 26 November 1990, pp. 4, 62); Debra Goldman, Robyn Griggs, Barbara Holsomback, and Kevin McCormack in *Adweek* (November 1990, pp. 1, 4, 5, 8, and 26 November 1990, pp. 1, 4, 20, 22); and Joshua Levine in *Forbes* (27 May 1991, pp. 319–22).

23. The landmark supreme court legal case in this area is *Federal Trade Commission v. Colgate-Palmolive Co. et al.*, 380 U.S. 374, 85 S. Ct. 1035.

24. Vol. 65, No. 1 (September–October 1983): 103–108. This episode was subsequently used as the basis of a video dramatization prepared by the Harvard Business School. The facts and dialogue reported here are drawn from both sources.

25. Goodpaster introduces this term in his article "Ethical Imperatives and Corporate Leadership," in *Ethics in Practice*, ed. Kenneth R. Andrews (Boston: Harvard Business School Press, 1989), p. 217. He has expanded on this concept in lectures at the Dartmouth Institute.

26. For a discussion of the complex processes of rationalization that can lead managers astray, see Saul W. Gellerman, "Why 'Good' Managers Make Bad Ethical Choices," *Harvard Business Review* 64, no. 4 (July–August, 1986): 85–90.

ETHICS
AND
EXCELLENCE

✦

✦IN THE PRECEDING CHAPTERS WE LOOKED AT SPECIFIC MORAL OBLIGA-tions that managers and firms owe their stakeholders. Most of the dilemmas we have examined involve painful conflicts among obligations owed to stakeholders, as when a manager like Alexander Gavin finds himself torn between concerns for the safety of his family and the welfare of his company, or when Phil Cortez must juggle obligations to a previous and present employer. In cases like these, ethical management involves determining which policy will cause the least harm to all stakeholders.

Although resolving moral conflict is an important part of managerial responsibility, business ethics involves more than putting out moral fires. It also comprises a positive vision of corporate responsibility. It addresses such questions as what role can business play in enhancing human life and how can corporations and their stakeholders work together for mutual benefit.

A generation ago, when the field of business ethics was just getting started, this positive side was usually discussed under the heading of "corporate social responsibility," the question of whether corporations are obligated to use corporate resources to address pressing social needs. For example, it was common to ask whether businesses have a responsibility to contribute funds and managerial time to address the problem of hard-core unemployment. On one side of the debate were those who believed that businesses have a duty, above and beyond the bottom line, to return value to the communities in which they operate. On the other side were thinkers like Milton Friedman, who objected to corporate benevolence as a waste of shareholder wealth and a distraction from what business does best. Between these two positions were those who believed that we should regard socially responsible business as an investment that could benefit the company in the long run, whether by ensuring a flourishing social environment in which to operate or by improving the public's image of the business community.

Implicit in these discussions was a distinction between the clear moral duties possessed by business firms and supererogatory obligations—matters above and beyond the call of duty that belong to the sphere of ethical altruism or moral heroism. Although there was a consensus that managers have a series of minimal obligations they must uphold, such as avoiding injury to customers and respecting commitments made to employees or other stakeholders, there was far less agreement on whether business has a positive obligation to go out of its way to enhance the quality of life for people inside or outside the firm. Since there is little consensus on the extent to which even individuals are required to act in supererogatory ways, there was naturally little agreement on whether businesses are morally required to exhibit generosity and altruism in ways not directly related to increasing profits.

In the decade or two since these debates, the world of business has changed dramatically. An increasingly competitive global environment and new economic pressures have placed stress on corporate programs of philanthropy. Pointing to some large companies, like Control Data or IBM, whose corporate giving and programs of communal involvement have been accompanied by decreased competitiveness and declining economic fortunes, some have asked whether firms can be "too ethical."[1] Within companies, downsizing, restructuring, and the use of contract employees have impacted on established loyalties and made it harder, in many people's minds, to establish or maintain a corporate culture based on ethical values.

But trauma and ethical stress are only one part of the story. The same period has seen a series of developments that, in their own way, have accentuated the importance of ethics in business life. During this period companies in different industries have flourished by incorporating into their mission statements ethical commitments to all stakeholders, including the communities in which the companies do business. From tiny Ben & Jerry's Homemade Ice-cream in Vermont to software giant Microsoft, successful companies are showing that ethics and business excellence are closely related phenomena.[2]

Driving these developments are changes associated with an increasingly competitive business environment. In a world of rapidly advancing technology and constant innovation in products and services, competitive advantage increasingly lies with those companies that can stay closest to the needs of their customers and clients. Computer technology has opened up new ways of providing highly specialized products and services, combining the advantages of mass production with custom manufacture. In all areas, more sophisticated customers with an expanded array of firms to choose from have come to expect quality and commitment with every product or service they buy. As a consequence, all firms, even those in traditional manufacturing areas, find that they are becoming service companies for which the quality of client–customer relationships is a major factor in business success.

Meeting the needs of customers and clients, however, requires complex changes within the company and in its relations with key stakeholders. Customers are increasingly involved directly in corporate decision making, often playing an active role in determining which products and services a company should develop. "Just in time manufacture" and other new inventory procedures require close and cooperative relationships with suppliers. In some cases these relationships involve giving suppliers a substantial role in everything from product design to the billing and payment process. Quality customer service and the reliance on sophisticated technologies also place a premium on employee involvement and motivation. There is little room for a disgruntled or hostile work force in a world where employees' creativity and enthusiasm, and their active response to the needs of customers, constitute the company's competitive edge.

According to William H. Davidow and Michael S. Malone, these developments have begun to fashion a new type of business organization that they call "the virtual corporation."[3] The virtual corporation lacks many of the features we have come to associate with business firms. Relying heavily on information technology, it is dedicated to the cost-effective instantaneous production of mass-customized goods (or services). Instead of maintaining strict divisions between functional areas such as design, marketing, manufacturing, and finance, it puts a premium on flexible, collaborative task forces that bring together employees from various organizational levels and with a variety of skills to accomplish specific projects. It replaces the older "command and control" hierarchies of the past, which assumed that only managers could make decisions and that employees could only take orders, with an emphasis on empowerment for people at all levels. Life in the virtual corporation requires employees and managers constantly to upgrade skills and assume new responsibilities.

Davidow and Malone observe that the virtual corporation maintains "an environment of teamwork, one in which employees, management, customers, suppliers, and governments all work together to achieve common goals."[4] Within this environment, corporate ethics is not just a matter of avoiding wrongdoing; nor is it merely a philanthropic afterthought to the primary process of pursuing profit. Instead, it is an essential component in the pursuit of business success and organizational excellence. In the words of Davidow and Malone, "The virtual corporation is built upon unprecedented levels of trust. Between the company and its suppliers and customers. Between management and labor. Between senior and middle management."[5] Davidow and Malone point to the special importance of the ethical integrity of the firm's leadership and the culture this leadership helps create. "Ultimately," they say, "it comes to this: the chief executive of a virtual corporation must be able to trust employees in the firm to make responsible decisions. Those employees must in turn trust in the vision for the corporation as devised by the CEO."[6]

Many leading companies in the manufacturing and service sectors fit this description. They are characterized by consistently good to outstanding economic performance and high employee morale. These are the companies that consistently win accolades as among the best places to work. One such company is the large New Jersey–based pharmaceutical firm, Merck, Inc. A series of events in Merck's recent corporate experience, the development of a miracle drug named Mectizan, provides a window into some of the dynamics that mark the changing environment of business today. We can better understand the role played by ethics in the virtual corporation by focusing in detail on the way that Merck's management handled a series of complex decisions during this remarkable episode.

Case 10.1 (A)

✦ MERCK & CO., INC.[7] ✦

In 1978, Dr. P. Roy Vagelos, then head of the Merck research laboratories, received a provocative memorandum from a senior researcher in parasitology, Dr. William C. Campbell. Dr. Campbell had made an intriguing observation while working with ivermectin, a new antiparasitic compound under investigation for use in animals.

Campbell thought that ivermectin might be the answer to a disease called river blindness that plagued millions in the third world. But to find out if Campbell's hypothesis had merit, Merck would have to spend millions of dollars to develop the right formulation for human use and to conduct field trials in the most remote parts of the world. Even if these efforts produced an effective and safe drug, virtually all of those afflicted with river blindness could not afford to buy it. Vagelos, originally a university researcher but by then a Merck executive, had to decide whether to invest in research for a drug that, even if successful, might never pay for itself.

RIVER BLINDNESS

River blindness, formally known as *onchocerciasis*, was a disease labeled by the World Health Organization (WHO) as a public health and socioeconomic problem of considerable magnitude in over thirty-five developing countries throughout the third world. Some 85 million people in thousands of tiny settlements throughout Africa and parts of the Middle East and Latin America were thought to be at risk. The cause: a parasitic worm carried by a tiny black fly that bred along fast-moving rivers. When the fly bit humans—a single person could be bitten thousands of times a day—the larvae of a parasitic worm, *Onchocerca volvulus*, entered the body.

These worms grew to more than two feet in length, causing grotesque but relatively innocuous nodules in the skin. The real harm began when the adult worms reproduced, releasing millions of microscopic offspring, known as microfilariae, which swarmed through body tissue. A terrible itching resulted, so bad that some victims committed suicide. After several years, the microfilariae caused lesions and depigmentation of the skin. Eventually they invaded the eyes, often causing blindness.

The World Health Organization estimated in 1978 that some 340,000 people were blind because of onchocerciasis, and that a million more suffered from varying degrees of visual impairment. At that time, 18 million or more people were infected with the parasite, though half did not yet have serious symptoms. In some villages close to fly breeding sites, nearly all residents were infected and a majority of those over age 45 were blind. In such places, it was said, children believed that severe itching, skin infections, and blindness were simply a part of growing up.

In desperate efforts to escape the flies, entire villages abandoned fertile areas near rivers, and moved to poorer land. As a result, food shortages were frequent. Community life disintegrated as new burdens arose for already impoverished families.

The disease was first identified in 1893 by scientists and in 1926 was found to be related to the black flies. But by the 1970s, there was still no cure that could safely be used for community-wide treatment. Two drugs, diethylcarbamazine (DEC) and Suramin, were useful in killing the parasite, but both had severe side effects in infected individuals, needed close monitoring, and had even caused deaths. In 1974, the Onchocerciasis Control Program was created to be administered by the World Health Organization, in the hope that the flies could be killed through spraying of larvacides at breeding sites, but success was slow and uncertain. The flies in many areas developed resistance to the treatment, and were also known to disappear and then reinfest areas.

MERCK & CO., INC.

In 1978, Merck & Co., Inc., was one of the largest producers of prescription drugs in the world. Headquartered in Rahway, New Jersey, Merck traced its origins to Germany in 1668 when Friedrich Jacob Merck purchased an apothecary in the city of Darmstadt. Over three hundred years later, Merck, having become an American firm, employed over 28,000 people and had operations all over the world.

In the late 1970s, Merck was coming off a 10-year drought in terms of new products. For nearly a decade, the company had relied on two prescription drugs for a significant percentage of its nearly $2 billion in annual sales: Indocin, a treatment for rheumatoid arthritis, and Aldomet, a treatment for high blood pressure. Henry W. Gadsden, Merck's chief executive from 1965 to 1976, along with his successor, John J. Horan, were concerned that the seventeen-year patent protection on Merck's two big moneymakers would soon expire, and began investing an enormous amount in research.

Merck's management spent a great deal of money on research because it knew that its success ten and twenty years in the future critically depended on its present investments. The company deliberately fashioned a corporate culture to nurture the most creative, fruitful research possible. Merck scientists were among the best-paid in the industry and were given great latitude to pursue intriguing leads. Moreover, they were inspired to think of their work as a quest to alleviate human disease and suffering worldwide. Within certain proprietary constraints, researchers were encouraged to publish in academic journals and to share ideas with their scientific peers. Nearly a billion dollars was spent between 1975 and 1978, and the investment paid off. In that period, under the direction of head of research, Dr. P. Roy Vagelos, Merck introduced Clinoril, a painkiller for arthritis; a general antibiotic called Mefoxin; a drug for glaucoma named Timoptic; and Ivomec (ivermectin, MSD), an antiparasitic for cattle.

In 1978, Merck had sales of $1.98 billion and a net income of $307 million. Sales had risen steadily between 1969 and 1978 from $691 million to almost $2 billion. Income during the same period had risen from $106 million to over $300 million.

At that time, Merck employed 28,700 people, up from 22,200 ten years earlier. Human and animal health products constituted 84 percent of the company's sales, with environmental health products and services representing an additional 14 percent of sales. Merck's foreign sales had grown more rapidly during the 1970s than had domestic sales, and in 1978 represented 47 percent of total sales. Much of the company's research operations were organized separately as the Merck Sharp & Dohme Research Laboratories, headed by Vagelos. Other Merck operations included the Merck Sharp & Dohme Division, the Merck Sharp & Dohme International

Division, Kelco Division, Merck Chemical Manufacturing Division, Merck Animal Health Division, Calgon Corporation, Baltimore Aircoil Company, and Hubbard Farms.

The company had twenty-four plants in the United States, including one in Puerto Rico, and forty-four in other countries. Six research laboratories were located in the United States and four abroad.

Although Merck executives sometimes squirmed when they quoted the "unbusinesslike" language of George W. Merck, son of the company's founder and its former chairman, there could be no doubt that Merck employees found the words inspirational. "We try never to forget that medicine is for the people," Merck said. "It is not for the profits. The profits follow, and if we have remembered that, they have never failed to appear. The better we have remembered it, the larger they have been." These words formed the basis of Merck's overall corporate philosophy.

THE DRUG INVESTMENT DECISION

Merck invested hundreds of millions of dollars each year in research. Allocating those funds amongst various projects, however, was a rather involved and inexact process. At a company as large as Merck, there was never a single method by which projects were approved or money distributed.

Studies showed that, on the average, it took twelve years and $200 million to bring a new drug to market. Thousands of scientists were continually working on new ideas and following new leads. Drug development was always a matter of trial and error; with each new iteration, scientists would close some door and open others. When a Merck researcher came across an apparent breakthrough—either in an unexpected direction or as a derivative of the original lead—he or she would conduct preliminary research. If the idea proved promising, it was brought to the attention of the department heads.

Every year, Merck's research division held a large review meeting at which all research programs were examined. Projects were coordinated and consolidated, established programs were reviewed, and new possibilities were considered. Final approval on research was not made, however, until the head of research met later with a committee of scientific advisors. Each potential program was extensively reviewed, analyzed on the basis of the likelihood of success, the existing market, competition, potential safety problems, manufacturing feasibility, and patent status before the decision was made whether to allocate funds for continued experimentation.

THE PROBLEM OF RARE DISEASES AND POOR CUSTOMERS

Many potential drugs offered little chance of financial return. Some diseases were so rare that treatments developed could never be priced high enough to recoup the investment in research, whereas other diseases afflicted only the poor in rural and remote areas of the third world. These victims had limited ability to pay even a small amount for drugs or treatment.

In the United States, Congress sought to encourage drug companies to conduct research on rare diseases. In 1978 legislation had been proposed that would grant drug companies tax benefits and seven-year exclusive marketing rights if they would manufacture drugs for diseases afflicting fewer than 200,000 Americans. It was expected that this "orphan drug" program would eventually be passed into law.

There was, however, no U.S. or international program that would create incentives for companies to develop drugs for diseases like river blindness, which afflicted millions of the poor in the third world. The only hope was that some third-world government, foundation, or international aid organization might step in and partially fund the distribution of a drug that had already been developed.

THE DISCOVERY OF IVERMECTIN

The process of investigating promising drug compounds was always long, laborious, and fraught with failure. For every pharmaceutical compound that became a product candidate, thousands of others failed to meet the most rudimentary preclinical tests for safety and efficacy. With so much room for failure, it became especially important for drug companies to have sophisticated research managers who could identify the most productive research strategies.

Merck had long been a pioneer in developing major new antibiotic compounds, beginning with penicillin and streptomycin in the 1940s. In the 1970s, Merck Sharp & Dohme Research Laboratories were continuing this tradition. To help investigate for new microbial agents of potential therapeutic value, Merck researchers obtained fifty-four soil samples from the Kitasato Institute of Japan in 1974. These samples seemed novel and the researchers hoped they might disclose some naturally occurring antibiotics.

As Merck researchers methodically put the soil through hundreds of tests, Merck scientists were pleasantly surprised to detect strong antiparasitic activity in Sample No. OS3153, a scoop of soil dug up at a golf course near Ito, Japan. The Merck labs quickly brought together an interdisciplinary team to try to isolate a pure active ingredient from the microbial culture. The compound eventually isolated—avermectin—proved to have an astonishing potency and effectiveness against a wide range of parasites in cattle, swine, horses, and other animals. Within a year, the Merck team also began to suspect that a group of related compounds discovered in the same soil sample could be effective against many other intestinal worms, mites, ticks, and insects.

After toxicological tests suggested that ivermectin would be safer than related compounds, Merck decided to develop the substance for the animal health market. In 1978 the first ivermectin-based animal drug, Ivomec, was nearing approval by the U.S. Department of Agriculture and foreign regulatory bodies. Many variations would likely follow: drugs for sheep and pigs, horses, dogs, and others. Ivomec had the potential to become a major advance in animal health treatment.

As clinical testing of ivermectin progressed in the late 1970s, Dr. William Campbell's ongoing research brought him face-to-face with an intriguing hypothesis. Ivermectin, when tested in horses, was effective against the microfilariae of an exotic, fairly unimportant gastrointestinal parasite, *Onchocerca cervicalis*. This particular worm, although harmless in horses, had characteristics similar to the insidious human parasite that causes river blindness, *Onchocerca volvulus.*

Dr. Campbell wondered: Could ivermectin be formulated to work against the human parasite? Could a safe, effective drug suitable for community-wide treatment of river blindness be developed? Both Campbell and Vagelos knew that it was very much a gamble that it would succeed. Furthermore, both knew that even if success were attained, the economic viability of such a project would be nil. On the other hand, because such a significant amount of money had already been invested in the development of the animal drug, the cost of developing a human formulation would be much less than that for developing a new compound. It was also widely believed at this point that ivermectin, though still in its final development stages, was likely to be very successful.

A decision to proceed would not be without risks. If a new derivative proved to have any adverse health effects when used on humans, its reputation as a veterinary drug could be tainted and sales negatively affected, no matter how irrelevant the experience with humans. In early tests, ivermectin had had some negative side effects on some specific species of mammals. Dr. Brian Duke of the Armed Forces Institute of Pathology in Washington, D.C., said that the cross-species effectiveness of antiparasitic drugs is unpredictable, and there is "always a worry that some race or subsection of the human population" might be adversely affected.

Isolated instances of harm to humans or improper use in third-world settings might also raise some unsettling question: Could drug residues turn up in meat eaten by humans? Would any human version of ivermectin distributed to the third world be diverted into the black market, undercutting sales of the veterinary drug? Could the drug harm certain animals in unknown ways?

Despite these risks, Vagelos wondered what the impact might be of turning down Campbell's proposal. Merck had built a research team dedicated to alleviating human suffering. What would a refusal to pursue a possible treatment for river blindness do to morale?

Ultimately, it was Dr. Vagelos who had to make the decision whether or not to fund research toward a treatment for river blindness.

QUESTIONS TO CONSIDER

1. What ethical considerations must Dr. Vagelos keep in mind as he decides how Merck should respond to the challenge posed by this new drug for river blindness?
2. What would you advise Merck to do?
3. What view of the role of ethics in corporate decision making underlies your recommendation?

MORAL INSIGHT AND BUSINESS JUDGMENT

✦

Several different models of managerial responsibility are available to help us think about the decision facing Dr. Vagelos. One is the familiar model advocated by Milton Friedman, according to which the primary responsibility of corporate managers is to maximize shareholder wealth. Although Friedman's model does not strictly rule out acts of social responsibility that enhance the long-term interests of the company, he would presumably look critically on the kind of major investment being contemplated by Merck. Not only does it involve a substantial commitment of corporate resources with little prospect of profit, but it also poses some risk to the company through liability and damage to a profitable major line of veterinary products.

Opposing Friedman's view is a model of corporate social responsibility that would call on companies to aid in the solution of social problems. For some theorists, this appeal is purely philanthropic. For others, corporate social responsibility is grounded in a notion of justice according to which large business firms are expected to "give back" to society some of the wealth they generate. Despite their sharp differences, these two models assume that corporate ethics is somehow *separate from* the concerns that are at the center of business decision making. Ethics is an "add on" to a firm's core task of producing competitive products and services and making a profit for its owners. Opposing these two models, however, is a third possibility suggested by our discussion of the virtual corporation. According to this model, ethical concerns play a part in building relationships of trust that are necessary for productive endeavor. They are what makes active and creative collaboration possible.

Working on this third model, Dr. Vagelos has to bring both ethical insight and organizational sensitivity to his thinking. On the ethical level, for example, he has to make an independent moral assessment of the importance of the effort to develop a human application of iver-mectin. Could Merck reasonably abstain from this effort, either waiting until the picture of risks and benefits cleared up or leaving the drug's development to others?

Applying **NORM** to this question, we can see that there are over-whelming moral reasons for Merck to proceed with the drug's development. Reasoning omnipartially, it makes good sense to encourage this initiative. Thinking of ourselves as possible victims of river blindness, we confront a disease condition so horrible that, even if we should actually enjoy a less vulnerable situation, we would be prepared to assume some burdens to develop a cure. For example, if it turns out that we live in one of the world's better-off nations we might reasonably accept a modest tax to "protect ourselves" should fate dictate that we were born in less fortunate circumstances and were exposed to this disease. As it is, we do not have this option. Although a widespread effort at sharing this bur-den would be desirable, Merck alone possesses the means and knowl-edge to develop this drug. The burden of deciding whether to do so thus falls on the shoulders of Dr. Vagelos and his colleagues. This analysis nevertheless shows that, given the stakes, and so long as this burden does not seriously jeopardize Merck's viability as a creative and profit-making company, we might omnipartially advocate that Merck under-take this task.

The importance of this project to some extent also qualifies any con-cern over the drug's side effects. Merck has good reason to be worried about possible unknown harms to human and animal populations. These risks must be seriously assessed, though they probably will not be entire-ly understood until human trials have been run. Nevertheless, because of the enormous suffering associated with river blindness, these risks are worth taking and we can assume that omnipartial persons would sup-port Merck's research initiative. From Merck's corporate point of view, this moral conclusion is important. It tells Merck's managers that even if the drug proves to have some serious side effects and some research sub-jects are harmed, the company's good-faith efforts will be respected and Merck will probably be spared destructive criticism.

Organizational considerations follow from and are reinforced by this central moral insight. Dr. Vagelos heads up a team of dedicated scientific researchers whose enthusiasm and dedication flow, in part, from their belief that their work serves important human purposes. These people are also realists. They know that Merck is a profit-making company and that it cannot go off on tangents trying to solve all the world's problems. But ivermectin is a different matter. This drug represents an opportunity that grows directly out of Merck's cutting-edge research. Can Dr. Vagelos and Merck put this opportunity aside without seriously disappointing and demoralizing some of the company's most creative people? Can he continue to attract and motivate the top-quality creative staff that Merck requires if, when challenged, the company fails to live up to the high aspirations it encourages? It is important to note that this organizational question would be less acute if the promise and importance of this drug were not so great. In that case, Merck's managers and scientists might be persuaded that there are better uses of corporate resources. But precisely because the moral stakes here are so clear, Dr. Vagelos, as a manager, must anticipate and respond to strong feelings on the part of some of Merck's most valued employee-stakeholders.

Vagelos's decision is not easy. Apart from its impact on employee morale, he must measure the financial costs and legal exposure this decision involves. Good intentions are not enough. Better information about the drug's risks and its legal and commercial liabilities is vital. But no reckoning of costs will make sense if the moral stakes of the drug's development are not clearly appreciated. As is so often the case in managerial decision making, moral insight about a key issue is a crucial first step in thinking.

Case 10.1 (B)

✦ MERCK & CO., INC. ✦

MERCK DECIDES TO DEVELOP MECTIZAN

In 1978, Dr. P. Roy Vagelos, then head of Merck's research labs, approved initial funding for research into a potential treatment for river blindness.

Vagelos believed there were several reasons Merck ought to go forward with the research, the first being the potential impact of a negative decision on the Merck culture. Failure to investigate Dr. Campbell's tantalizing hypothesis could demoralize Merck scientists, especially since the inquiry focused on a widespread, intractable disease that produced great suffering.

Vagelos also believed that the prevalence of the disease in the third world would motivate someone—third-world governments, private foundations, or even the U.S. government—to buy a successful drug and donate it to the victims.

The fact that a successful drug for onchocerciasis would not generate much revenue for Merck was a secondary concern to Dr. Vagelos and his associates. "Until you can demonstrate that the drug is capable of doing something," Dr. Vagelos noted, "you don't even bring the marketing people into it. Because, until you can characterize a drug, they can't put numbers on it." Dr. Vagelos admitted, however, that "we knew that it was going to be a borderline economically viable project at the start."

Finally, Dr. Vagelos believed the company should proceed because the project would further Merck's knowledge of parasitology, already an established field at Merck. Even if the research failed to produce a treatment for river blindness, it might produce findings of future use to the company.

For Dr. Vagelos and Dr. William C. Campbell, the scientist who had proposed the research, investing in the development of the drug for this third-world disease was an irresistible possibility. "Emotionally, you become very involved in what you can accomplish, as a research group and as a company," Dr. Vagelos explained. "And so we could hardly wait to start these experiments." It made sense for Merck, Dr. Vagelos believed, to learn as much about its fledgling class of compounds, avermectins, as possible.

CLINICAL TRIALS APPROVED

By 1980, ivermectin had traversed quite a distance on its journey to becoming a river blindness therapy: from the original parasitological research (led by Dr. Campbell) to the microbiology and chemical identification programs (led by Drs. Tom Miller, Richard W. Burg, and Georg Albers-Schonberg) to the chemical synthesis of ivermectin (by Drs. John C. Chabala and Michael H. Fisher) to development of the animal drug formulations. Eighteen months had elapsed since the compound's potential human application was first suspected.

Then, in January 1980, the baton was passed to Dr. Mohammed A. Aziz, senior director of clinical research at Merck. A quiet man of steely determination, Dr. Aziz was widely credited for championing the drug, which would come to be known as Mectizan, within Merck and shepherding it past numerous scientific and corporate obstacles. His obsession with developing Mectizan, cited by all who knew him, was due in large part to his personal background. As a tropical disease expert, native of the region now called Bangladesh and former World Health Organization (WHO) scientist with experience in Sierra Leone, Dr. Aziz knew firsthand what river blindness meant for third-world people. Dr. Aziz got his chance to proceed in January 1980, when Merck research management agreed to move forward with human clinical trials.

It was a momentous decision for Merck. The company was now committed to a lengthy, expensive set of tests for a drug that was not likely to generate much, if any, revenue. "We had never undertaken the development of a drug that was going to be broadly used, such as 18 million patients, with the idea that we were not going to make money," Dr. Vagelos later explained. In general, drugs that earn $20 million or less a year are at risk of being discontinued, he said, and certainly no one expected Mectizan to generate a fraction of that sum.

"On the other hand," Dr. Vagelos continued, "the company is so large and the laboratories so prolific, that one can never guess what is going to come out." A clinical investigation of ivermectin, however problematic, could yield useful knowledge.

At the outset of research, Dr. Bruce M. Greene, a prominent university scientist associated with the development of Mectizan, recalled, there was "a lot of turmoil in the company about whether we should expose this fabulous commercial product to the risk of human usage." Dr. Vagelos, who became chief executive in 1985, quieted the debate, and, as it turned out, Merck's concerns regarding negative side effects of ivermectin on humans were unwarranted.

The clinical trials would pose a special challenge. Victims of river blindness rarely lived within hailing distance of modern medical facilities. Yet clinical trials needed to be held in such settings to ensure the proper medical oversight of test subjects and the collection of rigorous data.

COOPERATION WITH WHO

Realizing that it would need help in this phase of the drug's development, Merck turned to the World Health Organization (WHO), the Geneva-based consortium of 166 member nations. Talks began in July 1982 to determine the most appropriate approach to the problem—from medical, political, and commercial points of view.

There was a certain incongruity in Merck's working closely with WHO. On some policy issues, the U.S. drug industry and WHO had had bitter disagreements. In the 1970s and 1980s, for example, multinational drug companies generally resisted WHO-backed standards for international drug marketing. They also denounced a WHO "essential drugs list" initiative designed to help third-world nations spend their limited resources on the most basic, widely needed drugs.

Notwithstanding such policy clashes, WHO had often collaborated with private drug companies to develop drugs for third-world nations, which typically did not have the marketplace clout, despite their large populations, to stimulate such research. According to a 1988 WHO report, less than 4 percent of the global drug industry's research expenditures focused on diseases endemic to developing countries, even though 25 percent of the world's population lived in the third world. In developing ivermectin, Merck and WHO complemented each other's needs quite well. Merck had a compound that might treat river blindness, and WHO had access to a global network of government health officials and scientists who could help run clinical trials.

Despite these common interests, the initial collaboration between WHO and Merck was at times strained. WHO was already deeply invested in a $26-million-a-year program to eliminate black flies through aerial larvacide spraying. WHO officials were initially concerned that this program might be abandoned if ivermectin looked promising. Merck officials reassured WHO that they would continue to support spraying as well as the development of the new drug.

WHO scientists also questioned the medical promise of ivermectin. "Initially, when Merck came to us and said it had this fancy new drug," recalled Dr. Duke, who then headed the WHO filariasis disease program, "my reaction was, 'We've got several drugs and they all incite violent reactions.'" There was skepticism that any drug could overcome the side effects induced by these drugs, which required close medical supervision. Furthermore, WHO scientists believed that any new drug for river blindness must attack the adult parasite, not the microfilariae offspring, because only then could new generations of microfilariae be conclusively stopped.

Notwithstanding periodic clashes of scientific judgment and institutional cultures, a working collaboration evolved over time. Working with Professor Michel LaRiviere of the University of Paris, Dr. Aziz eventually decided to conduct the first human tests of ivermectin at the University of Dakar, Senegal, in February 1981. Merck supplied the drug, grants-in-aid for the studies, and the resources to apply for regulatory approval; WHO provided scientists and research facilities.

Dr. Aziz and his associates moved ahead with great caution, administering extremely small doses. One scientist recalled how Professor LaRiviere personally stayed up all night with test subjects to monitor for adverse reactions. By the end of 1981, the early results were promising: no adverse reactions, and a single, extremely small dose of ivermectin dramatically reduced microfilariae counts. A second study in Paris was conducted to confirm the Dakar results.

But the skeptics remained. In November 1982, Andre Rougemont, a highly respected scientist at the University of Geneva and former WHO official, wrote a stinging letter to *Lancet*, the prestigious British medical journal. Rougemont charged that ivermectin "brings no really new or interesting feature to the treatment of onchocerciasis," and accused Dr. Aziz and his colleagues of being "over-optimistic."

Prodded by such a public attack, Dr. Aziz redoubled his efforts to prove that ivermectin was indeed superior to the existing drug of choice, DEC. With the help of Drs. Bruce Greene, Hugh Taylor, and other university scientists, Aziz plunged ahead with Phase II tests in Senegal, Mali, Ghana, and Liberia in 1983–84. The complex tests further confirmed the promise of ivermectin, and led to a subsequent set of trials in 1985. With mounting excitement, Dr. Aziz and his associates planned the final Phase III tests for the following year with 1,200 patients in Ghana and Liberia. These tests succeeded in establishing the optimum dosage level and in further confirming the drug's safety.

APPLICATION FOR APPROVAL OF DRUG

By early 1987, nearly seven years after Merck executives had authorized the first clinical trials and nearly ten years after Dr. Campbell first proposed the research, the company had the clinical data needed to seek final regulatory approval for Mectizan. The materials were submitted to the French Directorate of Pharmacy and Drugs, whose judgments are widely accepted by Francophone African nations where onchocerciasis is a major public health problem. Final approval came in October 1987.

It was a buoyant time at Merck, especially for Dr. Campbell, Dr. Aziz, and Dr. Vagelos. It was also a critical turning point. Less than two months after the last regulatory hurdle had been cleared, Dr. Aziz died at age 58 of cancer. And Merck, which had spent nearly a decade developing a remarkable treatment for river blindness, could not simply bask in the glory of its triumph. Its achievement would be of little consequence unless it could surmount another daunting challenge—delivering the new wonder drug to the people who needed it.

SELLING THE DRUG

As early as 1982, after Dr. Aziz's first clinical trials proved successful, Merck knew that some unorthodox plan to distribute Mectizan would be needed. Early research confirmed what many had suspected: no conventional market for the drug was likely to materialize. The victims were too poor; they lived in utterly isolated locations; and they had no access to pharmacies or routine medical care.

From this point on, according to Dr. Vagelos, Merck moved forward in developing Mectizan with a blind faith that some third party, at some point in the future, would step forward with funding. The anticipated funders included foundations, international health or development organizations, third-world governments, and the U.S. government.

When regulatory approval for Mectizan seemed certain in 1986, Dr. Vagelos, then Chairman and CEO, set out on a series of trips to Washington, D.C., searching for parties to buy and distribute Mectizan. His first stop was Deputy Secretary of State John Whitehead. Later he visited Donald Regan, then President Reagan's White House Chief of Staff. "Each of these people understood the potential importance of the drug, and they thought it must be distributed," recalled Dr. Vagelos. "And each of them referred the project to the U.S. Agency for International Development" (AID—a foreign assistance agency that makes grants and loans for various third-world development projects).

Whitehead introduced Dr. Vagelos to M. Peter McPherson, the head of U.S. AID at the time. As Dr. Vagelos recalled, Whitehead said, " 'Now, Peter, we've got to do this program.' And McPherson looked up at him and said, 'Mr. Secretary, we don't have any money.' " Follow-up conversations yielded the same answer.

Dr. Vagelos was highly skeptical—and disappointed. The proposed distribution program would require an initial commitment of only $2 million a year, eventually growing to a sum of $20 million a year. It would be hard to imagine a more cost-effective way for the United States to curry goodwill with third-world nations.

Dr. Vagelos was disappointed by the U.S. government's failure to come up with funding because he was spending so much time on the matter. He felt that it was beginning to detract from his normal responsibilities as Merck Chairman and CEO. "I was doing more for this than I'd done for any other drug," he said. "I mean, this [advocacy for a specific drug] is normally covered by our regulatory affairs and marketing people."

A series of visits to other potential funders—African health ministries, foundations, and others—were also to no avail. Merck even called upon noted international figures to advise them, but none of these efforts succeeded.

SHOULD MERCK SIMPLY GIVE THE DRUG AWAY?

At this point, an impertinent, offhand suggestion made several years earlier resurfaced at Merck headquarters. In 1983 or 1984, Dr. Brian Duke had made a provocative suggestion—with no authorization from WHO—that Merck simply donate Mectizan outright. To his chagrin, Dr. Duke saw his casual remark to a reporter turn up in print in *South*, a third-world business magazine. The suggestion was not appreciated by Merck management, who were still hoping to find third-party funding.

"That's not the way you do things in a commercial organization," Dr. Vagelos said in 1991. "You don't start out by thinking you're going to give something away. . . . We hadn't gone through our process of determining what it would take [to distribute the drug]." When the search for third-party funding failed, however, Dr. Duke's suggestion began to sound much more plausible. Dr. Aziz had long favored such a solution. As Dr. Campbell recalled, "Aziz was constantly pushing the idea that Mectizan should be given away with pride."

The idea of a drug company donating an unlimited supply of a breakthrough drug to millions of people was unprecedented. It was a proposed commitment that would prompt any company to think long and hard. As senior executives debated the issue internally and consulted with peers in the drug industry, they wondered: Would this set a "bad precedent"—an expectation that future drugs for third-world diseases should also be donated, which could itself discourage companies from conducting research on such diseases? Would Merck face intolerable legal liability if some Mectizan recipients suffered adverse reactions? Would the sheer cost of administering such a program and manufacturing the drug be prohibitive?

QUESTIONS TO CONSIDER

1. What were the business costs and benefits of Merck's decision to proceed with Mectizan's development?

2. In your view, can Merck now responsibly set a precedent of giving Mectizan away for free?

ASSESSING PRECEDENTS
✦

Many people believe that business is all about competition. Certainly it is true that firms must provide goods and services efficiently enough to be attractive among a field of competitors. But this emphasis on competition obscures the frequently more important fact that business is also very much about *cooperation*. In order to produce and deliver products and services, businesses depend on the constant support and collaboration of many stakeholders. These can be customers, employees, financiers, suppliers, communities, governments, trade associations, or regulatory bodies. Unless a firm can marshal the energies and resources of these stakeholders on its behalf, it will not long remain competitive.[8]

Merck's handling of Mectizan provides a complex illustration of this point. Once committed to the drug's development, the company found itself compelled to negotiate a series of hurdles created by key stakeholder groups. Inside Merck, the drug's proponents had to deal with constituencies who feared the harm that might be done to a "fabulous" veterinary product by exposing it to the risk of human use. Here, the leadership of Dr. Vagelos proved decisive, and subsequent research bore out his confidence in the drug. Like any new head of an organization, Vagelos had to win the confidence and support of his subordinates. Championing Mectizan provided him with an important opportunity to do so.

Outside Merck, the World Health Organization posed a formidable obstacle. For two decades tensions over standards for international drug marketing and other issues had marred relationships between WHO and multinational drug companies. WHO's leadership was also deeply invested in programs to control river blindness through larvacide spraying and was skeptical about Mectizan's efficacy and safety. Yet both Merck and WHO needed each other. WHO was interested in stimulating private drug companies to greater involvement in drug research in the third world. On its side, Merck needed access to WHO's network of government health officials and scientists in order to test Mectizan. By paying careful attention to the concerns of WHO's administrators and scientists, and by supporting WHO's ongoing programs in this area, Merck managed to overcome these obstacles. The Mectizan effort again thus provided an opportunity for a unique collaboration that was solidified by the drug's eventual success. What is the long-term value of the relationships and trust established between Merck and WHO during the

Mectizan effort or between Merck and other third-world researchers and scientists? Although hard to quantify, it had to be substantial. Here is yet another important business implication and benefit to Merck of the Mectizan program.

Merck's leadership in this area may also have yielded benefits for *all* multinational firms by providing WHO and third-world health officials with a vivid expression of goodwill on the part of a multinational drug company. Such exemplary initiatives help break through the layers of antagonism, fear, and ideological opposition that hobble business activity and investment all over the world. By setting an undeniable example of corporate commitment to people's welfare in less-developed nations, Merck helped expand opportunity for other members of the business community in this part of the world. Normally, companies are not called on to go out of their way to aid their competitors. They are even allowed to act in ways that put competitors at a disadvantage, as long as doing so better serves their clients' or customers' needs. In Chapter 7 we observed that, when dealing with competitors as stakeholders, companies have an obligation to avoid acting in ways that degrade the playing field for all members of an industry and also reduce consumer choice or value.[9] It follows from this, however, that companies are permitted to act in ways that *improve* the playing field and increase value for everyone. Merck's efforts here set a positive precedent of this sort.

What about the negative precedent that would be set by Merck's giving away a drug that cost millions of dollars to develop? Dr. Vagelos expressed this concern when, as funding sources dried up and Merck was forced to consider donating the drug, he said in some frustration: "That's not the way you do things in a commercial organization." His concerns here are not trivial. Just as Merck's collaboration with WHO can set an example of good business practice that can aid companies, so can a "give-away" program generate expectations that prove unfortunate in the longer run. If profit-making companies feel compelled by Merck's example to donate or underprice drugs in the third-world market, they may eventually decide to avoid this market—and research in its health-care needs—altogether. In the end, people in these countries could suffer as a result of Merck's generous impulse.

NORM tells us that we must always examine our conduct in terms of the precedents and practices it establishes, and that we must also look at these precedents in terms of the full gamut of their likely implications and consequences. Repeatedly, we have seen that some proposed moral rules that initially look good prove unacceptable because, once put into practice, they undermine or defeat the very purposes they seek. Is Merck's generosity here another example of this perverse dynamic?

The answer to this question lies in clearly identifying and understanding the moral rule Merck fashions by its decision. We should try to state this rule in all its specificity, including in our formulation of all the morally relevant general features that would be of interest to omnipartial persons.[10] The following looks like a good candidate for the rule describing Merck's choice:

✦

Proposed Moral Rule: When in the course of its research a profit-making drug company discovers and develops a drug that can significantly reduce human suffering, and when, after making strenuous efforts, it proves unable to locate public or private purchasers of the drug, it may give the drug away for free as long as it reasonably believes it can do so without damaging the company's financial health.

✦

It is not hard to understand the attractiveness of this rule and why it would be acceptable to omnipartial people. For one thing, an opposite rule, one that required a company *not* to give a drug away in these circumstances, would leave serious suffering unabated and would present a sorry and inhumane example of waste. For another, this rule is crafted narrowly enough to avoid imposing unfortunate pressures on other profit-making companies. The rule does not require companies to go out of their way to research, discover, or develop drugs like Mectizan. It only applies to products arising as a side effect of other profit-oriented research. It also allows companies to try to secure independent funding or customers for these drugs. Finally, by giving companies latitude in determining the impact of these activities on their long-term financial health, it spares them from commitments that may damage their growth or stability.

Some may object that although this moral rule may be acceptable, Merck's behavior will predictably be misread as a general precedent for corporate altruism by drug companies in the third world. Citizens of these countries cannot be expected to understand the finer nuances of the Mectizan initiative and, as a result, Merck's conduct will still result in fostering unreasonable and harmful expectations. *This objection is important. It reminds us that we are always responsible for considering all the implications of our conduct and the moral rules implicit within it, including foreseeable misinterpretations and abuses of these rules. In fact, we are just as responsible for the unwanted but foreseeable abuses of the good examples we set as we are for the consequences of the bad precedents we establish.*

Despite this reminder, the actual estimation of the misuse or misinterpretation of a practice is a complex matter. It depends in part on the force and evident clarity of the considerations that justify the conduct in the first place. Merck is able to donate Mectizan to needy people because a reasonable calculus of costs to the company and benefits to recipients points so overwhelmingly in this direction. Although Merck, to avoid creating unrealistic expectations concerning its own or others' future conduct, may be advised to make this clear in its publicity, the facts here are easily understood by leaders and health-care workers in the third world—the people who influence national policies and opinions. For all these reasons, Merck probably does not have to fear setting a dangerous precedent in donating this drug. It can make this substantial gesture of goodwill without creating an environment of unwarranted expectations for other companies or other drugs.

Case 10.1 (C)

✦ MERCK & CO., INC. ✦

MERCK DECIDES TO GIVE MECTIZAN AWAY

At press conferences held in Washington and Paris on October 21, 1987, Merck and Co. announced it would supply Mectizan, its new drug for treatment of river blindness, to everyone who needed it, for as long as necessary, at no charge. The announcement came soon after the French government's formal approval of Mectizan.

Dr. P. Roy Vagelos, chief executive, and other senior Merck executives were willing to proceed despite concerns over setting a bad precedent and potential legal liability. One factor that helped Merck come to its decision was the astonishing success of ivermectin as a veterinary drug. Even if the Mectizan donation ended up costing tens of millions of dollars, at that time ivermectin was reaping more than $300 million a year, with sales growing by 15 percent annually. Ivermectin-based products went on to become the largest selling animal drug in the world. When Merck announced the Mectizan donation, Jerry Jackson, a Merck senior vice-president and then president of Merck's international operations, was quoted in the *Wall Street Journal* as saying, "Merck can easily afford this."

Although some officials said WHO might have bought the drug for a few cents, far less than the official price of $3 per dose adopted by the French government when it approved Mectizan, Merck decided simply to give the drug away. Merck felt this was the best way to get the drug to as many people as quickly as possible. In addition, the donation would not only burnish the company's already-stellar image, it would represent a serious and substantial goodwill gesture to third-world nations and WHO.

Under general Internal Revenue Service rules for corporate donations, the costs of producing Mectizan would presumably be deductible. To minimize the threat of liability suits, Merck planned to distribute Mectizan only under close medical supervision.

And the "bad precedent"? Merck officials later concluded that the Mectizan donation did not appear to have discouraged research into third-world diseases, which was quite limited in any case. Indeed, the Mectizan precedent may have subtly made drug-company executives more open-minded about innovative collaborations, reported Dr. Colin Ginger of the WHO Onchocerciasis Chemotherapy Project. After the Mectizan donation, Ginger said that Ciba-Geigy, the Swiss drug company, agreed to perform pre-clinical tests on promising compounds if WHO would perform the animal and human tests. The agreement, a generous improvement over a prior one, saved Dr. Ginger's research program about $2 million.

In contrast to the initial concerns, the Mectizan donation elicited great admiration and imitation from other companies. In an effort to kill Guinea worm, a parasite spread through contaminated drinking water, American Cyanamid donated millions of dollars worth of Abate, a larvacide, to developing nations. For the same purpose, DuPont donated several hundred thousand square yards of nylon, which could be easily used to filter drinking water to remove Guinea worms.

Merck's donation may also have altered some expectations about pricing policies for drugs to be used in third-world nations. For example, a number of tropical disease experts complained about the high cost of Praziquantel, the drug of choice for treating schistosomiasis, a parasitic disease that affected an estimated 200 million people. "If Merck can give away Mectizan," said these scientists, "why can't Bayer, the German maker of Praziquantel, show a similar humanitarian concern by lowering its price?"

A Merck spokesman was quick to point out that Mectizan is a very special case. Here was a drug of almost miraculous safety and efficacy that could be taken only once a year in tablet form, with minimum supervision. These unusual circumstances enabled Merck to make an open-ended, long-term donation. Dr. Vagelos seized this rare opportunity, despite its substantial costs, to help millions of people.

THE DISTRIBUTION PROBLEM

At this point, however, Merck began to see the pragmatic limits of its good intentions. Developing Mectizan as an offshoot of its normal research activities was one thing—an ambitious challenge that lay within its expertise and budget. Manufacturing the drug was also a natural Merck activity. Now the problem of the effective distribution of the free drug suddenly became the most critical problem.

Most of the people who needed Mectizan lived in some of the most remote locations on earth. Some villages in the West African bush could be reached only after several days of travel over marginal dirt roads; still others were accessible only by footpaths. There were no pharmacies, doctors, or conventional systems of commerce. The third-world countries had not developed the medical systems that could deliver such a drug.

Merck realized, however, that some distribution system would need to be established if Mectizan was going to reach large numbers of those afflicted with river blindness. But then, who would run the system? And how would it operate?

Some suggested that Merck itself get involved in the distribution, but there were longstanding barriers to such a step. Governments were not eager to have multinational drug companies establish distribution systems that might conflict with government plans or that might represent a monopolistic threat. Other pharmaceutical firms believed that involvement in distribution might create a dependency that would place more demands on the company or restrict its options in the future.

However, relying on the embryonic—or nonexistent—drug distribution systems in many countries and regions seemed unacceptable. Where no distribution systems existed, free supplies of the drug would simply languish in government warehouses. Where fragile distribution systems existed, the distribution could be haphazard and even unsafe. Merck would not learn of adverse reactions or even have an accurate record of the areas that had received Mectizan. In the worst cases, supplies of Mectizan might be diverted into a black market or sold as substitutes for animal formulations of ivermectin.

Case 10.1 (D)

✦ MERCK & CO., INC. ✦

AN INDEPENDENT
DISTRIBUTION COMMITTEE

After considering the pros and cons involved if the distribution of their new drug, Mectizan, were handled by Merck itself, Chairman Vagelos and his senior executives came up with a creative solution. Merck created the Mectizan Expert Committee, a panel comprising seven internationally recognized experts on tropical medicine and public health. The Expert Committee established guidelines and procedures for public health programs that wished to distribute Mectizan, and encouraged groups of all types to take part in the distribution.

In this way, Merck could help ensure that Mectizan would be used appropriately. "Rumors go a long way in the third world," explained one Expert Committee member. If Mectizan were given out indiscriminately or used improperly, it could tarnish the drug's reputation and cause people to shun it. The committee also wanted to make sure that any adverse reactions were identified, that medical records were kept, that distribution programs were logistically feasible, and that program sponsors had a serious, long-term commitment to distribution.

As an extrabureaucratic, nonpolitical entity, the committee could set its own rules and get supplies of Mectizan out quickly, avoiding the internal politics and bureaucratic delays of WHO and individual governments. Although funded by Merck, the committee also served to insulate Merck from potential criticism if, for example, an applicant was denied Mectizan because the distribution plan was inadequate.

Much of the committee's strength resided in the expertise and stature of its members, who were among the world's top authorities in parasitology, tropical diseases, and public health. The Expert Committee's chairman was Dr. William H. Foege, who served as executive director of the Carter Center in Atlanta as well as being a former director of the U.S. Centers for Disease Control. Dr. Foege was singularly equipped to supervise the Expert Committee; he had previously played a key role in organizing the worldwide eradication of smallpox. Other members were Dr. Bruce Greene of the University of Alabama; Dr. Adetokunbo O. Lucas of the Harvard School of Public Health; Dr. Eric Otteson of the National Institutes of Health; Professor Michel LaRiviere of the University of Paris; and Dr. Guilermo Zea-Flores of the Guatemalan Ministry of Health. Dr. Brian Duke, who had formerly been with WHO and then with the Armed Forces Institute of Pathology, and Dr. Hugh Taylor of the University of Melbourne later joined the Expert Committee. Between 1988 and 1990, the committee had approved treatment plans covering more than one million people. Through a companion effort designed to reach those unable to participate in mass treatment programs, Merck distributed Mectizan to another half a million people. Although as many as 18 million people were already infected by onchocerciasis, WHO estimated that the most urgent challenge was to reach the 6 million people who were at greatest risk of blindness from the disease.

Because the drug not only halted the chronic worsening of the disease but quickly stopped any itching, villagers immediately appreciated the value of Mectizan and clamored for it. At one mass treatment in a village in Togo, a great number of people were roaming nearby, demanding to be treated as well. These people had traveled from a village ten kilometers away, on a dirt road built expressly for the purpose of getting Mectizan, and had walked through the night to arrive in time. But because program officials had not planned on the village's participation—the settlement was not even on any maps—there were not enough supplies to treat them that day. After a quick conference with the angry village chief, plans were hastily made to ensure that the people would be treated at a later date.

On a 1990 visit to Africa to see the fruits of his earlier work in the laboratory, Dr. Campbell recalled the joy, relief, and good humor of people when the drug was being handed out: "I remember one village chief saying something in his native dialect, which was then translated into French. Each time it was translated, there was a little laughter. Finally, it was translated into English. And what the chief was saying to me was, 'This is great! Now go back and find the cause of death and put it in a box, and put a lid on it!'"

THE UNFINISHED CHALLENGE

Although 1.5 million individuals had been treated by 1991, it was still only a small percentage of the people who needed Mectizan. Two significant problems still remained: (1) to find the money to finance distribution and to physically transport Mectizan supplies to remote villages, and (2) to ensure the effectiveness of distribution systems. The costs of resolving these exceeded the costs of manufacturing the drug.

The burden of distribution fell primarily upon government health ministries, which were also worrying about malaria, AIDS, and other prevalent diseases. In some cases they were also dealing with civil war (Liberia) and famine (Sudan, etc.). Some of this burden was eased by a special $2.5 million appropriation for Mectizan distribution and technical support in the 1991 budget of the United States Agency for International Development. These monies enabled a number of nongovernmental organizations, such as the

International Eye Foundation and the Helen Keller Foundation, to start their own distribution projects.

A number of private efforts were also initiated. Perhaps the most promising was the River Blindness Foundation, an organization started by a wealthy Texas businessman who committed millions of dollars to the effort. The foundation planned to raise more money and publicize the need for assistance. Lions International, the civic group, planned a major drive to distribute Mectizan in the nation with the most cases of onchocerciasis: Nigeria, Africa's most populous country. Even a third-grade class in Center City, Iowa, was inspired to help. Dr. Vagelos likes to tell the story of how children pooled their allowances and sent Merck a check for $32.47 to help with the distribution.

Skeptics asked Dr. Vagelos and other Merck officials why the company endured the costs, aggravation, and complexities to develop and make Mectizan available. At this, Dr. Vagelos turned reflective. "When I first went to Japan fifteen years ago, I was told by Japanese businesspeople that it was Merck that brought streptomycin to Japan after World War II, to eliminate tuberculosis which was eating up their society. We did that. We did not make any money. But it is no accident that Merck is the largest American pharmaceutical company in Japan today. The long-term consequences of acts of goodwill are not always clear," he said, but "somehow I think they always pay off."

The same rationale lay behind the decision by Merck in 1986 to sell a sophisticated vaccine-manufacturing technology to the Chinese. The recombinant hepatitis B vaccine would help China prevent liver cancer, the second largest cause of death among adult males there. After intense negotiations, Merck consented to sell the technology for a mere $7 million, a fraction of its value. The technology would allow the Chinese to vaccinate all newborns. Dr. Vagelos believed that in thirty or forty years, when China would be more integrated in the world marketplace, "the Chinese will remember that it was the Merck vaccine that saved all those kids."

Would Mectizan have such a long-term payoff for Merck? Only time will tell. But as of 1991, the company was simply proud that one of the offshoots of its fertile research program could prevent a horrible disease that afflicted millions of people.

CREATING VALUE FOR
STAKEHOLDERS

✦

The healing of disease, the wish that the lame might walk and the blind see, is one of humankind's oldest dreams. Merck's role in developing and delivering a cure for river blindness is worth celebrating in its own right. But it also provides a rich and complex illustration of the importance of ethics in business today. On the one hand, it indicates how the moral conduct of business can benefit us all and enhance society's respect for business professionals. On the other hand, it illustrates how closely linked are ethics and excellence in business performance.

From a purely ethical standpoint, Merck's experience again reveals the weakness in Milton Friedman's view that business managers are incompetent to address social problems, which are best left to governments or charitable organizations. The fact is that no one outside Merck was really able to appreciate the prospects for a solution to this problem. No one in government, international health agencies, or charitable foundations possessed Merck's clear sense of what could and should be done. In the end, others joined Merck in the effort to combat this disease. But it was Merck's vision and leadership that empowered them to do so. Merck served as the initiator and as the catalyst for change.

The lesson here is that business companies are sometimes *best* able to address social needs because they are often closest to the problems and most adept at assembling the people, knowledge, and financial resources for solving them. This does not mean that businesses must regularly devote some portion of their resources to philanthropy, as early proponents of corporate social responsibility believed. Most of the time, managers will properly direct corporate energies to meeting the needs of consumers and clients in ways that yield profit. What it does mean is that in the course of their profit-making activities managers should be alert to the ways that the skills and resources of their company can help create value for other stakeholders. When opportunities arise for a business— out of the depths of its experience and expertise—to make a contribution, managers should not be put off by narrow admonitions to attend only to the immediate "bottom line."

Reinforcing this advice are the links the Mectizan episode reveals between business ethics and business excellence. We have already considered some of the ways Merck's initiative contributed to the enhancement of a series of stakeholder relationships that are important to Merck's commercial success. Perhaps foremost among these is Merck's relationship with its employees. Like other employees of virtual corporations, many are skilled professionals whose career goals include meaningful work in an environment reflective of their values. Companies offering challenging and rewarding projects are better able to attract, motivate, and retain employees of this sort. Dr. Aziz is one example. As a researcher and manager with roots in the third world, his commitment to Merck was connected with the company's responsiveness to his concerns. To the extent that Merck's competitive advantage lies partly in the talents of hundreds and thousands of people like Dr. Aziz, it must factor their values into its decision making.

Another way of putting this is to say that there is a deep *human* connection between Mectizan and the successful line of veterinary products from which it sprang. The same talent, energy, and enthusiasm that created Mectizan also produced the whole line of avermectins. In view of this, we can see how misguided it can be to urge companies to concentrate on maximizing profit and to ignore endeavors that engage the moral imagination of key stakeholders. This wrongly assumes that the things that inspire and motivate dedicated, creative, and skilled people have no relationship to profits.

The Mectizan effort also contributed to reinforcing other key stakeholder relationships connected with Merck's long-term corporate success. We have touched on the positive implications for Merck's relations with WHO. To this we might add the complex array of technical specialists, research scientists, and government regulators Merck drew into the efforts of the Expert Committee. Another feature of the virtual corporation is relevant here: the relatively permeable and shifting boundaries between the company and its external constituencies. In a world of high-technology business, it is hard to draw lines between university research centers, corporate laboratories, and the governmental bodies whose decisions affect both. By drawing committed people together from all these sectors to work on a project valued by all, Merck was able to forge bonds of respect between itself and people who on one day might be important customers, on another regulators, and on a third developers of products or technology that Merck might commercialize.

Finally, to all this, we must add the citizens and leaders of the third-world nations plagued by river blindness. As this case makes clear, Merck had already profited enormously from the goodwill earned by its early involvement in Japan. With China's economy expanding rapidly it is likely that Merck's goodwill efforts there will reap similar commercial benefits. At this time it seems less likely that this experience will soon be repeated in the desperately poor nations plagued by river blindness. But we should keep in mind that Merck's commitment to the welfare of its larger community of stakeholders is not reducible to a quid-pro-quo level of business calculation. It is primarily an ethical commitment, but one that has often benefited the company. In the words of George W. Merck, son of the company's founder, "We try never to forget that medicine is for the people. It is not for the profits. The profits follow, and if we have remembered that, they have never failed to appear. The better we have remembered it, the larger they have been." In ways no one can predict, the corporate goodwill Merck showed here may contribute to the company's flourishing in the next century of its existence.

Summary

This book began by looking at the challenges voiced to the idea of business ethics. We followed that with detailed attention to the ways that managers can make responsible decisions and maintain moral self-respect amid the conflicting pressures created by commercial realities and stakeholder claims. We have concluded with an example of business ethics at its best, an instance in which ethics and financial performance are closely connected. Throughout, we have argued that the kind of moral insight furnished by the **NORM** method can be a valuable guide to individual and organizational decision making. These discussions are only a beginning. Your task now is to choose from among these perspectives, ideas, and methods to forge and implement your own vision of what it means to be an ethical manager.

Notes

1. Andrew W. Singer, "Can a Company Be Too Ethical?" *Across the Board* 30, no. 3 (April 1993): 17–22.
2. Robert Levering and Milton Moskowitz, *The 100 Best Companies to Work for in America* (New York: Doubleday, 1993).
3. *The Virtual Corporation: Structuring and Revitalizing the Corporation for the 21st Century* (New York: HarperCollins, 1992).
4. Ibid., p. 8.

5. Ibid., p. 183.
6. Ibid.
7. This entire case was adapted by Stephanie Weiss from a monograph, "Merck & Co., Inc. (A), (B), (C), and (D)," by David Bollier, under the supervision of Kirk O. Hanson, President of the Business Enterprise Trust and Senior Lecturer at the Stanford Graduate School of Business. © 1991 by the Business Enterprise Trust, 204 Junipero Serra Blvd., Stanford, CA 94305. Reprinted by permission. The business Enterprise Trust is a national organization dedicated to documenting and promoting creative ways business is combining social concern and business purpose. A video presentation of this award-winning case is available from BET.
8. For a fuller discussion of the importance of stakeholder collaboration, see R. Edward Freeman and Daniel R. Gilbert, *Corporate Strategy and the Search for Ethics* (Englewood Cliffs, N.J.: Prentice-Hall, 1988).
9. See pp. 259–265.
10. See Chapter 3, pp. 96–98.

FURTHER READINGS

The following readings expand on selected topics introduced in the text.

BASIC INTRODUCTIONS TO BUSINESS ETHICS

✦

Andrews, Kenneth R., ed. *Ethics in Practice: Managing the Moral Corporation.* Boston: Harvard Business School Press, 1989.

Beauchamp, Tom L., and Norman E. Bowie, eds. *Ethical Theory and Business*, 3d ed. Englewood Cliffs, NJ: Prentice Hall, 1988.

Boatright, John R. *Ethics and the Conduct of Business.* Englewood Cliffs, NJ: Prentice Hall, 1993.

Bowie, Norman. *Business Ethics.* Englewood Cliffs, NJ: Prentice Hall, 1982.

De George, Richard T. *Business Ethics*, 3d ed. New York: Macmillan, 1990.

DesJardins, Joseph R., and John J. McCall. *Contemporary Issues in Business Ethics.* Belmont, CA: Wadsworth, 1990.

Donaldson, Thomas. *Corporations and Morality.* Englewood Cliffs, NJ: Prentice Hall, 1982.

Freeman, R. Edward, ed. *Business Ethics: The State of the Art.* New York: Oxford University Press, 1991.

Goldman, Alan H. *The Moral Foundations of Professional Ethics.* Totowa, NJ: Rowman & Littlefield, 1980.

Halbert, Terry, and Elaine Ingulli. *Law and Ethics in the Business Environment.* St. Paul: West Publishing Company, 1990.

Hoffman, W. Michael, and Jennifer Mills Moore, eds. *Business Ethics: Readings and Cases in Corporate Morality*, 2d ed. New York: McGraw-Hill, 1990.

Hosmer, LaRue Tone. *The Ethics of Management*, 2d ed. Homewood, IL: Richard D. Irwin, 1991.

Iannone, A. Pablo, ed. *Contemporary Moral Controversies in Business.* New York: Oxford University Press, 1989.

Kuhn, James W., and Donald W. Shriver. *Beyond Success: Corporations and Their Critics in the 1990s.* New York: Oxford University Press, 1991.

Matthews, John B., Kenneth E. Goodpaster, and Laura L. Nash. *Policies and Persons: A Casebook in Business Ethics*, 2d ed. New York: McGraw-Hill, 1991.

May, Larry. *The Morality of Groups: Collective Responsibility, Group-Based Harm, and Corporate Rights.* Notre Dame, IN: Notre Dame University Press, 1987.

Shaw, William H., and Vincent Barry. *Moral Issues in Business*, 5th ed. Belmont, CA: Wadsworth, 1992.

Solomon, Robert C. *Ethics and Excellence.* New York: Oxford University Press, 1993.

Stone, Christopher D. *Where the Law Ends: The Social Control of Corporate Behavior.* New York: Harper & Row, 1975. Reissued: Prospect Heights, IL: Waveland Press, 1991.

Toffler, Barbara Ley. *Tough Choices: Managers Talk Ethics*. New York: John Wiley & Sons, 1986.

Walton, Clarence C. *The Moral Manager*. Cambridge, MA: Ballinger, 1988.

Westin, Alan F., and John D. Aram. *Managerial Dilemmas: Cases in Social, Legal, and Technological Change*. Cambridge, MA: Ballinger, 1988.

ETHICAL THEORIES

✦

Baier, Kurt. *The Moral Point of View*. New York: Random House, 1965.

Derry, Robbin, and Ronald M. Green. "Method in Business Ethics: A Critical Assessment." *Journal of Business Ethics* 8 (1989): 129–141.

Donagan, Alan. *The Theory of Morality*. Chicago: University of Chicago Press, 1977.

Frankena, William K. *Ethics*, 2d ed. Englewood Cliffs, NJ: Prentice Hall, 1973.

Gert, Bernard. *Morality*. New York: Oxford University Press, 1988.

Gewirth, Alan. *Reason and Morality*. Chicago: University of Chicago Press, 1978.

Green, Ronald M. "The First Formulation of the Categorical Imperative as Literally a 'Legislative' Metaphor." *History of Philosophy Quarterly* 8, no. 2 (April 1991): 163–179.

Lyons, David. "The Correlativity of Rights and Duties." *Nous* 4 (1970): 45–55.

Rawls, John. *A Theory of Justice*. Cambridge, MA: Harvard University Press, 1971.

Ross, W. D. *The Right and the Good*. Oxford: Oxford University Press, 1930.

✦ JOHN RAWLS'S THEORY OF JUSTICE ✦

Barry, Brian. *The Liberal Theory of Justice*. Oxford: Oxford University Press, 1973.

Blocker, H. Gene, and Elizabeth H. Smith, eds. *John Rawls's Theory of Social Justice*. Athens: Ohio University Press, 1980.

Daniels, Norman, ed. *Reading Rawls: Critical Studies of a Theory of Justice*. New York: Basic Books, 1975.

Wolff, Robert Paul. Understanding Rawls: *A Reconstruction and Critique of a Theory of Justice*. Princeton: Princeton University Press, 1977.

✦ HUMAN RIGHTS ✦

Dworkin, Ronald. *Taking Rights Seriously*. Cambridge, MA: Harvard University Press, 1978.

Feinberg, Joel. *Rights, Justice, and the Bounds of Liberty*. Princeton, NJ: Princeton University Press, 1980.

Lyons, David, ed. *Rights*. Belmont, CA: Wadsworth, 1979.

✦ UTILITARIANISM ✦

Lyons, David. *Forms and Limits of Utilitarianism*. Oxford: Oxford University Press, 1965.

Quinton, Anthony. *Utilitarian Ethics*. New York: St. Martin's Press, 1973.

Williams, Bernard, and J. C. C. Smart. *Utilitarianism for and Against*. Oxford: The Clarendon Press, 1973.

EMPLOYEE RESPONSIBILITIES
✦

✦ WHISTLE BLOWING ✦

Bok, Sissela. "Whistleblowing and Professional Responsibility." Pp. 292–299 in Tom L. Beauchamp and Norman E. Bowie, eds., *Ethical Theory and Business*, 3d ed. Englewood Cliffs, NJ: Prentice Hall, 1988.

Glazer, Myron. "Ten Whistleblowers and How They Fared." *The Hastings Center Report* 13 (December 1983): 33–41.

Glazer, Myron, and Penina Glazer. *The Whistle-Blowers: Exposing Corruption in Government and Industry.* New York: Basic Books, 1989.

Westin, Alan, ed. *Whistle Blowing! Loyalty and Dissent in the Corporation.* New York: McGraw-Hill, 1981.

✦ EMPLOYEE LOYALTY ✦

Baram, Michael S. "Trade Secrets: What Price Loyalty?" *Harvard Business Review* 46 (November–December 1968): 66–74.

Blake, Harlan M. "Employee Covenants Not to Compete." *Harvard Law Review* 73 (1960): 625–91.

Davis, Michael. "Conflict of Interest." *Business & Professional Ethics Journal* 1 (1982): 17–27.

Lieberstein, Stanley H. *Who Owns What Is in Your Head?* New York: Hawthorn Books, 1979.

Luebke, Neil R. "Conflict of Interest as a Moral Category." *Business & Professional Ethics Journal* 6 (Spring 1987): 66–81.

Moore, Jennifer. "What Is Really Unethical About Insider Trading?" *Journal of Business Ethics* 9 (1990): 171–82.

EMPLOYEE RIGHTS
✦

Ewing, David W. *Freedom Inside the Organization: Bringing Civil Liberties to the Workplace.* New York: E. P. Dutton, 1977.

Ezorsky, Gertrude, ed. *Moral Rights in the Workplace.* Albany: State University of New York Press, 1987.

Gibson, Mary. *Workers' Rights.* Totowa, NJ: Rowman & Allanheld, 1983.

Shepart, Ira M., and Robert L. Duston. *Workplace Privacy: Employee Testing, Surveillance, Wrongful Discharge, and Other Areas of Vulnerability.* Washington, DC.: Bureau of National Affairs, 1987.

Smith, Robert Ellis. *Workrights.* New York: E. P. Dutton, 1983.

Werhane, Patricia A. *Persons, Rights, and Corporations.* Englewood Cliffs, NJ: Prentice Hall, 1985.

✦ PRIVACY IN THE WORKPLACE ✦

Bok, Sissela. *Secrets: On the Ethics of Concealment and Revelation.* New York: Pantheon, 1983.

DesJardins, Joseph R. "Privacy in Employment." Pp. 127–39 in Gertrude Ezorsky, ed., *Moral Rights in the Workplace.* Albany: State University of New York Press, 1987.

Duff, Karl J., and Eric T. Johnson. "A Renewed Employee Right to Privacy." *Labor Law Journal* 34 (1983): 747–62.

Fried, Charles F. *An Anatomy of Values.* Cambridge: Harvard University Press, 1970.

Marx, Gary T., and Sanford Sherizen. "Monitoring on the Job: How to Protect Privacy as Well as Property." *Technology Review* 89 (November-December 1986): 63–72.

Noel, Al. "Privacy: A Sign of Our Times." *Personnel Administrator* 26 (March 1981): 59–62.

Rachels, James. "Why Privacy Is Important." *Philosophy and Public Affairs* 4 (Summer 1975): 295–333.

Reiman, Jeffrey, "Privacy, Intimacy, and Personhood." *Philosophy and Public Affairs* 6 (1976): 26–44.

Warren, Samuel, and Louis D. Brandeis, "The Right to Privacy." *Harvard Law Review* 4 (1890): 193–220.

Wasserstrom, Richard A. "Privacy." Pp. 392–408 in Richard A. Wasserstrom, ed., *Today's Moral Problems,* 2d ed. New York: Macmillan, 1979.

Westin, Alan F. *Privacy and Freedom.* New York: Atheneum, 1967.

◆ EMPLOYEE TESTING ◆

Axel, Helen. *Corporate Experiences with Drug Testing Programs.* New York: The Conference Board, 1990.

Libbin, Anne E., Susan R. Mendelsohn, and Dennis P. Duffy. "The Right to Privacy, Part 5: Employee Medical and Honesty Testing." *Personnel* 65, no. 11 (November 1988): 38–48.

Murray, Thomas H. "Thinking the Unthinkable About Genetic Screening." *Across the Board* 20 (June 1983): 34–39.

"Scientific Validity of Polygraph Testing: A Research Review and Evaluation." Technical Memorandum OTA-TM-H-15. Washington, DC: Office of Technology Assessment, November 1983.

◆ JOB SECURITY AND DUE PROCESS ◆

Epstein, Richard A. "In Defense of Contract at Will." *The University of Chicago Law Review* 51 (1984): 947–82.

Ewing, David. *Justice on the Job.* Boston: Harvard Business School Press, 1989.

Gould, William B., VI. "The Idea of the Job as Property in Contemporary America: The Legal and Collective Bargaining Framework." *Brigham Young Law Review* (1986): 885–918.

Lee, Barbara A. "Something Akin to a Property Right: Protections for Employee Job Security." *Business and Professional Ethics Journal* 9 (Fall 1989): 63–81.

Peck, Cornelius J. "Unjust Discharges from Employment: A Necessary Change in the Law." *Ohio State Law Journal* 40 (1979): 1–49.

◆ OTHER EMPLOYEE RIGHTS ISSUES ◆

Draper, Elaine. *Risky Business: Genetic Testing and Exclusionary Practices in the Hazardous Workplace.* Cambridge, England: Cambridge University Press, 1991.

Machman, Tibor R. "Human Rights, Workers' Rights, and the Right to Occupational Safety." Pp. 45–50 in Gertrude Ezorsky, ed., *Moral Rights in the Workplace.* Albany: State University of New York Press, 1987.

McGarity, Thomas O. "The New OSHA Rules and the Worker's Right to Know." *The Hastings Center Report* 14 (August 1984): 38–39.

Nixon, Judy C., and Judy F. West. "The Ethics of Smoking Policies." *Journal of Business Ethics* 8 (1989): 409–414.

Wermiel, Stephen. "Justices Bar 'Fetal Protection' Policies." *The Wall Street Journal* (March 21, 1991), p. B1.

OBLIGATIONS TO CUSTOMERS OR CLIENTS

✦

✦ ADVERTISING AND ETHICS ✦

Federal Trade Commission v. Colgate-Palmolive Co. U.S. 374, 1965, 85 S. Ct. 1035.

Goldman, Alan H. "Ethical Issues in Advertising." Pp. 256–58 in Tom Regan, ed., *Just Business: New Introductory Essays in Business Ethics*. New York: Random House, 1984.

Hunt, Shelby D., and Lawrence B. Chonko. "Ethical Problems of Advertising Agency Executives." *Journal of Advertising* 16, No. 4 (1987): 16–24.

Hyman, Michael R., and Richard Tansey. "The Ethics of Psychoactive Ads." *Journal of Business Ethics* 9 (1990): 105–114.

Levitt, Theodore. "The Morality (?) of Advertising." *Harvard Business Review* 48 (July–August 1970): 84–92.

Nelson, Phillip. "Advertising and Ethics." Pp. 187–98 in Richard DeGeorge and Joseph A. Pichler, eds., *Ethics, Free Enterprise, and Public Policy*. New York: Oxford University Press, 1978).

Packard, Vance. *The Hidden Persuaders*. New York: David McKay, 1957.

Sach, W. S. "Corporate Advertising: Ends, Means, Problems." *Public Relations Journal* 37 (November 1981): 14–17.

Schuman, Ronald, and Howard Schuman. "The Portrayal of Blacks in Magazine Advertisements: 1950–1982." *Public Opinion Quarterly* 48 (1984): 551–63.

Sethi, S. Prakash. *Corporate Free Speech: Advocacy/Issue Advertising by Business*. Cambridge, MA: Oelgeschlager, Gunn, & Hain, 1982.

✦ PRODUCT SAFETY AND LIABILITY ✦

Beshada v. Johns-Manville Products Corp. 90 NJ 191, 447 A2d. 539.

Coleman, Jules L. "The Morality of Strict Tort Liability." *William and Mary Law Review* 18 (1976): 259–586.

Dubasi, Jagannath. "Insulated from Reality (Johns-Manville)." *Financial World* (June 27, 1989): 64–65.

Epstein, Richard A. "A Theory of Strict Liability." *Journal of Legal Studies* 2 (1973): 151–204

Epstein, Richard A. *Modern Products Liability Law*. Westport, CT: Quorum Books, 1980.

Gatewood, Elizabeth, and Archie B. Carroll. "The Anatomy of Corporate Social Response: The Rely, Firestone 500, and Pinto Cases." *Business Horizons* 24 (September–October 1981): 9–16.

Liebman, Jordan H. "The Manufacturer's Responsibility to Warn Product Users of Unknowable Dangers." *American Business Law Journal* 21 (1984): 403–38.

✦

Oakes, G. "The Sales Process and the Paradoxes of Trust." *Journal of Business Ethics* 9 (1990): 671–679.

OBLIGATIONS TO COMPETITORS
OR SUPPLIERS
✦

Conference Board,The. *Competitive Intelligence* (Research Report No. 913). New York: The Conference Board, 1988.

Forker, Laura B., and Robert L. Janson. "Ethical Practices in Purchasing." *Journal of Purchasing and Materials Management* 26, no. 1 (Winter 1990): 19–26.

Paine, Lynn Sharp. "Corporate Policy and the Ethics of Competitor Intelligence Gathering." *Journal of Business Ethics* 10, no. 6 (1991): 423–436.

Sonnenfeld, Jeffrey, and Paul R. Lawrence. "Why Do Companies Succumb to Price Fixing?" *Harvard Business Review* 56 (July–August 1978): 145–57.

ETHICS AND GLOBAL BUSINESS
✦

Donaldson, Thomas. *The Ethics of International Business.* New York: Oxford University Press, 1989.

Feld, Werner J. *Multinational Corporations and U.N. Politics: The Quest for Codes of Conduct.* New York: Pergamon Press, 1980.

Frederick, William C. "The Moral Authority of Transnational Codes." *Journal of Business Ethics* 10 (1991): 165–177.

Hoffman, W. Michael, Ann E. Lange, David A. Fedo, eds. *National Conference on Business Ethics* (6th: 1985: Waltham, MA). *Ethics and the Multinational Enterprise*: Proceedings of the Sixth National Conference on Business Ethics, October 10 and 11, 1985. Lanham, MD: University Press of America, 1986.

Kline, John M. *International Codes and Multinational Business: Setting Guidelines for International Business Operations.* Westport, Conn.: Quorum Books, 1985.

Kurzman, Dan. *A Killing Wind: Inside Union Carbide and the Bhopal Catastrophe.* New York: McGraw-Hill, 1987.

Shrivastava, Paul. *Bhopal: Anatomy of a Crisis.* Cambridge, MA: Ballinger, 1987.

Shue, Henry. "Transnational Transgressions." Pp. 271–91 in Tom Regan, ed., *Just Business: New Introductory Essays in Business Ethics.* New York: Random House, 1984.

Swinyard, W. R., H. Rinne, and A. Keng Kau. "The Morality of Software Piracy: A Cross-cultural Analysis." *Journal of Business Ethics* 9 (1990): 655–664.

✦ BRIBERY ✦

Carson, Thomas L. "Bribery, Extortion, and the 'Foreign Corrupt Practices Act.'" *Philosophy and Public Affairs* 14 (1985): 66–90.

D'Andrade, Kendall, Jr. "Bribery." *Journal of Business Ethics* 4 (1985): 239–48.
Phillips, Michael. "Bribery." *Ethics* 94 (1984): 621–36.

OPERATIONALIZING ETHICS
IN ORGANIZATIONS

✦

Edmonson, W. F. *A Code of Ethics: Do Corporate Executives and Employees Need It?: A Study of 100 Codes of Ethics from America's Largest Corporations.* Fulton, Missouri: Itawamba Community College Press, 1990.
French, Peter A. *Collective and Corporate Responsibility.* New York: Columbia University Press, 1984.
Gellerman, Saul W. "Why 'Good' Managers Make Bad Ethical Choices." *Harvard Business Review* 64, no. 4 (July–August 1986): 85–90.
Hoffman, W. Michael, Jennifer Mills Moore, David A. Fedo, eds. *National Conference on Business Ethics* (5th: 1983: Bentley College), *Corporate Governance and Institutionalizing Ethics*, Proceedings of the Fifth National Conference on Business Ethics. Lexington, MA: Lexington Books, 1984.
Jackall, Robert. *Moral Mazes: The World of Corporate Managers.* New York: Oxford University Press, 1988.

ETHICS AND BUSINESS EXCELLENCE

✦

✦ CORPORATE SOCIAL RESPONSIBILITY ✦

Anderson, Jerry W. *Corporate Social Responsibility: Guidelines for Top Management.* New York: Quorum Books, 1989.
Berle, Adolf A., and Gardiner C. Means. *The Modern Corporation and Private Property.* New York: Macmillan, 1932.
Davis, Keith, and Robert L. Blomstrom. *Business and Society: Environment and Responsibility*, 3d ed. New York: McGraw-Hill, 1975.
Dodd, E. Merrick, Jr. "For Whom Are Corporate Managers Trustees?" *Harvard Law Review* 45 (1932): 1145–63.
Friedman, Milton. *Capitalism and Freedom.* Chicago: University of Chicago Press, 1962.
Goodpaster, Kenneth E., and John B. Matthews, Jr. "Can a Corporation Have a Conscience?" *Harvard Business Review* 60 (January–February 1982): 139–40. Reprinted in Andrews, *Ethics in Practice*, pp. 155–167.
Heald, Morrell. *The Social Responsibilities of Business: Company and Community, 1900–1960.* Cleveland: Case Western Reserve University Press, 1970.
Simon, John G., Charles W. Powers, and Jon P. Gunnemann. "The Responsibilities of Corporations and Their Owners." Pp. 16–64 in Simon, Powers, and Gunnemann, *The Ethical Investor: Universities and Corporate Responsibility.* New Haven: Yale University Press, 1972.
Tuleja, Tad. *Beyond the Bottom Line: How Business Leaders Are Turning Principles into Profits.* New York: Penguin Books, 1985.

Walton, Clarence C. *Corporate Social Responsibilities.* Belmont, CA: Wadsworth, 1967.

✦ STAKEHOLDER THEORY ✦

Boatright, John R. "Fiduciary Duties and the Shareholder-Management Relation: Or, What's So Special About Shareholders?" Paper delivered at the Annual Meeting of the Society for Business Ethics, August 6–7, 1993, Atlanta, Georgia. Forthcoming in *Business Ethics Quarterly* 4, no. 4 (1995).

Freeman, R. Edward. *Strategic Management: A Stakeholder Approach.* Boston: Pitman, 1984.

Freeman, R. Edward, and Daniel R. Gilbert, Jr. *Corporate Strategy and the Search for Ethics.* Englewood Cliffs, NJ: Prentice Hall, 1988.

Goodpaster, Kenneth E. "Business Ethics and Stakeholder Analysis." *Business Ethics Quarterly* 1 (1991): 53–73.

✦ ETHICS AND BUSINESS EXCELLENCE ✦

Business Roundtable, The. *Corporate Ethics: A Prime Business Asset.* New York: The Business Roundtable, 1988.

Davidow, William H., and Michael S. Malone. *The Virtual Corporation: Structuring and Revitalizing the Corporation for the 21st Century.* New York: HarperCollins, 1992.

Levering, Robert, and Milton Moskowitz. *The 100 Best Companies to Work for in America.* New York: Doubleday, 1993.

Peters, Thomas J., and Robert H. Waterman. *In Search of Excellence: Lessons from America's Best-Run Companies.* New York: Harper & Row, 1982.

JOURNALS

✦

Business & Professional Ethics Journal
Business and Society Review
Business Ethics
Business Ethics Quarterly
Harvard Business Review
Hastings Center Report
Journal of Business Ethics

INDEX